A Certain Gesture: Evnine's Batman Meme Projects and Its Parerga!

OTHER BOOKS BY SIMON J. EVNINE

Donald Davidson (Polity Press and Stanford University Press, 1991)

Epistemic Dimensions of Personhood (Oxford University Press, 2008)

Making Objects and Events: A Hylomorphic Theory of Artifacts, Actions, and Organisms (Oxford University Press, 2016)

A Certain Gesture:
Evnine's Batman Meme Project and Its Parerga!

Volume I

Edited by
Simon J. Evnine

275 New North Road
Islington Suite 1181
London N1 7AA
United Kingdom

Email: TellItSlant@ACertainGesture.com
Web: www.ACertainGesture.com

© Simon J. Evnine 2022. All rights reserved.

ISBN 979-8-9874157-0-2 (paperback)
ISBN 979-8-9874157-1-9 (hardback)
ISBN 979-8-9874157-2-6 (ebook)

Library of Congress Control Number 2022922877

Cover design: Yuriko Zakimi, Design with Purpose, Inc.
Logo design: Jennifer Watson, Context Communications

10 9 8 7 6 5 4 3 2 1

Eperga to the Parerga

Parergon (pl. parerga): something supplementary to a work (ergon) of art; an embellishment to it; a framing element

Epergon (pl. eperga): something outside of, or additional to, a work of art

For additional material, including all the memes that are not included in volume I, both Batman meme movies, all the music that is mentioned in the book, and more, go to this special webpage:

https://acertaingesture.com/eperga-to-the-parerga/

To
my analyst Manuela Menendez
midwife to this.... whatever it is

ADVANCE PRAISE FOR *A CERTAIN GESTURE: EVNINE'S BATMAN MEME PROJECT AND ITS PARERGA!*

Just as a newspaper holds its form constant while it varies the news content, the author of *A Certain Gesture: Evnine's Batman Meme Project and Its Parerga!* finds a way to use a single meme in which Batman slaps Robin as a structure for conveying a sequence of reflections. Sometimes alternately, and other times all at once, these reflections are philosophical and picaresque, sarcastic and explanatory, literary and analytical, visual and discursive, musical and rabbinical, fragmentary and unified, continuous and interrupted. **Kierkegaard meets Calvino meets auto-theory.** The collision sweeps up some analytic philosophers, an avuncular joke-teller, and other characters who come and go. The pictures provide a rhythm, the captions start a melody, and the commentary improvises with chords, riffs, and surprises.

Professor Susanna Siegel, Harvard University, author of *The Rationality of Perception*

A Certain Gesture: Evnine's Batman Meme Project and Its Parerga! is, among other things, an extended exercise in what you're not supposed to write. If we are told not to explain our jokes, the whole thing is an explanation of the joke. If we're told to say, at every step, what motivates our choices of topic, the book is gleefully and inexplicably obsessive. It's a book about representation, pastiche, logic, Judaism, psychoanalysis, shame, music, Batman, and the characters we play in attempting to understand ourselves. It's a meticulous, midrashic, imaginative, funny, insouciant, sincere piece of work. Part of the joy of philosophy is the experience of trying on someone else's vocabulary, concerns, convictions, and habits of reasoning, and seeing how our own are transformed in the process. I think **I have never read anything that is so full of this joy.**

Professor Ian Olasov, CUNY, author of *Ask a Philosopher: Answers to Your Most Important and Most Unexpected Questions*

To open a volume of the Talmud is to be confronted more by commentary than by any primary source. The Talmud itself is a commentary to the Mishna, which itself is, in some sense or other, a commentary on scripture. The Talmudic text constitutes just one column in the middle of the page, surrounded by later commentaries. On the one side, a commentary by Rashi, the great French exegete. On the other side, a commentary that often comments on Rashi's comments, by the generation of sages that followed him. Comments on comments on comments. One sometimes wonders, by the time one reaches the depths of insight at the end of this chain of comments, whether the original source was really hiding these treasures, or whether they've been smuggled in by the imagination of the commentators themselves. The author of *A Certain Gesture: Evnine's Batman Meme Project and Its Parerga!* stands in this proud tradition of Jewish commentary. Evnine's memes are a form of commentary to begin with: social commentary and more. But the author's commentary on those memes offers so much more depth, in philosophy, psychology, and Torah. Were these treasures really lying in wait, in Evnine's memes, or has the commentator conjured them up, *ex nihilo*? Evnine himself is certainly Jewishly literate, but **"Evnine" the commentator is in another league entirely, a great Rabbi of the generation.** I have tried to contact the real Evnine to discover something of the identity of Evnine the commentator, but all I received was an instructive slap! ***A Certain Gesture: Evnine's Batman Meme Project and Its Parerge!* is funny and profound and profoundly funny.**

Rabbi Professor Samuel Lebens, University of Haifa, author of *The Principles of Judaism*

Imagine a joke that begins, "Sigmund Freud, Ludwig Wittgenstein, and Bruce Wayne walk into a Yeshiva...." and you will glimpse what awaits you in *A Certain Gesture: Evnine's Batman Meme Project and Its Parerga!*. Astonishingly creative, intellectually rich, and personally intimate, **Evnine's text shatters the boundaries of conventional philosophical writing, to enchanting effect**.

> Professor David Livingstone Smith, University of New England, author of *Making Monsters: The Uncanny Power of Dehumanization* and *Approaching Psychoanalysis: An Introductory Course*

Evnine's *A Certain Gesture: Evnine's Batman Meme Project and Its Parerga!* is a highly original work. We are invited to eavesdrop on a scholar-artist who, having undergone an extended process of psychoanalysis, is analyzing as well as psychoanalyzing his own work in front of our very eyes. **On display are Evnine's remarkable erudition and wit but also his insight, his sensibility, and his vulnerabilities.** Evnine plunges so deep, we reach what may be the common origin of the psyche's sadistic and masochistic impulses; a minute later, we are taken to rarefied air where Tarksi's theory of truth resides. This is the joint work of a philosophy professor and the young boy the professor once was. We are made privy to repressed desires but discover also that the voyeuristic pleasure an observer may get in such cases is mixed with the pain of recognizing ourselves in the movements of another person's bared soul.

Evnine's exploration is personal, but like the best personal explorations, it illuminates human psychology – *our* psychology.

> Professor Iskra Fileva, University of Colorado, Boulder, author of *The Philosopher's Diaries* at *Psychology Today*

Memes are jokes and jokes are creatures of context. To get them, you usually need to be familiar with the context that is presupposed. This brilliant edition of and commentary on Evnine's Batman Meme Project flips the script. The memes are presented as strange and opaque and as urgently in need of the background against which they might show up as funny or even intelligible; the surrounding commentary supplies the missing context. In this way the book makes art happen, right before our eyes, for what is art but this very kind of opportunity to make the passage from not getting it to getting it? **That it is the artist's life** – from his work as a philosopher and a musician, his psychoanalysis, his Jewishness and Englishness, embarrassing memories of childhood and accidental encounters on social media – **that supplies the needed background is what makes this book so intimate, even if always dizzyingly ironic, so generous, even if also challenging**.

> Professor Alva Noë, UC Berkeley, author of *Strange Tools: Art and Human Nature*

x

What generous soul has not experienced a yearning for self-humiliation?
Ivan Turgenev, *Rudin*

Turn it and turn it again, for all is in it.
Ben Bag Bag, in *Pirqe Avot*

Three parts in one, but all of discords fram'd.
Thomas Kyd, *The Spanish Tragedy*

Table of Contents

EPERGA TO THE PARERGA V

ADVANCE PRAISE FOR A CERTAIN GESTURE VIII

LIST OF FIGURES XV

PREFACE XIX

INTRODUCTION XXI

EVNINE'S BATMAN MEME PROJECT 1

    M.1 ... A MEME IN WHICH I'M BEING 2

    M.2 HIVEMIND 6

    M.4 BUFFALO 7

    M.5 GILBERT AND SULLIVAN 11

    M.6 IT'S BEEN DONE! 13

    M.8 THE MEDIUM IS THE MESSAGE 22

    M.9 BEST 27

    M.10 SEEK SIMPLICITY 30

    M.11 THEY'RE FORGETTING SLAPPY 35

    M.12 THE SIZE OF AN OLIVE 38

    M.13 SHOW SOME RESPECT, ROBIN! 42

    M.15 BARBARA CELARENT 65

    M.17 ODE TO NAPOLEON 74

    M.18 YOU DON'T LOOK JEWISH 76

    M.19 COUPLES THERAPY 78

    M.22 SOME IDIOT 80

    M.24 "A GLOVE SLAPPING A HUMAN FACE – FOREVER" 82

    M.25 MR. PEABODY 85

    M.28 LUNCHTIME 87

    M.29 WHO KNOWS TWO? 88

    M.30 THIRTEEN HOLES 97

    M.31 JAMAICA? 110

    M.32 NEVERMORE! 111

    M.36 HERE! 115

    M.37 MY SISTER! MY DAUGHTER! 121

    M.42 THE SOUND OF YOUR BLOOD 123

    M.43 MORE LESBIANS 127

M.45 I don't care!	131
AND ITS PARERGA!	**135**
M.46 Talk to the Hand	136
M.49 Jingle Bells	157
M.50 Say the Opposites	159
M.52 Fuenteovejuna	163
M.58 A Certain Gesture	164
M.60 The Sound of One Hand Slapping (11ignj.jpg)	166
M.62 Liar	171
M.63 These Shrooms are Strong	174
M.69 Text/Subtext	176
M.72 Vos iz ayer yidisher nomen, Batman?	184
M.74 Politeness is so important	204
M.77 find this out; but	208
M.78 Not a Strict Freudian	214
M.80 The Slap Itself	221
M.91 Transformative Experience	223
M.92 Transformative Experience (alternate version)	229
M.96 The Origins of Neo-Platonist Metaphysics	234
M.97 He Forgot the Meme	241
M.101 Even You?	252
APPENDIX: MEMES OMITTED FROM VOLUME I	**253**
BIBLIOGRAPHY	**260**
INDEX OF MEMES	**272**
INDEX OF NAMES	**274**
INDEX OF SUBJECTS	**278**

List of Figures

Figure 1 The image of Batman slapping Robin xxi
Figure 2 Musical score with random words and punctuation 12
Figure 3 Still from the artist's brother's home movie showing the young Evnine as Robin 18
Figure 4 POW! Batman breaks down the toilet door 19
Figure 5 Evnine's underpants 20
Figure 6 The results of the on-line poll 28
Figure 7 Increasingly Verbose Melanie Klein meme 34
Figure 8 The melody of Evnine's cumulative song on the names of his cat 90
Figure 9 Photo of Evnine's ancestors, Moscow, 1905 107
Figure 10 Monotelic branching flowchart 127
Figure 11 First alternate version - M.43a 128
Figure 12 Second alternate version - M.43b 128
Figure 13 Alternate version - M.45a 132
Figure 14 My measurement by a Pauline gauge 177
Figure 15 The title page of John Wilkins's *The Discovery of a World in the Moone* 178
Figure 16 Map showing the main dialects of Yiddish 190
Figure 17 An inscription in a copy of *Naḥalat Olamim* in the hand of Shmu'el Yevnin 200
Figure 18 An inscription on a copy of *Ma'aseh Rav* in the hand of Shmu'el Yevnin 201
Figure 19 Detail showing two exclamation marks in the reflection 239
Figure 20 The meme with only the words reflected in the mirror 240
Figure 21 Socratic dialog in the format of the American Chopper Argument meme 242
Figure 22 A one-off meme 244
Figure 23 A Drake meme 247
Figure 24 Wojak, or Feels Guy 247
Figure 25 A Woman Yelling at a Cat meme 248
Figure 26 Not the original template image for Socially Awkward Penguin 251

Writing, for us, is the image of language... Writing may not be the mirror of language, but it mirrors language's self-image. (Noë 2015: 32)

Now he screams: "No? Not at all? No, no, no?" He slaps his face, ribs, stomach. The spectacle looks like a fight between at least two men. Within the whirlwind of limbs and expressions I recognize the countenance that has passed over his face more than once this evening: he is uniting with his abuser. Beating himself with another man's hands. (Grossman 2017: 50)

It was an awful blow, that slap. An outburst of unexpected violence, a leakage of murky information that belonged somewhere completely different. (Grossman 2017: 13)

Shamelessness, shame: the roots of violence. (Rushdie 2011: 118)

I never read prologues. I find them tedious. If what the author has to say is so important, why relegate it to the paratext? What are they trying to hide? (Machado 2019: 3)

It is a perpetual triumph of fancy to expand a scanty theme, to raise glittering ideas from obscure properties, and to produce to the world an object of wonder to which nature has contributed little. (Johnson 1973: 437)

To be nothing - is that not, after all, the most satisfactory fact in the whole world? (Woolf 1933: 128)

I find that having released myself from the duty to say things I'm not interested in, in a language I resist, I feel free to entertain other people's voices. Quoting them becomes a pleasure of appreciation rather than the obligatory giving of credit, because when I write in a voice that is not struggling to be heard through the screen of a forced language, I no longer feel that it is not I who am speaking, and so there is more room for what others have said. (Tompkins 1987: 174)

"But," I also enunciate, "what you completely do not seem to catch on to about these two parts of the kid is that they are not separate. They are constantly whirlpooling around in each other—and the basic rule is this: that each one has the power to poison the other one. So what being a kid was like for me was, at the same time, like being an adult in bad drag as a child, and being a child in bad drag as an adult." I was abject, incompetent, and powerless. (Sedgwick 2000: 30)

To be witnessed in one's failure is to be ashamed: to have one's shame witnessed is even more shaming. The bind of shame is that it is intensified by being seen by others as shame. (Ahmed 2004: 103)

Elements that have nothing to do with the main subject... are called parerga in Greek, and examples would include paintings of our Lord being cruelly whipped at the column in which are added to one side, even if off in the distance, a boy playing with a dog, or a battle of birds, or a peasant catching frogs, or other things that painters imagine without caring whether or not they correspond to the main subject. (Paleotti 2012: 231)

Certain curiosities, perhaps especially those that arise out of childhood prohibition and transgression, are not sated by a lifetime's reading and thinking. (Stott 2012: xii)

There is in this struggle with a close enemy a strange sort of twisted pleasure, for it is like striking oneself, yet simultaneously dodging every blow. (Tokarczuk 2022: 354)

The Wunderkammer represents the old world, chaotic, filled with anomalies and incomprehensible to reason. (Tokarczuk 2022: 671)

Preface

Six years ago, in the Summer of 2016, I took it upon myself to produce a *catalogue raisonée* of the memes produced by a professor of philosophy, Simon Evnine, that use the image of Batman slapping Robin. Quickly paring down my ambition from a full *catalogue raisonée* of the *oeuvre*, I resolved to pick only the best of them, some 120, and present them with explanatory commentaries. The next step down came when I re-evaluated the memes and decided that quite a few I had originally included should be dropped and a smaller number of previously excluded memes be included. That left me with a definitive choice of 104 memes to present and comment on. So wide, however, is the erudition displayed in these memes that my editorial labors came to feel overwhelming. My project was turning into a *Key to All Mythologies* and threatened to outlive me. Consequently, I have decided to present to the public what I have so far accomplished. This includes the presentation of and commentaries on 48 of the 104 memes. I hope that when the reader remembers that it has taken me some six years to prepare not even half of the memes to be included, they will look indulgently on my unorthodox decision to publish work in progress.

What I have to show for my labors would be even more scanty were it not for the immense amount of help and generous cooperation I have received from many people. In the preparation of the manuscript for publication, Jennifer Watson has given her unstinting help and advice. I simply could not have done this without her and no amount of thanks would be too much. Joseph Dane has generously lent his considerable expertise with publication through KDP. Thanks also to Irene Olivero for the painting of the meme. Thanks for more specific help and cooperation as follows. M.1: Asya Passinsky for conversation on the ontology of traditions. M.4: Bernard Nickel for advice on generics, Mark Warren for permission. M.6: Bernard Kobes for permission, Duygu Aktaş for thinking about classification, and Jeremy Evnine for permission and tolerance. M.8: Liam Kofi Bright and Eric Schliesser for thought, advice, and permission. M.12: Alyssa Gray, Jeffrey Shoulson, and Gedalyahu Wittow for help understanding. M.13: Edward Beasely for information, Teresa Cherfas for hunting in the archives, Catherine Delafield for information and permission. M.15: Paul Vincent Spade for permission, Catarina Dutilh Novaes, Clinton Tolley, and Sara Uckelman for information. M.19: Jennifer Matey for permission and discussion. M.29: Oliver Black for German translation, and Robin Jeshion for discussion of her views. M.30: Israel Sandman, Gedalyahu Wittow, and Abigail Yevnin for translation and information. M.32: Sidharta Lokanandi for suggestions. M.42: Miranda Rée for help with 1980s English. M.50: Maria Galli Stampino for translation into Italian. The two readings of *Mentre vaga Angioletta* are due to Wistreich (2017), its translation is mine. M.69: Eric Schliesser for his contribution and discussion around it. M.72: Alexander Beider, Leyzer Burko, Baruch Davidson, Shmuel Elikan, Jeremy Evnine, Gennady Estraikh, Alyssa Gray, Shlomit Landman, Chaim Miller, David Roskies, Israel Sandman, Jeffrey Shoulson, Gedalyahu Wittow, and one who must remain nameless for help with translation and information about Yiddish, Hebrew, and family history, Kestenbaum & Company Auction

House and Kedem Auction House for permission. M.74: Mary Anne Franks, Dane Harris, and Tamsin Shaw for permission. M.77: Jennifer Ferris-Hill and John Kirby for discussion of Housman. M.80: Jennifer Watson for design of the image. M.91: Laurie Paul for discussion of her views. M.96: Miranda Rée and Richard Sorabji for help trying to find the relevant handout. M.97: Xen Wanda and Rosa Vince for suggestions, Ian Olasov for much advice, and Wiley-Blackwell for permission to reproduce my work from *Blackwell Companion to Public Philosophy*.

For copyright reasons, many of the images, including the Batman slapping Robin meme itself, cannot be shown. I have therefore taken measures, as you will see. The unadulterated memes can be seen on the website connected to this book:, noted above under "Eperga to the Parerga."

INTRODUCTION

At the beginning of 2016, from January 27th to March 19th to be precise, Simon J. Evnine, a professor of philosophy at the University of Miami, posted on Facebook a series of memes using a popular image of Batman slapping Robin:

Figure 1 The image of Batman slapping Robin, painted by Irene Olivero, used with the artist's permission

Towards the end of this period, he came to refer to these posted memes as his Batman Meme Project and he took the project to reach its climactic finale with the posting of a brief movie entitled *Evnine's Batman Memes: The Movie*. The movie uses many of the already posted memes and introduces some new ones. Despite having presented the movie as the end of his creative activity around this image, however, Evnine continued to produce many more Batman memes until sometime in June 2016, and, desultorily, a few more over the next three years. He also made another short movie, *Gone!*, using this image. Of this later work, only *Gone!* and a handful of memes were ever made public on Facebook. The current volume reproduces 28 of the memes from the Batman Meme Project and 20 others (the Batman Meme Project's parerga) produced during and after the period of the project (most of them hitherto unseen) and supplies commentary on them that will help the viewer understand and enjoy this rich and complex body of work.

The memes are not closely connected to each other (excepting a few cases) but there are several underlying themes that hold them together in a fragile, rhizomatic unity. Other readers may discern other themes but those that impress themselves on me are philosophy (both as activity and as academic discipline), psychoanalysis, Judaism, and music. Since I discuss all of these at appropriate places in my commentaries on individual memes, I shall not dwell on them here other than to bring out the degree to which all these themes are deeply present in the life and experience of the meme-maker. Evnine began his academic life taking a Bachelor of Music degree at King's College London. His intention was to become a composer or musicologist. These career goals were set aside when he followed up his music degree with an M.A., an M.Phil., and a Ph.D. in philosophy. He has since worked for many years as a professor of philosophy though his trajectory in the discipline has been somewhat non-standard. (I discuss this in greater detail in my commentary on *Transformative Experience (alternate version)* (M.92).) Around the end of his undergraduate career, he became interested in psychoanalysis, his interest stimulated by someone in the orbit of R.D. Laing. As a result, he went into therapy with an existential psychotherapist for about seven years, allegedly to little effect. Later, however, he returned to the couch and has been an analysand for about 10 years. With regard to Judaism, Evnine grew up in a family I can only think to describe as non-observant Orthodox. All the commandments were rigorously observed, most of them in the breach. Notwithstanding, his Jewish background has always been important to him and I quote, in my commentary to *Text/Subtext* (M.69), a piece he wrote that explains some of that importance.

The image that features in the memes derives from a 1965 DC comic, *World's Finest* #153, by Edmond Hamilton (text) and Curt Swan (art). Contrary to the orientation found in the meme, which has Robin on the left, initiating the interaction, and Batman on the right, slapping Robin in response, the original panel has Batman on the left and Robin on the right. Batman has come to believe Superman is responsible for his parents' death. He says, as he slaps, "Don't tell me I'm wrong, you brat... Proving Superman's guilt is my whole mission in life!" Robin replies: "Ow! Batman, your grief has obsessed you with this idea of vengeance. I beg you... give it up!" (Batman is suffering from an induced illusion regarding Superman.) The panel began its life as a meme in 2008 when a user reversed its original orientation and supplied the following text: "Hey Batman, what are your parents getting you for Christ-," "My parents are deeaaaaaaad!!!" (Cronin 2009). It is remarkable just how much of the sensibility of Evnine's work is presaged by these two prior occurrences of the image. In both, Batman's status as an orphan (a status that he shares with Robin) is front and center. Although Evnine's parents did not die when he was still young, they did emigrate from England when he was only 18, leaving him alone, without family nearby, to pursue his studies in London. This clearly had a profound effect on him and the sense of loss, abandonment, and loneliness saturates the memes and movies he produced with the image. Furthermore, the original panel has Batman dismissing Robin as a "brat" and Robin describing Batman as in the grips of an obsession. Evnine's use of the image in the memes clearly has something obsessive about it and it is often used to enact an intrapsychic drama in which Evnine represents himself, in the persona of Robin, as a brat.

The fact that the Batman slapping Robin meme uses a panel from a comic, a fact which makes it atypical among memes in general, is of immense importance in understanding its potential and the uses Evnine makes of it. It is common to think that writing always functions as a representation of speech. Only a little reflection is needed to see that this is wrong. But speech bubbles in comics *do* link writing to speech. They are a specialized device for indicating that some writing (or better, a picture of some writing) functions as the representation of a spoken utterance. Because they represent speech pictorially, speech bubbles offer multiple possibilities for play around the complex interrelation of speech and writing. Over and over again, we see Evnine engaging in such play. Indeed, the relation of speech to (images of) writing, although rarely rising to an explicit level, is probably the most pervasive theme explored by the *oeuvre* as a whole.

The most striking feature of the image is the slap. An older man is slapping a young boy who is in his care. It is a violent and disturbing scene and Evnine was clearly sensitive to this. By presenting the slap in dismal repetition, yet each time contextualized in a different dramatic frame, Evnine holds it up to us as an object of obsession, an object that is, as it were, rotated in one's hands until one has seen every facet of it. Sometimes the slap is, as such slaps generally are, **punitive**. Sometimes, it is **corrective**, which itself might be seen as punishment for error. In two cases, the slap is present as a form of **torture**, to extract information. There are, however, less obvious types of slap. A number of the memes have an **antiphonal** quality and, in these cases, the slap functions as a mark of the transition between the two voices. In some it merely emphasizes the **interruptiveness** of Batman's words. There are also many cases in which the slap really has no relation to the dialogue. Here its presence is **absurd**. Finally, there are not a few memes where the slap is, as we might say, **demonstrative**, i.e., the text is itself about a slap or, more broadly, a hand.

The memes were all made on Imgflip.com, whose watermark is visible in their bottom left corners. Like many such meme generators, the site offers the image and the ability to add text via fillable fields. This text can be formatted to some extent. The defaults yield the kind of text familiar from image macros of 15 or 20 years ago: large Impact font, in white with black outlines and some font shadow. This is what we see in Evnine's earliest memes. One can also add further text boxes to allow writing to show up at different points in the image, insert further images, and hand-draw in a range of colors and thicknesses. These features have been utilized by Evnine to good effect in quite a few memes. Further refinement of the output is not possible with the meme generator. I have, where relevant, pointed out the evolutions in Evnine's technique in my commentaries. Since one can upload to Imgflip any image one wants to use as a meme template, Evnine found the image in its original orientation, erased (not too skillfully, it must be said) the original text, and uploaded it to make memes with the original orientation as well as the more common reverse orientation.

I am not including all of Evnine's memes in this volume, not even all those that were part of the original Batman Meme Project. I have selected those that are either interesting or humorous in their own right or about which some useful commentary might be made. To offer some standardization, I have supplied each meme with a didactic. This includes an M number to allow easy cross-reference, the title provided by the artist (in the file description – I preserve his inconsistent capitalization), the dates of composition and, where applicable, of posting on Facebook (always 2016 unless specified otherwise), the orientation of the image, the font used for the text, the contents of the textboxes, and an annotation of the text's color and other effects. Ideally, one should be able to generate, in one's mind's eye, the appearance of a meme from its

didactic. This is especially important given the division of my work into two volumes. I sometimes refer here to memes which will appear only in volume II and to help the reader, these are listed with their didactics in an appendix. (The memes are visible on the website linked to above in Eperga to the Parerga.) I have also, occasionally, referred to commentaries that will appear only in volume II but, since they remain as yet unwritten, there is nothing to be done about that here. The nature of the text makes footnoting somewhat complicated. Any unannotated notes are mine. Where a footnote is to quoted material, I always indicate, in square brackets, who is its author, even when it is me, the editor.

It should go without saying, but I shall say it anyway, that this is not a book that needs to be read in order, from start to finish. It may be dipped into, it may be traversed by a reader's idiosyncratic path, it may be abridged by a reader if she finds herself bored or mystified. Above all, a reader's experience of the book should be fun.

Evnine's Batman Meme Project

The Batman Meme Project, as that expression was used by the artist himself, consists of 55 memes posted on Facebook between January 27th and March 19th, 2016, along with the first of the two movies he made, *Evnine's Batman Memes: The Movie*. I here reproduce 28 of those original memes, including one (M.45) that appeared only in the movie.

M.1 ... a meme in which I'm being...

M.1: ... a meme in which I'm being... Composed: January 27th. Posted: January 27th. Orientation: Reverse. Font: Impact, with font shadow. TB1: "I CAN'T HELP THINK OF EVERYTHING AS PART OF A MEME IN WHICH I'M BEING...", white, with black borders. TB2: "SHUT UP, ROBIN!", white, with black borders.

The technique of this, as of all the earliest memes (M.1-M.4), is crude. The default settings of the meme generator used by the artist (Impact font, with font shadow, all capitals, white letters with black borders) are left in place, almost certainly because at that stage, Evnine did not realize they could be changed. They are highly unsuitable settings where there is a lot of text (see the technically disastrous *A Character in a Novel* (M.3)). Even here, where there is not that much text, Robin's words are quite hard to make out.[1]

Notwithstanding its technical shortcomings, M.1 makes a delightful (and archly meta) start to the Batman Meme Project. When the artist composed it, he surely had no idea how prophetic Robin's words would be. We are certainly meant to understand that Robin is about to complete his sentence with the word "slapped." Thus, the slap in this meme is an instance of what I called, in the Introduction, a demonstrative slap. Batman's verbal response is brutish and unimaginative, as in many of the memes produced (by others) with this image; however, given Robin's statement, which clearly makes the meme depend for its humor on this multitude of

---

[1] In addition, the meme is marred by an embarrassing grammatical solecism. Evnine should have had Robin say either "I can't help but think" or "I can't help thinking."

already existing memes, that unimaginative response is quite suitable.[2] This is, though, the only place in all of the artist's work where he resorts to such a trite and clichéd response for Batman. It is something that could only be gotten away with once, and it is appropriate that that once is here at the start of the whole project. Although the project had not even been dreamt of yet, one could not have asked for a more auspicious beginning.

If the Batman Meme Project had not even been dreamt of, in any form, at the time of this (and the next) meme, is there any justification for including these memes as part of it? Even after the more or less steady composition and Facebook posting of memes began on February 20th, with M.3 (nearly a month after M.2), the idea of a 'project,' a single endeavor of which these memes were parts, was not yet there. But at least, with M.3, there is Evnine's paratextual remark (in the Facebook post accompanying the meme) that he was "continuing [his] ever more erudite series of Batman memes" (see commentary on M.3 for more discussion of this remark) – hence, some consciousness of a series or collection. M.1 and M.2 were composed and posted with no appearance of such a thought on the part of the artist. Is it not then, in a sense, anachronistic to include them as parts of the Batman Meme Project?

As it happens, Evnine himself has provided resources for addressing this worry in an article he published on science fiction and genre (Evnine 2015). In that paper, he argues that literary genres, such as science fiction, are historical particulars rather than, as the consensus view has it, regions in classificatory or conceptual space. In other words, a genre is not like a 'file,' with an associated set of criteria something must meet to be put in that file. It is a historical reality, located in space and time, with all sorts of things as parts: literary works (the works in the genre), people (authors, fans, publishers), publishing houses, conventions, etc. As such, a genre is a special case of a *tradition*. The Jewish tradition, for example, has as parts: Jews, the Torah, the Talmud, synagogues, ritual objects, events like the exodus from Egypt, traditional practices, and so on. Evnine makes the radical suggestion that something may be part of a tradition at one time but not at another, or vice versa.

The idea that parthood is relative to a time is not so controversial when we think about things like chairs and tables. These are objects that are spread out in space, occupying a given location in virtue of having parts that occupy that location. (The chair is, among other places, where its legs are.) But many philosophers hold that their relation to time is quite different. A chair does not exist now by having a part that exists now. All of the chair exists now, and also later. (See the commentary on *Are you even listening?* (M.47) for more on mereology, the theory of parthood.) A given piece of wood may not be part of a chair now, as it lies on the floor of the carpenter's workshop, but become a part later when it is used to repair the chair. But something like a tradition, or a performance of a symphony – what philosophers like to call events – do seem to relate to time (and space) in the way that chairs and other objects relate to space. The performance is occurring now in virtue of having a temporal part, the

---

[2] How different things would have been had this been the last, and not the first, meme of the Batman Meme Project. In that case, it would have been Robin's contribution that was unimaginative; Batman's response would have been, instead, highly ironic.

performance of its first movement, which is occurring now. For things like this, the idea that parthood may be relative to a time is more striking. It would be as if at one time, say a week after the performance of a symphony, the performance of the first movement was a part of the performance of the symphony, but at another, say two weeks later, it was not! But this is exactly what Evnine holds with respect to some events, including traditions (but not performances of symphonies). As an example, he suggests the event of the crucifixion of Jesus as something which was a part of the Jewish tradition at the time it occurred and for some time thereafter. It was an important event in the history of the Jews, a part of their historical existence. But it later ceased to be a part of the tradition. It was, in a sense, excised from that tradition so that, today, it would be very odd to think of it as constituting part of the Jewish tradition in the way in which we still think of, say, the destruction of the Second Temple by the Romans in 70CE as part of that tradition. What brings about that excision is, for the most part, the attitudes to the crucifixion of the Jews. In general, what is part of a tradition is affected by the consciousness of the people in that tradition (and possibly others, as well). In this way, traditions can remake themselves on the go and can extend their origins back in time after the event. And the reason they can do this is because a tradition is an entity that is directly tied to the views, values, and beliefs of the people whose tradition it is.

It might be suggested that an artistic project is something like a miniature tradition. It unfolds through time; it is very much tied in its nature to the views, values, and beliefs not, as in a tradition, of a multitude of people (it is after all in miniature, relative to a tradition) but of one person, the artist whose project it is (or to several, if it is the project of several artists). If this is so, then it might be true that M.1 and M.2 were not parts of the Batman Meme Project when they were composed and published. In fact, it might have been then true that the Batman Meme Project did not exist at that time. But when it came to exist at a later time, it was able to extend its origins back in time through its ability to acquire as parts things that were not parts of it at the time they were created. And it is clear, in fact, that the artist did come to see M.1 and M.2 as parts of the project whose existence only emerged into his consciousness slowly, over time.[3]

As another instance of this pattern think, now, not of an artistic project, not of a tradition, but of a career, specifically, the career of a superhero. At some point this career has unequivocally begun. But before this point is reached, there are glimmerings: a peculiar injury that brings with it a new power, still not fully tested or understood; training of some kind; tentative efforts at vigilantism; a costume that is still improvised and has not yet reached its iconic form; a name or persona still in flux. In short, the makings of an origins story. When these events transpire, there is, as yet, no career of the superhero. How can there be? The superhero him- or herself is in the process of being born. But once a career has clearly begun, it envelops, with a backward sweep of its Batcape, so to speak, these mythical origins, which themselves

---

[3] See, for more along these lines, *Transformative Experience* (M.91) and the commentary on it.

now become the first stages of that career. In this light, we can see M.1 and M.2 as the origins story of the Batman Meme Project.

M.2 Hivemind

M.2 Hivemind Composed: January 27th. Posted: January 27th. Orientation: Reverse. Font: Impact, with font shadow. TB1: "HIVEMIND, I NEED…", white, with black borders. TB2: "ARE YOU A GODDAM COMMIE? WORK IT OUT YOURSELF!", white, with black borders.

The less cluttered text boxes and the simple, though still effective, content make this (from a visual point of view) the best of the earliest, technically impoverished memes. The meme refers to the practice, common on social media, of appealing to one's friends for information or advice one cannot, or does not want to, provide for oneself. Such appeals are often made using the somewhat sinister-sounding term "Hivemind."

M.4 Buffalo

M.4 Buffalo Composed: February 21st. Posted: February 21st. Orientation: Reverse. Font: Impact, with font shadow. TB1: "BUFFALO BUFFALO BUFFALO BUFFALO BUFFALO BUFFALO BUFFALO BUFFALO", white, with black borders. TB2: "BUFFALO!", white, with black borders.

This is the first of several 'occasional' memes, memes composed in response to a Facebook post, either by the artist or one of his friends, and published as a comment to that post. Here, the occasion was a post by Mark Warren, a former student of Evnine's, to announce the good news that he had obtained a tenure-track job as a philosophy professor at Daemen College in Buffalo, NY. His announcement took the following form: "Buffalo buffalo Buffalo buffalo buffalo buffalo Buffalo buffalo. Soon I will buffalo them too." The first sentence here is a well-known puzzle sentence which, as unlikely as it seems, is both syntactically well-formed and meaningful. In the meme, Robin reproduces the puzzle sentence and Batman occupies the role of Warren, buffaloing Robin with a slap. Since the parsing of the sentence requires some instances of the word "buffalo" to function as the proper name of the city, and hence to take a capital letter, the fact that the artist has still not evolved beyond the default setting of the meme generator which produces all text in capitals means that a reader not already familiar with the correct parsing is prevented from being able easily to recover it. The typography of the meme frustrates the typographical requirements of its text. The meme is, therefore, a colossal technical failure! We should note, however, that since the first occurrence of the word is one in which it names the city, the orthographical convention of English of beginning a sentence with a capital letter also contributes to difficulty in parsing the sentence. The capitalization of the initial letter serves two functions and the more common by far is simply that it begins the sentence. This illustrates the way in which orthographic systems always run the risk of inadequacy.

How *is* the sentence to be parsed? The word "buffalo" has three different meanings in it: the name of the city, the name of a type of animal, and a verb meaning something like "intimidate someone in order to take advantage of them" (which henceforth I shall abbreviate to "intimidate"). The whole could be paraphrased like this: animals of the kind buffalo that come from the city of Buffalo, ones that are intimidated by such animals associated with the city, themselves intimidate the selfsame kind of upstate New York animal. Syntactically, it is on a par with "British philosophers (that) French writers admire (themselves) admire Italian singers."

So much for the sentence's parsing. What is required for the claim it expresses to be true? This is a tricky philosophical question. The claim is what philosophers call a generic, a claim that something is *generally* true of some kind of thing. Such claims can be expressed by three types of sentence in English:

> Dogs bark (bare plural)
> A tiger has stripes (indefinite)
> The elephant can be found in Africa and Asia (definite)

It is important to keep in mind that it is not actually sentences that are generic since sentences of the above forms could all be used to make non-generic claims in certain contexts. What is generic or not is the claim or statement such a sentence is used to make on an occasion. Nonetheless, it is often harmless to speak in terms of sentences. Sarah-Jane Leslie and Adam Lerner spell out the difficulties of dealing with such claims:

> Generics have proved quite difficult to analyze semantically. For example, "dogs are mammals" seems to require for its truth that all dogs be mammals. "A tiger is striped" or "ravens are black", however, are somewhat more forgiving, since they are compatible with the existence of a few stripeless tigers and white albino ravens. "Ducks lay eggs" and "a lion has a mane" are more forgiving still; these generics are true even though it is only the mature members of one sex that possess the relevant properties. Notice, however, that we do not accept "ducks are female", even though every egg-laying duck is a female duck. Finally, we accept "ticks carry Lyme disease", even though very few ticks (approximately one percent) actually have the property, while also rejecting "humans are right-handed", when over ninety percent of humans are right-handed. (Leslie and Lerner 2022)

Given that a straightforward analysis of generics in terms of quantity seems out of the question, philosophers have turned to more substantive approaches. Leslie (2007) argues, on the basis of psychological studies, that generics reflect a capacity for making certain kinds of generalization that develops in individual humans even before language and is thus the product of evolution and the transmitter of evolution's imperatives. For obvious reasons, such imperatives will be of great use to us even when they concern properties that not all members of a class have. So we should not be surprised that generics, the product of this capacity, do not require that all members of the class picked out by the subject term exhibit the property ascribed in the predicate. They can be true notwithstanding exceptions, as long as those exceptions are of certain kinds. Marshalling various strands of thought, she arrives at the following account that is supposed to a) respect what we think such a primitive capacity for generalizations would look like, and b) correctly predict our intuitions about which generic claims are true and which are not. "Ks are F" will be true if and only if:

> The counterinstances, if any, are negative, and:
> A. If F lies along a characteristic dimension for the Ks, then some Ks are F
> B. If F is striking, then some Ks are F and the others are disposed to be F
> C. Otherwise, the majority of Ks are F. (2007, 386; letters added by me)

Let us unpack this a bit. It gives three ways a generic can be made true, all of which tolerate counterinstances. But for all of them, the counterinstances must be what Leslie calls "negative." This means that Ks that are not F must "simply fail to have the property in question" rather than having "an equally vivid, concrete positive property instead" (385). The characteristic dimensions referred to in A are some determinate number of features associated with the kind to which the kind K belongs. For example, K is often a kind of animal. Associated with the super-kind *animal* are the characteristic dimensions: method of locomotion (flying, swimming, walking), method reproduction (viviparous, oviparous), kind of diet (carnivorous, herbivorous), etc. Where the F in question comes along one of these characteristic dimensions, the generic "Ks are F" will be true if just some Ks are F (subject to the stricture on counterinstances just noted). That is why "ducks lay eggs" is true. Some ducks do; and the ones that don't (the male ones, mostly) don't exhibit some vivid and positive alternative method of reproduction, like bearing live young. They just don't lay eggs.

B allows some generics to be true because they involve properties that are especially dangerous or striking to us. Carrying Lyme disease is such a property. Where some members of a kind have such a striking property and the ones that don't might (they are disposed to), a generic attributing the property to the kind will be true. This accounts for the truth of "ticks carry Lyme disease." Finally, as per C, for properties that are not striking and that do not occupy a place along a characteristic dimension, most Ks must exhibit them for the corresponding generic to be true. That is why the generic "cats like sleeping in the sun" is true.

Let us consider the truth or falsity of our buffalo puzzle sentence on Leslie's account. (There are, of course, other accounts which might lead to different conclusions about our sentence.) The kind in question is upstate New York bovids who are intimidated by upstate New York bovids, and what is being predicated of that kind is that they intimidate upstate New York bovids. I am sure there are counterinstances but are those counterinstances negative? They would not be negative if, for example, they exhibited some other behavior which was an equally vivid positive concrete property – for example, helping upstate New York bovids to resist such intimidation. But let us suppose that the counterinstances are negative. Any relevant bovids who do not engage in intimidation simply leave each other alone. If there are no members of the kind who satisfy the predicate in question, then the claim will come out as false (as it should) under all three conditions. But again, let us suppose that there are at least some relevant bovids who are intimidated who, in turn, intimidate. Does the claim come out true, then, by clause A? Does such behavior, for them, lie along a characteristic dimension for animals like them? It is certainly not a method of locomotion, or eating, or reproduction. It is hard to know how widely the notion of characteristic dimension might be taken. Perhaps there are dynamics of group behavior and pro-sociality that ethologists might find such intimidation to be involved with. In that case, on our assumption that there are members of the kind who satisfy the predicate and that counterinstances are negative, the generic in question would come out true. This will depend on ethologists' understanding of characteristic dimensions and their judgments about buffalo behavior.

Supposing the conditions do not obtain for our claim to be true under clause A, what about clause B? This will depend on two things, whether the intimidation in question is striking and, if so, whether all upstate New York buffalo are disposed to engage in such behavior even if, as a matter of fact, they do not. The second issue is, again, one for ethologists to determine. The first is more complex. Is the behavior striking? One immediately wants to ask, striking to whom? It might be very striking to the intimidated buffalo while passing entirely unnoticed by humans. There is a serious issue here. Being striking is clearly relative to someone or to some group. This suggests that the truth of generics might likewise be relative. Here is a possible case. Suppose a species of insect travels between two populations of humans that have no knowledge of each other, sometimes infecting them with a virus. One population has developed an immunity to the virus and the other has not. Is the carrying of the virus by the insect striking? To one population it is, to the other it is not. So is the generic "such and such insect carries such and such virus" true or not? Or are we to say it is true relative to one population and false relative to another? Returning to our buffalo, I assume, from absence of any reporting on it, that if they engage in the intimidation in question, it is not striking to humans, at any rate. If we exclude the points of view of creatures who cannot entertain the generic, then that would suggest that it comes out false according to clause B.

Clause C, again, requires the input of ethologists. Just how many of these buffaloed buffalo also intimidate? Is it a majority? Who knows?

My conclusion is that we cannot determine the truth of the puzzle sentence without hearing from ethologists but my sense is that it would turn out to be false, not satisfying any of the three ways of being true. Perhaps the most likely avenue for its truth, however, is clause A.

M.5 Gilbert AND Sullivan

M.5 Gilbert AND Sullivan Composed: February 21st. Posted: February 21st. Orientation: Reverse. Font: Impact, with font shadow. TB1: ""No matter how I try, I just can't say goodb..."", white, with black borders. TB2: "I said Gilbert AND Sullivan!", white, with black borders. Hand-drawn musical notation in Robin's speech bubble.

Here we see the artist's technique beginning to evolve. The text is no longer all in capitals. The most likely explanation for this step forward is the desire to emphasize the word "and" in Batman's text. The meme generator makes it impossible to use bold or italics; other means of emphasis must be sought. The use of capital letters is one such means, but only if the other words are not all in capitals. (See the problems with *Buffalo* (M.4) discussed in the commentary on it.) The artist may have realized at this point that the meme generator offers a number of options to customize memes and this, no doubt, also led him to realize the possibility of drawing onto the memes, which he has taken advantage of with some hand-drawn musical notation.

Actually, the appearance of musical notation here is quite interesting from the point of view of representation in the memes. The speech bubbles are conventional devices in which a picture of writing represents writing, which in turn represents speech. The function of the musical notation is quite different. Far from being a representation of some determinate musical event, as the writing is of a determinate speech event, it simply functions to indicate that the speech event represented by the writing is one in which the words, as it were, are spoken in song. Its function is adverbial but by means other than the representation of an adverb. Any musical notes can absolve this function. Here, there are two joined semi-quavers and a dotted minim but the absence of a staff and clef means they are of no particular pitch. (In this respect, the notation here differs dramatically in function from that in *My favorite notes* (M.55) where at least the relative pitches are of great significance. See the commentary thereon for discussion.) Imagine a musical score in which a melody is supposed to be sung with words that are either indeterminate or (as the melody is in this meme) determined only by context. In order to indicate this, the composer adds some random words above or below the staff, possibly words that are part of a contextually indicated text, if there is one, but possibly not. And perhaps, for good measure, they throw in some punctuation marks, just as the kind of musical indication we are discussing often includes random clefs or time signatures.

Figure 2 Musical score with random words and punctuation

This, in reverse, is just what we have in *Gilbert AND Sullivan*.

The scene depicted in M.5 is one in which Batman has apparently demanded that Robin sing for him something by Gilbert and Sullivan and Robin, either mishearing or, not knowing who Gilbert and Sullivan were and hearing only what he knew, has sung something by the Irish-born English singer Gilbert O'Sullivan – his 1971 release *No Matter How I Try*. Some of the humor of the meme derives from the fact that Batman should have demanded that Robin sing for him at all, some from the fact that he wanted to hear Robin perform Gilbert and Sullivan (was he hoping for the maudlin sentimentality of *Tit-Willow* or the comic bombast of *A Modern Major-General*?) and some, finally, from Robin's misunderstanding.

M.6 It's Been Done!

M.6 It's Been Done! Composed: February 21st. Posted: February 21st. Orientation: Reverse. Font: Impact, with font shadow. TB1: "I'm going to call it "Irony, Esoterica, and Violence in Evnine's Early Batman Memes".", white, with black borders. TB2: "It's been done!", white, with black borders.

Like *Buffalo* (M.4), this was an occasional meme. The occasion was a Facebook post by Evnine himself, made earlier on February 21st, which read: "I am an artist. My medium is the Batman meme." (Here is another sign, after the reference in the note added to *A Character in a Novel* (M.3) to a "series of Batman memes," of the seriousness that quickly came to characterize the artist's relation to his work. Although the post is clearly meant to be funny, it also demands to be taken at face value.) Bernard Kobes, a professor of philosophy at Arizona State University, commented on this: "One day a doctoral dissertation will be written on 'Irony, Esoterica, and Violence in Evnine's Early Batman Memes'."[4] *It's Been Done!* was posted by Evnine as a reply to

---

[4] Kobes's comment, by the way, illustrates an interesting linguistic phenomenon. The conjectured dissertation's title is *Irony, Esoterica, and Violence in Evnine's Early Batman Memes*. As a title, it is plausible to see it as a referring expression, the referent of which is the dissertation of which it is the title. That would mean Kobes's comment as a whole says that one day a doctoral dissertation will be written about the doctoral dissertation whose name is *Irony, Esoterica, and Violence in Evnine's Early Batman Memes*. But of course, that is not what he means to be saying. The dissertation's title functions simultaneously as a name of the work of which it is a title and a description of the subject of that work. If someone writes a book called *English Romantic Poetry*, think of the difference between writing something about that book, and writing something about English romantic poetry. (Notice the difference pattern of capitalization in the two options.) By contrast, if a title were something like *Study No. 1*, to say that someone will write a dissertation on Study No. 1 *can only* mean that they will write on the work of

Kobes's comment. (In addition, the original post on which Kobes commented inspired, and shows up in, another soon-to-appear meme, *The Medium is the Message* (M.8).) In *It's Been Done!*, Robin seems to be in the position of an anxious doctoral student suggesting a dissertation topic to his advisor. Batman responds with the dreaded words that hang over the heads of all researchers striving to find some unexplored terrain on which to plant a flag.

Surprisingly, perhaps, it *has* been done! Herewith are some excerpts from the dissertation *Irony, Esoterica, and Violence in Evnine's Early Batman Memes* written by a student whose name I have replaced with "the Anonymous Dissertator" for reasons of privacy. The first excerpt concerns the question of which memes count as early.[5]

> ...deny that as a class, Evnine's oeuvre is susceptible to different periodizations. And into a bipartite division of early and late? Or a tripartite one of early, middle and late?... Some possible division points include:
>
> a) Between the BMP and its parerga. This is not a precise chronological distinction, since there is some overlap around the time of the latest memes that are part of the BMP and the earliest of the parerga, but by and large, these categories would be earlier and later memes respectively.[6] (Bipartite.)
>
> b) The "origins story memes" (M.1 and M.2), the bulk of the memes (M.3 to M.100), and a few late stragglers (M.101 to M.104). (Tripartite.)
>
> c) The primitive memes (Impact font, white letters with black outlines - generally all capitals) (M.1 to M.8) and the technically more mature memes (M.9 to M.104). (Bipartite.)
>
> What does not seem to emerge is any basis for classification into early and late, or early, middle and late, in terms of content, style, or formal features independent of control of the medium. The memes do become more experimental over time but the introduction of new ideas and new techniques is gradual and often one-off - early on the use of musical notation and the use of languages other than English, later more formal experiments (the addition of images, including images of text, the image within an image within an image,

which "Study No. 1" is the title. See the commentary on *find this out; but* (M.77) for more on titles and some of the linguistic issues that surround them.

[5] Throughout the quotations from *Irony, Esoterica, and Violence in Evnine's Early Batman Memes* I have substituted the M numbers I supply in this volume for the Anonymous Dissertator's own cumbersome method of referring to individual memes.

[6] [Editor's note:] The Anonymous Dissertator is correct (though I can't say I approve of "BMP," presumably an abbreviation of "Batman Meme Project"). *Talk to the Hand* (M.46) and *Are you even listening?* (M.47) were both composed before the end of the Batman Meme Project proper on March 19th, 2016. The fact that the temporal overlap is confined to only two memes, however, is largely an artifact of my selection from among non-posted memes. There are many others that were made and not posted during the time of the Batman Meme Project. Had I selected more of them for inclusion in this work, the coincidence of the distinction between the Batman Meme Project and its parerga and between early and late memes would have been much less convincing.

the use of empty speech bubbles, or just punctuation marks, the introduction of animated gifs, hand-drawn and multi-colored memes, etc.). Right from the beginning, Evnine was obviously interested in the potentialities of his medium and restlessly strove for novelty and innovation. As for themes or types of content, there are some local clusters. M.67 to M.71 (though with the interruption of M.70) form what I call the Depressive Cluster. There is a largish group of Quotational Memes near the end of the *oeuvre* (M.76-77, M.84, M.86-7, M.89, M.97-100). But these do not provide any basis for a major periodization.

Another excerpt comes from the dissertation's chapter on violence in the early memes, though in fact, the Anonymous Dissertator ends up discussing the entire corpus of memes presented in this book.

We come, finally, to the topic of violence. Unlike irony and the esoteric, violence is ubiquitous in Evnine's corpus of memes since the image common to them all is of one person perpetrating violence upon another...[7]

The slap is the signifier of patriarchy. Batman's dual identity means that he embraces the worlds both of law and order (his vigilantism approved of, indeed relied upon, by the state, in the persons of Commissioner Gordon and Chief O'Hara) and of wealth and social capital (he is "millionaire socialite" Bruce Wayne). Robin/Dick Grayson is his ward, a young person whose welfare has been entrusted to him and whom he makes free to abuse on a regular basis in these memes. Batman manifests his privilege and power, flaunting his ability to punish his dependents.[8] The memes present a world in which Batman is the master of his house: his 'youthful ward' Dick Grayson (the object of his violence and possibly his sexual predations), the maiden aunt Harriet, and the old retainer Alfred Pennyworth.[9] Less a post-modern blended family, and more a ghastly, infantile (pre-Oedipal) reflection of the traditional patriarchal household, Batman holds sway with absolute power. His façade of laughing, winking good humor, when in the persona of Bruce Wayne, is just the ease of omnipotence...

Yet for all its political dimensions, the violence in the memes seems highly personal. Evnine's use of the violent image is, after all, obsessive and repetitive. Was he suffering from PTSD? Was the project an exorcism of some kind?

---

[7] [Editor's note:] For this you get a PhD?

[8] [Anonymous Dissertator's note:] See Graeber (2012).

[9] [Editor's note:] The Anonymous Dissertator is in error about Robin's aunt, Harriet Cooper. She was not a maiden aunt but a widow. In the comic books, as opposed to the TV series, Aunt Harriet and Alfred did not overlap as residents of Wayne Manor. Both Aunt Harriet and Alfred show up in at a couple of places in Evnine's memes.

Although we cannot be certain, I will present, below, hitherto unknown evidence that suggests...

... an image in which "a child is being beaten." Freud notes that the fantasy his patients report with the words "a child is being beaten" is "invariably cathected with a high degree of pleasure" (Freud 1919: 185) and Evnine's joyous obsession with the image certainly seems to suggest some kind of libidinal cathexis of it on his part.[10] Given the artist's own multiple references to psychoanalysis in his memes, we should examine this paper of Freud's.

Freud notes that among his patients, many reported that when they were children of around five or six, they had fantasies they now report with the words "a child is being beaten."[11] They are, at least initially, unable to supply much in the way of detail. Who is the child? Of what gender? Why are they being beaten, and by whom? But under analysis, it emerges that the fantasy typically (at least for his female patients) goes through three stages. In the first stage, the fantasizer imagines that her father is beating an indeterminate child (not the fantasizer herself). The beaten child may be of either gender. Freud says the fantasy may be described, in this first stage, by the phrase "my father is beating the child" but quickly goes on to add that the fantasy may often arise in connection with jealousy of a younger sibling who is despised and hated by the fantasizer but inexplicably "attracts to itself the share of affection which the blinded parents are always ready to give the youngest child" (187). (Evnine, we know, was the youngest of four children.) Thus he introduces the description of the first stage: "my father is beating the child *whom I hate*" (185).

The second stage supplants the first as a result of an upsurge of guilt associated both with the child's Oedipal desires and the sadistic elements of the first stage. Freud says of the second stage that "it is the most important and the most momentous [phase] of all. But... it has never had real existence. It is never remembered, it has never succeeded in becoming conscious. It is a construction of analysis, but it is no less a necessity on that account" (185). It is the most important and momentous of all the fantasy's stages for at least three reasons. Firstly, the fantasizer now identifies with the child being beaten. Secondly, the fantasy becomes sexualized and pleasurable, and hence clearly of a masochistic nature. Third, it is its sexualized pleasure that underlies the third stage.

---

[10] [Editor's note:] If the Anonymous Dissertator is implying that the sequel Freud describes has any application at all to the artist and his memes, they are badly (very, very badly) mistaken!

[11] [Anonymous Dissertator's note:] My discussion of Freud's paper is far from systematic and I simply ignore parts of it that do not seem illuminating to me. In addition, most of what I refer to in it concerns Freud's remarks on the fantasies of four female patients (one of whom was his daughter Anna – see Eifermann (1997)). His interpretation of the fantasy in his male patients is somewhat different and has less to offer in understanding Evnine's work.

In the third and final stage, the stage in which, Freud intimates, it is preserved into adulthood, the fantasy again excludes the fantasizer (but she may describe herself as 'looking on' at the scene); the beater is not the father, but a paternal figure such as a teacher; there may be many victims, who are now always boys; and the beating may have been replaced by other punishments or humiliations. About this phase, Freud says "only the *form* [of it] is sadistic; the satisfaction which is derived from it is masochistic" (and hence fueled by the identification of the fantasizer with the child being beaten in the unambiguously masochistic second stage) (191).

The valuable points derived from Freud's discussion, with respect to the image in Evnine's work, are these. First, there is the sense of the fluidity of identification – sometimes the viewer "merely looks on," sometimes she identifies with Robin, the child being beaten. And, in a way, in its sadistic aspects, she does something like identify with the beater, Batman. Secondly, there is the reminder of how important our potential identification with Robin is and hence how masochistic the viewer's (and Evnine's) pleasure in the image may be. Of the three stages of the fantasy, Freud at times describes both the first and the third as sadistic and only the second as masochistic. But he also qualifies both attributions of sadism. The first stage is at first denied that epithet; only later, without comment, Freud begins to apply it.[12] The third is at first unambiguously marked as sadistic, but is later declared to be sadistic in form only. Although in many of Evnine's memes there is a strong identification with Batman, and although this identification is in some cases unqualified, nonetheless the sadistic potential of the meme, as the sadistic potential of Freud's patients' fantasy, is dwarfed by the potential for masochistic pleasure. Thirdly, the high degree of flexibility in Freud's treatment of the fantasy alerts us to what is a very important potential in the image, one that is clearly operative in Evnine's case, namely, its ability to represent *intra*-psychic conflict. The viewer may identify with both Batman and Robin at the same time. In this case, the masochistic and sadistic aspects become inseparable: a single psyche projects onto the image its own self-loathing, its own desire to slap itself across the face! Finally, the fantasy highlights the importance of the generational, or age, difference between the beater and the beaten, a feature also prominent in the Batman image (and emphasized in several of Evnine's memes). An older person is beating a younger one. Where the meme represents intra-psychic conflict, this difference of age is crucial. The image presents the adult slapping his or her childish self. To adapt further the phrase in Freud's title, we could say that at this stage, the fantasy/image should be described by the words: "*I am*

---

[12] [Anonymous Dissertator's note:] See Mahony (1997) for a good discussion of the literary aspects of Freud's essay.

beating the child whom I hate – myself!" Let us take up each of these points in turn…

… some remarkable evidence. Sometime in 1967, Evnine's oldest brother Jeremy (the second of the four siblings) made a number of inventive home movies with two friends, P. and R., and several other volunteers from the family. In the beginning of one of these movies we see the following scene. The long, narrow corridor of Evnine's childhood home (a beautiful Edwardian flat in the Kensington area of London) is used to portray a train carriage. Four people are shown journeying in this 'train,' playing cards.[13] Having previously tried to access the toilet with no success (the door was open but it was occupied), an 'elderly gent' (played by R.) gets up to try again and finds the door locked. He hammers on it ineffectively and slumps to the floor. At this point, at the end of the train/corridor appear – Batman and Robin! It will come as no surprise to learn that Robin is played by Evnine, as a boy of about seven years old. Batman, played by P., is wearing a dark sweater and black pants, with a plastic Batman mask and cape that belonged to Evnine (and are therefore comically small on the sixteen-year-old P.). He is using crutches for some reason. Robin wears slippers, red underpants, a long-sleeved blue top, and yellow scarf with red fleurs-de-lis as a makeshift cape.

Figure 3 Still from the artist's brother's home movie showing the young Evnine as Robin

---

[13] [Editor's note:] Having now seen this footage myself, I find it odd that the Anonymous Dissertator neglects to mention that one of the four card-players is young Evnine, got up to look like an adult.

As the Dynamic Duo burst onto the scene, Robin says "Holy Broken Bones, Batman" and Batman replies "Quick Robin, to the Batbog." ("Bog" is English slang for "toilet." The line, of course, is derived from the common line in the 1960's TV show, "Quick Robin, to the Batmobile." See M.15 for a meme that plays on this line.) Both voices in the soundtrack are done by Evnine's older brother, Robin's line being delivered in falsetto. They rush to the assistance of the slumped traveler and Batman uses a crutch to break open the door.

Figure 4 POW! Batman breaks down the toilet door

Inside the toilet is a woman, played by Evnine's other brother, David. Batman enters the toilet with lascivious intentions and shuts the door, leaving the now partially revived traveler and Robin beating on it futilely, both needing to relieve themselves. Robin gets down on all fours, crawls back down the train/corridor, and lifts his leg against the wall, peeing like a dog! He finally crawls off camera. End of scene.

This primal scene, I conjecture, involving a lack of access to the toilet is surely the key to unlocking Evnine's obsession with the image.[14,15] His older brother may have despised and hated him for being the youngest, may have

---

[14] [Anonymous Dissertator's note:] The theme of lack of access to a toilet may be behind M.45. See the interesting commentary on that meme in *A Certain Gesture: Evnine's Batman Meme Project and Its Parerga*, an invaluable resource for anyone thinking about the Batman Meme Project.

[15] [Editor's note:] I do indeed speculate that *I don't care!* (M.45) may be about lack of access to a toilet, though it is surely absurd over-reach to find in this theme the key to the artist's entire oeuvre. (And while the Anonymous Dissertator's generous (if somewhat condescending) citation of this volume is welcome, they sloppily omit its title's final exclamation mark!)

fantasized about his being beaten, but what a revenge he has concocted here for the young upstart! He has taken away Evnine's own Batman costume – awarded as a 'trophy' to his bravo P. – and 'demoted' him to playing Robin. He has harnessed Evnine's eagerness (after all, as a younger sibling trying to keep up with his older brothers and sister, he must have been eager to participate) to put him in a grotesque get up, to have him get down on all fours and pretend to pee like a dog. And what's that? Is there a stain on the bottom of the little boy's underpants? Has he been allowed to reveal himself as a dirty little boy? Was it, possibly, *placed* there deliberately by the 'director' for comic effect?

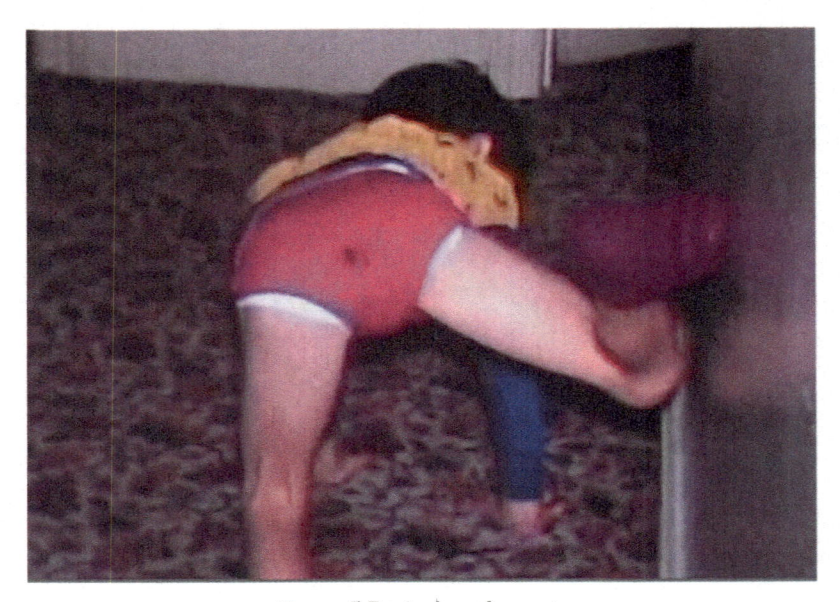

Figure 5 Evnine's underpants

One can only shudder in contemplation of Evnine's youthful embrace of his own humiliation, of his role in what was possibly his older brother's 'beating' fantasy, now with complex humiliations substituted for the ordinary beating. No wonder the image of Batman slapping Robin should have grabbed his imagination as an adult. It has become the site of his own fantasy. With this image, he may endlessly punish himself for his over-eagerness, his unthinking and unreflective childishness. The child, Robin, needs to be beaten down, beaten down by the adult he has become, for ever having been a child. Evnine is at once Batman (it was *his* costume, in the movie) and Robin, the beater and the beaten. The image, we may conjecture, captures the constant war against the child he was and the child who still resides within; it offers both the sadistic delight of the adult in punishing his younger self for offering himself in this way, for colluding in his own humiliation, *and* the masochistic delight of that child for finally being put in his proper place, for being instructed, in no uncertain terms, on *not* making a fool of himself.[16]…

The evidence uncovered by the Anonymous Dissertator is indeed valuable for understanding the significance that the image of Batman slapping Robin held for Evnine in his work with it. But the Anonymous Dissertator seems to have missed the final piece of the puzzle. Around the time of this home movie, the older Evnine was doing a trick for some visitors, a trick that depended on the use of a deck of marked cards. Who can now know why, but the younger boy felt compelled to hint at the deception. (If I had to hazard a guess as to motive, I would say the boy may have felt the hollowness of a victory achieved by such an obvious cheat.) The film-maker angrily declared that someone should spank the child and then proceeded to shoulder the obligation himself in the presence of guests and family alike. No help from the parents saved the youngster and only by dint of much wriggling was the sentence avoided.

---

[16] [Editor's note:] "One can only shudder…" One can only wonder! Wonder how the Anonymous Dissertator's supervisors let pass this dazzling flight of fancy! So much built on so little! And where is the scholarly tone so pedantically (yet reassuringly) present in other parts of the dissertation? Where the apparatus? Where the footnotes?

M.8 The Medium is the Message

M.8 The Medium is the Message Composed: February 22nd. Posted: February 22nd. Orientation: Reverse. Font: Impact, with font shadow. TB1: "I'm an artist. My medium is…", white, with black borders. TB2: "…the message!", white, with black borders.

As noted in the commentary on *It's Been Done!* (M.6), Evnine had posted, on February 21st, a Facebook status update that read "I am an artist. My medium is the Batman meme." *The Medium is the Message* clearly picks up on this and relates it to Marshall McLuhan's famous slogan "The medium is the message." The artist's subtlety is evident here in a small detail. Many of the memes, as discussed in the Introduction, have an antiphonal quality in which Batman's response completes what Robin says. That would have been the case here if the text had been divided thus: "I am an artist. My medium…"/"…is the message." However, this rhythm is disrupted by the fact that Robin gets as far as "is." He is definitely being interrupted rather than collaborating with Batman. Batman is hijacking Robin's assertion, which would, almost certainly, not have been completed with "the message" (but perhaps, who knows, with "the Batman meme," making this one of a small group of meta-memes in the corpus).

~~Given the breadth of meaning McLuhan accords to both "medium" and "message," his catchy slogan is practically devoid of content and resists any serious analysis. Insofar as one can get any handle at all on what it means, it is clearly false. Take, for example, this passage from "The Medium is the Message":~~

> ~~The electric light is pure information. It is a medium without a message, as it were, unless it is used to spell out some verbal ad or name. This fact,~~

> characteristic of all media, means that the "content" of any medium is always another medium. The content of writing is speech, just as the written word is the content of print, and print is the content of the telegraph. If it is asked, "What is the content of speech?," it is necessary to say, "It is an actual process of thought, which is in itself nonverbal." (McLuhan 1964: 8)

First, if the medium is the message, how can any medium be "without a message," as the electric light is alleged to be? Will it not always have itself as message? (Assuming, of course, that the electric light *is* a medium. The term "medium" has just been glossed in McLuhan's text as "any extension of ourselves." Presumably, the electric light extends us in the sense of extending our ability to see.) Secondly, if the electric light is used to "spell out some verbal ad or name," then the medium is not without a message (at least on that occasion), having that "verbal ad or name" as a message. But, as per the slogan, it also is "the message" itself. The use of the definite article before "message," in "the medium is the message," however, implies a singularity to messages associated with a given medium. So, in a case where the electric light spells out some verbal ad or name, ought not the slogan to read "the medium is a message" and not "the medium is the message"?[17] Thirdly, how does it follow ("this fact... means that...") from the first two sentences that the "content" of any medium is *another* medium? Is not each medium supposed to be its own message? (If not, then why not put the slogan as "a medium is the message" (but the message of what? another medium?) or "a medium is a message"? And is having something as content (or "content," but is '"content"' the same as "content"?) the same as having it as a message? Fourthly, in what sense is the content (or message?) of writing speech? Is writing always thought to be a representation of spoken language? Perhaps this is a traditional view of the nature of writing but it is far from obvious. (Indeed, it is obviously false. See the case of non-alphabetic writing systems, and also the commentary on *Show Some Respect, Robin!* (M.13), where this topic is taken up in earnest.) And fifthly, in what sense is the content of print the written word? Presumably "written" should not be taken here literally, as opposed, say, to printed. If it is, then it seems false that the content of print is the written word. But if "written" is not taken literally, then the relation of print to the written word hardly seems captured by saying that the latter is the content (or message?) of the former. Print is made up of written (i.e. printed) words. That seems a truism. And sixthly, in what sense is print the content (or message?) of the telegraph? Why shouldn't the telegraph, like writing, have as its content speech? Or, like print, the written word? And seventhly, why and in what sense is the content of speech an actual process of non-verbal thought? Is McLuhan expressing the old Lockean view that in speaking we are simply expressing the contents of our minds? (But why

17 The implication of uniqueness of the singular "the" is part of the 'orthodox' view of definite descriptions (expressions of the form "the such-and-such") in Bertrand Russell's theory of definite descriptions. Russell thought that in cases where there are no such-and-suches, or more than one such-and-such, any sentence of the from "the such-and-such is so-and-so" is false. Hence, if a medium has both itself as a message, and something else (such as a verbal ad or name), it will be false that the medium is *the message*. See the commentaries on *I thought your boat* (M.33) and *Perimeter* (M.79) for more on Russell's views on definite descriptions.

~~must that content be non-verbal?) What about all the functions of speech that are not expressing the contents of our minds? (See the commentary on *Not a Performative* (M.82).) And eighthly, is it even remotely plausible that there is some single relation (*having as content*) that obtains between the members of each of the following ordered pairs: <speech, non-verbal thought>, <writing, speech>, <print, writing>, and <the telegraph, print>? Is it not much more likely that the relations between the members of each pair is distinct from, though perhaps comparable to in some way or other, the relations between the members of the other pairs? In fact, the whole passage by McLuhan seems a farrago of unwarranted assumptions, hasty assimilations, dubious claims, and logical confusions.~~

~~Notwithstanding these copious problems with McLuhan's "the medium is the message," there is some limited truth to the slogan as it applies to *The Medium is the Message* itself, and Evnine's Batman memes more generally. If the image of the memes is itself counted as a medium, as the artist's Facebook status update of February 21st suggests, then it clearly is, if not *the*, at least *part of the* message conveyed in the memes in general since each, in its own way, attempts to enact the pure form of the slap represented in the image alone. In *The Medium is the Message*, of course, *almost* nothing else is added to this thought; hence here, the medium may indeed be the entirety of the message! That would render this meme the epitome of Evnine's entire endeavor in the Batman Meme Project – a status not even attained by the 'cleanest' or 'purest' memes, *The Sound of One Hand Slapping (11ignj.jpg)* (M.60), *Il n'y a pas de hors-texte* (M.76), and *The Slap Itself* (M.80) (all of which, I shall argue, are about quite different themes). That would arguably be the case if Robin had said only "My medium is...". But something else *is* added – his claim to be an artist. This, of course, echoes Evnine's own appropriation of the epithet in his Facebook comment. What Robin may take his art to consist in is something we get no clue about. Perhaps he is an artist in the medium of being slapped? If so, Batman's slap becomes the message, the meme offers (despite appearances) an instance of a demonstrative slap and resolves itself again into pure epitome of the whole meme project.~~

This was my original commentary on *The Medium is the Message* but it cannot stand. The problem is not with the stuff about the meme's being the epitome of the whole of the artist's endeavor. That is certainly too-clever-by-half but the same can be said for many other things I have written in these commentaries and I haven't thought to strike through them! No, the problem lies with the treatment of McLuhan's famous pronouncement "the medium is the message." There is this thing that analytic philosophers (at least this one) are prone to do. It involves taking some sentence or sentences from a piece of writing belonging to some other discursive tradition – post-structuralism, art criticism, continental philosophy, literary theory, historiography, media studies, etc. – and, stripping them of all context, attempting to make a particular kind of sense of them. Since it is probably already understood that the texts in question will not bear this kind of scrutiny, this practice is a kind of academic 'concern trolling.' It is supposed to look like a good faith attempt to engage with work outside our narrow boundaries but is really a bad faith occasion for the channeling of less wholesome motivations. As if one were to find someone looking pale and, in an apparent effort to revive their animal spirits, slap them hard in the face.

It is a practice connected with discipline, in three senses of that term. The analytic philosopher is, in the first instance, appalled by what he perceives as a lack of *discipline* in the target passage. The distinction between using words and talking about them is often obscured. Points are over-generalized, ambiguities left unresolved. Things that are complex are treated as if they were simple and things that are simple, as if they were complex. One could make a taxonomy of the kinds of things that will strike an analytic philosopher as evincing a lack of intellectual discipline. These are symptoms of the *disciplines* in which these provoking texts are situated. Disciplines can be thought of in terms of norms: encouraged or discouraged subjects, expected or frowned upon types of treatment of those subjects, and so on. The norms associated with those disciplines are what allow to go unchecked the things that activate analytic philosophers. Analytic philosophy itself, as a discipline, is immune (or at least much less subject) to those kinds of breaches of discipline (or so it likes to tell itself). So, finally, the analytic philosopher feels called upon to *discipline* the wayward texts, to admonish where admonishment is appropriate, to punish (by the shaming associated with the over-careful treatment to which the texts are subjected) the recalcitrant authors.

This whole drama, of course, is in reality a farce in which the analytic philosopher plays Punch, throwing his fists around, jeered at and despised by other characters and on-lookers alike. As the analytic philosopher Liam Kofi Bright writes (in a wholly different context):

> one should resist the analytic philosophy instinct: don't keep searching for some fine distinctions which explain why it's ok for you to be punitive… Nobody has ever been fooled by analytic philosophy. People see right through it. (Facebook post of May 19th, 2018)

No-one is grateful for the effort made by the analytic philosopher in dispensing discipline; nothing is illuminated thereby.

Research shows that people's division into liberal and conservative camps is correlated with their degree of fearfulness and sensitivity to disorder and threat:

> Psychologists have found that conservatives are fundamentally more anxious than liberals, which may be why they typically desire stability, structure and clear answers even to complicated questions. (Laber-Warren 2012)

Tools for alleviating fear include "cleaning and organizational items":

> examining the contents of 76 college students' bedrooms, as one group did in a 2008 study, revealed that conservatives possessed more cleaning and organizational items, such as ironing boards and calendars, confirmation that they are orderly and self-disciplined. Liberals owned more books and travel-related memorabilia, which conforms with previous research suggesting that they are open and novelty-seeking. (*ibid.*)

What Bright describes as "the analytic philosophy instinct" might be viewed in this light. My compulsion to deploy the "cleaning and organizational" distinctions that are the medium of analytic philosophy on texts like McLuhan's is probably generated by a sense of fear or anxiety:

over their trickster-like quality, their willingness to jerk and twist around, careless of consistency, open to the possibility of nonsense. Analytic philosophers who are prone to the kind of move I demonstrated (and then cancelled through the typographical device of, not just generically strikethrough font, but specifically "slapthrough" font) need to find some better way of dealing with their anxiety and being more "open and novelty-seeking" in their intellectual lives when they confront texts like McLuhan's.

And yet, and yet…. Here is McLuhan's text again, this time unstruckthrough:

> The electric light is pure information. It is a medium without a message, as it were, unless it is used to spell out some verbal ad or name. This fact, characteristic of all media, means that the "content" of any medium is always another medium. The content of writing is speech, just as the written word is the content of print, and print is the content of the telegraph. If it is asked, "What is the content of speech?," it is necessary to say, "It is an actual process of thought, which is in itself nonverbal."

How *can* that be allowed to stand? By what method of reading *can* one approach it? What hermeneutic key will unlock its excitement and its novelty? And is there no such thing as a charlatan? Is all caution misplaced? These are not rhetorical questions.

M.9 Best

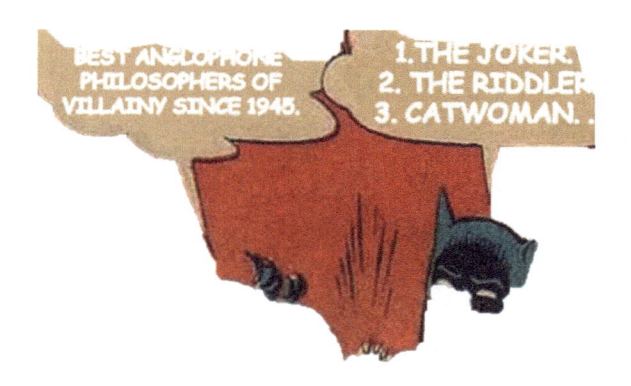

M.9 Best Composed: February 23rd. Posted: February 23rd. Orientation: Reverse. Font: Comic Sans. TB1: "BEST ANGLOPHONE PHILOSOPHERS OF VILLAINY SINCE 1945.", white. TB2: "1. THE JOKER. 2. THE RIDDLER. 3. CATWOMAN. ..", white.

At last the artist has realized that there are other fonts besides Impact and that one need not have borders around the letters. For some reason, however, he has reverted to using all capitals here. The content of the meme is clearly intended as a parody of the many polls that were being run around the time of its composition (and at many other times too) by Professor Brian Leiter on his blog *Leiter Reports: A Philosophy Blog*. These polls typically were cast as polls for "Best X [i.e., epistemologists, political philosophers, etc.] since 1945," with the further restriction that living candidates had to be at least 60 years old (or in some cases, at least 55 years old). Leiter would start with a personally selected list of candidates, allow a period of time for people to write in further candidates, and then determine a fixed time for voting. At the end of this period, he would publish the results, with some commentary on them of his own. Evnine evidently felt, as did many in the philosophical community, that such polls, especially if they included living philosophers, were invidious and of no real positive value to compensate.

In response to a comment from Kris McDaniel (a philosophy professor at Notre Dame University) asking where the poll was, the artist actually created a poll on the site Condorcet Internet Voting Service, the same internet platform used by Leiter. The post with the meme was edited with the text: "OK folks, the poll is live. Go vote at http://civs.cs.cornell.edu/cgi-bin/ vote.pl?id=E_17 cfd7cfc28c780e&akey=215be17f9408b129." Write-in candidates were allowed. (As the reader can see, there were many. The Penguin was written in by Evnine himself.) The meme was reposted, with further encouragement to vote, on February 27th. Finally, on March 1st, the results of the poll were published with the following commentary.

1. **The Joker** (Condorcet winner: wins contests with all other choices)
2. The Riddler loses to The Joker by 10–4
3. Catwoman loses to The Joker by 9–3, loses to The Riddler by 9–4
4. The Penguin (write-in) loses to The Joker by 12–1, loses to Catwoman by 7–6
5. Lex Luthor (write-in) loses to The Joker by 9–4, loses to The Penguin (write-in) by 8–5
6. *Tied*:
    Mr Freeze (write-in) loses to The Joker by 12–1, loses to Lex Luthor (write-in) by 7–4
    Ra's al Ghul (write-in) loses to The Joker by 12–1, loses to Lex Luthor (write-in) by 8–3
8. Vandal Savage (write-in) loses to The Joker by 12–0, loses to Mr Freeze (write-in) by 9–2
9. Dr Evil (write-in) loses to The Joker by 11–2, loses to Vandal Savage (write-in) by 10–2
10. Hannibal Lecter (write-in) loses to The Joker by 12–1, loses to Dr Evil (write-in) by 10–1

Figure 6 The results of the on-line poll

Best Anglophone Philosophers of Villainy Since 1945: Poll Results and Interpretation.

Total of 14 votes cast. No surprise to see The Joker in the top spot, though I'm sure he was aided by the representations of him in films by Jack Nicholson and Heath Ledger (and a recent offer from Harvard).[18] (Holy Crimson, Batman![19]) It also seems right that the other three of the top four spots went to The Riddler, Catwoman and The Penguin since these, together with The Joker, are my personal favorite philosophers of villainy.

Dr. Evil was surely never a serious contender and I'm surprised to see him beating out Hannibal Lecter. This may have been because Lecter was a last-minute write-in and no-one other than the fourteenth voter had a chance to vote for him.

UPDATE: In the making of this poll, no-one was betrayed by their youthful looks.

Several features of this commentary reflect Leiter's own polls: the confident assertion by the pollster that his own assessment is authoritative, the attentiveness to prestige and position,

---

[18] [Editor's note:] Owing to his founding of and long involvement with the Philosophical Gourmet Report (a ranking of philosophy graduate programs in terms of reputation), Leiter has always been very on top of offers, moves, promotions, etc. in the philosophy profession.

[19] [Editor's note:] Crimson is the Harvard color.

the slightly 'chaotic' quality that often means some important contenders are omitted – sometimes betrayed by their youthful looks (i.e., they did not appear to make the minimum age qualification for living philosophers).

Incidentally, sometime after the composition of this meme, Evnine had occasion to correspond by email with Professor Leiter on an entirely unrelated matter. In the course of their exchange, Leiter wrote that he thought of Evnine as "an odd and somewhat humorless chap." Who knows but that this very meme might lead Leiter to revise one part of his judgment, while strengthening the other. (I leave as an exercise for the reader to determine which parts.)

M.10 Seek Simplicity

M.10 Seek Simplicity Composed: February 23rd. Posted: February 23rd. Orientation: Reverse. Font: Arial. TB1: "Seek simplicity...", black. TB2: "...and distrust it!", black.

Seek Simplicity is unassuming in appearance but is technically important for several reasons. After the move away from Impact to Comic Sans in *Best* (M.9), yet a new font, Arial, is introduced here. Almost all the remaining memes are in Comic Sans and Arial, so this completes the roll out of the fonts and decisively leaves behind the clunky Impact, resurrected only a few times for special purposes. *Seek Simplicity* is also the first appearance of black lettering which from now on is the norm. Further, although *The Medium is the Message* (M.8) does quote from a well-known source, the disruptive rhythm noted in the commentary on it means that the quote does not really function *as* a quote. Here, however, for the first time we have the appearance of a well-known quotation (discussed below) functioning as, in some sense, the point of the meme. Finally, *Seek Simplicity* is the first instance, and a beautiful, classic, elegant one at that, of the antiphonal style in the memes. Batman completes what Robin is saying, almost in a call-and-response pattern, or as in a piece of antiphonal music. The size and placement of the text (always the most problematic technical feature) has been carefully controlled to echo this verbal antiphony and the three dots both at the end of Robin's text and at the beginning of Batman's quietly highlight the antiphonal quality. Unassuming and unflashy as it is, this is really a fine meme from all points of view.

The meme's high quality owes not a little to the text, a brilliant aphorism. Evnine added, in the first comment to the post: "Text from A.N. Whitehead (by way of Peter Simons)." In fact, Peter Simons uses the aphorism as an epigraph to his book *Parts: A Study in Ontology* (2000), which book, we know from the artist's syllabi, he taught more than once. (See *Are you even listening?* (M.47) and commentary thereon for something about mereology, the topic of Simons' book.) Whitehead's thought, and his means of expressing it, are breathtaking.[20] The idea of simplicity as a magnetic pole, capable of both attracting and repelling, is very profound. There is a good sense in which all philosophical activity should be aimed at achieving simplicity. It is the Holy Grail! And yet, as we all know, when things appear simple, one should immediately be suspicious. (Whitehead's use of the faintly archaic-sounding "distrust" is so good here.) Intellectual activity, at least philosophy, is forever caught in a loop of seeking precisely what it must distrust. How could one describe philosophy better?[21]

As a matter of fact, Evnine sounds this theme himself in a blog post he published in *The Parergon* (July 3, 2021). There he talks about the two-facedness of clarity, not the same as simplicity yet closely related. Here is some of what he has to say:

That is not it at all: clarity and sadism

Throughout my philosophical career, one virtue my writing has been consistently praised for is its clarity. Just about every journal referee and every book reviewer has used that very word or one of its cognates. Not its profundity, not its wisdom, not how interesting it is. It's always clarity, clarity, clarity. And I'm OK with that. I value clarity very highly. Moreover, my discipline, analytic philosophy, is founded on and built around the quest for clarity so my personal virtue is syntonic with the standards of my profession.

But things have been shifting for me lately and, without revoking my approval of clarity, I have come to see it also in other ways. Part of writing clearly is anticipating, and forestalling, potential ambiguities, misunderstandings, and irrelevant but tempting byways. Clear writing, in other words, serves to direct the reader's thought along *exactly* the path the author

---

[20] It is, somewhat disappointingly, not improved by context. The paragraph in which the aphorism appears, in *The Concept of Nature* (1920) is this: "I agree that the view of Nature which I have maintained in these lectures is not a simple one. Nature appears as a complex system whose factors are dimly discerned by us. But, as I ask you, Is not this the very truth? Should we not distrust the jaunty assurance with which every age prides itself that it at last has hit upon the ultimate concepts in which all that happens can be formulated? The aim of science is to seek the simplest explanations of complex facts. We are apt to fall into the error of thinking that the facts are simple because simplicity is the goal of our quest. The guiding motto in the life of every natural philosopher should be, Seek simplicity and distrust it" (142). The paragraph runs together distrust of simplicity with distrust of the "jaunty assurance with which each age prides itself that it at last has hit upon the ultimate concepts in which all that happens can be formulated," a distinct object of distrust, rightly identified but much less interesting than simplicity as such.

[21] This dialectic may also be part of the background to *Squiggle* (M.103). An equally brilliant, though much more flippant, aphorism to similar effect is J.L. Austin's: "we must at all costs avoid over-simplification, which one might be tempted to call the occupational disease of philosophers if it were not their occupation" (1975: 38).

wishes. I would put it in even stronger terms. Clear writing is designed to occupy the reader's mind, to colonize it, forcing it to renounce its freedom and follow slavishly the writer's direction of thought.

Deploying a psychoanalytic concept developed by Melanie Klein and her followers, clarity in writing seems to me to be a mechanism of projective identification. Here is part of the definition of projective identification from the *New Dictionary of Kleinian Thought* ([Spillius *et al.*:] 2011):

> Projective identification is an unconscious phantasy in which aspects of the self or an internal object are split off and attributed to an external object. The projected aspects may be felt by the projector to be either good or bad. Projective phantasies may or may not be accompanied by evocative behaviour unconsciously intended to induce the recipient of the projection to feel and act in accordance with the projective phantasy.

In analysis, the patient projects parts of their mind into the analyst and then, subtly and unconsciously, strives to get the analyst to act in conformity with them. If the patient, for example, has aggressive and sadistic phantasies they cannot assimilate, they will attempt to elicit aggressive and sadistic behavior from the analyst. It is both a dangerous and valuable game.

Clear writing, too, is aggressive and sadistic - not in its content but in the domination it attempts. The reader is 'forced' to look *here* and not *there* (where their own phantasies might take them), to disregard *this* but to give *that* a lot of weight, to understand something polysemous in *one* way and not *another*. I imagine that what is being projected through this mechanism is the writer's own anxiety, anxiety about confusion, about uncertainty, about getting lost, about being swallowed up by a messy, stinking pile of conceptual detritus. Writing clearly makes the writer work hard to control what they produce and at the same time, disallows anyone else the freedom to just let it all go.

I, certainly, whose care and intellectual hygiene so routinely earns me praise from my readers, am beset by these anxieties.

... Free association is a mode of talking which deliberately tries to set clarity aside... One thing leads to another not through linear logic but through chance associations, phantasy, and play...

[My] anxieties about free association in analysis have been gradually soothed so that now, after 8 years, I finally find myself occasionally able to talk freely. It's a great feeling. I look forward, too, to writing philosophy that is no longer 'clear' but manages to be interesting or profound instead.

The post ends with a meme by Evnine that is not in the Batman format. It is what is known as Increasingly Verbose. An image and text are associated in the top panel, below which are two or three more iterations in which the picture becomes more abstract and the text more verbose. It is the figure of Melanie Klein that provides the link between the meme and the body of Evnine's post.

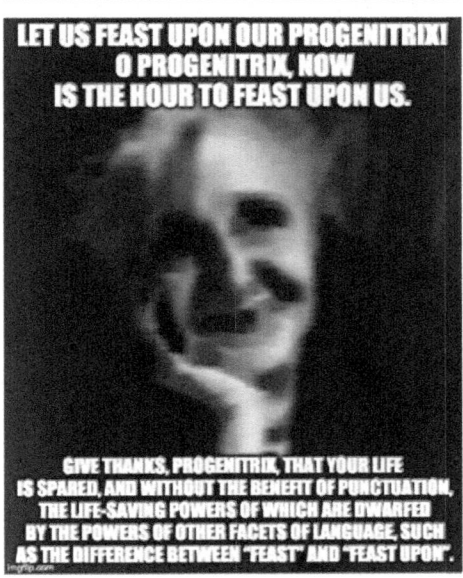

Figure 7 Increasingly Verbose Melanie Klein meme. First Panel – Let's eat, Grandma! Let's eat Grandma. / Punctuation saves lives! Second Panel – Let us feast upon our progenitrix! O progenitrix, now is the hour to feast upon us. / Give thanks, progenitrix, that your life is spared, and without the benefit of punctuation, the life-saving powers of which are dwarfed by the powers of other facts of language, such as the difference between "feast" and "feast upon". Third Panel – Owing to an unusual family circumstance, my chief care-giver as an infant was not my mother, but my mother's mother. I was often fed unpunctually by her and I experienced murderous rage as a result, against which I defended myself in the only way I knew how at that tender age, by splitting it off and projecting it on to my grandmother. Later, as my psyche developed, I had to find a way to reclaim the anger my care-giver had looked after for me, and I introjected her as an object both rageful and loving. That conjunction of rage and love still haunts me. Now, years later, I have anxiety dreams in which I am late (unpunctual) for an endless test in which I must insert commas and semi-colons into the text of Finnegans Wake. I wake up from these dreams famished. (The photograph of Melanie Klein belongs to the Wellcome Institute and its use here is authorized under a Creative Commons BY 4.0)

M.11 They're Forgetting Slappy

M.11 They're Forgetting Slappy Composed: February 24th. Posted: February 24th. Orientation: Reverse. Font: Arial. TB1: "It's great! Now there's also Love, Haha, Wow, Sad…", black. TB2: "They're forgetting Slappy!", black.

This was created and posted on the day that a range of new reactions, to augment the thitherto solitary Like, were introduced by Facebook. Evnine seemed to devote a lot of thought to Facebook reactions. On the same day on which this meme was posted, he wrote another status update in which, because the number of available reactions were now six, he suggested using a die to determine which reaction to use. Later, on May 8th, Facebook rolled out another reaction, Thankful (only available in some places, and temporarily, in honor of Mother's Day), and this prompted the artist to post the following remarks:

> I see today Facebook has a rolled out a new 'reaction' option – Thankful. My first thought was to post a joke about being thankful for the new option. But I'm not a thankful person in general and I will never use it – so I'm not thankful for it. However, all those who are likely to use it will, no doubt, be thankful for it!
>
> What about the self-applicability of the other options? I do like the Like option, but I don't love the Love one; I merely like it, and use it frequently. I do not laugh at (or with), or find funny, the HaHa option, though if it had been designed differently, with more verbal panache,[22] I might have.

---

[22] [Editor's note:] "Verbal" does not make much sense as applied to the panache proper to an image. Possibly the artist meant to write "visual." On the other hand, the memes themselves contain images of

I am not wowed by Wow (though I often use it); it's really commonplace in both design and function. And I am definitely not angry about Angry! As long as there are people who applaud between movements in classical concerts or who park across the sidewalk and force disabled people into the grass to get around them, we need Angry. So I'm thankful for Angry.

Am I sad about Sad? I am sad that there is sadness, and hence a need for Sad. But, as Gavin Lawrence[23] used to ask (and maybe still does! I hope so, because it made a big impression on me, so thanks Gavin!), am I sad that I or others experience sadness when their loved ones are sick or dying? Do I wish for a world in which no-one dies? Would that mean wishing for a world in which no-one was born, or one in which the world got more and more crowded? I don't know. So I don't know whether I'm sad about Sad.

Finally, a plea for a new reaction button (are you reading this Ariel?[24]): Grelling Paradoxical!

The piece shows a keen rhetorical sense, undercutting its initial disavowal of thankfulness first with the explicit but playful thankfulness for the Angry reaction and then with the heartfelt acknowledgment of a former teacher.

The reference to Grelling's Paradox is cute but not really appropriate. The paradox is one of the Semantic Paradoxes, so-called because they arise out of specifically semantic concepts. (The most famous semantic paradox is the Liar Paradox. See *Liar* (M.62) for a meme based on the Liar Paradox. Russell's Paradox, a paradox for set theory rather than semantics, is described and discussed in *Dialetheism* (M.20).) In the case of Grelling's Paradox, the semantic concept at work (and what makes it, at least superficially, relevant to Evnine's reflections on the Facebook reactions) is self-applicability. Some linguistic expressions apply to themselves and some do not. To say that an expression applies to itself means that the sentence you get by predicating the expression of itself is true. In English, a standard way to obtain a sentence that predicates an expression of itself is, first, to obtain a name for the expression (which we typically do by enclosing the expression in quotation marks or by italicizing it); and second, to write the expression itself, adding or not adding "is" where necessary to make a grammatical

---

words, thus problematizing the relation between the visual and the verbal. (One might think that all writing consists of images of words and, in a highly qualified sense, that is so. (See the commentaries on *Show Some Respect, Robin!* (M.13) and *Groovy* (M.102) for more discussion of this.) But in the memes, the visual aspects of the represented words are prominent in a way that goes beyond the typical visual aspects of writing: text color, outline, font, arrangement on the page, and, of course, the ubiquitous issue of the representation of punctuation marks. (See the commentary on *Not a Performative* (M.82) for more extensive discussion of this last point.)) Although this text was not written during the period of the Batman Meme Project itself, the artist was still composing memes at that point and it is possible that he is making some allusion to this fact about them.

[23] [Editor's note:] Gavin Lawrence was a teacher of Evnine's when he was in graduate school at UCLA.

[24] [Editor's note:] Ariel Evnine is the artist's nephew and works at Facebook (hence the "are you listening?").

sentence. (Obviously, this procedure will only produce a grammatical sentence in English if the expression we start with is capable of functioning as a predicate in the final sentence. We cannot predicate "the" of itself. Neither "'the' the" nor "'the' is the" is grammatical.)

Here are some examples. "a linguistic expression" applies to itself. The following sentence, in which we predicate the expression of itself, is true:

1) "a linguistic expression" is a linguistic expression.

So also the result of predicating "in the English language" of itself is true and hence the expression applies to itself:

2) "in the English language" is in the English language.

Most expressions, however, do not apply to themselves (even if we restrict ourselves to those that can be predicated of themselves). "in the German language" does not. The following is false:

3) "in the German language" is in the German language.

Other expressions that do not apply to themselves include "a table," "an adverb," and so on. The following are false:

4) "a table" is a table,
5) "an adverb" is an adverb.

Now for the paradox. Consider the expression "does not apply to itself." Does it apply to itself or not? If we predicate the expression of itself, is the resulting sentence true, like 1) and 2) above (in which case the expression does apply to itself) or false, like 3)-5) (in which case it does not)? Here is the sentence in question:

G) "does not apply to itself" does not apply to itself.

Suppose that G) is true. If it is true that the expression does not apply to itself (as G) tells us) that means that the sentence that results from predicating the expression of itself is false. But G) *is* the sentence that results from predicating the expression of itself. Hence, if G) is true, then G) is false! So suppose, instead, that G) is false. Since G) tells us that the expression does not apply to itself, if G) is false, then the expression does apply to itself. That means that the sentence we obtain from predicating the expression of itself is true. But, again, G) *is* that sentence. Hence, if G) is false, then G) is true!!

Of course, all of this is, as noted, irrelevant to the question of whether the artist is thankful for the Thankful reaction, likes the Like reaction, and so on. Each of *those* claims might be true, or false, without paradox.

M.12 The Size of an Olive

M.12 The Size of an Olive Composed: February 24th. Posted: February 24th. Orientation: Reverse. Font: Arial. TB1: "Rabbi Meir says "the size of an olive"", black. TB2: "Rabbi Yehuda says "the size of an egg!"", black.

Evnine posted this with the paratextual remark: "How much food must be eaten to engender the obligation of reciting the grace after meals?" Although a small number of memes were posted with some further text either in the post or in the comments, this is either the only, or one of only two (depending on how you take the paratext in *Some Idiot* (M.22)) in which text that appears outside of the meme actually affects the interpretation of the meme itself. In later memes, where further text is needed to set the stage, the artist adds a third text box to the meme in which to place it, making the memes themselves self-contained (surely a preferable solution to the one employed here).

This is the first meme to introduce Jewish themes into the Batman Meme Project. The topic (and ultimately the text of the meme) is complex and the difficulty in understanding it is increased by the fact that the artist has made a mistake in his paratext. Let us begin by clearing up the mistake. The dispute represented in the meme is not over how much must be eaten to make it obligatory *to say* the grace after meals, but how much must be eaten to make it obligatory, when three or more have eaten together, *to preface* the grace after meals with a *zimmun*, a call by one of them to the others to form a *mezuman* (a prepared gathering) to say the grace after meals. Rabbi Me'ir says the amount of food eaten to render a *zimmun* obligatory must have (at least) the bulk of an olive; Rabbi Yehuda thinks the obligation only kicks in when the diners have eaten food (at least) the bulk of an egg.

The dispute occurs in the Talmud, the fountainhead of rabbinic Judaism as practiced after the exile of 70CE. The Talmud consists of two elements, the *Mishnah* and the *Gemara*. The *Mishnah* is a compendium of extra-Biblical precepts that were committed to writing by Rabbi Yehuda HaNasi around the beginning of the 3rd century CE. (An individual precept from the *Mishnah* may be described as "a *Mishnah*.") The *Gemara* is a commentary on (parts of) the *Mishnah* by the generations of scholars who lived after it was redacted. The *Gemara* itself was committed to writing (in two slightly different forms – the more common Babylonian Talmud and the Jerusalem Talmud) sometime around the beginning of the 6th century CE. (See Evnine's blog post quoted in the commentary to *Text/Subtext* (M.69) for some of his thoughts about the Talmud.)

In the *Mishnah* (*Berakhot* 7:2), we read, concerning the obligation to convene a prepared gathering: "How much is needed [to be eaten in order] to convene? At least an olive['s volume]. Rabbi Yehuda says at least an egg['s volume]." Here we see the dispute enacted between Batman and Robin but, as yet, with only one of the protagonists, Rabbi Yehuda, named. The *Gemara* on this passage from the *Mishnah* begins as follows:

> Is that to say that Rabbi Me'ir considers an olive-bulk significant and Rabbi Yehuda considers an egg-bulk significant? (*Berakhot* 49b)

Now both protagonists are named. But where does the *Gemara* get Rabbi Me'ir's name from? It is, as we have just seen, not given in the *Mishnah* that is being commented on. However, at another point in the Talmud (*Sanhedrin* 86a), we read "R. Yoḥanan said: [The author of] an anonymous *Mishnah* is R. Me'ir." In the original *Mishnah* passage, the opinion "at least an olive['s volume]" is indeed anonymous. Hence, the Talmud is here applying its own interpretive principle to attribute the opinion to R. Me'ir. We now have enough to explain the text of M.12– the competing opinions, concerning the amount needed to require a *zimmun* before the grace after meals, attributed to Rabbis Me'ir and Yehuda.

But why does the *Gemara* ask this question ("Is that to say…") when it has just quoted the *Mishnah* saying exactly that? The reason, we go on to read, is that elsewhere in the *Mishnah*, R. Me'ir answered a (different) question with "the size of an egg" and R. Yehuda with "the size of an olive." Wouldn't the rabbis most likely have answered all questions relating to the amounts of food eaten necessary to impose some obligation with the same standard? One might wonder, then, whether some kind of inconsistency has crept in. The transmission of the *Mishnah* by mouth, until its final redaction, and thereafter its transmission in written sources (and no doubt also by mouth) was a long and complex process during which there was ample opportunity for corruptions of the text to arise. The sages of the Talmud had also to be concerned, therefore, with matters of textual criticism. (See the commentary on *find this out; but* (M.77) for further reflection on the question of amending a text on the basis of perceived inconsistency.) In this spirit, R. Yoḥanan asserts "The opinions are reversed." We should suppose that it was R. Me'ir's view that the quantity of food eaten necessary to impose the obligation of *zimmun* is "the size of an egg" and R. Yehuda's that it was "the size of an olive."

R. Yoḥanan's support for textual emendation, however, is opposed by Abaye, who argues that there is no inconsistency and the opinions should not be reversed here. This is because, Abaye says, the reasoning in the two cases is not of the same kind. In the case of the *zimmun*, R. Me'ir and R. Yehuda have a difference of opinion over how to interpret the Biblical verse that is offered as the basis for the requirement. *Deuteronomy* 8:10 says: "And you shall eat and be full, and you shall bless the LORD your God for the good land he has given you." (RSV). R. Yehuda takes "eat and be full" as a single unit and reasons that one could not be full from eating anything less than the size of an egg. Anything less and you would not fulfill the condition in *Deuteronomy* for the commandment to bless God (by saying the Grace after Meals). R. Me'ir, by contrast, takes "you shall eat" to refer to food and "you… shall be full" to refer to drink. Even food the size of an olive will fulfill the first conjunct and hence (its being taken for granted that you will have drunk as well) lays on one the obligation. The implication is that if the two rabbis agreed on how to interpret "eat and be full," they would agree on the amount of food.

In the case in which their opinions are reversed, the disagreement does not turn on diverging interpretations of another text, but on diverging legal principles. In another part of the *Mishnah* (*Pesaḥim* 3:7-8), the rabbis are discussing the question of one who has left his home to travel, on the eve of Passover, and remembers that he has left some leaven in his home. (Before Passover, all leaven must be removed from the home.) For what quantity of leaven is he required to turn back to throw it away? A similar question arises about an analogous situation. If one leaves Jerusalem with meat taken from a ritual sacrifice in the Temple, and one has traveled beyond Mount Scopus, for what quantity of meat must one return to dispose of it ritually in front of the Temple, and for what quantity can one simply burn it on the spot. Here R. Me'ir opines that only if the food is of the size of an egg must one return. R. Yehuda says one must return even if it is the size of an olive. Abaye, in the Talmud (*Pesaḥim* 50a and *Berakhot* 49a) explains their disagreement in this way. R. Me'ir thinks the quantity of sacrificial meat requiring the traveler to turn back should be related to the quantity that makes it susceptible to ritual impurity. Ritual impurity can only affect a quantity of meat at least the size of an egg. R. Yehuda, on the other hand, thinks that the quantity necessitating return should be correlated to the minimum quantity of consecrated meat which a ritually unclean person is prohibited from eating. This quantity is as small as the size of an olive. Hence in this case, the disagreement turns not on interpretation of a verse but on conflicting ways of conceptualizing the situation. There is thus no reason at all to expect consistency in the answers given by each rabbi to this question and to the question about the *zimmun*.

So much for the dispute between Rabbis Me'ir and Yehuda. Turning now to the meme itself, one very interesting feature calls for comment, namely, Evnine's decision to punctuate Batman's representation of R. Yehuda's words with an exclamation mark. Not only that, but the exclamation mark appears inside the quotation marks that surround R. Yehuda's words, in violation of the usual contemporary convention of placing periods and commas within, but other punctuation outside, quotation marks. There are many ramifications of this small detail but I defer to a later commentary a full discussion of them. I will add here to that discussion only one point that is pertinent to this meme in particular. Punctuation is a writerly *techne* but in the speech bubbles of the comic strip, we use writing as a direct representation of speech. (In fact, we use pictorial representations of writing as representations of speech.) How this should work is already something that Evnine is clearly exploring in his memes. But in the present instance, a further level of complexity is added owing to the fact that the *Mishnah* and Talmud themselves are redactions of what is called the Oral Law (supplementing the Written Law of the Torah). So we have writing that represents speech that quotes writing that represents speech. It is, consequently, doubly perplexing what to make of the exclamation mark within the quotation marks.

M.13 Show Some Respect, Robin!

M.13 Show Some Respect, Robin! Composed: February 24th. Posted: February 25th. Orientation: Reverse. Font: Arial. TB1: "[IN A BAD ENGLISH ACCENT:] "I'M ALFRED AND I'M A BUTLER."", black. TB2: "SHOW SOME RESPECT, ROBIN! HE WIPED YOUR SHITTY ASS WHEN YOU WERE A KID!", black.

In some ways, this meme lies at the heart of Evnine's entire project. To understand why, though, we must start some way back, in 1843 to be precise. In that year, Sir Charles James Napier (1782-1853), commander of the British forces in India, having been ordered to punish rebels in the independent province of Sindh, greatly exceeded his orders and ended up bringing the whole province under British rule. To communicate both his accomplishment and his disobedience, he sent to his superior, the Governor of India Lord Ellenborough, a single-word message - *Peccavi* – Latin for "I have sinned," a homophone of "I have Sindh." The story of this event first appeared in the new satirical magazine *Punch* on May 18th, 1844. It is stated that thitherto, the "most laconic military despatch [sic] ever issued" was Caesar's "*Veni, Vidi, Vici.*" Napier set a new record (presumably an unbeatable one) with a dispatch of one word only. From *Punch*, the story became widely known, made its way into many historical works, and spawned many variants of Napier's joke.

Like many good stories, it is untrue. But the truth, in this instance, is better than the fabrication! In July 1907, the journal *The East and the West* (vol. 6, number 19) ran a story by T. A. Gurney called "The Influence of Laymen on Missions" in which an allusion to the Napier anecdote was made. In the issue for October 1907, the editors report:

> Mrs. C. Mackintosh writes to us to say that this message was never sent by Sir Charles Napier, but was invented by her cousin Catherine Wentworth, the translator of 'Lyra Germanica.' Catherine Wentworth was then a young girl just out of the schoolroom, and was receiving lessons from Mr. Gaskell, to whom, after discussing with him Sir Charles Napier's conquest, she made the remark, '"*Peccavi*," I have Sindh.' On his suggestion the joke was sent to *Punch*, the editor of which sent her a cheque in acknowledgment.

A.L. Mayhew (1907), who quotes this passage in *Notes and Queries* for November 1907, notes that the author of *Lyra Germanica* (a translation into English of German hymns) was, in fact, Catherine Winkworth (1827-78), not Wentworth (evidently an error on the part of *The East and the West*) and it is to her, at the tender age of 16, that this ingenious, cross-lingual joke, a joke that has surfaced and resurfaced for nearly two hundred years, is to be attributed.[25,26] As

[25] Having attempted, and failed, to corroborate this attribution and determine the amount of the cheque in the archives of *Punch* (many thanks to Teresa Cherfas for searching on my behalf), I was alerted to a letter by A.C. Yate, published in *The Spectator* on June 1st, 1918. I abridge the letter here:

> ... Many, and among them persons of eminence in the world of letters—notably the late Sir William Lee-Warner, who sought in vain for some trace of [Napier's authorship] in the Calcutta records—have diligently taken up the quest for the origin of that which stands as the most laconic of all known military despatches... No Life or Memoir of Sir Charles claims the *bon mot* as his... At that time [May 1844] Miss Catherine Winkworth, afterwards known as the author of *Lyra Germanica* and other works, was under the tutorship of Mr. Gaskell, the husband of one of the most talented of British lady-novelists; and from Mr. Gaskell's pupil-room emanated "Peccavi—I have Sin(ne)d"... The present editor and the proprietors of *Punch* have admitted that their records are innocent of any reference to "Peccavi" and its origin. The historian of *Punch* adopts a less tolerant attitude and treats the claim of "a Miss Winkworth" in a tone of airy *persiflage*, if not of ridicule. There is no justification for such an attitude. Miss Catherine and her sister Miss Susanna were women of character and ability. Their niece and biographer (Longmans in 1908 published *Memorials of Two Sisters*), Miss M. J. Shaen, specially remarks upon the humour that characterized Miss Catherine's eyes and mouth... My acquaintance with Miss Shaen enabled me to invite her to make inquiries among the relatives of the Misses Winkworth as to the accuracy or otherwise of Miss C. W. Mackintosh's statement [in her letter to *The East and the West*]. Miss Shaen has made inquiries, and authorizes me to say that "members of Miss Catherine Winkworth's family are still alive who can vouch for the fact that the *bon mot* ('Peccavi') was sent to *Punch* by her and an acknowledgment received by her from the editor." I think, therefore, that it is only right that the best-accredited originator of "Peccavi" should not go down to posterity as "a Miss Winkworth."

Many thanks to Catherine Delafield for alerting me to the existence of Yate's letter. Delafield notes (in private communication) that the then-still-living family members amongst whom Miss Shaen might have made inquiries would have included "Margaret's sister Agnes (1857–1918) and her cousin Susan Collie (1861–1932) but also the Winkworths's sister Alice (b. 1834) and their cousin Jessie (1834–1919) who was mother to Catherine Winkworth Mackintosh. Jessie and two of her sisters visited Europe with Catherine and Susanna."

[26] After the correct attribution was made, it was somewhat lost sight of. An article by Walter Woollcott, in *The Nation* from 1913, mentions it (along with other variants of the joke that may or may not have been independently arrived at). But in 1936, Lord Zetland, Secretary of State for India, speaking in the House of Lords, rejects the attribution to Napier not because he is aware of Winkworth, but because he has

Yate's letter suggests, the attribution to Winkworth is far from implausible. Even a brief perusal of the posthumously published excerpts from Catherine's diary and letters from around that time (Winkworth 1883 and Shaen 1908) leaves one in no doubt of her capacity for such a joke. These writings reveal a deeply religious, thoughtful, lively young girl, thirsting for knowledge of all kinds, delighting in studying. She studied, by herself or with tutors, chemistry, algebra, Italian, astronomy, and history, but also art, singing, and dancing.[27] The death of her mother when she was 14 clearly hit her hard and may partially account for a very slight morbid strain in her thought. Every New Year and every birthday, she writes in her diary "I am now one year closer to death." She suffered some sort of health crisis for several years in her teens but she persevered, with the obviously loving attention of her sisters and acquaintances, and rallied, though with a sense of fragility thereafter. She and her formidable sisters were deeply, and enthusiastically, immersed in the religious and intellectual life of mid-Victorian England. They were good friends with the novelist Elizabeth "Lilly" Gaskell (it was her husband who was Catherine's tutor and who suggested sending the Peccavi joke to *Punch*), Charles Kingsley, and Giuseppe Mazzini (during his London exile); they were on visiting terms with Dickens, Charlotte Brontë, Thackeray, and Carlyle.[28]

It is not Catherine Winkworth who concerns us now, however, but her equally remarkable elder sister Susanna (1820-84). Under the tutelage of the Chevalier Bunsen (1791-1860), she undertook an English translation of Bunsen's 1852 book about the diplomat and historian Barthold Georg Niebuhr, taking serious pains to improve her German for this purpose. Having accomplished this, she was keen to translate more and her religious bent led her to the *Theologia Germanica*. This anonymous work of German mysticism, probably from the 14th century, was discovered by Martin Luther, who published it for the first time in 1516 (and

---

"been told by men of an older generation that it is very unlikely that Sir Charles Napier had even as much knowledge of Latin as to enable him to send a dispatch of even one word in that language." (This was met with laughter. The report is from *The Guardian*, Feb 14th.) Then, in the May 1954 issue of *Notes and Queries*, H.T. Lambrick notes that during the previous year, the centenary of Sir Charles Napier's death, many publications mentioned that the witticism was not his, ascribing it instead to *Punch* (evidently without any consciousness of the origin of the joke in *Punch*). Lambrick then attributes the joke to Catherine Winkworth on the basis of an article by N.M. Billimoria, in the *Journal of the Sind Historical Society* (vol. III, no. 4, Dec. 1938), in which Billimoria, without citing his source, quotes verbatim from the report of Mrs. Mackintosh's letter that appeared in the *The East and the West* and in *Notes and Queries* itself, in 1907! (Apparently the latter was his source since he gives the correct form of Winkworth's name.) I am grateful to Professor Edward Beasley, author of a biography of Sir Charles Napier, for supplying me with a copy of Billimoria's article and for informing me about and sending copies of the 1907 *Notes and Queries* piece and the 1913 *Nation* treatment.

[27] Interestingly, we learn from a letter to her from an older sister that it was not until two years or so after the "Peccavi" joke that she thought about learning Latin. Her knowledge of the word "peccavi" must have been from some other source than a general familiarity with the language. This makes an interesting point of comparison with Lord Zetland's disparagement of Napier's knowledge of Latin, mentioned in the previous footnote.

[28] See Delafield (2020, chapter 5) for a sensitive discussion of how Susanna Winkworth frames her own and Catherine's lives in the texts referred to.

again, in a fuller version, in 1518). It lay, he said, closest to his heart, other than the Bible and St. Augustine. In 1843 (the same year as Peccavi) a new manuscript version of the work, from 1497, was discovered and, containing material not previously known, was thought to represent a more authentic version of the text than that formerly available. (Scholars now reject this view.) Again through the instigation of the Chevalier Bunsen, Susanna undertook to translate this new version. Her translation was published in 1857.

For the translation, she chose a deliberately archaic style. This can be seen in a beautiful passage that was used as an epigraph by Clemence Housman to her novel *The Life of Sir Aglovale de Gallis* (1905). Housman was the sister of the better-known A.E. Housman, poet and classicist, some of whose words appear in *find this out; but* (M.77). Critical opinion of the novel is sharply divided.[29] I, myself, embody both extreme reactions. To my shame, I have twice abandoned the book in the middle, while simultaneously being dumbstruck by content and intensity I have seen nowhere else. Perhaps the paradox is resolved if one thinks of the novel as a fractal. Any part of it recapitulates all the themes of the whole. There is, consequently, a sense that there is no narrative motion. The book is about a minor character from Malory's *Morte d'Arthur*, Sir Aglovale, brother to Parsifal here and in many versions of the Arthurian stories. It is written in the language of Malory, an archaic idiom not too dissimilar to that used by Winkworth in her translation of the *Theologia Germanica*. Aglovale, in the novel, blunders around from one shame to another. Every time he seems to be on the path out of it, he (it seems almost deliberately) plunges into further shame, debasing himself, searching for total abjection.

One can see why, therefore, Housman chose this striking passage from Winkworth's translation as the book's epigraph:

> When a man truly perceiveth and considereth himself who and what he is, and findeth himself utterly vile and wicked and unworthy, he falleth into such a deep abasement that it seemeth to him reasonable that all creatures in heaven and earth should rise up against him. And therefore he will not and dare not desire any consolation and release, but he is willing to be unconsoled and unreleased; and he doth not grieve over his sufferings, for they are right in his eyes, and he hath nothing to say against them. This is what is meant by true repentance for sin, and he who in this present time entereth into this hell, none may console him. Now, God hath not forsaken a man in this hell, but He is laying His hand upon him that the man may not desire nor regard anything but the Eternal Good only. And then, when the man neither careth nor desireth anything but the Eternal Good alone, and seeketh not himself nor his own

---

[29] The following summary appears in Schenk (2017: 53): "For critic Raymond E. Thompson, 'the plot... rambles'; for scholar John Christopher Kleis, the book is 'ostentatious, ill-plotted, and virtually unreadable.' However, the novelist Ellis Peters called it 'the finest work on an Arthurian theme since Malory,' and the left-wing writer Reginald Reynolds described it as 'the most amazing book' he had ever read."

> things, but the honour of God only, he is made a partaker of all manner of joy, bliss, grace, rest, and consolation, and so the man is henceforth in the kingdom of heaven. This hell and this heaven are two good safe ways for a man, and happy is he who truly findeth them.

Two good safe ways for a man. Not one good safe way that leads through these two stages, but two good safe ways. Abjection itself is a safe way. Or to be precise, total abjection is. If there is but one little space for consolation to creep in, one little care or desire for one's happiness, God will not lay his hand upon the wretch. Abjection is a path which, once started upon, must be followed to its bitter end. There are signs, here and there in Evnine's memes, of such abjection. Most prominent is his use of an image that is full of shame. Batman, of course, is committing violence on his young ward. He will certainly be ashamed when this is over. (And the slapping itself may be the product of shame, as we shall see below.) But Robin too will be full of shame, as any victim of violence will realize. Shame because he tells himself he must have done something to deserve this; and shame for allowing it to happen, for not fighting back. Can Evnine's, let us say it, obsession with this image possibly have nothing to do with the shame that drips from every pixel?

A few of the memes (I am thinking of *Ode to Napoleon* (M.17), *Some Idiot* (M.22), *Mr. Peabody* (M.25), *#JeSuisRobin* (M.59), and *I am no-one* (M.67)) seem to allude to incidents involving shame, either in Evnine's experience or fantasy. (It's not always easy to be certain; and there are many other memes for which a case could be made.) *Show Some Respect, Robin!* belongs to this category. It depicts a scene in which Robin mocks the elderly Wayne-family retainer, Alfred Pennyworth. In its portrayal of the callousness of youth, it reminds one of a story that Evnine has sometimes told of an incident in his childhood, an incident that obviously made a big impression on him. Going to school on the London underground (the Circle Line between High St. Kensington and Blackfriars), he was anxious to get a seat in order to make it easier to do his last-minute homework. When a seat did surprisingly open up, he raced for it, in competition with an elderly gentleman who had the bearing of an ex-military type. Young and nimble as he was, he beat the older man to the seat and sat down. The man, in exasperation, audibly muttered the words "little bastard." Evnine's youthful lack of consideration for the older man's needs – an older man who, almost certainly as a veteran of WWII had figuratively "wiped [the artist's] shitty ass" for him – was bad enough. But the man's bitter expression of pain and frustration had the effect of freezing the boy in his place, now disabled by a new shame from remedying his initial shame by simply getting up, apologizing, and offering the man the seat.

That shame like this should be represented by a scene with a slap in the face is hardly surprising. Both shame and the slap bring blood to the face. The link between shame and violence forms the centerpiece of Krista Thomason's (2014) discussion of that emotion. Thomason rejects the most common accounts that see shame as a matter of failing to live up to one's own standards or ideals. Such approaches, she argues, are unable to make sense of the deep connection between shame and violence: the tendency for someone in their shame to lash out violently towards themselves or others. Such violence would only take one further from one's ideals. Thomason argues for a different approach to shame, one which will, according to her, make sense of the link to violence. The key components of her definition are what she calls "identity" and "self-conception." "Identity" seems to encompass all facts about oneself. "Self-conception," on the other hand, contains only those facts (or myths) about ourselves that we use to think about and present ourselves to ourselves and others. Naturally, there are many features of our identity that form no part of our self-conception. Shame is what we experience when we feel that some aspect of our identity which does not form part of our self-conception (or forms only a part of it) comes to define us.

Thomason argues that this conception of shame allows us to understand the link between shame and violence. The experience of shame renders us passive. Thomason suggests two distinct reasons why. First, the very coming to be defined by some part of our identity that is not part of our self-conception (or is only one part of it and not all) is something that is done to us and with respect to which we play no active role. But secondly, it is often the case that the part of our identity to which we are reduced in shame is itself something over which we have no control. A disfigurement such as that suffered by the so-called Elephant Man is something that the person was simply born with. In reacting to shame with violence, Thomason suggests we find one way in which to assert ourselves, to seize control, to do something to others in response to their having done something to us. It thus serves as a means of restoring the balance between passivity and activity, between lack and exercise of control.

This seems to me implausible. Deliberate violence is no more active than any other kind of deliberate action. True, Thomason says that violence is just one way to alleviate shame and people can choose other forms of activity to perform a similar function, but then we give up the idea that there is a special link between shame and violence. And if anything, the examples of violence in shame that Thomason brings are ones where the violence is impulsive and manifests a loss of self-control. Such violence renders us more passive, not less! The passage from the *Theologia Germanica* quoted above and Housman's Aglovale show us another way of understanding the link between violence and shame. What Thomason gets wrong is in holding that violence's connection with shame is as a means of alleviating the unpleasant emotion. It is, I suggest, the opposite: a means of intensification, a first step in a journey of total abjection along one of those "two safe ways" for a man through which redemption may ultimately be found.

Changing tack, *Show Some Respect, Robin!* is also extremely interesting for one of its formal features. It is the only meme in the corpus in which Evnine includes in a speech bubble a direction as to how the speech represented is supposed to sound. (I speculate a little about how the Yiddish in the speech bubbles of *Vos iz ayer yidisher nomen, Batman?* (M.72) might be pronounced but that meme itself gives no indication.) This is, if one thinks about it, extremely bizarre. Speech bubbles in comics are images that depict written words, and the device of the speech bubble means that the written words depicted are themselves representations of speech. Nothing, therefore, should belong in the speech bubble that does not function as a representation of spoken words (spoken by whomever the bubble is attached to – though see the commentary on *Shhh* (M.71) for some reflection on the thought bubble variation). How much of writing is a representation of speech? Punctuation is one area where there is some doubt. Some theories of punctuation take it as stage directions for verbal delivery, in which case it would belong in a speech bubble in the same way that the letters do that comprise the words. Or strictly, as the letters would in a purely phonetic alphabet. (So there is a case to be made for using something like the International Phonetic Alphabet only in speech bubbles.) Others take punctuation as a feature of writing. This is a very tough philosophical question. However, even though "[In a bad English accent:]" does clearly function as a stage direction for verbal delivery – that is explicitly what it is - it does not, like punctuation would if we took it as characterizing verbal delivery, do so 'silently,' as it were. The stage direction itself is made of words, words which are pictured in the speech bubble. According to the conventions of comics, then, the stage direction ought to be 'heard' as part of Robin's verbal utterance. Issues of this kind crop up in various places in Evnine's memes and it is clear that it was, or became, an explicit theme for him. (See, among other memes, *Cicero**!* (M.56), of which there is a recording of a live performance orchestrated by Evnine.)

We started this commentary with Sir Charles Napier and Peccavi. Let us therefore finish it by returning to him. *Show Some Respect, Robin!* is, as noted above, about Alfred Pennyworth, the butler who faithfully, suavely, and knowingly serves both Batman and Robin and Bruce Wayne and Dick Grayson. In the live TV series of the 1960s, Alfred was played by the English actor Alan Napier – second cousin four times removed of Sir Charles Napier, the wrongly-alleged coiner of Peccavi.

M.14 Free Association

M.14 Free Association Composed: February 24th. Posted: February 26th. Orientation: Original. Font: Arial. TB1: "All you have to do is lie there and say whatever comes into your mind!", black. TB2: "I can't, Batman. It's so hard!", black.

This is the first of the small number of memes in which the image is in its original orientation with Batman on the left and speaking first. Evnine had to erase the original dialogue from the image himself and did so, in the case of Batman's speech bubble, very poorly. As a result, all the memes made in the original orientation are visually unappealing. The choice of font here seems only to make things worse. The content of the meme, however, is of great interest. As its title makes plain, it is about the psychoanalytic practice of free association. Perhaps because of the similarity between the beginning of Batman's text and the alleged advice to young brides of another era that "all they had to do was lie there" and think of England, and perhaps because of Robin's use of the word "hard," several commenters on the original posting were misled into thinking the meme was somehow salacious. True, it was, as all the memes were, posted without a title but one might still think these commenters were too disinclined to read what was in front of them and too inclined to free associate themselves!

In free association (about which I shall speak at greater length presently), a patient is supposed to say whatever comes into their mind without editing or censoring it. The method is intended to help reveal the contents of the patient's unconscious, both by relaxing the defenses that prevent these contents from becoming conscious and by allowing the analyst to note the uncontrolled juxtapositions of material and the exact places where resistance is encountered in blockages to the flow of speech. Batman may be depicted here in the role of friend/guardian or possibly even of analyst (a role he may occupy in *I don't care!* (M.45)). In either case, the slap emphasizes how unsympathetic his verbal response is to Robin's plight. (The original orientation of the image, which gives Batman the first word, seems subtly to highlight Robin's difficulties in becoming, as one must in free association, the prime mover in speech.) In fact, Robin's is the voice of wisdom here. Although free association might seem as if it is a simple method, it is not, either in theory or in practice. As Stephen Mitchell and Margaret Black put it, as psychoanalysis developed, "[f]ree association was increasingly viewed as an unavoidably compromised activity from the start, at best a goal of the analytic process rather than the immediately available vehicle it had been naively assumed to be" (2016: 27). One must work at being able to free associate – and the difficulties in doing it are as important as its successful accomplishment. When it is successfully accomplished, it can be, as Anton Kris (1996) emphasizes, the source of a unique and intense pleasure.

So much for the practical difficulties of free association. What about the theoretical understanding of it? To narrow down the focus of our discussion, we should begin by noting an important distinction between an absolute and a relative sense of free association (sometimes called in the analytic literature "directed free association"). In the absolute sense, a patient simply free associates. There is no guidance, no focus. This is the notion that will prove difficult to understand. By contrast, in the relative sense, one free associates *to* something (an image, idea, word, or dream element, etc.), often at the request of the analyst. Free association in the relative sense is both easier to understand from a theoretical point of view and easier for a patient to engage in. Before setting it aside to concentrate on the perplexing notion of absolute free association, we may illustrate the relative sense with two examples taken from a wonderful paper by the analyst Soazig Le Besco (2016). Here is the first passage from her paper.

> After some restlessness in the course of the patient's talk, the analyst says "You seem to be having a hard time staying with difficult emotions."
>
> The patient acknowledges this. He recalls that he told a niece about how his dog had a small part in a famous film but that he nonetheless warned her strongly against seeing it since it is entirely focused on a final wrenching scene in which a dog (not the one played by his own) dies. His niece said that she loved to have a good cry on a regular basis and would certainly seek out the film. The patient explains to the analyst what a revelation it was to him that anyone should positively want, or seek out, such experiences.
>
> The analyst asks if there are any difficult emotions the patient can stay with. He realizes that he does seek out, and enjoy, internet videos in which animals are found abandoned and sick and are then shown being cleaned up, cared for, and loved. Although such videos, unlike the movie in which his dog appeared, have happy endings, he finds them very sad but likes them nonetheless.

> The patient goes on to describe a video he saw several years before about two men who acquire a lion cub in London in the 60s.[30] They raise it but when it becomes too big, they arrange for it to be let loose in a safari park somewhere in Africa. A couple of years later they return to see if they can discover what became of it. They find the lion, which recognizes the men and goes crazy with happiness at seeing them. The patient explains how he finds this devastatingly sad – even though the whole story has such a good outcome: the lion living free in its natural habitat, the love remembered and expressed by both men and lion. He finds his own reaction mystifying and inexplicable.
>
> "You are the lion," says the analyst.
>
> The patient is amazed at his having failed to consider that possibility and immediately feels it is right.
>
> "Are you saying that I feel as if I was raised and then abandoned?" (This is related to events in the patient's life with which both he and the analyst are very familiar.)
>
> "You tell me." And, after a few seconds, "**What thoughts do you have about lions?**"
>
> The patient explains that in fact, he has very ambivalent thoughts about lions. On the one hand, they have great positive qualities: they are awe-inspiring and noble, but also potentially cuddly and sweet. On the other hand, he is always mindful of their great violence – not toward animals on whom they prey, but towards each other. Isn't it true, he asks, that male lions regularly kill the young of a female from another male if they form a pride together?
>
> The analyst observes how acting from instinct is like the "anti-[patient's first name]." (Le Besco 2016: 98; emphasis in bold is mine)

And here is the second, perhaps even better, example. (It is unclear whether this concerns the same patient as the first example.)

> The patient, who has alternated between lying on the couch and sitting face-to-face but at this point has been on the couch for a while, mentions that he had the idea before the session that he would sit up but then, when he came into the room, he either forgot or didn't care and so just lay down....
>
> Later, the patient brings up some ideas about a book he is writing and the analyst avoids engaging directly with the ideas and relates what the patient is saying back to himself. The patient becomes disinterested [sic] pretty quickly and says he finds talking about these self-related issues "dismal." After a bit of back and forth, the analyst says, graciously, "OK then, let's talk about whatever

---

[30] [Editor's note:] The story seems to be that told in Bourke and Rendall (1971).

you want."³¹ At this point the patient doesn't want to talk about his book anymore.

Analyst: "It seems like you're getting away from things today."

The patient acknowledges this and explains that he thinks the analyst means getting away from the couch, by wanting to sit up; and getting away from his psychological issues by wanting to talk about his book. But he adds that he's "getting away from things" in another sense. He had the idea of sitting up but then forgot or abandoned it. He got the analyst to agree to talk about his book but then didn't want to follow up on that opportunity.

The analyst agrees that there is indeed another level of "getting away from" and asks the patient **what he associates with that phrase**.

The patient replies that as a matter of fact, something definite comes to mind. He remembers that as a young man he was in a second-hand bookstore and came across a book on psychoanalysis, about which he knew almost nothing at the time. Browsing in it, he found an anecdote the author gave about an adult man who masturbated lying on his bed but with one foot on the floor. The analyst in the book had related it to the man's wanting to be able to *get away* in case he was caught (and perhaps to a childhood experience in which he had been caught). The patient says that this vignette has stayed with him and that it illustrates "what psychoanalysis can do."

The analyst asks if the patient **has any associations to feet**.

The patient again answers promptly: "My father used to say that human feet are incredibly ugly and it would be much nicer if we had little hooves."

"Do you feel like you have hooves?"

"No. Why?"

The analyst reminds the patient of how he has often compared himself to satyrs in Greek vase paintings (typically depicted with goat-like features) as a way of expressing how he experiences his sexuality.

The patient acknowledges the aptness of the connection but **goes on to say** that he has always found goats very sweet. **On further reflection**, however, he comes to the realization, by which he is very taken, that goats seem like the most ancient animals, conjuring up the earliest ages of humanity, sometimes in a sinister way. The patient **evokes the image** of ancient nomads with a couple of goats around a tent and **goes from there** to the biblical ritual of the scapegoat ("one goat for Azazel") and how archaic and frightening that seems. (Le Besco 2016: 93; emphasis in bold is mine)

---

[31] [Editor's note:] This is quite different from inviting the patient to free associate in the absolute sense.

In this second passage, the analyst twice asks for the patient's associations to particular elements (the phrase "getting away from" and feet). The patient himself engages in relative free association spontaneously in connection with goats. There is no big revelation in this excerpt or in the previous one, but they well convey the point of relative free association. Pregnant themes are raised and juxtaposed in interesting ways. There is a definite sense of the emergence of meaning from a welter of detail. Nor is the method particularly perplexing for a patient. Things may or may not come to mind but there is no unclarity about what is being asked of him.

The absolute sense of free association, by contrast, is considerably more difficult to understand and Evnine attempted to explore it in two places in his philosophical work, an early paper (1989) and an unpublished MS dating from the same time as the memes. At its simplest, one can see absolute free association as the refraining from censoring oneself because one is embarrassed or worried about hurting the feelings of the analyst, and so on. A step further would be to take it as refraining from imposing any narrative on one's thoughts.[32] This naturally leads to the idea that without the imposition of narrative and transition, the meaningfulness of the juxtapositions of ideas will be more clearly seen. But neither of these steps, valid though they are as characterizations of free association, fully gets to the heart of the matter.

In his 1989 paper, Evnine points out how Freud makes two claims about unconscious mental states which, taken together, have a very interesting consequence. On the one hand, such states are exempt from the demands of rationality (in the unconscious, Freud (1915: 134) says, there is "no negation, no dubiety, no varying degree of certainty"). On the other hand, a main reason for positing the existence of such unconscious states is because the demands of rationality on mental content in general are not fully satisfied by conscious mental states alone. These conscious states exhibit rational 'gaps' which can only be plugged by the attribution of unconscious states to the subject if her mental life as a whole is to meet the demands of rationality.[33] Free association is the primary method for making the unconscious conscious. Its character, therefore, is affected by the way in which unconscious mental states stand ambivalently with respect to the demands of reason. Free association is a kind of liminal activity. This leads Evnine to say that "[f]ree association is, paradoxically, the demonic possession of the patient by himself, which is yet the very opposite of self-possession" (1989: 96-7).

He goes on:

---

[32] The historian Robert Brentano memorably writes that a historian should present "a series of images and ideas whole, clear, bright, and let the transition occur, as it should, without the dullness of written words. Without words, transition becomes beautiful. If I ever have enough nerve, I shall write history completely without transition" (1988: 378). Despite some unclarity (an apparent conflation of transition without words and absence of transition), these are stirring words. They invite one to think of the patient in analysis as working up the nerve to attempt to write his or her own history without transition.

[33] Evnine draws here on the views of the philosopher Donald Davidson, on whom he wrote his first book (1991). I have occasion to say a bit about Davidson in my commentary on *Snow is white!* (M.70).

> One could say that the practice of free association turns the space of the analysis into the unconscious itself. In everyday life, our interaction with other people takes the form of what we might call discourse [an activity governed by principles of rationality]... But if the unconscious enters into the analysis, and if the unconscious is, as Freud claims, exempt from the principles of rationality, then it follows that analysis itself is no longer a form of discourse. (97)

The puzzling nature of the patient's speech in the analytic session is taken up in much greater detail in a later unpublished paper by Evnine, "Free Association and Expressive Limitations: A View from the Philosophy of Language." Taking off from an article by the Slovenian analyst Savo Spacal (1990), Evnine develops three conceptions of free association, all based on existing psychoanalytic theories. These are the Observational, the Productive, and the Relational Conceptions. Spacal associates the Observational Conception with Freud and Breuer:

> Even before Freud, Breuer had an important insight, according to Spacal: "a patient... is able to understand the latent meanings of her own symptoms and behavior, provided that she is left free to investigate her own inner world" (421). Breuer used hypnosis to help the patient investigate. Freud replaced Breuer's use of hypnosis with free association, which "was instituted primarily as an introspective modality" (423). Free association meant leaving the patient alone to investigate something only she could adequately access: the contents of her own mind.
>
> There are several components to the Observational Conception. 1) The patient has privileged access to a realm of data, her thinking, that the analyst can know about only indirectly. 2) If the patient lets her mind wander without conscious control, there will be information contained in the thoughts and their relations (mostly, the relation of temporal contiguity) that is valuable to the patient. 3) The analyst can help the patient see the value, but only if the patient can provide access to the data by means of verbalization. 4) The patient's task in free association is thus twofold – to let her mind wander freely in this way *and* to report the results to the analyst.
>
> A brief account of speech act theory, as propounded by the philosopher J.L. Austin, will allow us better to understand the nature of the patient's speech in all this. Austin (1975) distinguishes between a variety of different kinds of acts that a speaker performs when she speaks. One kind of act he calls "locutionary." A locutionary act is an act of uttering (either verbally or in writing) something with a particular semantic content. The specification of a locutionary act as such, therefore, is only by way of the semantic content involved and does nothing to address what the speaker is *up to* in making an utterance with that content on a particular occasion. But of course, when we speak, we almost always are up to something. We are asking a question, making an assertion, conjecturing, drawing a conclusion, giving an order, making a threat or a promise and so on. Acts of these kinds Austin calls "illocutionary" (since they

are acts we perform *in* performing *locutionary* acts). And asserting, denying, promising, asking, etc. are varieties of illocutionary force that a given utterance can have. We can promise *that the night will end*, assert *that the night will end*, or question *whether the night will end*. A single kind of locutionary act, making an utterance with the semantic content *that the night will end*, can be done, on different occasions, with different types of illocutionary force.

Certain illocutionary forces are conventionally associated with types of syntax – the imperative mood for a command, the interrogative for a question, the indicative for an assertion. But the syntax of an utterance is neither necessary nor sufficient for determining its illocutionary force. An excellent illustration of this point is provided by the game show *Jeopardy*, which calls itself an answer-and-question quiz show on the grounds that the host speaks in the indicative while contestants must reply in the interrogative mood. Notwithstanding that requirement, it is clear from an illocutionary point of view that the host is asking questions and the contestants giving answers. So the indicative mood is not necessary for making an assertion nor the interrogative sufficient for asking a question.

Returning to free association, the Observational Conception is dramatically expressed by Freud in his famous image of a train traveler. Freud would say to a patient: "act as though... you were a traveler sitting next to the window of a railway carriage and describing to someone inside the carriage the changing views you see outside" (1913: 135). So, think of the railway traveler following this injunction. Her face is pressed to the window, her back is towards the someone inside. She says things like "there are some cows in a field... the clouds are thickening... there is a waterfall...." Each of these utterances has the illocutionary force of an assertion and is a report of an observation (or as we might say, is an observation). If the person inside starts distracting her, she might turn away from the window and say "Please be quiet!" or "Stop tickling me!" but these requests/orders are *interruptions* of her activity, not *parts* of it. And she never has occasion, either, to ask any questions as part of her activity. (Though she might use the interrogative form to make an observation by means of a rhetorical question such as "Is that a pheasant?".)

Now think of the patient engaged in free association understood this way. She says "I am remembering that time that such and such... I am feeling cold in my left foot... I am looking at that picture..." and so on. These are reports of her thoughts, feelings, and perceptions. Like the train traveler, she never has occasion to order or request or ask questions. If the analyst distracts her, she might say "Please be quiet!" but that is an *interruption* of her activity not a *part* of it.[34] And she never questions. If she observes, within herself, some curiosity about something, say about whether the analyst has read a certain book, she can offer an observation to the effect that she has that curiosity, but to report that one is curious about whether the analyst has read a certain book is quite different, a different kind of illocutionary act, from asking the analyst whether she has read that book. The first does not call for an answer, the second does. (The analyst's silence, for example, would have a quite different meaning in the face of a question from the meaning it would have in the face of an observation of curiosity.)[35]

In some ways, this nexus between the epistemological idea that the patient, but not the analyst, has privileged access to the material essential to analysis (the patient's thoughts and their relations) and the illocutionary role of the patient as reporting that information to the analyst must have been virtually forced on psychoanalysis in its earliest moments. For the first analyst had (and could have had) no other analyst than himself. Freud's self-analysis involved, as the basis for his attempts to gain understanding, close observations of his own thoughts – the empirical observation of the phenomena under study. Whatever he did, his patients, in principle, could have done themselves. What corresponded to the speech of his patients was his own writing down of his self-observations. This writing down was, for him, like a scientist keeping a record of an experiment and served to make his data available to others, just as the patient's speech does on the Observational Conception.[36]

---

[34] [Evnine's note:] It was, of course, an interruption of this kind that practically inaugurated the method of free association when Frau Emmy von N. told Freud "in a definitely grumbling tone that I was not to keep on asking her where this and that came from, but to let her tell me what she had to say" (Breuer and Freud 1893-5: 60).

[35] [Evnine's note:] Bollas (2009: 10) gives a very different spin to Freud's train analogy, linking free association to the pursuit of a "train of thought." This seems to me to focus entirely on what is outside the window, so to speak, and ignores the role of reporting going on inside the train, which is integral to Freud's theorization of the relation between thinking and speaking in free association.

[36] [Evnine's note:] Patrick Mahony (1987) offers an interesting suggestion (though not one I find compelling) about why Freud, and some precursors in the history of free association like the Kabbalist Abraham Abulafia, might have written their associations down rather than spoken them aloud: "Writing is much slower than speech and could well have acted as a security device for those solitary forerunners who were fascinated and yet anxious before the torrential movement of an unleashed unconscious" (32). One reason I am not convinced, at least in the case of Freud, is that for Freud, his self-analysis was part of a scientific investigation. Writing down one's observations is just good scientific practice. Speaking them aloud, if he was alone, would not function to make the data available to others. Indeed, it would have been quite pointless. I think, however, that Mahony is probably conceiving of free association along the lines of the Productive Conception - as being primarily the production of language, not as a kind of thinking which is then reported. Certainly, the expression "the torrential movement of an unleashed unconscious" and the coupling of Freud with the experiments in automatic writing of Abulafia suggest this.

On the Observational Conception, when an analyst enjoins her patient, at the start of their work together, to follow the Fundamental Rule of free association – that "analytic patients are to put into words all their thoughts, feelings, and perceptions" (Lichtenberg and Galler 1987: 48) – she essentially has the role of an experienced scientist exhorting a tyro: "Don't be afraid to publish the data, to say what you've seen, even if you worry that I or your colleagues will ridicule you and you will lose professional standing! Stay true to the data! And no datum is too small or insignificant."[37]

The idea that "putting a thought into words" involves reporting that one has had that thought is, however, rather peculiar (and hence Freud's train analogy so inadequate). Such reporting is quite different from what we may call "expressing a thought." This is when one thinks in speaking, rather than speaks about thinking, something that is wittily captured by E.M. Forster (1927) when he writes "How can I tell what I think till I see what I say?" More seriously, many philosophers have advanced what they call a Transparency Thesis. In the words of Gareth Evans (1982), "[i]n making a self-ascription of belief, one's eyes... are directed outward – on the world." Evans goes on to give the following example:

> If someone asks me 'Do you think there is going to be a third world war?', I must attend, in answering him, to precisely the same outward phenomena as I would attend to if I were answering the question 'Will there be a third world war?' I get myself in a position to answer the question of whether I believe that *p* by putting into operation whatever procedure I have for answering the question whether *p*. (225)

If one finds the Transparency Thesis plausible, then the idea that one puts one's thoughts into words by reporting on them will appear perverse.

However, the matter is complicated by the fact that some thoughts can *only* be reported on and not, in the sense at issue, expressed. As Evnine explains:

> A prominent category of such thoughts [i.e., those which can only be reported on] is those that have already occurred. One cannot spontaneously express a thought one had yesterday. The best one can do is report that one had it.[38] There are two noteworthy special cases that fall under the rubric of thoughts that

---

[37] [Evnine's note:] See the language used to initiate a discussion of free association, as reported in Hoffer and Youngren (2004): "whether, in the rapidly changing field of psychoanalysis, 'free association' remains 'a basic tool of *data gathering*'" (1489, emphasis mine). The language of honesty and the patient's having made a promise also resonate here. Cf. Freud (1913): "Never forget that you have promised to be absolutely honest, and never leave out anything because, for some reason or other, it is unpleasant to tell it" (135); and M. Guy Thompson (2004).

[38] [Editor's note:] Of course, one might still have the thought or have it again, in which case it could be expressed and not merely reported on.

have already occurred. One is dreams. (In fact, their having already occurred is only one reason why they cannot be spontaneously expressed. The other is that sleeping inhibits one's ability to perform any illocutionary acts.) Another case is when several thoughts occur simultaneously. Irwin Hoffman (2006) raises this issue:

> What if, subjectively at least, the patient feels he or she has several things coming to mind *simultaneously*, several things that he or she *could* speak of, so that *only* by *choosing* will it be possible to speak at all? If that's the case, some judgment will be necessary in order to make that choice. (45; emphasis in the original)[39]

In cases like this, one would almost certainly not be able to express all the thoughts by a single utterance and hence would have to express some and then subsequently report on the others.[40]

Other thoughts that cannot be expressed, or cannot be adequately expressed, but can be reported on, include those that, unlike cognitive states (what philosophers call propositional attitudes), have no propositional content to be put into words: bodily sensations, moods, and things like that. If one has the thought that the weather looks nice, one can fully express it by saying "The weather looks nice" (or report on it by saying "I am having the thought that the weather looks nice"). But if, during a session, one gets a headache, the most one can do in expressing it is to say "ouch" or groan. In such a case, a report such as "I have a headache" may be much more valuable. And some such thoughts cannot even be inadequately expressed. Mild hunger, for example, could really only make its way into the session by being reported on.

Here is what Evnine says about the Productive Conception of free association, a conception that Spacal associates with Melanie Klein.

---

[39] [Evnine's note:] It may be that by writing "subjectively at least," Hoffman intends to back off from the claim that it actually is possible to have several thoughts simultaneously. Examining this issue would be too much of a diversion but see Peacocke (2023) for an argument that it is possible.

Hoffman is arguing in his paper that we should see a role for agency in free association. He is, in my terms, challenging the Productive Conception (which he takes to be widely accepted) since, as we shall see, it is only on that conception that free association might be thought to exclude agency. One would, for example, not be tempted at all to deny agency to Freud in writing down his observations of his own thoughts.

[40] [Editor's note:] Why does Evnine write "almost certainly" rather than leave his claim unqualified? Presumably, he is, in his tiresome way, alive to the possibility of ambiguity. If one simultaneously thought one was at the edge of a river and that one was at a financial institution, one could simultaneously express both thoughts by an utterance of "I am at a bank." One would not need to express one and then report the other.

One can immediately see that Klein's conception of free association must be enormously different from the Observational one from the continuity she asserts between free association in adult patients and play in child patients. The reason is obvious: play does not generally contain acts that have the illocutionary force of assertions. The elements of a child patient's play, therefore, cannot be *reports* on her states of mind. What the child is doing, in the context of analysis, is producing material for the analyst to interpret. Anything one does, of course, might be (and often is) interpreted by the analyst, but the point of play is that its particular conditions make it especially fruitful as a source of interpretable material. (It also has the advantage of by-passing the possibly still poor language skills of the child.) I take the 'particular conditions' to be something like this: play is an activity that the player can become lost in, and this becoming lost in the activity enables unconscious forces and ideas more easily to shape the character of that behavior. The same holds, *mutatis mutandis*, for free association in the adult patient, on the Productive Conception. Free association is the adult counterpart of playing. It is supposed to be, ideally, not just talking but "getting lost in" talking, aided by the supine position and the analyst's being out of sight. Talking, under these conditions, is a privileged mode of production that allows unconscious forces and ideas more easily to shape the talking and in which the product is, therefore, especially apt for interpretation by the analyst.

Talk (or other forms of language production) is generally superior to play because of the richness of what can be expressed by it. Someone can express a belief that Mark Twain was an author and a simultaneous belief that Samuel Clemens was not an author, even though Samuel Clemens was Mark Twain. It is hard to envisage anything short of language enabling someone to express those two beliefs. But if a child does not have the language skills, or if a patient of any age for some reason finds language production hard, then other behaviors, which may already be on the analyst's horizon, might take on a greater role as part of the field of free association. In this light, we can note that in their survey article about free association, Lichtenberg and Galler (1987) report how many analysts have found it useful to enlarge the scope of the fundamental rule, advising patients that if they feel they can't talk, they may express themselves in other ways.

> When analyzing patients with severe blocking of speech, Scott [(1958)] encouraged his patients to make noises within the analytic hour by reformulating the fundamental rule: "Try to talk, etc., and if you can't talk, try to make some kind of noise, and if you don't know what kind of noise to make, just guess" (p. 108). ... Gedo (1981) indicated that, at times, whistling was an appropriate communication for the therapist, and, by analogy,

> a satisfactory communication by the patient. Balint (1959) [sic] encouraged an inhibited patient to perform a somersault within her analytic hour. (53-4)[41]

> These features of free association, on the Productive Conception, are allied with further differences between the theoretical contexts of the Observational and the Productive Conceptions. The patient is no longer the expert, keeping the analyst apprised of her observations. Rather, as Melanie Klein (1955) writes: "the psycho-analytic procedure consists... in understanding the patient's mind and in conveying to him what goes on in it" (10). This goes hand in hand with the development by Klein and her followers of the notion of projective identification and attention to the utility of the countertransference, both of which are avenues by which the analyst's own thought processes come to contain information about the patient's mind. The analyst's initial exhortation to patients to "to put into words all their thoughts, feelings, and perceptions" is not to be heard, as it is with the Observational Conception, as back-stiffening encouragement from a senior fellow to help the patient's investigation into her own mind, but rather as the call of the taskmaster to the worker to keep up production. In words from the first movie version of *Dune*, here giving rise to an apt *double entendre*, "the Spice must flow"! The analyst needs lots of rich material to work on and the patient is the one to produce it.

Evnine goes on to draw from the Productive Conception potentially alarming consequences for the patient engaged in free association, again basing himself on the continuity of play and free association.

> I said above that this showed that the Kleinian conception of free association must be different from the Observational because in play, a child is not making observations at all. But we can go further than this. In play, a child is not generally engaged in genuine illocutionary acts of any kind – not asserting, questioning, commanding, entreating. This is not just because play does not have to involve language. It holds equally in cases where the play does involve language. Consider this passage from a case history. A therapist reports how a young patient "*appointed me his assistant* and equipped me with an endless number of space guns... Every now and then... he would... order me to execute

---

[41] [Evnine's note:] As it happens, two of the three examples referred to in this paragraph are problematic. Scott's "just guess" strikes a very jarring note. Guessing, if one doesn't know something, is an activity aimed at getting the right answer, which seems wholly alien to the Productive Conception of free association (and can also have no place in the Observational Conception if what one is guessing is the right noise to make). And Balint's patient's somersault is not at all spontaneous, being undertaken at the instigation of the analyst. It seems to constitute an interruption of the process of free association rather than a part of it. It would be quite another matter if the patient just got up and did a somersault without encouragement. (Lichtenberg and Galler's reference to Balint is mistaken. The anecdote appears in his (1968: 127-32) and not in (1959).)

some maneuver, since he was so busy shooting" (Sidoli 1996: 169-70; emphasis mine). Consider first the non-illocutionary action-description: "equipped me with an endless number of space guns." Perhaps the child gave the therapist some toy guns or perhaps he merely mimed an action of giving. But it is clear that he did not actually equip his therapist with space guns. He merely pretended to. Now consider the phrases I have italicized, which are illocutionary action-descriptions. Does the child actually order the therapist to execute some maneuver? He may utter the sentence "Fire the port lasers!" (i.e., perform a locutionary act with that content) but he no more orders the therapist than he equips her with space guns. He cannot order his therapist to do things. He doesn't have that kind of authority over her. In the play, he pretends to order her. Finally, consider "appointed me his assistant." This is ambiguous. In one sense it might be expanded along these lines: "lifted me from the lowly rank of deck hand in recognition of my bravery in battle." In this sense, the child cannot actually appoint the therapist as his assistant. Once again, we would be dealing with a pretense of illocution. But the phrase "appointed me his assistant" might mean something like: assigned me the part of assistant in the game we were about to play. This is a real illocutionary act the child can perform. It's his game. He has the standing to assign the therapist a particular role in it. But equally, the real illocution is not *part* of the play but a precondition to it. In sum, even when it involves language use, play does not generally involve real illocution but merely pretend illocution.[42]

My contention is that something like this applies to the adult patient who primarily speaks rather than plays. That this should be so is evident from the model of free association as the production of material. Illocutionary force characterizes social interaction. If a patient produces speech as material, then the words are not part of a social interaction, though the act of producing them might be. As material, the sounds of the words may be of interest, the syntax, the semantic meaning (related to the locutionary acts the patient performs). But none of this adds up to insertion of the patient's speech into an illocutionary context. Rather shockingly, it turns out that, although the patient may, as part of her free association (and unlike on the Observational Conception) apparently ask questions, issue commands, speculate, fantasize, and assert,

---

[42] [Editor's note:] This is surely a vast overstatement about play in general since not all play involves pretending.

none of that matters for the goals of free association.[43] The patient is, as it were, illocutionarily disabled.[44]

A big difference between the child engaged in play and the adult engaged in free association, however, is that the adult is not pretending anything. It is the nature of play and of the related activity of pretense that blocks the child's illocutionary range.[45] What is it, exactly, about free association, on the Productive Conception, that does the same for the adult? It is the environment created by the analytic frame.[46] There are two ways of bringing this out and I am genuinely unsure whether or not they are ultimately equivalent. It could be that in free association the patient successfully brings off the various illocutionary acts she seems to herself to be performing – making assertions, conjecturing, asking questions, etc. – but the frame leads the analyst simply to ignore them. But we might also say that the frame includes the analyst's deliberate denial of the appropriate uptake to the attempted illocutionary acts in such a way as to render the patient literally unable to make them. The patient can, of course, utter whatever words she wants, in whatever tone she wants, and take herself to be asserting or questioning, but in reality, the frame of the analysis renders such acts impossible.

On the second way of putting things, and on the first too if they are equivalent, there is something decidedly sinister about this conception of free association. In her study of "disempowered speech," Jennifer Hornsby (1995) characterizes a notion of what she calls "inaudibility." The performance of a "successful speech act" requires a certain kind of uptake. Uptake is not to be confused with a desired response. Taking up a question does not entail offering

---

[43] [Evnine's note:] This requires an important qualification. On the Productive Conception, if the patient seems to ask a question, for example, the context is such that its illocutionary force is somehow blocked. As part of the material produced for interpretation, it does not call for an answer. But the fact that the patient may be appearing to ask a question is part of the material. So illocutionary force is not wholly irrelevant. It just doesn't work in the usual way.

[44] [Evnine's note:] This is one way of understanding Freud's remark in "Negation" that "in our interpretation, we take the liberty of disregarding the negation and of picking out the subject-matter alone of the association" (1925: 235). If "negation" is understood as "denial" (which in fact is the more usual translation of the word *verneinung* used here) and "the subject matter of the association" is taken as the propositional content of what the patient says, then Freud is saying exactly that he disregards the illocutionary aspect of the patient's speech and attends only to its locutionary aspect.

[45] [Evnine's note:] As, analogously, it is the nature of sleep to disable the sleeper illocutionarily. A sleeper may perform a locutionary act, say of uttering a sentence the content of which is that a clock in another room be set seven minutes slow. But someone completely asleep cannot, by virtue of their being asleep, make a request to set that clock seven minutes slow. We would not, overhearing the sleeper, take ourselves to have even a *prima facie* reason to adjust the clock.

[46] [Editor's note:] See the commentary on *Not a Strict Freudian* (M.78) for Agnès Fabrikant's (1997) remarks about the relation between the analytic frame and the parergon.

an answer to it. Rather, uptake includes (and is perhaps exhausted by) the recognition that the speaker is, in some sense, performing, or able to perform, a speech act of the kind she is attempting. When a failure of this kind of uptake obtains, Hornsby describes it as a violation of "reciprocity." One of her examples is how women's refusal of sexual advances becomes impossible in a context in which it is widely believed that women will say "no" when they mean "yes." To the extent that the Productive Conception of free association treats patients as producers, there will be a failure to take them as being in a position to perform illocutionary acts at all. They are illocutionarily inaudible, just as the sleeper is in her sleep-talking or the child in her play.

We come finally to what Evnine has to say about the Relational Conception of free association, associated by Spacal with relational trends in the development of psychoanalysis.

In this context, the patient's speech is neither a scientific report on the contents of her mind nor the production of illocutionarily inert material to fuel the analyst's activity but is rather part of the development of a relationship. It is, therefore, talk of a kind that is much more familiar to us than talk as understood according to either of the other two conceptions. In one sense, that of fostering a relationship, it is of exactly the same nature as the analyst's own talk. The two parties *talk to each other*. There is no violation of reciprocity.

The analyst's statement of the fundamental rule should be heard, on the Relational Conception, as an encouragement to a kind of intimacy. "Open yourself to me as much as is possible. There's no need to hold back in here. Don't worry about hurting or shocking me. Say whatever you happen to feel. It's all good." Self-censorship on the part of the patient is not like suppression of the data (as it is on the Observational Conception) nor like slacking in the production of Spice (as it is on the Productive Conception) but a failure of trust, a holding back from the development of the right kind of relationship....

A relationship between two people is sensitive to all their behavior together, verbal and non-verbal. Indeed, it is so all-inclusive as to become almost invisible. Spacal says, "the method of free association simply loses its importance in the face of the operative principle of an optimum relationship" (431). I would prefer to say, free association becomes less of a method and more a way of relating. Insofar as free association is still seen as a method or technique there is therefore some tendency to downplay its significance from a relational perspective.[47]

---

[47] [Evnine's note:] In this context, see the framing of Hoffer and Youngren (2004) and Hoffman (2006). Ogden (1996) is a more complex case. He disavows the fundamental rule, which he considers a dispensable "aspect of technique," but at least part of his reason for disavowing it is to qualify the Relational Conception itself in the name of the patient's 'right' to privacy and non-communication. For

To return to M.14, it is evident, given this welter of complexity, that Batman's 'encouragement,' his "all you have to do," is woefully inadequate and simplistic.

someone like Ogden, the main fault of the otherwise anodyne Relation Conception is a tendency to overbearing intrusiveness.

M.15 Barbara Celarent

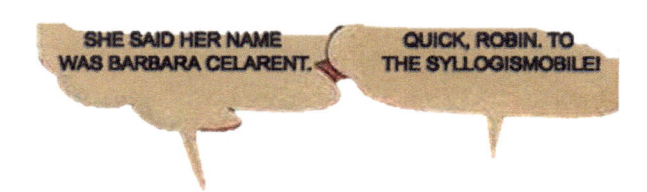

M.15 Barbara Celarent Composed: February 26th. Posted: February 26th. Orientation: Reverse. Font: Arial. TB1: "SHE SAID HER NAME WAS BARBARA CELARENT.", black. TB2: "QUICK, ROBIN, TO THE SYLLOGISMOBILE!", black.

Visually, a rather ugly meme. The text looks even worse than text all in capitals usually does, perhaps because of the flattened appearance of the two lines in the middle of each speech bubble. But notwithstanding its visual deficiencies, it is, as we shall see, interesting and amusing. We should also note that it is the first appearance of the theme of names and naming that is so dominant throughout the whole meme project. Like *Lunchtime* (M.28), *I am Spartacus!* (M.65), *Vos iz ayer yidisher nomen, Batman?* (M.72), *Too Easy, Robin!* (M.75), and *A Girl Has no Name* (M.94), it explicitly involves a question or statement about what someone is called.

Who is Barbara Celarent and why does her name elicit this response from Batman? To understand what Robin says, we must examine Aristotle's theory of the syllogism.[48] The word "syllogism" has passed into ordinary language as synonymous with "deductive argument," or even "argument," but for Aristotle and for logicians who have followed him, even into the 20th century, a syllogism is a particular kind of deductive argument. It consists of three sentences (two premises and a conclusion) each of which is of one of the following four forms:

(A) Every S is P (Universal Affirmative)

---

[48] I have drawn on a number of sources for the following, but special mention must be given to Spade (2007) on which I have relied greatly.

(E) No S is P (=Every S is not P) (Universal Negative)

(I) Some S is P (Particular Affirmative)

(O) Some S is not P (Particular Negative)

These forms consist of "terms" (S, P), a copula ("is"), and a quantifier ("every," "some") and, in the cases of E and O, a negation operator ("not").[49] The quantifier and the term that it governs ("Every S" or "Some S") together make the subject of a sentence (though I shall sometimes refer to the term in question itself as the subject); the other term is its predicate. A syllogism involves three distinct terms, each of which appears in two of the three sentences. The term that is the subject in the conclusion is called the minor term and that which is the predicate of the conclusion is called the major term.[50] The term that appears only in the premises is called the middle term. Evidently it, in its relation to the major and minor terms, in conjunction with the particular forms of the sentences in question, is what 'mediates' the terms in the conclusion so as to make the syllogism valid or invalid. As an example, consider the following:

1) Every human is mortal;

2) Every musician is human;

3) Every musician is mortal.[51]

"Musician" is the minor term, "mortal" the major term, and "human" the middle term. All the sentences are of the A form (universal affirmative). And the syllogism is clearly valid – if its premises are true, then the conclusion must be true as well. (Note that this condition holds whether or not the premises or conclusion are actually true. Validity is about the relation of the conclusion to the premises, not its or their truth.) We may call the premise with the major term (1), the major premise and that with the minor term (2), the minor premise.

There are many types of syllogism. Let us consider them under four figures (as they were traditionally called): the middle term is the subject in the major premise and the predicate in the minor premise (our sample argument above is of this kind); the middle term is the predicate in both premises; the middle term is the subject in both premises; and the middle term is the subject in the minor premise and the predicate in the major premise.[52] For each figure, we are dealing with arguments with three statements, each of which can take one of

---

[49] Or one could distinguish two distinct copulas – "is" and "is not" – and simply say that each of these forms contains terms, a copula, and a quantifier.

[50] Terminology on this point was unsystematic in Aristotle and his followers. As most modern writers do, I follow the practice of the ancient commentator John Philoponus (6th century CE).

[51] For many people, the paradigm of a syllogism is "All men are mortal; Socrates is a man; Socrates is mortal." It will be immediately evident that this does not, strictly, count as a syllogism at all by the conditions we have laid down since the subject of one of the premises and the conclusion is "Socrates" and not a quantifier followed by a term. No matter. Just treat the name as a term that happens to apply only to its bearer (or think of it as abbreviating some general term that only applies to that bearer, such as "husband of Xanthippe") and treat it as "every Socrates" (or "every husband of Xanthippe").

[52] It was not until after the Middle Ages that the fourth figure was regularly distinguished from the first figure. As will be evident, the first and fourth together are aptly described as having the middle term as subject in one premise and predicate in the other.

four possible forms (A, E, I, O). That means that, for each figure, there are 4^3=64 combinations, or 256 kinds of syllogism across all four figures. For example, let us pick, at random, the second figure (so the middle term is in the subject position in both premises), with the sentences being of the forms O for the major premise, A for the minor premise, and I for the conclusion. Choosing as our major, minor, and middle terms our previous assignments ("mortal," "musician," and "human" respectively) that would give us a syllogism like this:

4) Some human is not mortal (O form, with the predicate of the conclusion, hence the major premise)
5) Every human is (a) musician (A form, with the subject of the conclusion, hence the minor premise)
6) Some musician is mortal (I form, without the middle term)

This is not a valid syllogism as one can see if one thinks about a situation in which no human is mortal and all musicians are humans. Of course, the first of these suppositions is false (and the second is at least controversial, depending on whether one thinks birds, for example, are musicians). But the validity of the syllogism requires that if the premises are true, the conclusion *must* be true as well. In the imagined circumstances, the premises might be true but the conclusion would be false.

In fact, of the 256 varieties of syllogism, only 24 are valid. These 24 varieties are known as "moods." (Sometimes the count is given as 19 because five moods – known as subalternate – are trivial variants of others. Take the mood illustrated by 1)-3) above. If we changed the conclusion to "Some musician is mortal" we would have a distinct valid mood, but it is trivial because, for Aristotle, any statement of the form "Every S is P" implies a statement of the form "Some S is P."[53] Some tallies omit the subalternate moods and some do not.) How is one to remember which the valid moods are? Here we get, finally, to Barbara Celarent. Medieval logicians gave names to the valid moods, names that encode information about them.[54] The names have three syllables (or, in a couple of cases, more that are non-functional) and the vowel for each syllable is either A, E, I, or O. These give the forms of the major premise, the minor premise, and the conclusion. So the name of the mood illustrated in 1)-3) has three "A" vowels, because its premises and conclusion are all in the A form (universal affirmative). Its name, in fact, is "Barbara." Of the six valid moods of the first figure (the middle term is the subject in the major premise – the premise in which it is paired with the predicate of the conclusion – and the predicate in the minor premise – the premise in which it is paired with the subject of the conclusion), two are subalternate and hence not of primary importance. The

---

[53] This is one respect in which Aristotle differs from modern logicians who take sentences of the form "Every S is P" to be equivalent to "No S is not P" and hence to be true if there are no S's at all and hence if the sentence "Some S is P" is false.

[54] The precise origin of these names is unknown. They are sometimes associated with William of Sherwood, from around 1250, but they can be found in two earlier anonymous manuscripts from around 1200 or just before. See Kretzmann (1966: 66 n.27 and 67 n. 28). Uckelman (2017) has an excellent, thorough discussion of the early textual evidence for medieval syllogistic mnemonics.

remaining four are given the names "Barbara," "Celarent," "Darii," and "Ferio."[55] All the names of the other moods begin with B, C, D, or F to indicate that they can be converted (or 'reduced,' as it is often put), by means of certain transformations, into syllogisms of one of the original four forms.[56] The names of the other moods encode the information about how the conversion is accomplished. For example, if a vowel is followed by an S (except at the end of the name), the preceding sentence should be converted by reversing the subject and predicate terms. (This works with sentences of the E and I forms. If no S is P, then no P is S and if some S is P, then some P is S.) If the letter P follows a vowel (except at the end of the name), then the preceding sentence should be converted in the following way: exchange the subject and predicate, and 'lower' the quantifier from "Every" to "Some." (This works for the A form. If every S is P, then while it is not necessarily true that every P is S, it must be true that some P is S.) These, plus a few further rules, suffice to show how any valid syllogism (with the exception of two, as noted) can be converted to a syllogism of the first figure, either Barbara, Celarent, Darii, or Ferio. (We shall illustrate this in the next paragraph.) The great 19th century logician Augustus De Morgan said these syllogistic names were "magic words... more full of meaning than any that were ever made" (1847: 130).

[55] The basic four moods of the first figure use, in order, the first four letters of the alphabet, minus the vowels "A" and "E," which are already used by the system to indicate universal positive and universal negative sentences respectively. This is not generally commented on in expositions of the mnemonic system. (Perhaps it is considered too obvious to need pointing out – but it took me, personally, years to realize it; and an informal survey of specialists in ancient and medieval logic revealed that many scholars had not noticed this fact.) The history of alphabetization is a highly interesting topic in its own right. It probably developed first in Alexandria, in connection with that city's great library, as a way of organizing information for easier retrieval in scholarly and administrative contexts (Daly 1967). In the Middle Ages, and especially in the second half of the 12th century (just around the time we begin to have evidence of the syllogistic names) alphabetization really began to take off in scholarly circles (Rouse and Rouse 1982). It was not, however, embraced without reservation. Alphabetical order was seen as a makeshift way of accommodating human frailty, an ordering at odds with the superior rational order of things, which hung on as a rival to alphabetical order for some time. Given this background, it is somewhat puzzling why the inventor of the syllogistic mnemonic should have used alphabetical order for the first four moods. Since the names were not independently in use, alphabetization does not serve to organize an existing body of knowledge. It also probably does little in the way of rendering the mnemonic verse easier to remember. In his logical works, Aristotle introduced the variable and generally used as his variables the first three letters of the Greek alphabet, alpha, beta, and gamma. In a case like this, the alphabetic ordering of the three letters chosen, letters which, in the very nature of the case, are completely arbitrary, has the effect of making something otherwise surd at least somewhat rational. In other words, far from there being an opposition between alphabetic and rational ordering in that case, the alphabetic ordering *is* a rational ordering when choosing letters to function as variables. I suggest that the choice of names for the first four syllogistic moods works in the same way. Given the absence of any other principle of choice among made up, three syllable names, a resort to the alphabetic provides at least some sense of obedience to reason.

[56] Two of them cannot be converted by these rules but require a slightly different process of conversion. We shall ignore them in what follows. See Spade (2007: 24 n.41) for a good explanation of why these recalcitrant two moods cannot be converted in the usual way.

Finally, verses were written to help students remember the names, with all the information they encode. William of Sherwood's version, from his mid-13th century *Introduciones in logicam* gives the 19 count thus:

> Barbara celarent darii ferio baralipton
> Celantes dabitis fapesmo frisesomorum;
> Cesare campestres festion baroco; darapti
> Felapton disamis datisi bocardo ferison.[57]

One obvious weakness of this mnemonic device is that the names in question mean nothing. Most of them look like names of characters in a fantasy novel by L. Sprague de Camp (on whom, more below)! But in truth, it would be hard to devise a system that carried as much information which, in addition, actually meant something. A second weakness is that the names themselves do not tell you which figures the valid syllogisms they name belong to. Given just a name, Festion for example, we know it designates a mood in which the major premise has the form "No … is …," the minor premise has the form "Some … is …" and the conclusion the form "Some … is not …" And we know that it can be reduced to a syllogism of the form Ferio by converting the first premise by exchanging the subject and predicate terms. (The "f" at the beginning and the "s" after the first vowel tell us these things.) Since Ferio has the following form

> No B is C;
> Some A is B;
> Some A is not C,

we learn that Festion has the form

> No C is B;
> Some A is B;
> Some A is not C.

Here, the middle term, the one not appearing in the conclusion, is the predicate in both premises, hence Festion is of the second figure. However, the name itself did not carry that information. We had to work to extract it.

Later authors sought to remedy this defect. Some composed versions of the mnemonic verse that included the reference to the figures explicitly. Here is a common version that seems to have been composed by Henry Aldrich, in his *Artis Logicae Compendium* (1691), an enormously influential logic textbook which "remained in use until the second half of the nineteenth century" (Kneale and Kneale 1962: 298):

> Barbara, Celarent, Darii, Ferioque *prioris*.
> Cesare, Camestres, Festino, Baroko *secundae*.
> *Tertia* Darapti, Disamis, Datisi, Felapton,
> Bokardo, Ferison habet. Quarta insuper addit

---

[57] Note the organization into three figures only, separated by semi-colons. The first group is large since it contains all those moods (minus the three subalternates) that would later be distributed amongst the first and fourth figures.

> Bramantip, Camenes, Dimaris, Fesapo, Fresison[58]

(Some of the names have slightly different forms here. For example, Festion shows up here as Festino. I have italicized the words that are not names of syllogisms. They mean "of the first," "of the second," "the third has...," and "the fourth adds in addition... .") Others amended the names in such a way that each name itself would contain the information of which figure the syllogism it named belonged to. One such scheme was devised by the important late 19th and early 20th century mathematician, logician and psychologist, Christine Ladd-Franklin (1847-1930) in her paper "On the Algebra of Logic":

> If there were ever any occasion to use the mnemonic verses of syllogism, it might be worth while to put them into a form in which each word should bear the mark of its figure, as well as of its mood and its method of reduction. By some slight changes in the words, the first, second, third, and fourth figures might be indicated by the letters r, t, l, and n respectively: –
>
> (r) Barbara, Cegare, Darii, Ferioque prioris
> (t) Cesate, Camestes, Festivo, Batoko secundae.
> (l) Tertia, Dalipi, Disalmis, Dalisi, Felapo.
> (l) Bokalo, Feliso, habet; quarta insuper addit,
> (n) Bamanip, Camenes, Dimanis, Fesanpo, Fesion. (Ladd-Franklin 1883: 40 n. 1)

(The period after "Felapo" should probably be a comma.)[59]

Now let us turn to Batman's response. It is obviously modeled on the common phrase, from the 1960's Batman TV series: "Quick, Robin, to the Batmobile!" (This mode of expression was, as our Anonymous Dissertator quoted in the commentary to *It's Been Done!* (M.6) revealed, adapted by the artist's brother in his home movie.) But the vehicle invoked in *Barbara Celarent* is a "syllogismobile." This must surely be an allusion to the Harold Shea stories by Fletcher Pratt and L. Sprague de Camp. (The bibliography for these stories is somewhat complex and I shall not pursue it here.) The term is introduced in the first such story, *The Roaring Trumpet* from 1940. The first speaker is the character Reed Chalmers:

> "As you know, you can build up a self-consistent logic on almost any set of assumptions... To contrive a vehicle for transportation from one world to another, we face the arduous task of extracting from the picture of such a world as that of the *Iliad* its basic assumptions, and expressing these in logical form —"
>
> Shea interrupted: "In other words, building us a syllogismobile?" (Sprague de Camp and Pratt 1975: 8-9)

---

[58] Many thanks to Professor Clinton Tolley for help in tracing this back to Aldrich.
[59] See Uckelman (2021) for an in-depth assessment of Ladd-Franklin's work on the syllogism.

When one has extracted these basic assumptions, one impresses them (somehow!) on one's mind and thereby travels by syllogismobile to the world thus epitomized. Shea decides to send himself to the Ireland of Cuchulinn and Queen Maev in this manner. He recites the "basic assumptions" of such a world, expressed in logical form:

> "[1] If P equals not-Q, Q implies not-P, which is equivalent to saying either P or Q or neither, but not both. [2] *But* if not-P is not implied by not-Q, the counter-implicative form of the proposition... [3] The full argument thus consists in an epicheirematic syllogism in Barbara, the major premise of which is *not* the conclusion of an enthymeme, though the minor premise of which may or may not be the conclusion of a non-Aristotelian sorites... [4] If either P or Q is true or (Q or R) is true then either Q is true or (P or R) is false—"...
>
> He had done it. The formula worked! (12-3; I have added the numbers in square brackets)

In fact, the formula has not worked, at least not in the intended way, for Harold finds himself in the world of Norse mythology, a far colder and more brutal destination than he was hoping for!

The passage is of some interest. (It should be noted that each set of ellipses displaces a paragraph or so of intervening description of the process of Shea's 'translation' to his destination and that the whole set of assumptions is itself said to be six pages long.) The most interesting thing to notice is how different [3] is from the rest of the text. [1], [2], and [4] are all couched in the idiom of modern symbolic logic.[60] [3], on the other hand, is couched in the idiom of traditional, syllogistic logic, with its attendant obscure terminology ("epicheirematic," "enthymeme," "Barbara," and "sorites"). In some ways, the juxtaposition of these two idioms here, as the moving parts of a syllogismobile, stands as a good emblem for the sensibility of writers like Fletcher Pratt and L. Sprague de Camp. On the one hand, they inhabited the world

---

[60] This is evident in a couple of features. Traditional logic, deriving ultimately from Aristotle's syllogistic but stretching all the way into the early 20th century, usually represents propositions or sentences as having internal structure – usually of the subject-predicate form "S is P" – even when considering the use of those propositions as wholes (in conjunctions, negations, and so on) where the internal structure is not relevant (as it *is* in the syllogism) to the logical relations being studied. It was a development of modern, mathematically-inspired logic, toward the end of the 19th century, to treat inferences that do not depend on the internal structure of propositions by using single letters to represent the propositions involved. And the use of the letters "p," "q," and "r" as the primary propositional letters (as we see in the excerpt from Pratt and Sprague de Camp) originated only (probably) in 1897 in the work of Giuseppe Peano. It became completely standard after it was taken up by Bertrand Russell in his 1903 *Principles of Mathematics* and by Russell together with A.N. Whitehead, in their monumental *Principia Mathematica* (1910-3). (See *Seek Simplicity* (M.10) and *Dialetheism* (M.20) for memes that refer to Whitehead and Russell respectively.) Finally, the development of this so-called propositional logic required the careful use of some device to resolve ambiguities in parsing. Peano et al. used a system of dots but the now-standard parentheses (used somewhat haphazardly in the quotation from Pratt and Sprague de Camp) quickly caught on. It is these features, propositional letters, specifically "p," "q," and "r," and the use of parentheses, that make [1], [2], and [4] belong to the world of the then-relatively-recently developed mathematical logic rather than that of traditional logic.

of high fantasy, full of mages, wizards, and bizarre names. In such a world, [3] would feel right at home. At the same time, Pratt was a serious military historian and Sprague de Camp was trained as an aeronautical engineer. The scientific milieu of modern mathematical logic is also important to them. (Sprague de Camp was a stickler for not playing fast and loose with science, and as outlandish as the idea of a syllogismobile is, it also represents a sense of the importance of logic and reason even in the realm of high fantasy; such worlds are expected to be internally coherent.) The very yoking of the genres of fantasy and science fiction seems to be embodied in this passage.

As for the details of Shea's invocation, it is, unsurprisingly, hard to make much sense of what is supposed to be going on. Reed Chalmers speaks of expressing in logical form "the basic assumptions" of some fictional or mythological world. One might naturally think that these assumptions would have substantive empirical content: "there are gods of the following kind…," "magic works in the following way…," etc. But the syllogismobile, as constructed, seems devoid of any empirical content. Is the difference between, say, the actual world and the world of Norse mythology simply that the worlds obey different logical principles? Even if there could be different worlds that obeyed different logics, there is no reason to think that each mythology, each fictional world, would have its own proprietary logic. Must there be a *logical* difference between the worlds of Norse mythology and the Ireland of Cuchulinn and Queen Maev? In any case, [1] is a tautology (true regardless of the truth or falsity of P and Q) according to the logic of Whitehead and Russell.[61] [2] is a fragment and cannot be evaluated for truth or falsity.[62] [4], finally, has some bite since it is, in fact, false. So maybe [4] is where we find the difference between reality and the world of Norse mythology!

What about [3]? An epicheirematic syllogism is a syllogism in which one or both of the premises is enhanced by the inclusion of a reason why it should be accepted. We have seen what is meant by saying it is "in Barbara." We are therefore talking about a syllogism that looks something like this:

> Every B is C, because… (major premise)
> Every A is B, because… (minor premise)
> Every A is C.

---

[61] But maybe that is the point! In the second Harold Shea story, *The Mathematics of Magic*, we are given two parts of the syllogismobile designed (successfully, this time) to get Harold and his friend Reed Chalmers to the world of *The Faerie Queen*. The first part is just [1] again, the second part is cast, again, in a more syllogistic idiom. So perhaps the trivial [1] is intended to guarantee some certain level of normality in the world aimed at, as if to say that whatever the differences, they will not contravene basic logic!

[62] The term "counter-implicative" comes from W.E. Johnson's *Logic* (1921-4). The counter-implicative of two propositions P and Q (or of the proposition "If P then Q") is the proposition "If Q then P." It is not clear, from the syntax, whether Shea is introducing "If not-Q then not-P" *as* a counter-implicative or is about to introduce *its* counter-implicative. In either case, the missing proposition would be "If not-P then not-Q."

The major premise, we are told, is not the conclusion of an enthymeme; an enthymeme is an argument in which one of the premises is not stated explicitly. And the minor premise may or may not be the conclusion of a non-Aristotelian sorites. A sorites is an argument constructed by chaining together syllogisms and suppressing all the but the final conclusion. An Aristotelian sorites has the form:

> Every A is B
> Every B is C
> .
> .
> .
> Every A is Z.

A non-Aristotelian (or Goclenian) sorites has the form:

> Every Y is Z
> Every X is Y
> .
> .
> .
> Every A is Z.

[3], therefore, does not say very much. Only that some argument has a certain form and that one of its premises is not the conclusion of a certain kind of argument and the other of its premises may or may not be the conclusion of a different type of argument! But clearly, the point is the profusion of esoteric terminology. All this terminology, and the identification of these forms, could have been picked up by the authors from any number of places since it was utterly standard for logic textbooks, at least as far back as Aldrich (1691) (to whom we credited an important variant of the mnemonic verse for syllogistic moods) to treat the enthymeme, the epicheirema and the sorites together in a single chapter. Sprague de Camp and Pratt may well have gotten it from Mansel (1849), Keynes (1884), or Joseph (1906), all very popular and much reprinted, but there are probably a dozen or so more possible sources.

M.17 Ode to Napoleon

M.17 Ode to Napoleon Composed: February 22nd. Posted: February 28th. Orientation: Reverse. Font: Comic Sans. TB1: "I'm sure I'll be able to step in tomorrow to conduct Schoenberg's "Ode to Napol..."", white. TB2: "Don't be an idiot! You know nothing about music.", white.

It is not clear why Evnine has "Schoenberg" here rather than "Schönberg" since the meme generator he used does accommodate the umlaut and that would have certainly been much funnier.

The content of the meme reflects an incident from the artist's early years as a music student at King's College London. (The incident probably occurred in 1980.) Several students and one faculty member were working, over a period of a couple of weeks, on Arnold Schönberg's 1942/3 piece *Ode to Napoleon Buonaparte* (op. 41), in preparation for a performance. (Schönberg makes another appearance, though unnamed, in *My favorite notes* (M.55).) The piece is scored for string quartet, piano, and reciter but notwithstanding the relatively small number of performers involved, the musicians were feeling the lack of someone to conduct. One day, the artist overheard them discussing this and cockily volunteered himself. In Batman's words, effectively, Evnine knew nothing about music. He certainly had never had experience conducting anything, let alone a work as complex as this one. But the faculty member involved went ahead and agreed, giving Evnine the score in preparation for a rehearsal the very next day. (There was some speculation that said faculty member, who was a rival of Evnine's for the affections of a fellow student, may have set up Evnine to fail.) Things went much as might have been expected. At the first pause, it was agreed all round that the arrangement was not working. (The musicians persevered without conductor and eventually performed the piece.) If only, the artist must have felt, his idiotic offer had been received as it deserved to be! The meme, therefore, can be seen as a kind of wish fulfillment. (See *Some idiot* (M.22) for a point of comparison.)

M.18 You don't look Jewish

M.18 **You don't look Jewish** Composed: February 28th. Posted: February 28th. Orientation: Reverse. Font: Arial. TB1: "Yes, my maternal grandmother.", black. TB2: "That's funny! You don't look Jewish.", black.

Robin is evidently claiming to be Jewish since, traditionally, Jewishness is transmitted matrilineally. Batman is right that Robin does indeed not look Jewish. The idea of Batman and Robin as Jews plays an important role in *Vos iz ayer yidisher nomen, Batman?* (M.72), where the Dynamic Duo speak Yiddish to each other despite their being archetypal WASPS. (See the commentary thereon.)

You don't look Jewish recalls an old joke that the artist may have heard from his late father, a great lover of jokes.

> A young, very English-looking man gets onto a bus. He has blue eyes, ruddy cheeks, and sandy hair. He sits near a little old Jewish lady. After a few moments she leans across and says:
> "Are you Jewish?"
> "No madam, I am not Jewish!"
> A few moments elapse and she tries again:
> "Are you sure you're not Jewish?"
> "Yes, I'm sure I'm not Jewish!"
> He is getting a bit irritated, now, but still maintaining a polite façade. After a few more minutes:
> "You're absolutely sure you're not Jewish?"

Finally giving way to anger, he shouts:

"I am absolutely sure I am not Jewish! And please stop bothering me!"

Undeterred, after a few more minutes, the old lady gives it one last try:

"You're sure you're not Jewish?"

In exasperation, and just to get the woman to stop bothering him, he says:

"Yes, yes. OK. I'm Jewish!"

"That's funny," says the lady. "You don't look Jewish!"

The form of the joke may be thought of as foisting on someone something they don't want, and then questioning them for having it. A wonderful example of this, from Jewish lore, is given by Rabbi Adin Steinsaltz (1976: 242):

A rabbi asked his disciple why the letter *peh* (*p*) was needed in the word *korah*. When the disciple replied that the letter did not appear in that word, the rabbi persisted: "Let us assume for a moment that the letter is placed in this word." "But why should it be needed there?" asked the disciple, to which the rabbi replied, "That is exactly what I asked you."

More generally, it echoes the pipulistic style of Talmud study that Steinsaltz says the anecdote just quoted was intended to parody. In *pilpul*, an expounder of a passage and a questioner joust in the following way.[63] After the expounder has expounded and the questioner has made a first question,

the expounder declares, "You have not understood my method properly, since I was referring to something else. But you are wrong even on the basis of your *own* method and way of understanding." The questioner presses on: "I have understood your theory very well, and my query, despite what you claim, is closely related to the question. But even if I accept your view that I have not understood you properly, my query is still relevant according to your approach." And so on, ad infinitum... (Steinsaltz 1976: 241)

---

[63] See Harris (2010) for more on the nature and history of *pilpul*.

M.19 Couples Therapy

M.19 Couples Therapy Composed: February 22nd. Posted: February 29th. Orientation: Reverse. Font: Arial. TB1: "How about couples therapy?", black. TB2: "I don't do feelings!!!", black.

Another therapy-related meme. Not only does Robin acknowledge some sense of dysfunctionality in his and Batman's relationship, he implies they are a couple. (See the commentary on *Nevermore!* (M.32) for further evidence that the two of them may be intimately involved. In general, their intimacy is manifest almost everywhere.) Given how they seem to be locked into a pattern of repeated abuse, it is brave of Robin to suggest couples therapy. Batman, however, contemptuously rejects the suggestion on the grounds that he "doesn't do feelings." As Jennifer Matey (a philosophy professor at Southern Methodist University) pointed out in the comments to the post, Batman most certainly does "do" one feeling, namely anger. This tension, between an attempt to renounce emotion altogether and the hypertrophy of one particular, often (though we should remember, not always) destructive emotion, is a staple of superhero culture – indeed, a staple of the culture of masculinity.

The toxic, hyper-masculine war on feelings and emotions also connects, in a roundabout way, with the logical and philosophical milieu of the artist. In graduate school, Evnine was drawn to a passage from Andrea Nye's book *Words of Power: A Feminist Reading of the History of Logic* (1990):

> Desperate, lonely, cut off from the human community which in many cases has ceased to exist, under the sentence of violent death, wracked by desires for

> intimacy that they do not know how to fulfill, at the same time tormented by
> the presence of women, men turn to logic. (175)

His interest in the passage, at the time, was as an object of ridicule, but given how well these words capture both Batman in this meme (and the superhero in general) and the stereotypical male logician (and analytic philosopher in general), we may perhaps surmise that the artist came to sense not a little truth in these words, at least as they apply to himself. Indeed, his very ridiculing of the passage as a much younger man probably betrayed an uncanny recognition of himself in an unexpected mirror. If such conjectures are not entirely ill-founded, this meme takes on an almost embarrassingly intimate and confessional tone.

M.22 Some Idiot

Some idiot has underlined nearly the whole book!

It was me.

M.22 Some Idiot Composed: February 22nd. Posted: March 4th. Orientation: Original. Font: Comic Sans. TB1: "Some idiot has underlined nearly the whole book!", black. TB2: "It was me.", black. Added Image: Cover of the Hackett edition of Kant's *Critique of Judgment*.

The posting of this meme was accompanied by the text: "Based on a real incident involving Professor Anthony Savile and me." Although this was posted after *Dialetheism* (M.20), which introduced the technique of adding textboxes to contain explanatory text, *Some Idiot* was composed as early as February 22nd, a whole week before *Dialetheism*. So we should not be surprised by the appearance of retrogression in the resort to the paratextual comment. On the other hand, the early composition date of *Some Idiot* is remarkable for the presence of a new technical innovation, the addition of an image to the meme – in this case, the cover of Kant's *Critique of Judgment*, in the Hackett edition. Though Evnine has positioned the book over Robin's hand, he has made no attempt to place it in that hand. The meme generator does not enable this and he would have had to resort to other means to accomplish it (something he does get around to, in *The Language of Flowers* (M.51), *Not What You're Thinking* (M.93) and, with some virtuosity, in *The Origins of Neo-Platonist Metaphysics* (M.96).

The paratext tells us the meme is based on a real incident and there is no reason to doubt this. The artist was at Bedford College, London, between 1981 and 1983, doing an M.A. in philosophy without previously having had any acquaintance with the subject. Anthony Savile was a faculty member there at that time and given Evnine's background in music, it is quite likely he studied with Savile, who specializes in aesthetics. *Some Idiot* seems to be a relatively straightforward depiction of the artist's humiliation as a young man. It is intensely puzzling why Robin should, in response to Batman's angry or contemptuous allegation, out himself as the underliner. Is he simply shocked into the honest disclosure? Might he, perhaps unconsciously, welcome the prospect of humiliation the occasion offers?

This meme seems to pair with *Ode to Napoleon* (M.17), another meme based on a real incident from Evnine's life as a student, in which Robin, representing the artist, is called an "idiot." However, *Ode to Napoleon* has a wish-fulfillment aspect to it – what in real life led to the artist's humiliation is met, in the meme, with a firm response the effect of which is to head off that humiliation. Here, in *Some Idiot*, no such intervention is present. The humiliation itself is depicted, *in flagrante delicto*. (This may have something to do with the fact that *Ode to Napoleon* uses the usual, reverse orientation of the image whereas the present meme uses the original orientation.) One might conjecture that the longish interval between composition and publication of this meme was a result of the artist's reluctance to publish such a humiliation for all to see.

M.24 "a glove slapping a human face – forever"

M.24 "a glove slapping a human face – forever" Composed: March 2nd. Posted: March 4th. Orientation: Reverse. Font: N/a. TB1: N/a. TB2: N/a. Added Images: In both textboxes, iterated versions of an earlier meme.

After the previous meme, *Whereof one cannot speak...* (M.23), which was the first to have a speech bubble without text, we now, with *"a glove slapping a human face – forever"*, suddenly find ourselves with no text at all and with complex images galore! One might describe this meme as technically exuberant. It certainly could not have been produced in one go on the meme generator. Rather, an image would have to be taken and inserted into the speech bubbles to produce another image, which itself would then be inserted into the speech bubbles of a third to produce the finished product. Has the artist missed an opportunity here by having the same number of image-iterations in both Robin's and Batman's speech bubbles, rather than, for instance, having one further round of iteration in Batman's? I am uncertain as to whether that would have been better or worse. On the plus side, it would have injected some drama into the image. On the minus side, it might have assimilated the logic of the image too much to the logic of conversation and so made more pedestrian this bold technical development.

The meme gains so much from the brilliant title, which was suggested to the artist by Professor Michael Rosen, of Harvard University. It is adapted, of course, from George Orwell's *1984* and Rosen posted a fuller quotation, with adaptation, in a comment to the original posting of the meme on Facebook:

> All competing pleasures will be destroyed. But always — do not forget this, Winston — always there will be the intoxication of power, constantly

> increasing and constantly growing subtler. Always, at every moment, there will be the thrill of victory, the sensation of trampling on an enemy who is helpless. If you want a picture of the future, imagine a glove slapping a human face — forever.

(The original has "a boot stamping on" instead of "a glove slapping.") So wonderful is this quotation here that it was a hard choice for me, as editor of this volume, whether to use the title of this meme as a title for the whole volume, or to go, as I did, with the title given by the artist to another meme, *A Certain Gesture* (M.58).[64]

One thing that Rosen's adaptation of Orwell makes salient is something which, surprisingly, arises nowhere else in Evnine's memes – the fact that the slap given by Batman to Robin is with a gloved, rather than a bare, hand. In fact, Evnine came to see this as an important point and, several years after the Batman Meme Project, wrote about it on his blog, *The Parergon*. Here is what he wrote:

> I am currently reading Carolyn Korsmeyer's recent book *Things: In Touch with the Past* (OUP, 2019). Korsmeyer writes:
>
>> Dan Lewis, Senior Curator of the History of Science and Technology at the Huntington Library in California, described the thrilling privilege of handling the books housed in the collection... Lewis, who does not wear gloves, says that being able to handle such rare documents is like "being present at the moment of creation." (25)
>
> On reading this, I was arrested by that parenthetical comment about Lewis's not wearing gloves. Why doesn't he? The way the passage is written suggests that this is a remarkable fact, that one would expect him to wear gloves in handling these precious books. Lewis's haptic experience would be slightly different if he did wear gloves, but I assume it is not for that difference that he forgoes this form of protection. His goal is more likely – this is a key theme in Korsmeyer's book – to be in direct contact with these rare objects from the past. But is Lewis's pursuit of the frisson of unmediated touch so important to him that he ignores the damaging effects of his body's effluvia on these objects, of which he says "Just to be in their presence is an honor"?
>
> Having thought all this, my mind went (forgive my crudity) to men who fetishize not wearing a condom during sex. Their sensory experience will, like Lewis and his books, be different according to whether or not they use a condom. But one might easily speculate that it is not really for the sake of the haptic surplus that they so scorn the use of something that protects their

---

[64] Another friend of the artist, Professor Tim Watson, of the University of Miami, independently referred to the same passage in Orwell at the end of the Batman Meme Project, in a comment on the posting of *Evnine's Batman Memes: The Movie*.

partner from the damaging effects of their body's products, whether in the form of unwanted pregnancy or STD. Korsmeyer says that experiences like those of Lewis "evoke an impression that gaps of time have been momentarily bridged, bringing the past into the present" (25). It is hardly novel to see sexual relations in terms of bridging a gap not of time, but between persons. Perhaps the sexual cases should be subsumed under the wider rubric about touch, not the usual finger-as-phallus motif, but instead the phallus-as-finger. But men who prioritize the pursuit of unmediated contact over the well-being of their partner are often, rightly, reviled. How should this bear on how we think about putting our grubby ungloved hands on priceless relics from the past? The general public, naturally, is kept from defiling quasi-sacred relics in this way – but what of curators like Lewis who take to themselves the privilege and pleasure of intercourse with these hierodules?

What does all this have to do with Batman and Robin? Despite Rosen's reference to Orwell, it never really occurred to me until this very day, exactly four years after I began the Batman Meme Project (actually, tomorrow is the four-year anniversary), that Batman slaps Robin *with a gloved and not a bare hand*. In fact, gloved hands are very prominent in the image. We see two of Batman's and one of Robin's, densely clustered in the bottom left corner. How does this detail inflect the image? What does it mean for [the *Batman Meme Project*]? Should we praise Batman because, even in this moment of violence, he holds back from the further violation of Robin's bodily autonomy that hitting him with his bare hand would represent? Should we pity him because, even in this moment of perverse intimacy, he cannot bridge the gap with another person? I just don't know how to read it.

M.25 Mr. Peabody

M.25 Mr. Peabody Composed: February 22nd. Posted: March 5th. Orientation: Reverse. Font: Comic Sans. TB1: "Sometimes I touch myself.", white. TB2: "Hands off Mr. Peabody!", white.

The relatively long time between the dates of composition and posting, coupled with the subject matter, suggest that Evnine may have had doubts about posting this meme. And indeed, the temptation to engage in psycho-biographical speculation concerning the artist is well-nigh irresistible. As far as we can tell, however, parental attitudes to sex when the artist was growing up were sane and progressive. There is unlikely to have been excessive anguish over the inevitable rites of adolescence. This meme, then, unlike some others, is probably not best read as evidence of juvenile trauma.

Much more interesting to think about here is the language of the meme and its relation to the dramatic interaction. Robin is tentatively confessing his sexual self-exploration, perhaps because he is worried that he is not 'normal' and craves guidance and reassurance. Rather than reassuring Robin, Batman sternly admonishes him not to engage in masturbation. Batman, it must be remembered, is not Robin's father but his legal guardian. He speaks with the voice not of natural affection but of politically and legally constituted power, power over Robin. His policing of Robin's body and sexual behavior transmits that power. At the level of the dramatic interaction, then, we have an enactment of what the philosopher Michel Foucault calls the "anatomo-politics of the human body." This is one of the poles of social power exercised over life and its reproduction as such. (The other pole is called "biopower" and is manifest in policies enacted at a population-wide level.) The anatomo-politics of the human body is centered on

> the body as a machine: its disciplining, the optimization of its capabilities, the extortion of its forces, the parallel increase of its usefulness and its docility, its integration into systems of efficient and economic controls. (Foucault 1978: 139)

Historically, a large part of this exercise of power focused on masturbation. In masturbation, the body is undisciplined, according to this antiquated discourse, because masturbation involves inner desire left unintegrated into the economy of relations between people, relations that because of their interpersonal nature are visible and hence easier to control. As Richard Sennett puts it, "a person alone with his or her sexuality appeared to be a person alone with a very dangerous force" (Foucault and Sennett 1981). Not only is it the case that in masturbation, desire is undisciplined and the body's forces spent without being integrated into the efficient and (re-)productive economy of interpersonal relations; in addition, masturbation's linking of pleasure and solitude reinforces the already dangerous potential of a special kind of solitude – what Sennett calls the "solitude of difference… of having an inner life which is more than a reflection of the lives of others."

So much, then, for the basic shape of the encounter between Batman and Robin: an all too familiar exercise in social control dressed up as morality and hygiene. But all this is cleverly stood on its head by the *language* of the meme. The phrase that Robin uses to describe his self-exploration is not at all the language one would expect from him, given his age and gender. It is mature, languid, and in fact decidedly feminine.[65] It suggests lazy hours of unfocused and un-goal-directed activity, not the brief, telic urgency of the adolescent boy. Batman, by contrast, uses language that is not just unambiguously male, but also ridiculously, inappropriately childish, pitched at someone five-to-ten years younger than Robin. (The artist may have picked up the expression "Mr. Peabody" from Jodie Foster's film *Little Man Tate* in which a TV producer says to the seven-year-old title character, before he goes on stage, "no playing with little Mr. Peabody.") Thus, the meme transforms the clichéd scene of Victorian prudishness in which 'undisciplined' sexuality is policed and repressed into a site of subversion in which age- and gender-specific behaviors are reversed, the teenage boy expressing himself as an adult woman and the adult man, as a little child.

---

[65] One thinks of the Divinyls 1990 hit "I Touch Myself," sung by the late Chrissy Amphlett.

M.28 Lunchtime

M.28 Lunchtime Composed: March 4th. Posted: March 7th. Orientation: Reverse. Font: Arial. TB1: "What was that guy's name again?", black. TB2: "Lunchtime O'Boulez!", black.

A little piece of whimsy on the part of the artist, obviously created just to allow him to include the name "Lunchtime O'Boulez" in his project. (We see here again the obsession with naming and names.) Lunchtime O'Boulez, who indeed has a wonderful name, is the author of the regular column "Music and Musicians" in the British satirical magazine *Private Eye*. Lunchtime O'Boulez is, presumably, so-called on account of the similarity of his name to two others – "Lunchtime O'Booze," the name of another pseudonymous reporter from *Private Eye*, and "Pierre Boulez," the name of one of the titans of 20th century music both as composer and conductor.

M.29 Who knows two?

M.29 Who knows two? Composed: February 23rd. Posted: March 9th. Orientation: Original. Font: Arial. TB1: "Who knows two?", black. TB2: "I know two. Two tablets of the law...", black.

Who knows two? (M.29) and *Thirteen Holes* (M.30) form a pair, the second having been created and posted in response to comments made on the first, as will be explained in the commentary on it. The text of *Who knows two?* comes from the song traditionally sung at Passover, *Eḥad Mi Yod'ea* (*Who knows one?*).[66,67] The song has both an antiphonal and cumulative structure. For all the numbers n, from one to thirteen (in ascending order), there is a verse that begins "who knows n?" and an antiphonal response "I know n. n (is/are) F." With each answer, all the previous answers are included, in descending order, finishing with the answer to "who knows one?" Here is the final verse (it is, of course, a feature of cumulative songs that one need only ever quote the final verse to give the full text), the translation taken from Tabory (2008: 133) with my own glosses in square brackets:

Who knows thirteen? I know thirteen.

---

[66] A quite different Yiddish song of the same name is used in the soundtrack of the second Batman meme movie made by the artist, *Gone!*.

[67] It is noteworthy that the artist's great-great-grandfather, Nathan Neta Jewnin (c.1838-1914), a rabbi in Jewish Lithuania, wrote and published a commentary on the Passover Haggadah, including the song *Eḥad Mi Yod'ea*. (It is unclear whether the artist was aware of this when he composed this meme.) I shall discuss Jewnin's commentary in my remarks on *Thirteen Holes* (M.30).

Thirteen attributes [the merciful attributes of God[68]];
twelve tribes [of Israel];
eleven stars [in Joseph's dream[69]];
ten commandments;
nine months of pregnancy;
eight days till circumcision;
seven days of the week;
six orders of the Mishnah;
five books the Torah;
four mothers [the Matriarchs Sarah, Rebecca, Leah, and Rachel];
three fathers [the Patriarchs Abraham, Isaac, and Jacob];
two tables of the law[70];
One is God in heaven and on earth.

The antiphonal structure of the song makes it especially apt for use in the meme and should render the slap itself an instance of what I called in the introduction an antiphonal slap. And yet, the artist has used the original orientation of the image which has Batman asking the question and Robin giving the answer. The effect, therefore, runs counter to the antiphonal nature of the song and renders the question "who knows n?" not rhetorical, not investigative, but examinatorial (i.e., Batman seems to be testing Robin). (The slap cannot be seen as punitive, either, since Robin is able to answer the question correctly.) In fact, the meme would have worked as well, though perhaps rather differently, had the more common reverse orientation of the image been used. In that case, the slap would have expressed Batman's irritation at Robin's impertinence in 'testing' him. As it is, the overall integration between the roles (questioner vs. answerer), the figures playing those roles, and the slap is hard to find.

It seems that Evnine had a fondness for cumulative songs. There exists a digital recording in which he and his partner Giovanna Pompele sing a cumulative song, evidently of their own composition. The final verse is as follows:

I have a little grey cat
I have a little calico cat
And his name is Zemeckis
And his name is Tenbrooks

[68] From *Exodus* 34, 6-7. "And the Lord passed before him and proclaimed, 'The Lord, the Lord God, merciful and gracious, longsuffering, and abounding in goodness and truth, keeping mercy for thousands, forgiving iniquity and transgression and sin, by no means clearing the guilty, visiting the iniquity of the fathers upon the children and the children's children to the third and the fourth generation.'" As one might expect, the extraction of precisely thirteen attributes from these verses is contentious and there exist different ways of doing it. Evnine has said that, when he was a boy, the cantor in his synagogue sang this liturgically important passage to an unusual and extremely haunting melody.

[69] From *Genesis* 37, 9: "And he dreamed yet another dream, and told it his brethren, and said, Behold, I have dreamed a dream more; and, behold, the sun and the moon and the eleven stars made obeisance to me."

[70] Evnine, of course, uses "tablets" in the meme.

And his name is Boon Boy
And his name is Farabiano Butel
And his name is Macky Bee
And his name is Farabutles
And his name is Boxim
And his name is Bocca
And his name is Boyottles
And his name is Bunols.

And here is the melody:

I Have a Little Grey Cat

Simon Evnine and Giovanna Pompele

Figure 8 The melody of Evnine's cumulative song on the names of his cat

The song mentions two cats at the beginning but then goes on to give "his" names. These are almost certainly names of the grey cat since calico cats are very rarely male. But then why is the reference to the calico cat there at all? And while Evnine did have a grey cat (actually a Russian Blue), his name was "Celestino," which does not appear in the list at all. These puzzling anomalies give an air of authenticity to the song as a 'folk object.' Such songs are often cryptic and suggestive, as we shall see further in the commentary on *Thirteen Holes* (M.30).

The song touches on a very interesting philosophical issue. The philosopher Robin Jeshion proposes that the following rule is an implicit norm governing our naming practices:

Single Tagging: Fix the reference of a term [to be a name for something] only if, so far as you know, the named object is not already named. (2002: 65)

Put crudely, this says: don't name something if you think it has already got a name! *I Have a Little Grey Cat* seems to exhibit a phenomenon that flies in the face of *Single Tagging*, as I shall endeavor to explain. To do so, however, we must take a couple of steps back to see why Jeshion proposes *Single Tagging* in the first place.

Philosophers distinguish between two types of belief (and statement), *de re* and *de dicto*.[71] *De re* beliefs (beliefs *about a thing*) are about, or involve, some particular thing. *De dicto* beliefs (beliefs *about something said*) are ones that are entirely conceptual, or general, in nature. To give Jeshion's example: if, standing in front of Bessie the cow during time of famine, a farmer gives voice to a belief by asserting "Bessie is starving," her belief is *about* Bessie the cow. If a person in another part of the county, who has no knowledge of Bessie at all, thinks the famine is so bad that no cow will fail to be starving, even the fattest of them, and expresses her belief by asserting "The fattest cow is starving," her belief is not about, or does not involve, Bessie herself, even if Bessie *is* the fattest cow. She might have said, equivalently, "The fattest cow, whichever cow that happens to be, is starving." The example suggests a link between *de re* beliefs and proper names ("Bessie"), on the one hand, and *de dicto* beliefs and definite descriptions ("the fattest cow"), on the other. Although this alignment is controversial and in need of a lot of qualification if it is to be made plausible, Jeshion does wish to preserve a link between the *de re* and proper names. Proper names, she argues, are at bottom devices that enable us to think and speak of particular things, to have *de re* thoughts and make *de re* statements about them, even when they are not right in front of us.

Proper names may be bestowed on things either ostensively or by reference-fixing descriptions. Ostensively, we have the thing to be named within our cognitive (and sometimes physical) grasp and think or say something to the effect of "Let *its* (or *his* or *her*) name be N." We 'baptize' (and sometimes baptize) the object in question. Bestowing a name in this way obviously requires *de re* thought rather than enabling such thought. The bestower has to have the thing to be named in their cognitive grasp, perceiving it, thinking about it, in order to think or say "let *its* name be…" But once the name is bestowed in this way and used, it may enable others to have *de re* thought about the named object who did not previously or otherwise have it in their cognitive grasp. This is how most readers of this book get to have *de re* thoughts about Robin Jeshion herself via the name "Robin Jeshion." A historical connection exists between the original bestowal on her of that name and us now, who use that name to refer to her. (This is crucial to Jeshion's point about the function of proper names being to enable *de re* thought.) But names can also be bestowed on things by reference-fixing descriptions. We can say "Let N be the name of the F," where "the F" is some definite description intended to apply to what will become the referent of "N." A classic example in philosophy involves Leverrier's discovery of the planet Neptune. Before anyone had the planet itself in their cognitive grasp, Leverrier calculated that there must be a planet that was causing observed perturbations in

---

[71] "*De re*" is generally pronounced [deɪ reɪ] – using the International Phonetic Alphabet – or [day ray] – using the standard English pronunciations of these words. "*De dicto*" is pronounced as you would now anticipate.

the orbit of Uranus. He was then in a position to say something like this: "Let 'Neptune' be the name of the planet causing perturbations in the orbit of Uranus." The name, thus introduced, could then be used by himself and others to think and speak about Neptune itself, *de re* - even to enable them to think such things as that Neptune, that very planet, might, had the history of the universe been different, not have caused perturbations in the orbit of Uranus.

The possibility of descriptive reference-fixing, however, seems to create a problem. Having *de re* thought about something seems like a cognitive accomplishment. By some miracle, your thought is able to make contact with objects distant in time and space. It should not be thought of as something that comes too easily. Yet it seems that introducing a proper name by means of descriptive reference-fixing can be done at the drop of a hat. In a famous example of introducing a proper name by descriptive reference-fixing, Gareth Evans writes: "Let us use 'Julius' to refer to whoever invented the zip" (1985: 181). Can this simple assertion allow Evans, or us, to have genuine *de re* thought about some particular person who happened to invent the zip? For example, that that very person had a younger sister? (The point, of course, is not whether we can know this thought to be true, but whether we can even have it - about *Julius*! Of course we can have the *de dicto* thought expressed by "Whoever invented the zip had a younger sister.") Jeshion thinks that in the Evans case, as described, we are not enabled by the introduction of a proper name to have *de re* thought, but that this is not an objection to her claim about the way in which proper names enable *de re* thought. This is because she thinks that Evans does not actually succeed in introducing a proper name at all by his stipulation. Introducing a proper name, Jeshion thinks, is a distinctive kind of speech act (see the commentary on *Not a Performative* (M.82) for further explanation of speech acts) and as such, there are substantive conditions in place that must be satisfied for it come off successfully. One can no more name an object just by uttering "Let us use N to refer to the F" than one can perform a marriage just by uttering "I hereby pronounce you married." So simply uttering the words "Let us use 'Julius' to refer to whoever invented the zip" will not, by itself, be sufficient for me to name some particular person "Julius" and hence will not be sufficient for me to have *de re* thought about that person via the proper name "Julius."

In the marriage case, simply uttering the words is not enough. One has, in addition, to be authorized to perform marriages, the interested parties must be of age and not currently married, etc. What are the analogous substantive conditions on naming? The principal necessary condition on successful naming, in Jeshion's view, is that one must sincerely intend to use the introduced expression as a name and to use it to enable "psychologically neutral" thought about the thing named. By "psychologically neutral" Jeshion means something like "not via any of the named object's characteristics (i.e., not under any particular mode of presentation)." An ancillary condition on successful naming is the principle quoted above, *Single Tagging*. This is not offered as a strictly necessary condition since Jeshion allows there may be exceptions. It is, she holds, a norm that must be generally satisfied (or at least generally recognized as demanding general satisfaction) if naming is to work as it does.

We are now in a position to assess *Single Tagging* and the bearing on it of *I Have a Little Grey Cat*. Clearly Evnine named his cat many times over, knowing full well that the cat already had a name. His practice, therefore, did not conform to *Single Tagging*. Is it covered by the kinds of exceptions Jeshion contemplates? In the main text, she suggests three sources of exceptions to the principle: pet names ("pet" qualifying the kind of name, not the kind of thing named), names adopted solely for business purposes, and pen names. She then appends the following footnote:

> Reflections on exceptions actually helps bolster *Single Tagging*. Many pet names (e.g., 'Emmie' for 'Emily') are, not insignificantly, phonologically similar to the nonpet name. This mitigates the extent to which they count against the role of naming devices for interpersonal communication and psychologically neutral thought about individuals. Pen names are normally introduced to conceal the identity of the writer; their capacity to do so depends essentially upon the presence of a normative principle like *Single Tagging*. Notice that there is something not just semantically nonstandard, but semantically deviant about multiple aliases. (75)

It is not clear to me why Jeshion thinks the phonological similarity of pet names to their nonpet counterparts bolsters *Single Tagging*. Perhaps the thought is that here, where one does give a name (the pet name) to something that we know already has a name, we make it similar to the existing name so as to minimize the extent to which it is, genuinely, a different name. This places a lot of weight on phonology in individuating names, but in any case, it does not seem entirely to the point. Cases like "Emmie" for "Emily" or "Bob" for "Robert" are arguably not violations of *Single Tagging* at all since they are *conventionally* recognized as variants and hence not really distinct names from the full form. In naming someone "Emily" or "Robert" one is, as it were, already bestowing on them a selection of conventionally-determined forms for casual address. Real pet names, bestowed *ad lib* and not by convention, on the other hand, are not at all regularly phonologically similar to the official names of their referents.[72] With regard to pen names, it is perhaps not obvious that they are "normally" used to *conceal* a writer's identity since many writers use pen names even when their identity is known, but they clearly are often so used. But even in those cases, I do not see how their efficacy depends on the presence of something like *Single Tagging*. Supposing no such principle were in effect, we would not be able, from the fact that a book was published under the name "Mark Twain," to assume that its author had no other name; but that would hardly give us a clue that his other name was "Samuel Clemens," so his identity might remain concealed even so. Nor do I understand what is "semantically deviant" about multiple aliases.

Behind *Single Tagging* (or perhaps alongside it) is Jeshion's idea that names are ultimately there to give us psychologically neutral ways of referring to things. But lack of psychological neutrality affects naming in various ways. Children are regularly named after beloved grandparents or given patronyms. These names are given with the intention of activating at least some users (including, often, the bearers) emotionally. No doubt this is not essential to

---

[72] One hesitates to intrude on people's intimacy by giving real life examples but in one case, where I received permission to share, Ollie (a conventional and phonologically similar variant of "Oliver") calls Jenny ("Jennifer") "Fluffy" and Jenny calls Ollie "Baby Jesus."

their functioning as proper names, as such. It is an accretion to the practice of using proper names. But such uses of names are extensive and hardly anomalous exceptions to a practice governed by an ideal of psychological neutrality. Furthermore, and here we come finally to *I Have a Little Grey Cat*, the giving of names is often an act of love itself even where the names themselves may be fairly indifferent to us. It is actually quite common for pet owners to bestow an orgy of names on their beloved animals as a way of expressing their love. Names are not just ways of enabling psychologically neutral reference and *de re* thought and talk; they are also, often, the impress of our feelings onto the things so named, ways of connecting us to those things and (in the case of common family names) of connecting those things to each other. We use proper names to structure our world and the giving of multiple names to the same thing is important to that, both by allowing one and the same thing to occupy different places in our thus-structured world and by adding weight to the significance something has to us - a kind of turning up of the volume of that thing.[73]

It is, in fact, slightly mysterious why Jeshion advances *Single Tagging* as a condition on felicitous naming at all. In Evans's Julius case, we attempt to give a name to something that we know must already have one, hence violating *Single Tagging*. But surely what disqualifies it as an example of successful name-introduction, for Jeshion, is its off-handedness, the evident lack of any serious intention, on Evans's or our part, to use "Julius" as a name of whoever satisfies the description. And if the right intention were there, would the mere fact that we knew Julius already had some other name ("Whitcomb Judson" as it happens – so now you really *can* have *de re* thought about the inventor of the zip) really lead Jeshion to hold that no new name had been introduced? Surely not.

Although this plays no explicit role in her argument, and although (in personal communication) Jeshion rejects this, I conjecture that she is moved to propose *Single Tagging* by something of the same impulse that led to the tradition of "ideal" or "philosophical" languages that flourished in the 17th century but has surfaced at various other times, including during the beginnings of so-called analytic philosophy at the end of the 19th and beginning of the 20th centuries. (See *The Cheat of Words* (M.89) and its commentary for more about this.) In content, if not in proximate motivation, *Single Tagging* seems similar to the many complaints of ideal language enthusiasts that it is an imperfection in natural languages that they have multiple words for the same thing. For example, John Wilkins, who developed one of the best-known ideal languages in the 17th century, says of synonymous words that "they make language tedious, its purpose being utility" (bk. 1, ch. 5, section 2). The thought that everything should, ideally, have at most (and at least?) one name seems only to be plausible if one thinks that there should be some substantial isomorphism between language and reality, that language ought to be a rationally-ordered instrument rather than the furiously confusing *bricolage* that it actually is. Perhaps the goal to which *Single Tagging* aspires – that things should have only one name – is a worthwhile condition to impose on an ideal language. It

---

[73] Here would also belong a discussion of the distinction between using names to refer and to address. This is a fascinating topic I touch on briefly in the commentary on *Dinner's Ready* (M.104).

would, after all, prevent situations in which one or more people might be referring to the same thing but fail to realize that. Already having the name "Bruce Wayne," Batman would not be allowed to have the name "Batman" and hence Catwoman could not fall in love with Bruce Wayne while despising and working against Batman! But it seems just wrong-headed to suppose that the principles that might govern an ideal language turn up as normative principles governing how our actual language works. It is not a fault in language that Catwoman faces her predicament. Names can enable *de re* thought and psychologically neutral ways of referring to things, certainly. But they can equally well and legitimately serve as marks of possession, imprints of love and lineage, badges of honor, and many other things.

One might question the place for such conditions as *Single Tagging* in an account of naming at all. John Searle (1995) makes the point that many activities that are governed by uses of language in constrained conditions – such as the performance of a marriage or the declaration of a war – have counterparts that are not so regulated that precede and underlie them. So, a legally recognized marriage may be accomplished by various speech acts with their own felicity conditions. If the person pronouncing the words is not really authorized, if one of the parties is already married, etc., then the performance of the marriage is infelicitous - the couple is not, in fact, legally married. But quite apart from marriage is the existence of marriage-like relationships, established without such institutional requirements on the basis of mutual understanding and affection. And alongside formal declarations of war and the Geneva Conventions, there is war-like behavior with no formal structure. When Jeshion talks about the bestowing of a name as a kind of speech act, with its own felicity conditions, she is undoubtedly describing something real. There are procedures for naming ships of the Royal Navy, for baptizing children into a church, and so on, all of which require the satisfaction of a number of conditions to come off successfully (the namer must be the monarch, the namer must be a priest). But underlying all that is a practice of giving names that is conducted informally and does not require any special speech acts at all. People simply resolve to call something by a given name and then do so. Or they just start using names without any thought at all.[74] This is what happens when pet owners multiply names for their pets in incontinent bouts of affection. We can study official naming, as we can study official war or official marriage. And we can study 'common-law' naming, as we can study human conflict and familial bonding. Jeshion seems to be aiming for something in between - not a study of the actual conditions for legal recognition of a name, but still a practice governed by conditions on the model of such official naming. I doubt whether there is any such practice, but even if there is, names also exist that require

---

[74] Jeshion, in effect, anticipates this objection and says "I do not, however, hold that the namer must possess this intellectualized account of the function of names [as enabling *de re* thought and speech] and their psychological neutrality as her reasons for naming the object. A parent's own internal reason why she names her child might just be that people name their children. But I think that nevertheless, this must be her reason for introducing the name, even if she never conceives it as such" (64). But the objection I make isn't that Jeshion requires the namer to have an intellectual account of the *function* of names that she needn't, in fact, have, but that it requires her (explicitly so, in the wording of the felicity conditions on naming) to have intentions and aims that she might not have.

more stringent conditions (as with ships of the Royal Navy) or no conditions at all (the artist and his little grey cat - and his name *is* Bunols).

M.30 Thirteen Holes

M.30 Thirteen Holes Composed: March 9th. Posted: March 9th. Orientation: Original. Font: Arial. TB1: "Who knows thirteen?", black. TB2: "I know thirteen. Thirteen holes in Trotsky's head...", black.

Thirteen Holes is an occasional meme, prompted by a comment from Professor Michael Rosen on the original Facebook posting of *Who knows two?* (M.29). Rosen wrote ""Two, two the worker's hands/ Working for his living, O!"," quoting a line from a Marxist parody of a cumulative folksong, *Green Grow the Rushes, O*, that is often compared with *Eḥad Mi Yod'ea* for its numerical structure and some of the items enumerated. In response, Evnine posted M.30, which uses another part of the parody, the item associated with the number thirteen, inserting it into the "Who knows n? I know n" framework of *Eḥad Mi Yod'ea* (rather than creating a new framework based on *Green Grow the Rushes, O*). To interpret *Thirteen Holes*, then, we should say something about *Green Grow the Rushes, O* and the Marxist parody of it.

Here is the full text (or rather *a* full text, given that there are so many variants) of *Green Grow the Rushes, O*. (As noted in the commentary on *Who knows two?*, for a cumulative song, one need only give the last verse.)

> I'll sing you twelve, O
> Green grow the rushes, O
> What are your twelve, O?
> Twelve for the twelve Apostles,
> Eleven for the eleven who went to heaven,
> Ten for the ten commandments,

> Nine for the nine bright shiners,
> Eight for the eight bold rangers,
> Seven for the seven stars in the sky,
> Six for the six proud walkers,
> Five for the symbols at your door,
> Four for the Gospel makers,
> Three, three, the rivals,
> Two, two, lily-white boys,
> Clothed all in green, O
> One is one and all alone
> And evermore shall be so.

Variants of this song in English, and similar songs in other languages, are legion and any attempt to identify origins and lines of influence between versions must be nearly impossible.[75] Perhaps there are such lines of influence, or perhaps common forces (cultural, psychological, archetypical) have led to the development of such songs independently of each of other. (Most likely, elements of independent development have been overlain by cultural transmission of myriad kinds.) The American folklorist William Wells Newell, writing of a variant named "The Carol of the Twelve Numbers," says "Our song is everywhere familiar in Western Europe, where it is generally regarded as possessing something of a sacred character" (1891: 219) and gives references in a footnote to versions in German, Flemish, Spanish, and Provençal. There also exist versions in Latin, presumably translated from vernacular originals, one of which is very close to *Eḥad Mi Yod'ea* (*Dic Mi Quid Sit Unus*, which preserves the "who knows n?" format and, strikingly, has for the number three the Patriarchs and not the Trinity that Christian versions typically have).[76] And, of course, there is the Hebrew/Aramaic *Eḥad Mi Yod'ea*, which was first printed in 1590 along with a Yiddish translation in a Haggadah from Prague. (Our first sighting of it is from 1526, along with the Yiddish translation, as a hand-written addition to another Haggadah.) Evidence suggests it may have existed for a couple of hundred years before that but it is hard to be certain.[77] *Eḥad Mi Yod'ea* is very similar to a German folksong, *Guter Freund Ich Frage Dich*, though it is unclear which, if either, was the model for the other.[78] The text of the version in the Haggadah has, for obvious reasons, remained fixed, but there are a variety of folk versions, translations into Yiddish, Russian, and Ladino (Sephardi Jews began to incorporate the song and vary it more radically in the middle of the 19th century) that shade off into the realm of parody and play (see Adelman 2015 for some parodies), just as the Marxist version parodies or plays with *Green Grow the Rushes, O*.

---

[75] Waltz (2018) is invaluable and has a lot of information about variants and sources.

[76] See F.C.H. (1868) for its full text.

[77] See Tabory (2008) and Adelman (2015) for overviews of the scholarly state of play.

[78] The observation of their similarity is standardly attributed to Joseph Perles (1835-94) but in fact, it was noted already by the Swiss Hebraist Johann Caspar Ulrich in 1768 (Ulrich 1768: 138). (His German version is *Guter Gesell Ich Frage Dich*.)

What are we to make of the wonderfully evocative but often mysterious values given to the numbers in *Green Grow the Rushes, O*? For this song, unlike for the textually well-preserved and liturgically well-situated *Eḥad Mi Yod'ea*, we have little context other than a generically Christian one to guide us. (And even that might be misleading if one thinks, as one commentator does, that its references are pagan or Qabalistic, or somehow both![79]) Who are the lily-white boys (or babes, or maids), clothed in green? Who are the three rivals (or wisers, or riders, or thrivers, or tryers, or divers, or shrivers, or arrivals – this last being how a friend of mine was taught it by his mother)? Or the six proud walkers? The writing around this song is full of answers to these questions. For some numbers, there is a lot of consensus, for others, various flights of imagination.

A more significant question that confronts us, however, is not in interpreting the various numbers but in understanding what it means to offer an 'interpretation' of them. What is someone doing who says, for example, that "the 'two lilywhite boys' are believed to *refer to* Christ and St. John the Baptist" (Anon n.d.: 3; my emphasis)? Or that the five symbols at your door *are* the points of a pentagram to ward off evil? Discussing "The Carol of the Twelve Apostles," Newell says:

> The composer of this carol must have had some distinct idea in his mind with reference to the mystic meaning of each of these numbers, but it is not now, in all cases, possible to discover what this significance was. The correct reading for nine seems to be that last given ["the nine of the bridal shine"], the bridal shine having reference to the nine orders of angels, supposed to be present at the marriage of the Lamb… . The original explanation of six ["Six are the cheerful waiters"] may have had reference to the miracle of the turning of the six water-pots into wine at the marriage in Cana. Eight ["Gabriel angels"] appears to have denoted the archangels. The lily-white babes *may* refer to Christ and John the Baptist, and the three strangers ["Three of them are strangers"], etc., to the three men of the East, who came to worship Jesus. (1891: 216)

The premise that the song had "a composer" who "had some distinct idea in his mind with reference to the mystic meaning of each of these numbers" seems already to set us badly off on the wrong foot. Whatever one thinks about the so-called Intentional Fallacy with respect to authored artworks, the object of interpretation here is a folk-object.[80] Its forms have mutated

---

[79] Stewart (1977). Waltz (2018) pushes back against this strongly and effectively.

[80] Evnine wrote something on his blog *The Parergon* about the Intentional Fallacy, an excerpt of which it is relevant to quote here:

> The so-called fallacy was a creation of the New Criticism, in an article by William Wimsatt and Monroe Beardsley. As if in horror of their own mothers and the messiness and entanglement of our biological origins, those critics sought to elevate the work of art onto a cool, clean marble pedestal (like, oh say… a Grecian urn) and pretend that it didn't come from the womb of someone's mind. Indeed, their revulsion of origins extends, when taken to its logical conclusion, to the annihilation of a work's context altogether. For how can one

over time, misheard and misunderstood by countless people and communities, and assimilated again and again to some preconceptions of past William Newells about what 'must have been meant.' We cannot even ascertain the 'original' text, let alone find some individual who authored it and whose ideas will provide the meaning of these arcane enumerations. When an interpreter says that eight *denotes* this, or the lily-white babes *refer to* that, they surely cannot be attempting to recover a single person's ideas about anything.

Take one itself, the rock solid one. *Eḥad Mi Yod'ea* says explicitly "one is our God, who is in Heaven and on earth." But what about *Green Grow the Rushes, O*? Cecil Sharp, commenting on another variant of it (*The Ten Commandments*) which, like *Green Grow the Rushes, O,* also has for one "One is one and all alone and ever more shall be so," says "All versions agree in this line, which obviously refers to God Almighty" (Sharp 1916: xlii).[81] Why does it "obviously refer" to God and what does it even mean to say that? I have already said that it cannot (or at least should not) be taken to mean anything about the ideas of an original author. Is it supposed to mean, then, that in other comparable versions, God is referred to explicitly? So He is. But so also are Christ, "God, Baptism, Faith and Truth," "the righteous man," (which Newell says "must mean Christ" but of course, this just raises the very same issue), and the Virgin Mary (for all of which, see Newell 1891). Does it just mean something about what people who sing the song take it to refer to, each group of associated people forming what Stanley Fish (1980) calls "an interpretive community"? (If so, no evidence at all is presented to bear out the existence of such interpretive communities.) Most likely, it is no more than a way of indicating that this is what people now think it refers to.[82] But if the meaning of saying "refers to" is explained in terms of

---

separate the maker's intentions for her work from context in general? The philosopher Paul Grice, explaining how what a speaker means on a particular occasion is a function of what her communicative intentions are, makes the crucial point that we do not need to imagine a psychological examination of the speaker.

> An utterer is held to intend to convey what is normally conveyed (or normally intended to be conveyed) [by his words] and we require a good reason for accepting that a particular use diverges from the general usage (e.g., he never knew or had forgotten the general usage). Similarly in nonlinguistic cases: we are presumed to intend the normal consequences of our action.

So the attribution of personal intention and a knowledge of context (to uncover what is normal in it) are inextricably linked. Wimsatt and Beardsley have in their sights not just the so-called Intentional Fallacy but a much wider so-called Contextual Fallacy.

[81] Waltz (2018) echoes the consensus, but rather amusingly goes on to say: "Refers to God or Jesus *or both.* Clearly it is a reference to the essential *unity* of God" (my emphasis). (I here leave aside the question of whether Christianity, with its Trinity (on which, see *Filioque* (M.7) and its commentary), does subscribe to the essential unity of God.)

[82] Waltz continues after the quotation in the previous footnote that "Even Stewart [he of the Qabalistic/Pagan interpretation], p. 77, agrees with this, which tells you how certain it is," thus suggesting that what is at issue is no more than consensus among latter-day commentators.

what people think it refers to, there is an obvious problem of non-well-foundedness. What is it that they are agreeing on when they agree that one "refers to" God?

Let me be explicit that the problem I am grappling with here is not the epistemological one of how we could ever know, or come to know, what the enumerations mean or refer to. It is that when dealing with a folk-object like (the various versions of) this song, it is hard to know what is being said by claims to the effect that the lily-white boys refer to, or mean, Christ and St. John the Baptist, etc. Consequently, it is hard to understand what the people who make these claims, whether to agree or disagree with other scholars, are up to. What, precisely, are the nature and goal of their interpretative activity?

Possible answers to these questions may be suggested by treatments of such folk-objects that take a more systematic approach. I shall, therefore, compare two such approaches, Stewart's (1977) discussion of *Green Grow the Rushes, O* and one by Evnine's own great-great-grandfather, Nathan Neta Jewnin, on *Eḥad Mi Yod'ea* (published as part of a commentary on the entire Haggadah in Warsaw in 1914).[83] I shall present their commentaries on two, since two is the number at issue in *Who knows two?* (and the songs Stewart is concerned with do not go up to thirteen, the number in *Thirteen Holes*, but typically stop at ten or twelve).

R. J. Stewart, mystic, folklorist, and musician, presents himself, in his book *Pagan Imagery and English Folksong*, as an iconoclast, pushing past the dominant interpretative traditions which are shackled to the orthodoxy of a particular (patriarchal) religion (be it Christianity or Judaism). He, by contrast, draws on a plethora of sources that that reflect pre-Christian, pagan (and matriarchal) origins.

> Many attempts have been made to interpret the Dilly Song [another name for *Green Grow the Rushes, O*]. The usual process has been that of fitting each line forcibly into an orthodox framework and to call [*sic*] any details that do not fit 'corruptions'... The song is clearly religious, therefore most researchers conclude that it must be Christian. It obviously contains wild elements, therefore these must be traced to Hebrew influence in the same way as the New Testament follows on from the Old. A simple reading of the known Hebrew text [of *Eḥad Mi Yod'ea*] destroys this suggestion completely... From what source could the Orthodox Hebrew and popular Christian songs have derived? Why, in each quite distinctly separate case, was an acceptable variant tailored from a free source such as is noted in oral tradition?... The archetype of the song is an exposition of the Divine Universe through the various stages of manifestation. Once this simple fact has been realized, it is easy to understand why varying

---

[83] The question of the Romanization of the name of the artist's ancestor is vexed. Here I use the form found in the *Jewish Encyclopedia* of 1903, to be pronounced according to the principles of German orthography (i.e., as /Yevnin/, to use the International Phonetic Alphabet rendering). The name was, by its bearer, written with Hebrew characters in Yiddish or Cyrillic characters. See the appendix to the commentary on *Vos iz ayer yidisher nomen, Batman?* (M.72) for more about the spelling and pronunciation of the name and for the bibliography of R. Nathan Neta Jewnin.

faiths all have versions of their own, each apparently deriving from early forms which have in common a mystical concept. (74-5)

This passage reveals what lies at the heart of Stewart's endeavor. What he is about to discuss is not any particular version of the song, but an archetype that lies behind them all. Thus the questions of influence become redundant and the need to label some lines as "corruptions" of others disappears. The songs are all autochthonous manifestations of the same archetype, they all come from "the same region of deep mass-consciousness" (89).

This approach has several consequences. Since the approach is trans-cultural, Stewart is free to draw on any source of folk wisdom, including other variants of the song, and the echoes of folk wisdom that persist in subterranean form in organized religions. His main resource is what he calls "Qabalah," the tradition of Jewish mysticism, and its "prime emblem," the Tree of Life, which "unfolded or manifested in ten clearly defined stages… from heaven to earth" (76-7).[84] Stewart mistakenly treats Qabalah as a heresy with respect to traditional rabbinic Judaism, which fits with his proclivity to look for answers before, or behind, organized religions.[85] But besides the Qabalah, Stewart draws freely on druidic and pagan lore, numerology, Christian symbolism, Tarot, astrology, and so on. Despite the great freedom that this syncretistic approach affords, an interpretative burden is imposed by it on Stewart. If each version is a manifestation of the same archetype, and since no version can be dismissed as a corruption of another, all versions of the song must be shown to display a correspondence with the others. If one has "rivals" and another "strangers," then some connection must be found between rivals and strangers since both are performing the same archetypical function.

Let us see Stewart's approach in action. Here is what he says about two:

> TWO. 'Two of them are lily-white boys clothed all in Green Oh.' This immediately reveals links with *The Two Brothers* [another folk-song], but Baring-Gould surprisingly suggests that the 'lily-white boys' are the astrological sign of Gemini. In old calendar terms the Sun entered Gemini at the beginning of May, the time of the pagan Beltane feast. The possibility of developing an astrological implication from the song is tempting, especially with those variants having 12 verses, yet these versions were more probably built up [from versions with 10 verses] to suit Christian adaptation. The twelvefold system adapted by the Christian cult, however, was used to fit Apostles to earlier patterns which had astrological links. We are dealing here

---

[84] In fact, his qabalistic references are confined to the *Sefer Yetzirah*, ascribed by Jewish lore to Abraham but in reality, likely composed around 3rd to 5th centuries C.E..

[85] The relations between the rabbinic, legalistic side of Judaism and its mystical side are the subject of much scholarly work. Some, like Gershom Scholem, have emphasized the tension between them while others argue they are much closer in spirit. (Idel (1991) is a good overview.) Many important Jewish figures were both legal experts and revered mystics. While one cannot rule out that some rabbis sometimes called some qabalists "heretics," and although Qabalah may have spawned the genuine heresy of Sabbateanism, at no point has Kabbalah as such been considered a heresy within Judaism.

with a *synthetic* type of thought, which continually returns to a state or stage where systems such as music, mathematics, astrology and general imagery merge into one another. There is no contradiction in the Dilly Song even though we find it temporarily jumping from one type of symbolism to another, for it is still fulfilling its pattern of exposition, be it pagan or Christian.

In Mishnah[86] 10 of *The Sepher Yetzirah* we find "TWO: Air from Spirit." Gemini is an 'Airy Sign', of course, so perhaps Baring-Gould's inference, drawn from an early work on festal embroidery, is correct. The Second Sphere of the Tree of Life is said to be that of the Unity of Being, expressed in the First Sphere, now divided into action, into that of Doing, making 1 into 2. This is called the sphere of Wisdom. A great deal was made in early mathematics of the relationship between the numbers one to four, which add sequentially to ten. It is interesting to recall that the symbol of Cornwall[87] is not much different from the Pythagorean tetractys – a pyramid of ten dots (One for All, and All for One!). Ten was said to be the perfect number, as it was the sum of 1-4 reverting to its unity 1(0). We shall not expand upon this difficult art here, but it does reveal itself within the folksong. We can see why this second stage is also called 'God's own son' or 'Christ's natures' in some song-texts. Rather than delve into the murky depths of classified heresy, we can merely add that the reading of the Two Boys as Christ and John the Baptist is a rather unfortunate – though common – explanation of the second verse. It leads us into the whole issue of God, Father and Son, which caused so many heads to roll, including that of John the Baptist. That incident may well indicate the customary pattern that a priest or prophet was expected to die after he had handed on his power to his successor. John, of course, was a typical other-world seer, after the fashion of our native 'Bran' cult, while his divine successor Jesus was clearly a solar figure, after the nature of 'Beli'.

The Qabalistic attributes of Wisdom to this second stage or sphere links up well with the line 'Two was the jury'[88] from the Bristol variant, and the lily-white babes or maids are typical images to personify wisdom. (78-9)

I shall not attempt to tease out the logic of the argument here. Stewart, indeed, would approve of my reticence: "Throughout the centuries people have believed that such symbols

---

[86] [Editor's note:] An odd use of the word "Mishnah," on which, see the commentary to *The Size of an Olive* (M.12). The reference in Stewart is to chapter 1, section 10.

[87] [Editor's note:] Stewart is basing his analysis largely on a Cornish version of the song. Lest we jump to conclusions, however, he assures us that "It is not being suggested... that Cornish people are the lost tribes of Israel, or that British lore is in any way derived from Jewish tradition" (77).

[88] [Editor's note:] I am shocked that Stewart does not offer an interpretation for a variant of the Bristol version: "Two is the Jewry" (see F.C.H. (1868), who notes that this version is "sung by the children at Beckington, Somerset," but a scant 50 miles from Bristol).

lead to an awareness that is higher or better than straight-line logic, everyday disordered thinking" (84). He berates the orthodox commentators, "fitting each line forcibly into an orthodox framework and… call[ing] any details that do not fit 'corruptions'." The chief differences between Stewart and these hide-bound relics are a) that the framework into which each line is forcibly fit is not 'orthodox' but pagan and syncretistic; b) that his framework is supposed to explain *all* the variants and dismiss none as mere 'corruptions';[89] and c) that his method of forcing the multiple variants into the framework is a kind free-associative ramble through just about any body of ancient or mystical lore at hand. Still, there is a somewhat clear answer to the question "what does it mean to say X is/means/refers to Y." It is that Y is an element of the archetype underlying all versions of the song, the unfolding of the Tree of Life from heaven to earth in clearly defined stages, and that X is a particular manifestation of this element.

Now let us compare this with what Jewnin does with two. The text of his commentary is translated by Dr. Israel Sandman. I will mark his footnotes as translator's notes and his elucidatory insertions into the body of the text with square brackets and bold, to distinguish them from my own editor's notes and insertions, the latter marked only with the usual square brackets. Jewnin begins, like Stewart, with an introduction to his approach:

> Who knows one. I have seen that many interpret this riddle, but they do not do so in keeping with the theme of the day [**viz. Passover**]. However it is certain that since it was set for Passover, it is referring to that theme. Therefore, I shall likewise interpret it in keeping with the theme of the day. (1914: 54)

Amusingly, Jewnin starts off the same way as Stewart does, with a dismissal of other attempts at interpretation and a brief announcement of the right way to do it. But the task Jewnin sets for himself is considerably more circumscribed. The problem confronting an interpreter of *Green Grow the Rushes, O* is to say what the things are that are referred to in the song, where these are not self-evident. In the case of *Eḥad Mi Yod'ea*, this is much less pressing. The song has been textually stable for hundreds of years and the numbers are either self-evident or generally agreed upon.[90] Rather than trying to explicate what the things associated with the numbers are meant to be, Jewnin only seeks to find some reason why those things show up in a Passover song.

---

[89] Though see his own suggestion that "those variants having 12 verses… were more probably built up [from versions with 10 verses] to suit Christian adaptation."

[90] It is, however, instructive to remember the role of accompanying cultural knowledge. For example, the fathers, in the answer to "who knows three?", are always said to be the three Patriarchs – Abraham, Isaac, and Jacob. This is because those three are often referred to as "the fathers" in Jewish religious discourse. But without knowledge of that discourse, one might understand the language of the song perfectly and yet still be puzzled as to who the "three fathers" are in the same way we are puzzled as to who the "lily-white boys" are. The same goes for the answers to two, four, ten, eleven, twelve, and thirteen. It may seem as if there is little danger of the song's surviving (along with knowledge of its Hebrew (and occasional Aramaic)) while that cultural knowledge is lost. But this seems to be exactly what has happened with at least some versions of *Green Grow the Rushes, O*.

We should probably not count it against Jewnin's strategy to "interpret [the song] in keeping with the theme of the day" that in fact,

> The song has nothing to do with Passover, and it also appears as a table song for festivals… Goldschmidt noted that it was also sung at [Jewish] weddings in Cochin and Senegal, as evidenced in a volume printed in Amsterdam in 1757 for the use of those communities. Records of the Inquisition, from Majorca in 1678, show that this song was considered sort of a Jewish catechism.[91] (Tabory 2008: 64)

For the song *is* regularly sung on Passover (and in most communities at no other time) and the commentary is not an attempt to uncover its origins or anything like an original purpose.

I continue with the commentary on two:

> Why were these two, viz. the heavens and the earth [which have just been sung about in "who knows one?"], created? [**For the sake of**] the two Tablets of the Covenant [i.e. the answer to "who knows two?"], viz. for the sake of the Torah, as the verse (*Jeremiah* 33:25) states, 'Were it not for the sake of My covenant of day and night [**= the Torah**], I would not have established heaven and earth.'[92] So, too, is it stated in *midrash*[93] (*Exodus Rabbah* 41[:**6**]): "'Carve out for yourself two tablets' (*Exodus* 34:1). Why two tablets? Corresponding to the heavens and the earth." Therefore, when Moses our Rabbi made a stipulation about fulfilling

---

[91] [Editor's note:] And what a bizarre and unsystematic catechism the Inquisition must have found it! Which is not to say that one couldn't attempt to 'rationalize' it. One, of course, is the foundational belief of the religion – its monotheism; two, the historical event in which God communicates with the Jewish people through Moses (one cannot take this as a reference to what is written on the tablets without making ten a mere repetition); three and four, the historical origins of the Jewish people; five and six, the central texts; seven, the importance of the Sabbath, the seventh of the seven days (and perhaps by metonymy, the observances and rituals of regular life); eight, the covenant that God has made with the Jewish people; nine, the continuity of the Jewish people as part of that covenant; ten, the commandments placed on the Jewish people (and by metonymy, the *halakhah*, the code governing all aspects of everyday life). Eleven is anomalous, but perhaps can stand for the reality of prophecy (and hence also the authority of the books of the Prophets, and by metonymy, those parts of the Bible other than the five books of the Torah). Twelve is difficult to rationalize. The division of Jews into twelve tribes has long since lost any real significance – only the Levites are still recognized as such, but perhaps, then, twelve can stand metonymically for the sacramental role of the Levites and Cohanim. Thirteen, again, is somewhat random, but speaks to one aspect, mercy, of the character of the God whose existence stands at the start of the song. So, as a catechism, it does cover, albeit in some cases sporadically and incompletely, belief in God (one), God's nature (thirteen), history (two, three, four, eight, nine), ritual (seven), sacred texts (five, six, and perhaps eleven – but why no reference to the Talmud?), and sacramentality (seven, eight, ten, eleven, and twelve). The real sticking point is the fact that metonymy is a completely unsuitable rhetorical figure in a catechism.

[92] [Translator's note:] As interpreted in Babylonian Talmud, *Pesaḥim* 68b. See Rashi there: "'My covenant of day and night': viz. Torah study, about which is stated, 'you shall meditate upon it day and night' (*Joshua* 1:8)."

[93] [Editor's note:] "*Midrash*" is the name for the body of homiletical interpretations of scripture. It can also be used as the proper name for one particular such work, *Midrash Rabbah*, which Jewnin is quoting here.

the Torah and the Commandments, he called the heavens and earth as witnesses against them, as Rashi writes at the beginning of Torah portion *Ha'azinu* (*Deuteronomy* 32:1). In *Yalqut*[94] there, on the verse (*ibid.* v. 2) "Let my teaching drip like rain" [**it states**]: "Just as He set the heavens and earth as witnesses against them, likewise he set the four directions [***ruḥot/*** רוחות][95] of the world as witnesses against them." On this basis, it is possible to interpret the verse (*Amos* 4:13) "For behold! The One Who Forms the mountains and creates the wind [***ruaḥ/*** רוח] and tells to man what his conversations is" on the basis of what we say in *Pesiqta*[96] on the verse (*Mica* 4:1) "It shall come to pass in the latter of days that the mountain of the house of the Lord will be firmly set at the top of the mountains": In the future, the Holy Blessed One will bring [Mountains] Sinai, Tabor, Carmel, and Hermon, and build the Temple upon them. There (v. 2) he concludes, "for Torah will go forth from Zion." The Sages (of blessed memory) expounded the same [concept] regarding Mt. Moriah: It is called "Moriah" because from there instruction [***hora'ah/*** הוראה][97] goes forth to all of Israel. Thus we see that these mountains were created for the sake of the Torah; and thus did the four directions [***ruḥot/*** רוחות] of the world as witnesses against them regarding the fulfillment of the Torah. This is the intention of the verse, that even from the mountains and from the four directions [***ruḥot/*** רוחות] of the world a person is told what his conversation should be, namely that he should constantly be engaged in the Torah, as the verse (*Joshua* 1:8) states, "you shall meditate upon it day and night."

It is furthermore possible to explain "Who knows two" on the basis of what is stated in *Midrash Tanḥuma*:[98] In the merit of Jacob we were redeemed from Egypt; and of his name the letter B/ ב [**the numerical value of which is 2**] corresponds to the two tablets. This is the meaning of "who knows two?" It refers to the 2 = the letter B/ ב of "Jacob," being the two Tablets of the Covenant. He hereby alludes that in his merit they would be redeemed from Egypt, subsequently receiving the two Tablets of the Covenant.

The details of the reasoning here are, if anything, more vertiginous than they are in Stewart. Briefly, Jewnin offers two interpretations for why "two tablets of the law" is connected to the theme of Passover. In the first, longer paragraph (the paragraph break is my addition), the two tablets are connected, via a number of different routes (based on different interpretative resources) to the heavens and the earth. Since these were part of the answer to "who knows

---

[94] [Editor's note:] *Yalqut Shim'oni*, a medieval collection of midrashic comments on the Bible.

[95] [Translator's note:] The Hebrew term has several meanings, including: directions/compass points; winds; and spirits. For this passage, both "directions/compass points" and "winds" can work.

[96] [Editor's note:] Another work of *midrash*.

[97] [Editor's note:] Because the word for instruction (*hora'ah*) and the name of the mountain are similar.

[98] [Editor's note:] Another work of *midrash*.

one?" (one God who is in heaven and earth), whatever link that answer has with Passover is transmitted to the two tablets. The second interpretation is a little less tenuous, though somewhat more fanciful. Passover is about the exodus of the Jews from Egypt. It was owing to the merit of Jacob that they were redeemed, and the last letter of Jacob's name has the numerical value of two (in Hebrew, the numbers are represented by an assignment of numerical values to the letters of the alphabet), which numbers the tablets of the covenant. Hence, "two tablets" is linked, via Jacob's name and merit, to the exodus from Egypt commemorated at Passover.

Perhaps this is even less satisfying than Stewart's exposition. But the two styles of interpretation are quite different in nature and to be judged by quite different standards. Stewart is part of the modern world, responding to those (the plodding orthodox interpreters of the song) who would appeal to the 'science' of textual criticism (see the commentary to M.77 for more on textual criticism). Thus, he is connected to everyday and scientific reasoning, even if he eschews it for himself. His interpretation is supposed to displace, or be an alternative to, the fruits of science. His indiscriminate appeal to so many disparate sources, therefore, has an air of irresponsibility to it. Jewnin, on the other hand, was living in a tightly knit Jewish community in Lithuania. His exposition is not supposed to displace any scientific results and his wide use of sources, from different times and places, is nonetheless confined to the canon appealed to by all rabbinic scholars. He is part of a tradition of exegetes of similar nature. His goals are quite different from Stewart's and the means he uses to achieve them not at all inappropriate. One might say that Stewart's energy is centrifugal, Jewnin's centripetal.

I do not want, however, to place too much weight on the differences in the social milieux of the two interpreters. This photo was taken in Moscow in 1905:

Figure 9 Photo of Evnine's ancestors, Moscow, 1905

The patriarch in the family tableau is Bezalel Jewnin, the son of Nathan Neta and Evnine's great-grandfather. (His grandfather is the young man seated on the right.) Nathan Neta lived in Vilna, in the Pale of Settlement to which most Jews were confined in the Russian Empire. He almost certainly spoke Yiddish as his first language. His son Bezalel, on the other hand, lived in Moscow and was a merchant of the First Guild (which, among other things, entitled him to wear a sword). If he knew Yiddish, it is clear that he did not speak it with his family. This comfortable bourgeois family would have put their faith in science and industry, not in 'superstition.' Yet Bezalel saw to the posthumous publication of his father's commentary on the Haggadah in 1914, the year of Nathan Neta's death. When this photo was taken, Nathan Neta was alive and working as a rabbinic scholar. Nathan Neta and his son Bezalel straddled one moment in the Jews' entry into modernity. We shall return to this photo shortly.

Coming to the Marxist parody of *Green Grow the Rushes, O*, the final verse is:

> I'll sing you fourteen - O!
> Red Fly The Banners - O!
> What are your fourteen - O!
> Fourteen for the IQ of the average Trot
> And Thirteen for the holes in Trotsky's head.
> Twelve for the chimes on the Kremlin clock
> And eleven for the Moscow Dynamos
> Ten for the Days that Shook the World
> And Nine for the Days of the General Strike
> Eight for the hours of the working day
> Seven for the Seventh World Congress
> Six for the Tolpuddle Martyrs,
> Five for the years in Stalin's plans
> And four for the four years taken,
> Three, three, the Rights of Man!
> Two, two the workers' hands, working for a living, O!
> One is workers' unity and ever more shall be so!

Notice that one charming feature of the original has been preserved in the parody, though in relation to different numbers. When going down the list from twelve, the original has "Twelve for the twelve apostles; eleven for the eleven that went to Heaven." This presumably means the eleven of the twelve apostles that went to Heaven (i.e., all but Judas). The sense of the line for eleven is only evident, however, when one counts down to it from the higher number. When adding the numbers, one would add eleven before one got to its antecedent in twelve. In the parody, we have "Four for the four years taken," the sense of which is not evident until one counts down from the next line, "Five for the years in Stalin's plan"! Notice also that this version goes up to 14, extending by two its model. Most traditional versions go up either to ten or twelve. *Eḥad Mi Yod'ea*, by contrast, goes to thirteen. Cecil Sharp, quoting almost verbatim the entry from the *Jewish Encyclopedia* of 1906, notes that "It has been suggested that the Hebrew version was purposely extended to thirteen, the unlucky number, in order that the Jew might be able to feel that with him thirteen was a holy and, therefore, lucky number (1916: xliv). If the extension to thirteen was deliberate, I would suggest it was less to make the Jew feel that thirteen was lucky than simply to stamp the Jewish version with a characteristic that would never be found in Christian ones.

Why did Evnine choose thirteen and "the holes in Trotsky's head" for this meme? He could, after all, have responded to Rosen's invocation of the parody with any of its entries. Perhaps he chose thirteen partly because, as just noted, it is the number that distinguishes the Jewish *Eḥad Mi Yod'ea* from Christian variants of the song. But almost certainly, the predominant reason was this. The thirteen holes in Trotsky's head are surely meant to be the wounds he sustained during his assassination by ice pick (though as far as I know, he was struck just once with the pick so it is unclear why the song speaks of thirteen holes). The Soviet agent who organized the assassination and recruited and trained Ramón Mercader was Leonid (Naum) Eitingon. Leonid, with a truly astounding (and sinister) career in the Soviet secret services,[99] is just one of three famous Eitingons. The others are Motty, a fur magnate who likely worked as a conduit between America and a nascent Soviet Union before diplomatic relations were established, and Max, a psychoanalyst and close friend of Freud's, and one of the founders of the famous Berlin Psychoanalytic Institute. Another Eitingon, not famous at all, is Zissia, the matriarch in the photo above, thus making Evnine a relative of these remarkable men, including the one who put thirteen holes in Trotsky's head.

---

[99] Around 1943, Leonid trained Nikolai Khokhlov, an artistic vaudeville whistler, for over a year and a half to impersonate a German officer. When he was finally ready, Khokhlov parachuted into Minsk under the name "Lieutenant Otto Witgenstein" and successfully completed his mission of blowing up Wilhelm Kube, the "Butcher of Belorussia" (Wilmers 2009: 340-1).

M.31 Jamaica?

M.31 Jamaica? Composed: March 6th. Posted: March 9th. Orientation: Reverse. Font: Arial. TB1: "My analyst went on vacation.", black. TB2: "Jamaica?", black. TB3: "No, she went freely.", black (with hand-drawn speech bubble pointing to Robin).

Although we saw the introduction of a third textbox in *Dialetheism* (M.20), this is the first time it is used to furnish text for another speech bubble, thus increasing the dramatic potentialities inherent in the image exponentially. Evnine made a number of uses of a third speech bubble, allowing both Batman and Robin, and in two memorable cases, *Jingle Bells* (M.49) and *Dinner's Ready* (M.104), a third character, to get in an extra word. The text in *Jamaica?* is based on an old joke that can be found in printed sources as early as 1913 and (judging by the frequency of early print renditions) must have already been well known.[100] It is usually told about the joke teller's wife and goes something like this: "My wife went to the West Indies." "Jamaica?" "No, she went of her own accord." (Possibly the artist changed "of her own accord" to "freely" because of space constraints.) As Professor Michael Rosen happily commented on the meme's original Facebook posting: "[N]ote the subtle, post-modern note by which a very old joke is hybridized through a Woody Allen trope and 'my wife' becomes 'my analyst'."

---

[100] See Zimmer (2008), which is short but (with the updates that draw on the comments) very much worth reading. The joke has appeared in print many, many time and it has also made an appearance in several films, of which the relevant excerpts are given in Zimmer's blog post.

M.32 Nevermore!

M.32 Nevermore! Composed: March 9th. Posted: March 10th. Orientation: Reverse. Font: Comic Sans. TB1: "'Tis some visitor entreating entrance at my...", black. TB2: "Nevermore!", black.

Several of the memes contain quotations from poetry and this is the first of them. The words, of course, come from Edgar Allen Poe's *The Raven*. Robin's line should be completed "chamber door" but Batman, with some humor, interrupts Robin with the refrain of the poem, the ominous word spoken by the raven. His interruption displays humor because he is careful to preserve the rhythm of Robin's line, which makes the slap both antiphonal in form and interruptive in content.

What, exactly, is happening in the meme? Is Robin quoting the poem or using the words himself? (Perhaps the contrast should be between merely quoting and quoting and using together.) If Robin is quoting the poem, even reciting it, then Batman's response is humorous for another reason besides its rhythmic placement. For in that case, Batman would be directing Robin to desist (permanently?) from his poetic performances by *using* a quotation from the poem. He would be using and quoting the word in one breath.[101]

---

[101] The distinction between using words (to talk or write about whatever) and talking or writing *about* words (i.e., mentioning or quoting them) is often treated as a shibboleth of analytic philosophy but there is some reason to be skeptical. I investigate these issues further in the commentary on *"Sorry!" Not Sorry!* (M.83).

We should not, however, discount the possibility that it is the *artist* who is quoting the poem, putting its words into the speech bubbles where they are merely used, by Batman and Robin, to conduct a somewhat elliptical exchange. Making sense of the meme, in that case, becomes somewhat more difficult. It is not impossible, I think, to read it as having a sexual meaning. If the chamber to the door of which someone is seeking entrance were to be interpreted as the rectum, Robin might be commenting (whether approvingly or otherwise is impossible to determine) on an on-going history of sodomitic relations between Batman and himself. (In the context of sodomy, the anus is commonly called the "back door," casting the rectum in the role of a chamber.[102]) In that case, Batman's "Nevermore!" suggests self-loathing for his pedophilic behavior and a resolution never to repeat it. (The slap also fits here. For a discussion of the link between shame and violence, see the commentary on *Show some respect, Robin* (M.13).)

This reading of the meme is not at all outlandish. In one of his blog posts about his work, *Interview with the Author*, Evnine reveals that when he used to watch the live Batman series from the mid- to late-sixties, as a boy of around seven or eight years old, he learned the word "catamite" from his father in connection with it. And his father also used to refer to Robin as "Batman's little buggery boy." (Who knows what else may be illuminated by this precocious sexual knowledge!) But apart from the reference to the creator of the meme's personal psychology, the homosexual reading of the meme is borne out by objective factors. Fredric Wertham's 1954 book *Seduction of the Innocent* fired a broadside against comics culture and in the year of its publication, Wertham was invited to testify before Congress for hearings on juvenile delinquency. Here he is, writing about Batman and Robin:

> At home [Batman and Robin] lead an idyllic life. They are Bruce Wayne and "Dick" Grayson. Bruce Wayne is described as a "socialite" and the official relationship is that Dick is Bruce's ward. They live in sumptuous quarters, with beautiful flowers in large vases, and have a butler, Alfred. Bruce is sometimes shown in a dressing-gown. As they sit by the fireplace the young boy sometimes worries about his partner… It is like a wish dream of two homosexuals living together. (Quoted in Weldon 2016: 45)

While most of the writers of the Batman comics might have demurred, one, Grant Morrison, did not:

> Gayness is built into Batman. Batman is very, very gay. There's just no denying it. Obviously as a fictional character he's intended to be heterosexual, but the basis of the whole concept is utterly gay. (Quoted in Weldon 2016: 53)

This statement by Morrison raises interesting questions about what it is to give a reading or an interpretation of a text. (See the commentary on *Thirteen Holes* (M.30) for more about this

---

[102] Another kind of chamber is the tomb, or grave. One thinks, simultaneously, of Poe's own stories about being buried alive and David Watney's striking image, deployed in his discussion of homophobic discourse around AIDS, of the rectum as a grave.

issue.) Batman is intended to be heterosexual but has gayness built into him. What can this mean?

Glen Weldon, discussing precisely this issue, writes:

> 1) Intention doesn't matter. Imagery does..... 2) Gays have always looked for their reflections in media... by looking more deeply. Every exchange, every glance, every touch, is hungrily parsed for something they recognize, for fleeting glimpses of themselves, their desires, and the world they know... 3) Batman is a character who comes factory preinstalled with rich and varied ideas – ideas in which gay men historically find affinities: the constant threat of a secret self's exposure, the cloak of night, a muscular physicality, a homosocial friendship – and, yes, okay, fine, a flair for interior design... 4) Batman is an inkblot; we see in him what we want to. (2016: 54; enumeration mine)

Although the four ideas I have numbered here are not inconsistent with each other, they do focus on different phenomena. 1) contrasts intention with imagery. An artist may produce an image, say of Bruce and Dick waking up in the same bed,[103] which presents a gay couple even though it was not intended to. 2) describes an activity, "hungrily parsing," by which gay consumers find intimations of their lives and concerns. Here the readers' activity is highlighted and the idea given of employing interpretative acrobatics to yield the desired connections. 3) puts the focus on the created character. Batman comes with various features, placed there by the creators, that parallel important concerns of gay readers. (This seems closest to what Morrison suggests with his claim that Batman has "gayness built in.") Finally, 4) invokes the Rorschach test and likens the text to something that elicits revelatory material from us despite ourselves. I suggest it is 3) that gives the best understanding of what it is to offer a gay reading of Batman (or, *mutatis mutandis*, a reading of any variety, of any text). It is like 1), but of wider scope, not being confined to imagery. It captures the sense of deliberateness that is missing in 4). And it seems less strained than 2).

There is another interesting aspect to the meme. As we have noted, the meme has Batman speaking the very word uttered thrice by the raven in Poe's poem. This leads one to reflect on the similarities between the figures of the raven and the bat. In *Detective Comics* 33 (September 1939) we get, for the first time, Batman's origins story. (See the commentaries on *...a meme in which I'm being...* (M.1) and *Vos iz ayer yidisher nomen, Batman?* (M.72) for something about origins stories.) Young Bruce Wayne's parents are murdered and the boy vows to fight crime in response. As an adult, he is ready to begin fulfilling his vow but realizes he needs a disguise. Wearing a rich dressing gown and sitting in an armchair in the study of the mansion left to him by his father, he muses "Criminals are a superstitious cowardly lot. So my disguise must be able to strike terror into their hearts. I must be a creature of the night, black, terrible...a...a..." In the next panel, the caption text informs us: "As if in answer a huge bat flies in through the open window." A window flanked, be it said, by uncertainly rustling curtains. Bruce exclaims: "a bat!

---

[103] The first panel of "Ten Nights of Fear," *Batman* #84 (June 1954).

That's it! It's an omen. I shall become a BAT!" A black, ominous creature that strikes terror into people's hearts, entering into a room with rustling curtains to take a place in the morbid ruminations of a man in the comfort of his study. How similar are Poe's poem and the comic panels that make up Batman's origins story.

Fernando Pessoa was a great admirer of Poe and translated a number of his poems into Portuguese, including *The Raven*. George Monteiro (2010) discusses the similarities, both in form and content, between *The Raven* and one of Pessoa's own poems, *O Mostrengo* (The Monster). Like a raven, Pessoa's monster flies and this, Monteiro informs us, is the legacy of an earlier version of the poem, *O Morcego* (The Bat)! Linking the two versions of the poem Monteiro invokes a third figure – "a shrouded human figure, very far larger in its proportions than any dweller among men," as Poe describes the last thing seen by Arthur Gordon Pym of Nantucket, in the eponymous narrative – and concludes: "Had Pessoa morphed or melded his "morcego" and his "mostrengo," he'd have been the inventor of 'Batman'" (114).

M.36 Here!

M.36 Here! Composed: March 12th. Posted: March 13th. Orientation: Reverse. Font: Arial. TB1: "How about a hand job, Batman?", black. TB2: "Here!", black.

It seems that Robin is asking Batman to masturbate him. (See, in connection to Robin's sexuality, *Mr. Peabody* (M.25) and perhaps *Nevermore!* (M.32).) Batman responds, instead, with a slap, which is after all a job done by the hand, yielding a beautiful example of what I called in the Introduction a demonstrative slap.

I say that Robin is requesting a kind of sexual contact but it is, of course, possible that I am misreporting what he says (or what Evnine has him say). Perhaps he is requesting the very kind of hand job, a slap, that he in fact receives, attempting to inject some humor into the tired repetition of the meme's scene. Or perhaps he is using the expression "hand job" to mean nothing more than "job done by or to the hand," suggesting to Batman that he engage in some unspecified manual labor. Indirect quotation, the reporting of what someone says in a way that frees the reporter from having to stick to the actual words used by that someone (which I am doing with respect to the encounter depicted in the meme), is a perfectly ordinary and natural thing to do but, as we all know, it can be a very tricky business. When, in general, do we *correctly* report what another has said? Using the actual words of the person whose speech one is reporting is neither necessary nor sufficient for accurately reporting what it is they have said.[104]

[104] Insufficient – Speaker: "I am hungry." Reporter: "Speaker said that I am hungry." (Obviously an incorrect report despite using the speaker's exact words.) Unnecessary – Speaker: "I am hungry." Reporter: "Speaker said that she is hungry." (Obviously a correct report despite not using the speaker's exact

In our case, we are fortunate to have to hand a blog post by a former colleague of the artist's, Colin McGinn, to which we can turn for illumination. It opens like this:

> Morality, Reported Speech, and "Hand Job": A Refutation
>
> What kind of hand job leaves you cleaner than before? A manicure, of course. Why does this joke work? Because of the tension between the conventional idiomatic sense of "hand job" (a certain type of sex act) and its semantic or compositional meaning (in which it is synonymous with "job done by or to the hand").[105] When you think about it virtually all jobs are "hand jobs" in the second semantic sense: for all human work is manual work—not just carpentry and brick laying but also cookery and calligraphy. Indeed, without the hand human culture and human economies would not exist. So really "hand jobs" are very respectable and vital to human flourishing. We are a "hand job" species. (Are you now becoming desensitized to the specifically sexual meaning of "hand job"? Remember that heart surgeons are giving you a "hand job" when they operate on you; similarly for masseurs and even tax accountants.) (2013b)

McGinn goes on to draw out the consequences for indirect quotation of people using the expression "hand job" in certain contexts.

> Suppose now a professor P, well conversant in the above points, slyly remarks to his graduate student, who is also thus conversant: "I had a hand job yesterday". The astute student, suitably linguistically primed, responds after a moment by saying: "Ah, you had a manicure". Professor P replies: "You are clearly a clever student—I can't trick you. That is exactly the response I was

---

words.) These examples using pronoun change are, in a sense, trite but it is not hard to come up with other more interesting examples, involving substitution of synonyms, substitution of active for passive constructions (and vice versa), known idiosyncrasies in the speaker's or reporter's idiolect, and so on. Not to mention translation.

[105] [Editor's note:] For the purposes of this commentary, I go along with McGinn's claim that "hand job" does have, as a "semantic or compositional meaning," something synonymous with "job done by or to the hand." But in fact, this is at least questionable. In English, where two nouns join to make a compound noun, the way the semantic value of the result depends on the semantic values of the components is tricky. For one thing, why the prepositions "by" and "to"? Would the garish decoration of a bridge with the severed hands of criminals – a job done *with* hands in the same sense as a paint job is done *with* paint – be a hand job? Furthermore, the term "job" can mean both an episode of work (discrete or continuing) and a type of work. It would be surprising if that difference didn't affect the nature of the qualification associated with the compound noun "hand job." (In the idiomatic sense, "job" has to mean "episode of work" but in pre-idiomatic uses of the expression "hand job," as far as I can tell, "job" always functions in the "type of work" sense.) My point is not to quibble about particular claims here, but merely to indicate that things might be more complex than McGinn suggests with respect to the "semantic or compositional meaning" of the compound noun.

looking for!"[106] They then chuckle together in a self-congratulatory academic manner. Academics like riddles and word games.

But suppose a naïve eavesdropper, overhearing this witty conversation, jumps to the conclusion that "hand job" was being used in the narrow sexual sense. He then reports the speech act of Professor P as follows: "Professor P told his student that he masturbated yesterday". He has failed to see the joke and has no knowledge of the linguistic and intellectual background of the speech act he is trying so ineptly to report. He clearly misreports what Professor P said (oratio obliqua),[107] missing both the content and the humor. We might accurately paraphrase P's remark as follows: "I had a job performed on my hand yesterday". Perhaps the inept reporter's mistake is understandable, but it is still a mistake. (*ibid.*)

McGinn is right that the inept reporter does not correctly report what Professor P says to his student but I don't think it has anything much to do with the distinction between the "idiomatic sense" and the "semantic or compositional meaning" of the expression "hand job." Suppose, for example, that the professor and his student had come to use the noun "wank" to mean any job done by or to the hand.[108] If Professor P had said "I had a wank yesterday," would not the reporter have been equally inept had he said that the professor told his student that he had masturbated yesterday? And would he not equally have "failed to see the joke" because he had "no knowledge of the linguistic and intellectual background" of the speech act he was reporting on? Are you now becoming sensitized to the specifically sexual innuendo at work? Remember that heart surgeons are giving you a wank when they operate on you. Well, in this last sentence, I go too far. If Professor P said to his student "heart surgeons are giving you a wank when they operate on you," he would say something true since "wank" in the dialect formed by the two of them means "job done by or to the hand." (If it didn't, of course, then Professor P would have told his student that he had masturbated the previous day in the envisaged scenario.) But when *I* say "heart surgeons are giving you a wank when they operate on you," I am saying, falsely, that they masturbate you when they operate on you, since in my idiolect "wank" does not mean "job done by or to the hand." So I cannot truly utter the sentence "heart surgeons are giving you a wank when they operate on you" though Professor P could (at

---

106 [Editor's note:] There is an aspect of this imaginary encounter that plays no role in McGinn's discussion and may even cut against the moral he alleges to draw from it. "You are clever – I can't trick you" is what one says when one has tried to trick someone and they have not been fooled. So Professor P did expect the student to be offended. But Professor P goes on to say that the student gave the response that P was looking for. So he expected the student to be fooled but wanted them not to be. This has the structure of an initiation test. In the vignette, the student passes the test and is rewarded with a shared chuckle, a sign of the free-spirited camaraderie of those who 'get it,' who are not squares like the naïve eavesdropper mentioned in the next paragraph.

107 [Editor's note:] Indirect speech (i.e., indirect quotation).

108 I use the Anglicism "wank" since American English does not contain any semantically simple expression for an episode of masturbation with which I am familiar.

least to his poor student, forced to endure his attempt at edgy humor). But, come to think of it, McGinn too, addressing the general reader, does not say "heart surgeons are giving you a hand job when they operate on you." What he writes is: "heart surgeons are giving you a 'hand job' when they operate on you." Why the quotation marks around "hand job"?

I suggest the quotation marks are there because McGinn recognizes that although the "semantic or compositional meaning" of "hand job" is "job done by or to the hand," "hand job" is also an *idiom* and the notion of idiom requires careful treatment. An idiom is not just some language that is used, *ad hoc*, to express something other than its semantic or compositional meaning. Idioms are established and conventional. In becoming established and conventional, they acquire a *semantic* meaning which rivals, and may eventually even come to replace entirely, the "semantic or compositional" meaning of the language out of which they are constructed. Take, for instance, the expression "on the ball," which is an idiom in contemporary English that means "alert" or "sharp." The words "on the ball" have not lost their ability (in virtue of their "semantic or compositional meaning") to ascribe a location to something atop a round object manufactured for play (a tennis ball, for example) or warfare (a musket ball) or the like. ("Where did that butterfly land?" "It's there, on the ball.") But nor is their use to mean "alert" or "sharp" a metaphor or an *ad hoc* pragmatic effect achieved only by grace of the speaker's intentions and the context. That meaning is like a new, literal semantic meaning the expression, as idiom, has acquired. In its idiomatic sense, we can (if we like, still) hear the "semantic or compositional meaning" it has in its non-idiomatic sense. But we do not have to – and one day that might become almost irrecoverable.[109] It would be absurd to suggest that if I heard someone say to their student "I was on the ball yesterday – I caught many errors in a piece I was working on" that I would have ineptly reported them by saying that they said to their student that they were alert yesterday and that what they *really* said, strictly speaking, was that yesterday, they were located on (or had their eye on) a round object made for play, etc.

"Hand job," too, is an idiom, and its meaning "episode of masturbation" is no less literal, as such, than its "semantic or compositional meaning" of "job done by or to the hand." In another blog post, also devoted to the expression "hand job," McGinn writes:

---

[109] The history of the idiom "beg the question" is instructive from this point of view. The word "beg" used to have as one meaning "to take for granted without warrant" (OED). "Beg the question" thus meant, according to its "semantic or compositional meaning," "take for granted something under question that one did not have warrant for" or "assume something which was under question." That sense of "beg" disappeared from the language but "beg the question" (meaning to assume that which one was supposed to be arguing) persisted as an idiom in which one could not hear or recover the original "semantic or compositional meaning." This was evidently offensive to many speakers of the language who thus began to re-literalize the idiom using a different, and current, sense of "beg," namely "to ask for." The phrase is now used, not as an idiom (or perhaps only with a lingering sense that it used to be one) but according to its "semantic or compositional meaning," to mean "ask for some question [usually explicitly supplied] [to be asked]."

> ... The phrase is now virtually taboo... yet semantically it is perfectly innocuous.
> Even to use the phrase "job done by the hand" now risks sniggers and censure.
> Can we not recover it for "respectable" use? Must it be indelibly associated with
> sex acts?... [I]ndeed it is not difficult, by repetition and suitable intonation, to
> rid the phrase of its contemporary narrow meaning (and some amusement is
> to be had by such an exercise). Again we can employ the phrase "hand job" in
> its original meaning and not be found coarse or worse. (McGinn 2013a)

My point about idiom is to suggest that "hand job" is not "perfectly innocuous" semantically. It need not be indelibly associated with sex acts – no bit of language need be indelibly associated with anything! Meanings change, of course. But right now, it is part of the *semantic* meaning of "hand job" that it refers to an episode of masturbation. It is true that the idiom, having come to exist, now threatens to over-shadow the non-idiomatic use of the phrase, rendering it risible. Such, regrettably, is the power of the salacious. But we cannot, in anything more than the most local way, negate the meaning of the idiom by performing the hand job of pounding our fists on the table, or the hand job of gesturing at the sea like King Canute ordering back the tide, and saying "hand job," "hand job," "hand job," over and over again.

Notwithstanding the idiomatic sense of "hand job," I do hand it to McGinn, as I said a couple of paragraphs back, that it would be inept to report Professor P as having said that he masturbated yesterday, in the scenario envisaged. Not, as I have been explaining, because a correct reporting of the speech act ought only to confine itself to the semantic or compositional meaning of "hand job," since I think it does have "episode of masturbation" as a semantic meaning, but because a) Professor P and his student have repurposed the expression, as they could repurpose any expression, to mean something other than "episode of masturbation," and they are speaking in their *ad hoc* dialect at the time;[110] and because, b) as McGinn also notes, the expression "I had a hand job yesterday" would be a clumsy way of saying "I masturbated yesterday." The natural way to use the expression to say "I masturbated yesterday" would be "I gave myself a hand job yesterday." The anomalous phrasing ought to give any reporter pause in reporting what an utterer of the sentence said in uttering it. (In fact, the phrasing much less anomalously suggests that Professor P was telling his student that he sought professional help on the previous day.)[111]

---

[110] Whether they already have constructed their idiolect or whether they are in the process of doing it depends on what is referred to by "the linguistic and intellectual background of the speech act [the naïve eavesdropper] is trying so ineptly to report."

[111] If one were to charge Professor P with speaking to his student inappropriately, as the inept reporter evidently does, none of the forgoing, however, would be enough to get Professor P off (to exculpate him – be careful how you paraphrase me!). The problem would lie not with what Professor P said to his student – I have agreed he has not said that he masturbated – but with how he says it. Specifically, he says it using an expression that, in his and the student's regular language, as opposed to their *ad hoc* dialect, means "episode of masturbation," and hence *suggests*, albeit in that riddlesome, word-gamey way apparently so loved by academics, that he is saying that he masturbated or that he got someone else

Returning to the text of the meme, then, there is no anomalous phrasing in Robin's speech to give us pause in reporting its content by saying that he is inviting Batman to masturbate him. The question remains of whether 1) we should take there to be some pertinent "intellectual or linguistic background" to the speech act captured in the meme, so that "hand job" might refer either to any job done with the hand or even specifically to a slap, in which case Batman is straightforwardly complying with Robin's request, or whether 2) Robin is, as it appears, actually suggesting a sexual act and Batman is having some fun with him by taking "hand job" not in its idiomatic (but still literal) sense but in the non-idiomatic (and contextually inappropriate) sense of "job done by or to the hand." Insofar as the meme would be quite flat-footed on the first option, and given that it provides no hint at all of any previous intellectual or linguistic background, I think we should assume the second option. Robin is indeed talking about a hand job and Batman is just being an obnoxious smart aleck at the expense of one whose welfare is entrusted to him.

to masturbate him. That is something that, generally speaking, one ought to avoid knowingly and winkingly suggesting one is saying to one's students. Merely avoiding actually saying it is not enough. (See, on inappropriate teacher-student relations, the early text by the artist quoted in the commentary on *The Origins of Neo-Platonist Metaphysics* (M.96).)

M.37 My Sister! My daughter!

M.37 My Sister! My daughter! Composed: March 13th. Posted: March 13th. FIRST PANEL Orientation: Reverse. Font: Arial. TB1: "My sister!", black. TB2: N/a. SECOND PANEL Orientation: Original. Font: Arial. TB1: N/a. TB2: "My daughter!", black.

This is the first of several animated GIFs, a huge departure from the standard format. When viewed appropriately (for example, as posted on Facebook) the two panels alternate within the

121

same space. The meme enacts a famous scene from the Roman Polanski film *Chinatown* (1974) in which Evelyn Mulwray (played by Faye Dunaway) is slapped by Jake Gittes (played by Jack Nicholson) repeatedly, with alternating hands, until she confesses that the same woman is both her sister and her daughter, thereby revealing the fact that her father had raped her when she was a teenager. One cannot help but feel that the artist has gone too far here. The violence of the image he works with is always there, bubbling right under the surface, occasionally breaking through (see the commentary on *Couples Therapy* (M.19) for some discussion of this). But to harness this awful scene, in which the violence of the slapping is used to extort a confession of the even worse violence of the rape and incest, for a cheap laugh? Shameless.

M.42 The Sound of Your Blood...

M.42 The Sound of Your Blood... Composed: March 13th. Posted: March 17th. Orientation: Reverse. Font: Comic Sans. TB1: "I can't stand this noise. If only we had an anechoic chamber, its six walls...", white. TB2: "Fool! You'd be deafened by the sound of your blood in circulation and your nervous system in operation.", white.

The language used in this meme clearly echoes a story the composer John Cage told in a number of places of a visit he made to an anechoic chamber at Harvard University. For Cage, the moral of the story seems to have been that where there is life, there is music ("until I die there will be sounds") – something he took to be a joyous state of affairs. The artist, apparently, was fascinated, perhaps even obsessed, by this story, or by the thought of an anechoic chamber, but seems to have made of the whole thing just about the opposite of what Cage took it to mean. As a young man, he wrote what he called a "book," entitled *The Incoherence of the Incoherence* (after the work by the Islamic philosopher Averroes). This piece of near-juvenilia is a strange jumble and we shall defer until the commentary on *Incoherence* (M.95) a closer look at it. But the book contains a passage we will quote here in which the artist gives us his own perspective on Cage's anecdote:

> "Darkness there was, but no silence."[112] Such might be an apt description of being in an anechoic chamber with the lights off.
>
> "For certain engineering purposes, it is desirable to have as silent a situation as possible. Such a room is called an anechoic chamber, its six walls made of

---

[112] [Editor's note:] This quotes the beginning of the artist's 'book.'

special material, a room without echoes. I entered one at Harvard University several years ago and heard two sounds, one high and one low. When I described them to the engineer in charge, he informed me that the high one was my nervous system in operation, and the low one my blood in circulation. Until I die there will be sounds."[113]

Think what this means. One day, here in the city, listen to the noises around you. Music blares, the traffic roars, people shout. What a din! What a hubbub! In order to escape this inconvenience, remove yourself to the countryside. Enjoy the bird song and the murmuring of the brook (never mind the hurdy-gurdy and the loutish accents). Enjoy them. Sing them to yourself, once, twice, then again, and again and on and on until they grow into a clamorous uproar, until the cricket booms in your ear at night and the whippoorwill screams to you of death.

Then take up thy substance and get thee hence; take thyself and go.[114] Go to the wastelands or the deserts where not even the beasts and insects live. Ah desolate solitude. Let us live together in silent ceremony. But what is this? Can it be that I hear something? Yes, it is coming from over there. No, now it's here. And there, and there, and there. It's everywhere. "Yes, everywhere," howls the wind, in hollow mockery. "As long as this planet moves about the sun there will always be alternate patches of hot and cold air. And the hot air will always displace the cold air and I, yes I, the wind will live forever. And for me, living is screaming. From now on, for you who have seen the barren places of the earth, will my slightest stirring, unheeded by all else, be as the trumpeting of a thousand elephants and when I raise my voice you shall stop your ears and cower, lest you are overcome."

Fly, fly from here quickly! But where can I go? Where shall the wind not find me? Shall I take refuge from mankind with the wind, or from the wind with mankind? But wait! Has not the ingenuity of man provided me with that with which I can avoid both man and the wind? Is there not the anechoic chamber, its six walls made of special material, a room as silent as technologically possible? But imperiously, the voice of Being laughs: "Get thee to an anechoic chamber, and hear there thy nervous system in operation and hear there thy blood in circulation."[115]

The piece is strange and somewhat overwrought (and involves a jarring switch from second to first person in the course of the penultimate paragraph) but it strikingly illustrates the

---

[113] [Editor's note:] Cage (1961: 8). The passage continues: "And they will continue following my death. One need not fear about the future of music."

[114] [Editor's note:] Possibly a reference to *Genesis* 12,1.

[115] [Editor's note:] Cage (1961: 51).

artist's constant, almost existential, struggle against noise, something that also makes itself felt in *Shhh!* (M.71). It is indeed curious that of all the senses, we are, in a way, most vulnerable through hearing. We can avert our gaze from something we do not wish to see, or simply close our eyes; we can stop our mouths and noses, at least for a time, to protect from taste and smell. Only touch leaves us as potentially exposed to the violence of the other as sound. But we can at least fight against unwanted touch. Against noise, against other people's music and screaming, against broken car alarms, we can do next to nothing. And what we can do is often only to produce an even greater noise, preferable only because of our choosing.

There is more to the story of the artist's interest in the anechoic chamber and John Cage. We are in possession of a letter he wrote, almost certainly at the end of May or in early June, 1982. Here is the relevant part:

> You'll never guess what happened. It was brill-to-the-max ciudad.[116] I went with Miranda to some of the 70th birthday bash for John Cage at the Almeida.[117] Between two of the events we went to the caff across the road for a cup of tea. We sat down at a large table and then noticed that right next to us, was Cage himself, being interviewed by a couple of wankers.[118] As you know, I'm obsessed by the story he keeps telling about that time he was in an anechoic chamber. So I asked him if he'd been in one in London. He said he'd been photographed in one but it wasn't operational! What a pity. If only it was working I could go myself. Then we got talking about philosophy. He was absolutely sold on Norman Malcolm's memoir of Witters.[119,120] Only he pronounced it as "meeeeemoir," the first vowel long, in both the phonetic and temporal sense. It sounded so strange. Then, cos me and Miranda are trying to eat a macrobiotic

---

[116] [Editor's note:] Brilliant to the max city. On the model of "weird city," a construction the artist learned from the American conductor John Morris Russell when they were students together at King's College London some time between 1978 and 1981.

[117] [Editor's note:] "Cage at 70," the opening event of the Almeida Festival of 1982, was a series of performances at St James' Church, London N7 (not at the Almeida Theatre itself, as Evnine suggests in his letter) from Friday May 28th to Sunday May 30th.

[118] [Editor's note:] A strangely (or perhaps not) uncharitable reaction to two perfectly innocent people who, no doubt, had banked on this time with Cage and felt it was the artist and his companion who were the 'wankers.'

[119] [Editor's note:] Norman Malcolm's *Ludwig Wittgenstein: A Memoir*. For the style of abbreviation manifested in "Witters," see the commentary on *Distinguo, Batters* (M.34). The philosopher Grice recalls J.L. Austin's having said "Some like Witters... but Moore is *my* man" (Grice 1991: 381). Given that Grice's book was not published until 1991, the artist's use of this slang is almost certainly coincidental.

[120] [Editor's note:] Cage's enthusiasm for this work around that time is borne out by a passage from a letter he wrote to Ornella Volta, the author of two works on Satie, on May 25th, 1983, a year after the conversation reported here: "I have finished reading your book (in French; no English has arrived); I love it. I can say that for few others. Like yours they are profoundly touching: Norman Malcolm's *Memoir of Ludwig Wittgenstein* [sic] and Templier's *Erik Satie* (not in the English translation, which I find impossible to read). This making reading matter touching must be what death does to biography" (Cage 2016: 529).

diet, and he wants to write a macrobiotic cookbook(!), he gave us this recipe.[121] (I quote, almost *verbatim*.) "Take a carrot, a turnip, and a parsnip. Put them in the oven and roast them. It's delicious." Ha ha ha. We tried it and do you want to know what it was like? A carrot, a turnip, and a parsnip that had been roasted. Not too thrilling. I hope his cookbook has some recipes in it that are more exciting and tastier than that![122] Anyway, he was really nice and it was so amazing to chat with him. I feel like a scrofulous peasant that's been touched by royalty! It'll be a story to put in a meeeeemoir of my own.[123]

[121] [Editor's note:] Again from a letter not long after the reported conversation (Feb 28th, 1983, to Lindsey Maxwell): "Through John [Lennon] and Yoko [Ono] I changed my diet and that of Merce Cunningham to the macrobiotic diet" (Cage 2016: 528). This makes the artist a kind of culinary grandchild to John and Yoko.

[122] [Editor's note:] Cage says this, of his projected cookbook: "instead of just being about cooking, it will be about everything that interests me. But I will arrange the use of chance operations so that cooking comes up more than anything else" (Montague 1985: 206). (How can one do anything other than love that second sentence.) The book was never written but on the website of the John Cage Trust there is a page with Cage's notes on macrobiotic cooking and a selection of recipes. Amazingly, one can find on the page, under the heading "Root Vegetables," the following: "Carrots, Turnips, Jerusalem Artichokes, etc. Place in a Rohmertopf (clay baking dish) in a hot oven for an hour or more with a little, very little, sesame oil. They may be covered with leeks and topped with a mixture such as one of those suggested for roast chicken" (http://johncage.org/blog/cagerecipes.html, quoted here with the permission of the John Cage Trust). It is possible that Cage did not recommend to Evnine the use of sesame oil, or that he did, but that the artist ignored the advice.

[123] [Editor's note:] Though the present work is hardly a memoir of Evnine, it is, perhaps, a meme-oir, as Cage would have called it, so the artist's prediction is, literally in a manner of speaking, here being fulfilled.

M.43 More Lesbians

M.51 More Lesbians Composed: March 12th. Posted: March 18th. Orientation: Reverse. Font: Arial. TB1: "There already *are* lesbians in it.", black. TB2: "Good. Consider adding more lesbians!", black. TB3: "Advice for the aspiring novelist", white.

This meme seems to have been inspired by an image one can find on the internet:

Figure 10 Monotelic branching flowchart

(I have found instances of it as early as 2013 but have not been able to ascertain its first appearance or its creator.) We might call the form that provides the humor here the *monotelic branching flowchart* – i.e. a flowchart that provides alternative paths only to end up with the same outcome (*telos*) for all paths, thus making the original division retrospectively unnecessary.

There are two alternates to the published version of this meme. I reproduce them both because they provide insight into the artist's creative process and indicate just how much care he took to get the wording exactly right.

Figure 11 First alternate version - M.43a

Figure 12 Second alternate version - M.43b

We do not have direct evidence of the order in which the three attempts were made but if we assume, supposing there exists no evidence to the contrary (and see the commentary on *find this out; but* (M.77) for just how important such qualifications are), that each attempt was an improvement over the previous version in the eyes of the artist, and if we assume that his eyes would judge improvement in a way similar to mine (or indeed, anyone's), then I conjecture that the order of composition was M.43a, M.43b, and M.43. Certainly, M.43 must have been adjudged by Evnine as the best, since it was the one he eventually posted. (I discount the possibility that he made alternate versions after having posted M.43 though that is not strictly impossible.)

Each meme in the artist's output can be thought of as the solution to a problem – how to realize some idea in the highly restricted parameters the image provides. In this case, the problem is how to render the flowchart in the source material, with its two branches, in a way that preserves as much of its humor as possible. Because of the multiple versions, we can see the artist trying out different solutions. In all versions, the artist has, wisely, concentrated on the first, and funnier, branch of the flowchart (though we shall see that the final version also gives a nod to the second branch). In both M.43a and M.43b, the fact that the advice pertains to writing fiction (here a novel rather than the more generic "story" of the original source) is incorporated into Robin's text. In M.43a, the clunkiest of the three versions, Robin devotes a whole sentence to saying that he is writing a novel. This has the encounter, effectively, beginning *ab novo*. No previous context need be inferred. The whole is self-contained. The result is that the meme is stodgy and undynamic, something improved upon by M.43b, where the information about writing a novel is slipped into an adverbial expression and the opening "Yes" implies that Batman has asked whether Robin has lesbians in his novel. Not only is this more dynamic, it also successfully incorporates something of the format of the flowchart, based, as it is, around an original question to that effect. In both the alternate versions, Batman has the same text. The force of the imperative matches the slap, while both slap and imperative are in tension with the approval suggested by "Good." This, again, captures part of the humor of the flowchart, in which the approved answer - "yes" - still gets the response that one hasn't done enough. (The simple advice "add more lesbians to your story" is like the sign in an actual library that reads "Quieter please!")[124]

The final version, M.43, represents a notable improvement over the other two in several respects. First, the artist has off-loaded the background information that the whole exchange concerns the writing of a novel into text at the bottom of the meme. This is the first meme to use text outside of the speech bubbles in this way, as a sort of caption or title that explains the *mise-en-scène* of the meme. (Later such uses include *Too Easy, Robin!* (M.75), *The Origins of Neoplatonist Metaphysics* (M.96), and *Synthesis* (M.98).) Two previous memes (*Dialetheism* (M.20) and *The Incredulous Stare* (M.38)) use extra text outside of speech bubbles but rather as labels for specific elements of the meme than as captions for the meme as a whole. (Perhaps

---

[124] I relegate to this footnote the observation that the font switches from Comic Sans, in M.43a, to Arial, in M.43b and M.43. As far as I can tell, the change makes little difference to the overall feel of the meme.

one could argue that the extra text in *Dialetheism* is somewhere between a label and a caption.) This frees up space in Robin's text box but instead of trying to add more words to it, the artist has left the space, giving a lightness to the whole and allowing the text to be larger. Like M.43b, we start *in medias res*, with Robin replying to Batman, but now not to the question "Are there lesbians in your novel?" but to evidently unsolicited advice (something like "Make sure to have lesbians in your novel"). This is very clever of Evnine. Batman would not give such advice if he thought there were, or might be, lesbians in Robin's novel. Hence, if we think of him as starting with the flowchart's question in his mind, his implied admonition itself suggests the content of the flowchart's second branch. Robin's response and Batman's follow up to that, both present in the meme, then deliver the content of the first branch. Batman's text is also improved upon, relative to M.43a and M.43b. Instead of now saying simply "Good. Add more lesbians!", he echoes more closely the language of the original (in surely one of its finer details) by using the word "consider," which like "good" is in tension with the imperatival form and the slap. The effect is to make the whole encounter funnier and more absurd, but also lighter and more natural. The artist's instincts were good and the improvements charted through the three versions (assuming we have ordered them correctly) shows his sensitivity and the soundness of his judgment.

Batman's and Robin's (or is it the artist's?) keen embrace of lesbians, in this meme, is also manifest in *Not What You're Thinking* (M.93).

M.45 I don't care!

M.45 I don't care! Composed: March 3rd. Posted: March 19th. Orientation: Reverse. Font: Arial. TB1: "You gave me the wrong code for the bathroom!", black. TB2: "I don't care!", black.

This meme was not posted directly on Facebook like the preceding ones. I include it as part of the Batman Meme Project, nonetheless, since it appears in the first of the artist's two movies, *Evnine's Batman Memes: The Movie*, which he himself described on more than one occasion as the finale of the Batman Meme Project. One can infer that the meme was important to the artist from its prominence in the movie. Other than the memes appearing with the movie's title and at its end, it is the only meme in the movie that did not appear on Facebook. It appears, in its entirety and without any distracting effects, at a central and dramatic point in the musical accompaniment and remains visible for nearly three seconds, longer than any other meme. Notwithstanding this heavy emotional freighting, the meme's particular meaning is elusive. A possible slender clue, however, is supplied by an alternate, never-published version of the meme. Composed on the same day as M.45, M.45a has the same text for Robin but a different response from Batman.[125]

[125] The positioning of the text inside Robin's speech bubble is very slightly different in the two versions. In M.45, the "f" of "for" just crosses the line around the speech bubble; in M.45a, it sits well inside that line. I cannot tell whether this means the artist deliberately repositioned Robin's text between the first and second attempt (we have no way of knowing in which order they were composed, though if the repositioning were deliberate, that would suggest M.45 was made first, since why would Evnine have moved the text from its perfect location in M.45a when he tried out a new text for Batman?) or whether

Figure 13 Alternate version - M.45a

The clue is that Batman's response in the alternate version is a well-recognized trope associated with talk therapy (often, it must be said, by way of ridiculing such therapy and its practitioners). M.45a, therefore, casts the Dynamic Duo as the Psychodynamic Dyad, that strange, ephemeral unity that allegedly emerges from the patient and therapist in psychoanalysis. (See the commentary on *Not a Strict Freudian* (M.78) for a bit more on the analytic Dyad.) Obviously, bathroom-related matters feature prominently in psychoanalysis (another trope used to ridicule psychoanalysis is its purported tracing of all of a patient's problems to their toilet training), so once we see Batman using the language of the analyst, it is hardly surprising to see Robin talking about some kind of experience concerning the bathroom. But what, exactly, would the meaning of Robin's accusation be and what its psychoanalytic significance?

Alessandra Lemma has a fascinating discussion of the uses a patient in psychoanalysis can make of the consulting room toilet. She summarizes her findings thus:

> I have found two qualitatively different uses of the toilet in the context of the analytic relationship. First is the perverse use of the toilet to enact sexualized, hostile, intrusive dynamics in relation to the analyst. Here the patient alternates between being the voyeur, fantasizing the analyst in the toilet, and being the one in the toilet who is looked at by the analyst.
>
> The second use involves anxieties about fantasized damage done to the object[126] should the patient expose parts of the self felt to be messy and

---

it is an inconsistency in how the meme generator produced the final images from the user input. (The meme generator is definitely inconsistent in how it renders colors.)

[126] [Editor's note:] A technical term here referring to the analyst.

unacceptable. Here the patient may at first be altogether unable to use the analyst's toilet, displaying phobic avoidance of it lest a messy, dirty part of the self contaminate the longed-for, good, "clean" relationship with the analyst... Their eventual use of the toilet may be a first step toward giving expression to warded-off dangerous feelings before they can be more safely integrated into the analytic relationship. (2014: 37)

Lemma's discussion, however, is specifically about the use of a "consulting room" toilet, that is, a toilet potentially, and (at least more or less) exclusively, used by an analyst and their patients. (In fact, she notes that for many patients, it is "felt to be quite specifically, and very personally, the 'analyst's toilet'" (36); interestingly, she herself refers to it as "the analyst's toilet" in the sub-title of, and throughout, her paper.) In the case of M.45 and M.45a, Robin talks of a "code" for the bathroom and this suggests a rather different scenario that may raise somewhat different issues – not a consulting room toilet, which would not typically require a code for access, but a toilet in an office building in which an analyst has an office. In these cases, the building's management often makes members of the general public go through the professionals who rent office space there. So an analyst may display a code to enter the bathroom or hang out a key in the waiting room. This renders moot (or less intense) the ways Lemma describes that a patient may 'use' a consulting room toilet. If the patient and analyst were of different genders, they would not even use the same common bathroom, typically. On the other hand, the scenario of the public bathroom raises a different set of issues. If such a bathroom allows multiple simultaneous uses, the possibility arises (depending on the genders of the analyst and patient and the gender-configuration of the public bathroom) of the analyst's and patient's meeting in the bathroom or even using it at the same time. Finally, coming to M.45 and M.45a (if we lean heavily on the exiguous clue provided by the latter), the scenario of the public bathroom raises the issue of the analyst's controlling, and possibly impeding, the patient's corporeal 'self-expression' in the toilet.[127] Here, one might wonder about countertransference and the 'use' made by the analyst of the 'patient's' toilet! By providing the wrong code, or none at all, or failing to provide a key, the analyst is in a position to deny a certain level of physical ease and comfort to the patient. Of course, innocent mistakes can happen. But if such a situation were to be unrectified, having been brought to the attention of the analyst, one really would have to consider the countertransferential implications. If, in these two memes, we are to take Robin as alerting the figure of the analyst to the problem for the first time, one has to say that the prognosis is not good! In M.45a, Batman responds to Robin's distress at having been impeded in his access to the bathroom with the clichéd therapist's formula, its very quality as a cliché indicating a lack of real concern. In M.45 itself, that lack of concern is made brutally explicit.

[127] Interestingly, one other meme in which Batman may possibly be seen as occupying the role of analyst and Robin that of patient, *Free Association* (M.14), also concerns difficulties in Robin's, the patient's, self-expression. Batman, in *Free Association*, is portrayed as encouraging it, in theory, but in such harsh and unempathetic terms as, in effect, also to be impeding it. And see *Bibliophagia* (M.88) and the commentary thereon for more on the relation between language production and excretion.

Though it seems unlikely an analyst would ever respond as Batman does in M.45, is there any reason to think, if we follow the idea of reading M.45 through the therapeutic lens suggested by M.45a, that its themes are rooted in the realities of the artist's life? It is hard to say. Evnine, we know, saw his analyst in two locations. In the first, the office was in a small suite, originally a two-bedroom apartment, shared with another analyst. The suite did have a "consulting room toilet," a toilet that would be used by both the analysts and their patients. The waiting room was what had been the living room, the two offices the bedrooms, and the small toilet was wedged between the two offices. (A real 'family romance'!) Lemma's thoughts on the uses made by the patient of the analyst's toilet would certainly have had purchase in this situation – if the patient could only have made it that far! Just getting to this toilet would require an immense intrusion into the space of the analyst(s) (and fellow patients). One would risk encountering the analyst or other patients (or both) in a space that was too small for two, let alone three, people to share who might have reasons to avoid casual physical contact. There would be no way of determining to what degree the smells and noises attendant on bathroom use might permeate the actual consulting rooms. Thus, although the patient was, in theory, free to use the toilet, in practice, a not insignificant price would have had to be paid in anxiety, potential embarrassment, and the willingness to set aside consideration of other patients. In such a situation, the "phobic avoidance" that Lemma talks about might have been amplified by this different set of considerations around location.

The second office in which the artist saw his analyst was in a public building and so there was no "consulting room toilet." As in the meme, a code was required to gain access to the toilet. Presumably, this was somehow supplied by the analyst and, if we are reading the meme correctly, perhaps not always the right one. If such a code seems an odd thing for an analyst to make a mistake about, I might offer a case I have knowledge of in which an analyst gave the wrong address to a new patient that made it impossible to find their office. And they had business cards printed with the wrong address! In the case of the artist's analyst's second office, a search of city records reveals that around the time M.45 and M.45a were composed, there was a permit active (PL-15-09-3973) for alterations to the bathrooms in the building, suggesting that there may indeed have been some disruption to access to the bathroom and/or the installation of a new system of access. Might PL-15-09-3973 be the right code to allow us to unlock this otherwise quite mysterious meme and enter its fraught precincts?

AND ITS PARERGA!

Evnine produced a number of memes during the period of the Batman Meme Project which he elected, for whatever reasons, not to publish on Facebook as part of it. (Many are, quite frankly, not very good.) He also continued to produce new memes after the official end of the project, intensively until about June 2016 and thereafter sporadically for several years. Only a few of these later memes, mostly those that are animated GIFs, were ever posted on Facebook. All of these contemporaneous but unposted and subsequent memes constitute the parerga of the Batman Meme Project.

M.46 Talk to the Hand

M.46 Talk to the Hand Composed: February 22nd. Orientation: Reverse. Font: Impact, with font shadow. TB1: "My therapist says you're…", white, with black borders. TB2: "Talk to the hand!", white, with black borders.

This meme, never published by the artist, is instantly recognizable in style as belonging with M.5-M.8 (all created around February 20th-22nd) – the use of Impact with font shadow, white letters with black borders, but no longer all in capitals, as M.1-M.4 were. Perhaps it remained unpublished owing to its similarity to another published meme (not included in this volume) in which Robin says "According to my therapist, I'm…" and Batman replies "T.M.I.!". Unlike the version published on Facebook, where Robin is about to say something that his therapist says about him, here in *Talk to the Hand* he is about to report something his therapist thinks about Batman. This is clearly more threatening to Batman than the merely boring prospect of hearing about the therapist's views on Robin. (Though can the two really be distinguished? Were Robin's thoughts about the therapist's thoughts about Robin to the effect that Robin was a masochist, would that not be tantamount to Robin's thoughts about the therapist's thoughts about Robin's thoughts about Batman being to the effect that Batman was a sadist?)

The use of the colloquial expression "Talk to the hand!" (usually said by someone holding up their hand in front of them, as in a halting gesture, and not by someone slapping) in Batman's rejoinder makes this, in many ways, a superior meme to the published version (which accounts for my omitting the published version from this volume). For the colloquialism renders the slap in the meme a demonstrative slap, but in a figurative way. This is something that none of the other demonstrative slaps achieve; they are always demonstrative in a literal register.

NOTICE OF WITHDRAWAL

A decision has been made to withdraw the meme that was to have been M.48. (Consequently, the meme which follows *Are you even listening?* (M.47) is, through an error in the reckoning, numbered M.49.)

Why has it been decided that the meme should be withdrawn? Is it offensive? Is it libelous? Not at all. It is a never-published take on the nature of the Trinity, in the manner of *Filioque* (M.7). In the usual reverse orientation, in large, black Arial font, Robin says "Three persons." and Batman replies "But one hypostasis!". It was composed on March 3rd.

Image 1 The withdrawn meme. One can appreciate the artist's decision to hold back from publishing the meme on Facebook. How much Trinitarian humor could the Batman Meme Project sustain? And Filioque *(M.7) is far superior to this relatively pedestrian bit of erudite-theology-as-Batman-meme. What is more remarkable is that the artist took the trouble to compose it in the first place.* Filioque *was published on February 22nd while this meme was not composed until March 5th. Why did Evnine revisit the Trinitarian theme with nothing better to offer?*

A bit weak, but inoffensive. Why, then, has it been withdrawn? The answer lies in its content: "Three persons. But one hypostasis!". Perhaps not the makings of a scintillating meme, but it contains a very important point with respect to the meme project as a whole. The distinction has already been made between the artist, who composed the memes, and the editor, who has selected them, written the commentaries, and attempted, on behalf of the reader, to disentangle the thicket of the artist's mind. This, even though no attempt has been made to hide the fact that it is Simon Evnine who is both artist and editor. In creating this notional distinction, however, two consequences were set in motion. First, some things that needed to be said became unsayable. For they could not be said by the artist. He is the producer of a corpus of work that is the subject-matter of this volume. He has occasionally spoken about the works, when they were posted on Facebook (those that were); but these paratexts were few and far between. Almost no help was given, no interpretation offered. The art was to be sufficient; those who had ears might hear what it had to say. He may as well be dead – in any case, he has no business speaking up here about his work. But they also could not be said by the editor because the editor is, precisely, not responsible for the memes themselves and approaches them like any other reader, albeit with access to unspecified sources of information the average reader (though not every reader) will lack. But where memes and commentary bleed into each other, where themes introduced in a meme are developed in a commentary, neither artist nor editor is fitted to speak. The second consequence set in motion by the notional split between artist and editor is that, inevitably, there was drawn into the whole business a third person, neither artist nor editor: he who envisaged the whole of the project, who composed the memes knowing that they would be edited and presented by... himself. The two, the artist and editor, once distinguished from each other, have necessarily, between them, engendered the third, the authorial voice of the whole project, emerging, by double procession, equally from the artist and editor (as the Holy Ghost proceeds from both the Father and the Son). The bifurcated artist and editor make the project unstable without the synthesizing presence of the *auteur* (reports of whose death have been greatly exaggerated). (See *Synthesis* (M.98) for the language of synthesis.) It belongs to *him* to say the things that are unsayable by either the artist or the editor. Three persons (artist, editor, *auteur*). But one hypostasis (Simon Evnine)!

But where, in this whole project, was the *auteur* to say these things? Not in the memes themselves and not in the commentaries. A special preface was considered, prior to the editor's preface, but the idea was rejected. Such a thing would appear at the very beginning of the work, cutting the legs out from under the editor before he had even found his own voice. No, a special interstitial space had to be created for the *auteur* to speak, a place that was both *inside* and *outside* his own creation; so it was he, or as I may as well now say, it was I, who decided to withdraw this meme that speaks to the issue of three-in-one-ness and put in its place, in the interstices opened up by its withdrawal, a space in which I can discuss the three-in-one-ness of the Batman meme project, understood in its widest sense, and say what would otherwise remain unsayable.

This space will remain interstitial. Although there are multiple cross-references throughout this whole work, and although in this Notice of Withdrawal, I shall refer to other parts of the book, there are no references *into* it even though, at several points, it would be a courtesy to the reader to direct her here. Nor will any of what is said here be cited in the indices to the work, neither the index of names, the index of subjects, nor the index of memes. There is no road in except the one you have taken, of merely coming upon it.

Author's Preface

Like Michael Dummett and *The Interpretation of Frege's Philosophy*, this is a book I wrote "without meaning to." I had always gotten a kick out of the memes I had encountered that used the image of Batman Slapping Robin and it was a pleasurable discovery, in January 2016, that I could make them myself. I made two, posted them on Facebook, and thought to let the matter rest. But the meme had not done with me and, after a month, I resumed making them with an ever-increasing sense of obsession. Somewhere along the way, I began to think of them as constituting the Batman Meme Project, an indication of the growing seriousness with which I took them. So many had esoteric or personal meanings which I refused to make explicit, when I posted them on Facebook, that it came to seem like a good idea to gather them all together and explain them when I had finished. Such was the origin of this book. However, just as the memes had taken the reins from my hands, so the book too, once begun, drove me towards something much more ambitious than I had originally envisaged – nothing less, in fact, than "a new conception of philosophy, a new image of the thinker and the thought," to quote Deleuze on Nietzsche. Just quite what this new conception of philosophy is has eluded me (and eludes me still) but I fairly early stopped even trying to spell it out to myself and became content with just doing what I was doing. I (try to) remain confident that in there, rattling about, is something like a new conception of philosophy. Perhaps its whole point is that it is ineffable.

I conceive of the book under three principal metaphors: free association, the cabinet of curiosities, and the folly. The memes and the book were all composed during my psychoanalysis and they and the analysis became inextricably bound up with each other. The great pleasure I took in memes using this image was clearly indicative of underlying psychological processes and it didn't take long for them to surface as I talked about my project. Batman and Robin, in turn, gave me a lens through which to come to understand parts of myself. (And it emerged, interestingly, that they had deep roots in my life.) At the same time, in the analysis, I was struggling with free association. It is widely recognized, by both patients and analysts, that it is remarkably difficult to pull off, despite its seeming that there should be nothing easier. But what was difficult on the couch was, by contrast, easy at the keyboard and I allowed myself, in writing this book, pretty much to be led wherever my mind took me and to worry about what, if anything, it all meant later. Writing with this kind of freedom is one big way in which my work on this book is so different from my work in a more traditional philosophical vein. I am also happy for the book as a whole to present itself as a kind of symptom, apt for interpretation of whatever kind anyone wishes to employ. Everything anyone thinks about it and me is likely to have some truth to it.

One of several books that have profoundly influenced my own writing here is W.G. Sebald's *The Rings of Saturn*. Sebald, in that book, discusses Sir Thomas Browne. The work of both of these authors is often on the model of a cabinet of curiosities, a collection of eccentric and interesting things that form a unity through no other principle than that of having been collected by a given person. So too, in my book, I have put on display a lot of the detritus of my mind, detritus that I have accumulated through frustrated ambitions to scholarship and a broad but shallow learning. Perhaps most of this detritus is junk but some, I venture to hope, may have a little value.

The folly, to me, stands for a project that ostensibly has little point, that is the product of obsession, that is labored on in obscurity for a great length of time but which, if completed, is magnificent simply because of its excess and the fact that it exists despite the inauspicious signs governing its protracted birth. Whether this book does have little (or any) point, and whether it is in any way magnificent, must be left for others to determine. But surely enough, I have labored on it in obscurity for many years, in the grip of an obsession. As my principal avenue of philosophical research for the last six years, it has been next to impossible to give it the exposure which comes naturally to more conventional work in progress. I have consequently lacked almost all forms of feedback and external validation and that, as we know, is bound to drive one a little crazy. This preface marks the moment at which I hope to emerge from obscurity and present my little folly to the light of day.

Simon Evnine
Miami
December 2022

Acknowledgements

The editor has thanked many people who with great kindness have facilitated his editorial labors. But there remain others to thank who helped either with the creation of the memes themselves or with the overall project. They could not be thanked 'out in the open' and I turn to that pleasurable task here.

First and foremost I must thank my analyst Dr. Manuela Menendez. As the dedication of the book indicates, she has been the book's midwife. Indeed, we have not infrequently joked that she is its co-parent – though I always retain the maternal role for myself! Without her the book would not exist. And without her, I would be in much worse condition than I am.

I must also thank profoundly my partner Giovanna Pompele. She supported this project through good times and bad, keeping a faith in my ability to pull it off which I often lacked myself. She also pushed me to think much more deeply about what I was trying to do, especially with regard to what might be called the auto-theoretical aspirations of the book. And she read and improved many parts of the text.

Others have also played important sustaining roles. My former student Ted Locke has been a partner in thinking about auto-theory. My siblings Sharon Sokoler, Jeremy Evnine, and David Yevnin have provided much enthusiasm. Caterina Gualco and Marcello Frixione have given me unexpected opportunities to develop the artistic aspects of my project. Susanna Siegel has taken seriously the philosophical ambitions of my work and provided support and advice from the beginning.

Jenny and Oliver Black twice offered me their home in Chedington, Dorset, where I spent many happy weeks laboring in obscurity. With their home came their love and their amazing hospitality.

Ben Chiriboga and especially Miriam Richter offered legal advice that kept me going when I worried the book would be illegal (for copyright reasons)!

I have had institutional support from the Center for the Humanities at the University of Miami, where I worked on the book as a Fellow in AY 2017-8. Thanks to the Center, its then Director Mihoko Suzuki, and to the other Fellows: Juan Chattah, Tracy Devine Guzman, Catherine Judd, Brenna Munro, Dominique Reill, Stephanie Skenyon, and Lindsay Thomas.

I was the recipient of a Residential Fellowship from the Emily Harvey Foundation in Venice, where I was able to work on the book, in spectacular surroundings, in Fall 2018. Thanks to them, especially Zofia Chilicka, Henry Martin, Silvia Scattolin, and Berty Skuber, and also to the staff at the Caffè del Doge.

Marc Brudzinski helped with the French in *And this is not a slap* (M.61). Arman Agadjanian gave me the Armenian in *Maudlin Trash* (M.40). And Susanna Shavelson, as recounted in the commentary, helped with the Yiddish in *Vos iz ayer yidisher nomen, Batman?* (M.72). Getting help with the Yiddish and with the commentary on that meme was actually an adventure and I include here the text of a blog post I wrote about it. I place it in this section since, as you will see, it is in its way a heartfelt, though of necessity anonymous, acknowledgement.

*Image 2 Vos iz ayer yidisher nomen. Robin: What is your Jewish name, Batman? Batman: Call me *Mr* Batman, Boy Wonder. And my Jewish name is Simcha Bunim.*

The Savage Detectives and My Irascible Yiddish Expert

About one year ago, I had some contact with an onomast and linguist specializing in Jewish languages. (There are many Jewish languages: Hebrew ancient and modern, Aramaic, Yiddish, Ladino, Judeo-Arabic, Judeo-Persian, Italkian, and others.) I wrote about this in several previous posts about the Yiddish meme in my book *A Certain Gesture: Evnine's Batman Meme Project and Its Parerga!*. I have been wanting to write more about that experience for some time but have hesitated owing to ethical concerns that make it difficult, concerns that arise mostly (though not exclusively) from my irascible expert's having forbidden me from publishing any part of their emails.

Yes, you read that right. This expert ended by invoking the law, asserting their rights over the contents of their emails, and forbidding me from quoting anything from them!

The whole episode was on the way to becoming quite upsetting to me when my partner enabled a Gestalt switch that led me to find it both entertaining and enriching. "This is like something out of *The Savage Detectives*," she said, referring to the Roberto Bolaño novel I was reading at the time. And it was! A literary 'feud' over esoteric scholarship, one party becoming more and more enraged precisely as the other party tries to assuage them. The affair was both heated and absurd!

Here follows as much of the story as I can bring myself to relate. (And even this makes me uncomfortable - not, I should add, on my own account.)

Jews have a practice of giving double names to their children, one a religious, Jewish name, the other a secular one. Batman, in the meme, gives as his Jewish name "Simcha Bunim." But is "Simcha Bunim" a Jewish name? Or is "Simcha" a Jewish name and "Bunim" a secular one? This was to be a major theme in the commentary on the meme but I was finding it hard to get good scholarly information on the nuances of this double naming practice and its historical vicissitudes. One expert on Jewish names whom I consulted suggested I contact the irascible expert. Tracking them down was not easy but I eventually found a mailing address and wrote them a letter. Surprisingly (but as it turned out, wholly in keeping with their generosity), they replied quite quickly by email, letting me know they had received my letter and would respond at greater length shortly. And so they did, offering a lot of very helpful material concerning the distinction between Jewish and secular names, including a passage I wished to quote in the commentary.

The meme represents Yiddish in Roman letters and another major theme in the commentary is the different methods used for doing this. (The native orthography of Yiddish uses Hebrew letters.) Since my correspondent was also an acknowledged expert on this topic, I decided, in my pushy way, to send them, a couple of weeks later and with the excerpt from their email incorporated, a draft of the entire commentary on the meme. I sent the commentary out to quite a few people at that point to get feedback. It is long - seventeen or so pages - and a crazy mixture of scholarship (somewhere between mock and aspiring), a bibliography of the rabbinic works of my ancestors in the old country, and Batman-related nonsense.

Reader, the expert read it! They were, indeed, the only person I had any reason, at that time, to believe did read it. I was overjoyed and so very, very grateful. Nor was my gratitude in any way diminished by the expert's opinion that my piece was so riddled with error as to be barely rectifiable! Since I cannot quote their verdict, let me give you some of my response:

> First of all, thank you so much for taking the time to read my piece. And thank you also for your frank appraisal of its deficiencies, which I truly appreciate. I can't help but feel that your willingness to help me will put you in violation of the Yiddish proverb you cite: *af a nar makht men nit kin peyresh*.

Image 3 Specially made meme for the irascible expert

As you can infer from my reply, the expert had, again I say, with amazing generosity, offered to help me remove the errors from my wretched commentary. There was, however, a Faustian element to the offer: I would have to promise, in advance, not to include anything they thought unworthy of publication and to include only what they thought to be correct.

I explained, at some length, why I could not agree to this. There was a very specific problem, which I shall not go into, but the more general point I tried to convey was that although the scholarship in my commentary was important to me, and I wanted it to stand up in its own right, nonetheless my goals were not primarily scholarly but literary and philosophical. For example, in the commentary I explain how 'the artist of the memes' (i.e., me) arrived at the text that appears in the meme. That involved composing the text in English, putting it through Google Translate, and then getting help to put it into real Yiddish. I was able to recognize that what Google Translate had yielded was awful but it served my purposes to include it in the story of how the final text was reached. But for the irascible expert, it was offensive to give any space to the obviously deficient output offered by Google Translate.

Having audaciously made my case for why I wanted both the expert's help and the right to make my own decisions about the content of the commentary, I waited. I was hoping that the charm with which I explained all this, the playfulness of including a specially composed Batman meme incorporating the Yiddish proverb they threw my way, the slyness and subtlety of my whole project, would win them over. I was a little boy trying to coax a stern and severe parent into indulgence. It was at this point, if I remember correctly, that my partner staged her Bolaño-inspired intervention.

And a good thing she did! The reply I received, far from manifesting the fondness I was trying to elicit, was now not just impatient and dismissive but positively outraged and angry. The expert, apparently, had *not* previously read the commentary, but merely skimmed it. Now that they had read it properly (but how grateful I am that they did, after all, not just leave it skimmed but read it properly) they found what I had written highly offensive. They felt I was poking fun at Yiddish by implying that there was something intrinsically funny about seeing Batman and Robin talking Yiddish. There would be nothing funny, the expert said, about seeing them talking French or German. So why should it be a source of humor to see them speaking Yiddish, a real language into which Shakespeare, Whitman, Einstein and many, many others have been translated. Would I also find a source of fun the articles of Kant- and Hegel-scholarship written in Yiddish and published in Yiddish journals?

It seems I had well and truly brought us to a pass in which I was Robin, receiving a slap, and the expert Batman, delivering it. And who is to say I had not unconsciously aimed at just this? As I reflect on it now, I see how inappropriate my reply was to the expert's reaction to my shoddy scholarship. Could I realistically have thought they would be amused by the meme I made in their honor? What a misjudgment of tone on my part! So perhaps I was, after all, trying to provoke them.

I wish I could quote from what I can only describe (with but the tiniest exaggeration) as the irascible expert's torrent of indignation and rage. Alas, I cannot. But here is my reply, the last salvo in this strange *folie à deux*:

As always, thanks for your thoughtful engagement with my work. I am not sure why I have been so unsuccessful in communicating my ideas to you but let me say categorically that it is not my intention, in any way, to make fun of Yiddish or its speakers. Quite the opposite! All these days, I have been straining my eyes trying to make out the Yiddish, to the small extent I can, in digital archives of the Yiddish press finding out about some of the ancestors whose works I list at the end. I daily curse the fact that I do not know Yiddish properly and have, at various times in my life, seriously thought about learning it.

In the piece I have written, I say at one point "Starting in the second half of the 18th century, Jewish proponents of the Enlightenment began to stigmatize Yiddish as a merely debased form of German that kept its native speakers from accessing European high culture. **The image of Yiddish as a comic, backward, folksy language began to take shape, in contrast to dominant European languages, on the one hand, and Hebrew, on the other – an image that even many subsequent supporters of Yiddish have been happy to accept**." In an earlier version, I then referred, in a footnote, to a recent book on Yiddish (I won't say which one though I'm sure you'll recognize it from what I go on to say) that exemplifies "a supporter of Yiddish" being happy to accept this comic image of Yiddish… This made me angry for just the reason I have made you angry…

So, I heartily share your indignation on behalf of Yiddish and its speakers and I was using this commentary as a way of linking myself to both of them. (Hence the whole discussion of Lita [Jewish Lithuania] and my ancestors there.)

HOWEVER, none of this is to say that I haven't myself been guilty of the thing you and I both condemn. I will have to think hard about whether I have unintentionally mocked Yiddish in saying that there was something humorous about seeing Batman and Robin speaking that language. I will say that in another meme, I have them speaking Latin and find that humorous for similar reasons, though of course, the nature of the contrast between Batman and Latin IS different from that between Batman and Yiddish - and that's where it's possible I have fallen into error.

I seem to have made things worse with every email I have sent you and for that, I am deeply sorry. (I hope this email

> doesn't make things even worse.) I approached you with respect in my heart and I have admired your erudition and hoped to learn from it. But I will certainly excise the quotation from your email and altogether stop bothering you!

Even now, I sometimes find myself wishing I received some word from the irascible expert. It would hardly matter whether it was conciliatory or angry. If the former, I would have finally succeeded in replacing the slap with a loving caress; if the latter, my exciting and Bolaño-esque 'feud' would continue. I have loved this irascible expert and love them still. They paid attention to me and they offered to help me; they *saw* something in me. I hope I have seen something in them, too.

Epigraphs

I find it almost impossible to say which of the three persons chose the epigraphs for this volume. But there are three of them and, by coincidence (and it is, if not coincidental, at least entirely undeliberate), each seems like it could have been the choice of one of the three persons – artist, editor, *auteur*. The first epigraph, from Turgenev's novel *Rudin*, seems to be spoken in the voice of the artist, for whom some of the memes were clearly an exercise in self-humiliation. (I leave it to the editor to say which are, and which are not, best seen in this light.) The second, from the *Mishnah*, is an editor's choice, an editor either confident that he has done a good job and included in his edition "all" that is necessary or, more likely, overwhelmed by the abundance of what needs commenting on! Finally, the third epigraph, from Thomas Kyd's *The Spanish Tragedy*, speaks of the discordant intertwining of three "parts" or voices, the three voices being those, precisely, of artist, editor, and *auteur*. This is something that only I, the *auteur*, could be in a position to comment on.

I discovered quite recently that if quotations from copyrighted works are used as epigraphs, one needs permission while if the same words are quoted in the body of a work (assuming the quantity lies within the limits of fair use), one does not. What, I wondered when I learnt this, about the vast catalogue of whale-themed quotations at the beginning of *Moby-Dick*? Somewhat in the spirit of Melville, I have included, after and distinct from the epigraphs, a list of largely slap-themed quotations, not as epigraphs but before the main text, hoping thereby to open up a new kind of parergonal space that eludes the thorough treatment given to the paratext by Gérard Genette (1997).

M.76 Il n'y a pas de hors-texte

M.76 Il n'y a pas de hors-texte Composed: April 13th. Orientation: Reverse. Font: Comic Sans. TB1: "This meme will be explained in the accompanying book.", black. TB2: "Il n'y a pas de hors-texte!", black.

M.76 is the only meme to mention this book. Though I certainly knew, in composing it, that I was destabilizing the distinction between the memes and the commentary on them – indeed, that was its point – I had not anticipated how it would, with the strict distinction between artist and editor I gradually developed, become almost Escher-like in its impossibility. (I was still uncertain about whether to write the commentary in the voice of the meme-maker or, as I eventually decided, in a different voice.) It is, of course, out of the question that the editor should be in a position to comment on its impossible quality so I provide its commentary here, myself.

In response to Robin's shattering of the fourth wall, Batman quotes a well-known sentence from Derrida (2016). Its translation into English is contested and Derrida's translator, Gayatri Spivak, provides two versions: "There is nothing outside the text" and "there is no outside-text." The second, placed in square brackets along with the French, is evidently intended to convey the original more literally and less idiomatically. Setting aside entirely the question of how to interpret Derrida, the sentence's occurrence in his work highlights two ways in which it is of interest to us, as we seek to understand the meme.

The claim appears in Derrida's discussion of Rousseau's thoughts on writing and language. Rousseau sees writing as something added to the proper field of language, which is speech. For cases in which person-to-person speech, full of emotion in inflection and sound, is not enough, people develop an adjunct technology which, as he says, substitutes intellect for emotion. Derrida describes how a supplement both adds to the original but also stands in for some deficiency in the original. The pure presence, the fulness of being, that communication via speech aspires to is already failing. It is as if the mediation of writing is always already there, making up for the ways in which the spoken word inevitably falls short. To adapt Sartre's striking phrase, we might say that writing "lies coiled in the heart of being – like a worm" (1956). "*Il n'y a pas de hors-texte*" (the sentence, not the meme) is supposed, in some way, to show that the appeal to the 'proper' order of things in which speech is primary and writing nothing but an added *techne*, is illusory and that in fact writing, text, is already presupposed by speech. There is no field in which pure presence rules. There is no communication that escapes the mediation of writing, nothing outside the text.

"Supplement," of course, is just another word for parergon.[128] The parergon is central to my book – although it assumed this centrality only gradually. At first, it appeared in the book's title

---

[128] Max Deutscher (2014) notes that one definition of "*hors-texte*," introduced by Derrida in connection with the supplement, as given by *Le Petit Robert*, is "engraving inserted late in assembling a book, not included

simply as a way of indicating that I would be writing about more than the Batman Meme Project in its strict sense. I had declared the project finished but then continued to produce more memes. They too would have a place in the book. This function is preserved in the division of the book into two parts: The Batman Meme Project and Its Parerga! But the book has the form of an art catalogue. All its writing, outside the relatively few words that appear in the memes, is parergonal to the memes themselves. They are the editor's comments on what is ostensibly the main *raison d'être* of the book – the memes. The form of the book, therefore, and its association with the distinct voices of the creator of the memes and the editor of the catalogue, attempts to reinforce, to use Derrida's terminology, the supplementarity of writing. And yet, of course, the supplemental writing really *is* the book.[129] The supplement displaces what is supposed to be the main content of the book.

As if all this were not enough, I soon began to blog about my book-in-progress and found myself thinking of these blog posts, sometimes, as parts of the book. And the same for occasional talks I gave about the work, talks for which I sometimes even created new Batman memes! The very boundaries of the book became vague and indeterminate. As you will see in perusing this book, I have found ways of incorporating some of these blog posts and excerpts from presentations into the text. Several appear in this Notice of Withdrawal but others, mostly attributed to the artist of the memes, have been quoted in the editorial commentaries (a practice which has required me slightly to alter the posts when they mention the book-in-progress). It is certainly hard for me always to distinguish ergon from parergon, text from paratext. And that difficulty itself become an unspoken (other than here) central theme of the work.

The second respect in which Derrida's "*il n'y a pas de hors-texte*" is of interest to us is not its generic connection to supplementarity and the parergon but its particular attention to the relations between writing and speech. Since the exploration of these relations is carried out within the memes themselves, however, this is a topic the editor has been able to identify and write about on a number of occasions in his commentaries. I shall consequently not belabor the point here. The interested reader can consult the commentaries on *Show Some Respect, Robin!* (M.13), *Cicero**!* (M.56), *Vos iz ayer yidisher nomen, Batman?* (M.72), and various other memes.

Auto-Theory

At a certain point in my work, I began to think of it as a kind of auto-theory. The appropriation of this term, developed in a feminist context, is somewhat problematic. Here are some blog

---

in the pagination." This seems a paradigm example of a parergon though, frustratingly, it is not discussed in Genette's (1997) encyclopedic treatment of the paratext.

[129] The editor, from his constrained perspective, seems to be gesturing at this idea in his commentary on *Transformative Experience (alternate version)* (M.92). He writes: "If the artist could only have found a way to write *around* the memes, and not just *in* them, he could have transformed his way of doing philosophy even more."

posts I wrote trying to come to terms with whether, and to what extent, it is legitimate for me to use this expression to describe my work.

On auto-theory: Can it be done by the privileged?

For some years now, I have thought of my writing, in and around my book project, *A Certain Gesture: Evnine's Batman Meme Project and Its Parerga!*, as auto-theory. I even occasionally use the term in my parergonal writings, some of which will be quoted in the book.

I would like to tell you something about auto-theory at this point, but I am absolutely unqualified to do so. First, I simply don't know enough of it, or about it. I can speak in vague generalities - the creative mingling of self-writing and theory/philosophy, with both formal and thematic implications - and I can point to some prominent examples - Maggie Nelson's *The Argonauts*, Sara Ahmed's *Living a Feminist Life*, Audre Lorde's *The Cancer Journals*. But for anything better, you will have to consult the experts. (I have found these recent writings by Lauren Fournier (2021) and Arianne Zwartjes (2019) helpful, as also this much earlier piece by Jane Tompkins (1987).)

But a more profound reason why I am unqualified to speak about auto-theory is that it is a practice that springs, initially from feminist theory, and now from other identity-based approaches: queer theory, critical race theory, disability studies, trans studies, and others. It has, in my understanding, been developed as a tool of the oppressed, who have felt their oppression extended through the traditional idioms and norms of academic discourse, which privileges mind over body, abstraction over concretion, the general over the particular, the impersonal over the personal. Auto-theory's formal novelties, its genre-b(l)ending intertwinings of the personal and the theoretical, are thus allied to a political project of liberation. Although this political project is, or should be, everyone's, it belongs to different people in different ways. Given my position of privilege along so many dimensions, it does not belong to me, I feel, to say what auto-theory is.

I worry, too, that it does not belong to me to write it.

Arianne Zwartjes says that auto-theory's

> imaginative act is putting body on the same plane as intellect. What the term *autotheory* describes are ways of mixing "high theory" with our panting, sweating physicality, the embodied experience.

Panting and sweating. Sara Ahmed calls a "sweaty concept" "one that comes out of a description of a body that is not at home in the world" (2017: 13). The body of a cis straight able-bodied white male tenured professor is not, typically, one that would be imagined as "not at home in the world."

Image 4 When I was a child, my father often quoted the saying: "Horses sweat; men perspire; ladies feel the heat." In auto-theory, the 'ladies' are definitely sweating.

Consider the bravura opening of Maggie Nelson's *The Argonauts* which within ten lines gets to a brief, raw, somewhat abject description of a sexual encounter ("my face smashed against the cement floor of your dank and charming bachelor pad... a stack of cocks in a shadowy unused shower stall" (2016: 3). Three years ago, I promised my readers they would never have to endure such writing from me. What is edgy and cool in Nelson's work could only be sad and sordid (both in the wrong way) coming from one situated as I am.

Or take this example from Sara Ahmed. Talking of her first feminist essay, written at university, she adds this footnote:

> Though one funny detail: I spelled *patriarchy* wrong throughout! *Patriarchy* became *patriachy*. Maybe that was a willful desire not to get patriarchy right. (2017: 271)

This anecdote is simultaneously charming and weighty. How can the anecdote pictured in this meme, from my own early educational days, compare?

Image 5 Batman represents the philosopher Anthony Savile, my tutor for one term in AY 81-2 at Bedford College London.

It has some charm but none of the weight of Ahmed's story, which comes from someone who has fought on the front-lines against patriarchy. Ahmed writes:

> It should not be possible to do feminist theory without being a feminist, which requires an active and ongoing commitment to live one's life in a feminist way. (2017: 14)

Perhaps her point applies more generally: it should not be possible to do auto-theory without being committed to a life of emancipatory political work, work deriving from one's body, from the very fabric of who one is.

Am I, then, just an interloper, wearing the vestments of auto-theory like an organ-grinder's monkey, preening itself in an ill-fitting red military-style jacket and turquoise fez?

On auto-theory: Bodies that are (not) at home

In my first post on auto-theory in my book-in-progress, *A Certain Gesture: Evnine's Batman Meme Project and Its Parerga!*, I raised the question of whether auto-theory, arising as it does out of emancipatory political struggles, is something a multiply-privileged person like me can properly engage in. Auto-theory is the insurrectionary intrusion of the personal into the theoretical. One way it works, according to some feminist theorists, is by orienting theory to the lived bodily reality of the author. I quoted Sara Ahmed, who describes a "sweaty concept" as "one that comes out of a description of a body that is not at home in the world" (2017: 13). I remarked that the body of a cis straight able-bodied white male tenured professor is not one that is generally imagined as "not at home in the world."

But the reality is that I do not experience my body as being at home in the world at all. There are many reasons why my body does not feel at home in the world. If I were braver, and if the anticipated result were less pitiful, I would describe a number of them. As it is, I will mention just one: how I hate the sound of my own voice. I cannot listen to recordings of it and when, as occasionally happens, I catch an echo from the inside of what it sounds like from the outside, I cringe. (I believe this is quite a common experience.)

To speak in more general terms, Plato's claim that the body is like a prison to the soul has always resonated strongly with me. I feel my body to be an alien thing, beset by inconvenient (this is hardly the right word) needs and desires.

At this point, though, my thoughts about 'at homeness' in the world become confused. Feminist scholars such as Genevieve Lloyd and Andrea Nye (among others) have persuasively argued that such images of alienation from the body, along with the attendant prioritizing of mind over body, reason over emotion, action over passion, etc. (the very priorities auto-theory is aimed at overturning) are staples of specifically male-dominated philosophy. If being at home in the world means embracing the values of white men that are promulgated to the benefit of white men, then my very not feeling at home in the world (manifested in such things as hating the sound of my own voice) is part of what makes me at home in the world!

In one of the commentaries in the book, on a meme entitled *Couples Therapy*, I quote a passage from Andrea Nye's book *Words of Power: A Feminist Reading of the History of Logic* (1990). As a graduate student, I used to be fond of quoting this passage as an object of ridicule.

> Desperate, lonely, cut off from the human community which in many cases has ceased to exist, under the sentence of violent death, wracked by desires for intimacy that they do not know how to fulfill, at the same time tormented by the presence of women, men turn to logic. (175)

Now, older, a little wiser, and more humble, I look at myself and see only its truth. (And of course, I contemn the younger man who laughed. But could my fascination have indicated, even then, some shameful self-knowledge?)

The man described in Nye's passage is both at home and not at home in the world. Can he write auto-theory? What are the terms under which he can join, should he want to, the emancipatory struggle with which auto-theory is linked? As "at home" in the world in the sense of finding refuge in the scared hidey-hole that has been the headquarters of patriarchy, he surely has nothing to say. As "not at home" in the sense of being "desperate, lonely, wracked...," he should surely keep his mouth shut if he doesn't want to fall into the "we cis white men have it so hard - if only you knew - in fact, we probably have it harder than trans people, people of color, women mode." Is nothing the only thing he can say?

On auto-theory: Form as dress-up

A recent call for papers by a journal planning a special issue on auto-theory asked contributors to remove any identifying information and prepare their submissions for anonymous review! Not quite a paradox, since the submissions were not intended to *be* auto-theory, but nearly one, since one might expect even academic journal articles, if they are about auto-theory, to be somewhat personal.

I suppose it is sometimes appropriate to think of auto-theory as coming from the 'auto' side of things and sometimes from the 'theory' side. (Though no doubt there are cases that cannot be happily classified in either way.) The infusion of theoretical writing into memoir or autobiography need not, though it might, leave the surface form of the writing undisturbed. For example, *The Argonauts*, by Maggie Nelson, reads as, indeed is, a memoir, but one that happens to contain a lot of theoretical writing. The inclusion of the theory does not make it anomalous as a memoir. It is there as a manifestation of its author's own understanding of the events she writes about. But I suspect that auto-theory is more frequently thought of as the infusion of personal writing into theoretical work or theoretical contexts. In this case, disruption to the surface form is likely to be more problematic, as my opening anecdote illustrates.

In another example of auto-theory, Eve Sedgwick writes, quoting herself speaking to her therapist:

> "What you completely do not seem to catch on to about these two parts of the kid [my gloss: the childish and the precocious] is that they are not separate. They are constantly whirlpooling around in each other—and the basic rule is this: that each one has the power to poison the other one. So what being a kid was like for me was, at the same time, like being an adult in bad drag as a child, and being a child in bad drag as an adult." (2000: 30)

How perfectly this captures the spirit of my own book-in-progress, *A Certain Gesture: Evnine's Batman Meme Project and Its Parerga!*! I have already reproduced on this blog the following meme and commentary. (The commentary takes the form of embedding the meme as the top panel in another meme format known as *Increasingly Verbose* in which an image and text are iterated, with the image becoming progressively more abstract and the text becoming progressively more verbose.) I put it here again, now letting it resonate with Sedgwick's beautiful description of the mutual impersonation of her adult and child personae.

> A child is being slapped by Batman. Robin is that child. What, if anything, do I add to my knowledge when I come to know that I am Robin? Do I know who I am? Who Robin is? Do I want this?

> The proposition BATMAN IS SLAPPING ROBIN is being entertained by Batman in a manner in which only he can entertain it. It is a first-personal manner. I am Batman. I am slapping Robin. I need this. With stunning regularity and despite my best intentions, I am Robin.

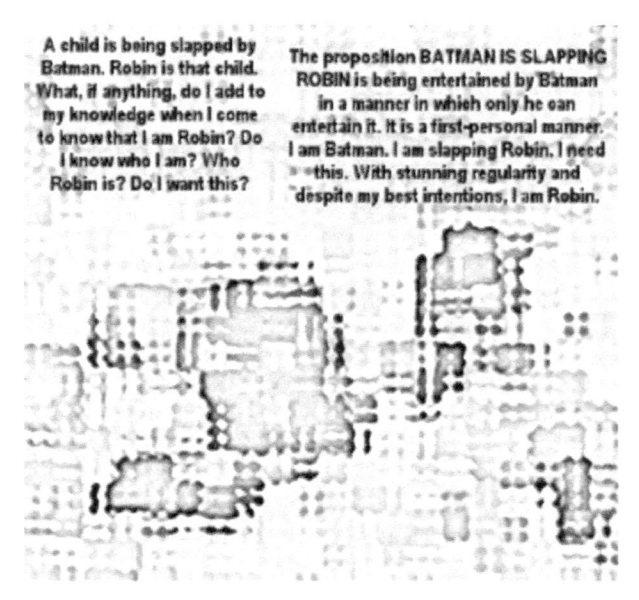

Image 6 The Slap Itself *plus two further panels that form the commentary on it, all in the form of an Increasingly Verbose meme in which an image become progressively more abstract while the words become increasingly verbose. Panel 2 – Robin: A child is being beaten. Beaten by Batman. Robin is that child. I like this. Batman: Despite his best intentions, and with stunning regularity, Batman finds himself caught up in the repetition of what happened to Robin. But what was it, exactly, that did happen to Robin? I don't want this. Panel 3 – Robin: A child is being slapped by Batman. Robin is that child. What, if anything, do I add to my knowledge when I come to know that I am Robin? Do I know who I am? Who Robin is? Do I want this? Batman: The proposition BATMAN IS SLAPPING ROBIN is being entertained by Batman in a manner in which only he can entertain it. It is a first-personal manner. I am Batman. I am slapping Robin. I need this. With stunning regularity and despite my best intentions, I am Robin.*

In thinking about Sedgwick's passage, I am struck by how often the notion of costume comes up in my writing about my book. In the two introductions to a lecture that I gave, the ideas of concealing oneself with a mask and of Batman's outfit as fetish wear both appear. In this first post of mine on auto-theory, I wonder if I am like "an organ-grinder's monkey, preening itself in an ill-fitting red military-style jacket and turquoise fez." In another post, I ruminate on the meaning of Batman's glove. (In one of the memes that I have since decided not to include in the book, there is a reference to cosplay as well.)

The form of a work is how it appears, how it shows itself, its costume. This form or appearance can, of course, be talked about within a work, but in being talked about, a new form or appearance is generated. Ultimately, as Wittgenstein says: "What can be shown cannot be said." For example, my book has the form, the appearance, of an art catalogue in which an artist's works are reproduced and commented on by an editor. But the artist and editor are, at bottom, the same person. Making this device explicit within the work is something neither the artist nor the editor can do, in their assigned roles. The attempt to articulate the work's two-facedness (in both senses of that expression) inevitably generates an unarticulated and even trickier threefoldness. (And somewhere in there, though I won't try to unearth it now, is a connection with the parergon.)

Putting Wittgenstein's "what can be shown cannot be said" together with the psychoanalytic commonplace that if there is something in an analysis that cannot be said, it inevitably becomes the crux of the whole analysis, one is led, inexorably, to the conclusion that for auto-theory, form is everything. Even relatively straight memoiristic writing, such as Sedgwick's, typically likes to dress itself up with some formal innovations. (In Sedgwick's case, passages from her therapist's notes, and haikus, often seamlessly integrated with surrounding text.) And in other cases, such as Kraus's *I Love Dick*, one cannot separate the formal innovations of the work from its auto-theoretical intent. In the best auto-theoretical writing, the personal and the theoretical are "whirlpooling around in each other," each appearing in the other's clothes, each with the power to poison the other, to deflate it with a slap. This is the thrilling risk of auto-theory.

M.49 Jingle Bells

M.49 Jingle Bells Composed: March 19th. Orientation: Reverse. Font: Comic Sans. TB1: ""Jingle Bells, Ba..."", black. TB2: "Who was it who laid an egg, bird boy?", black. TB3: "And I got away!", black, with a hand-drawn speech bubble leading to the Joker. Added Images: (i) The Joker speaking on a telephone and (ii) a wheel.

Composed on the very day the Batman Meme Project was declared over by Evnine, with his posting of *Evnine's Batman Memes: The Movie*, this exuberant and technically innovative meme shows that Evnine was anything but played out. It provides an auspicious start to the post-Batman Meme Project phase of his meme-making.

Robin's words are the beginning of a well-known children's song:

> Jingle Bells
> Batman smells
> Robin laid an egg.
> The Batmobile
> Has lost a wheel
> And the Joker got away!

One can follow the progress of the song by proceeding clockwise through the two speech bubbles, the image of a wheel, and the image and added textbox for the Joker (as played by Cesar Romero on the live Batman series from the 1960s). This is accomplished with great technical proficiency. The location of the wheel over the whoosh line of Batman's moving hand imparts a sense of motion to it, downwards and to the right, as if rolling out of the frame. The image of the Joker matches his red jacket to the background red of the meme, incorporating him organically into the whole. This and *Dinner's Ready* (M.104) are the only memes where text is assigned to someone other than Batman and Robin. In both cases the third speaker is the Joker. This is quite appropriate given his role as an agent of chaos.

M.50 Say the Opposites

M.50 Say the Opposites Composed: March 20th. Orientation: Reverse. Font: Comic Sans. TB1: "Say the opposites of these words: "Always coming from take me down..."", black. TB2: "I wasn't born yesterday!!!", black.

Among the many *accademie*, the coteries of intellectuals, that flourished in Italy in the 16th and 17th centuries, there was one which was especially select. Select, yes, though its members were not necessarily of the highest nobility or the most learned schools. This academy was nothing other than the psychotherapeutic establishment of the day; the regular, organized center of a science which was so completely 'underground' that even those upon whom therapy was practiced were often quite unaware of its existence. Its mythical patron was Orpheus and, as you will consequently guess, its members were musicians. The members of the *Accademia Orfica* included all the well-known (and many unknown) musicians of that era – Giovanni de' Bardi, Caccini, Peri, Vincenzo Galilei, Monteverdi, Emilio de' Cavalieri, Vittoria Archilei and she whom we now know only as *la vag'Angioletta*. This nymph, so famously be-rhymed by Guarini (an honorary member of the Academy) was, in fact, the most artful, the most subtle of those members of the Academy who were primarily practitioners as opposed to theoreticians. To give just one example, she cured the Duke of Mantua's son of an overly bellicose humor with the performance of a single aria in which, portraying the forsaken Ariadne, she lamented over the war-like ways of her lover Theseus and called the sun and the stars to witness that she would die of her grief, and called on the gently swaying trees to form a canopy through which she could join the shades of all her unfortunate brothers and sisters who had died of love (*amanti squarciati*). The Duke's son wept openly and vowed to donate all the funds he had amassed for the financing of a military expedition to a convent of Poor Clare nuns.

10 or 15 years prior to this, another spectacular, though largely unrecognized, success for the psychotherapeutic community had been at the nuptials of Ferdinando de Medici and Cristina of Lorraine in Florence in 1589. Rumors that the groom might not be able to consummate the marriage prompted a few knowledgeable courtiers to seek the intervention of the *Orfici*. Anyone who hears the opening two chords of the young Caccini's 'trial analysis,' conducted under the supervision of the arch-theorist Bardi (whose few incursions into the practice of analysis were barely on the fringes of orthodoxy), anyone, I say, who hears the opening of the aria *Io che dal ciel cader*, cannot fail to be struck by the power which was in the hands of these unseen guardians of renaissance spiritual health.

The theory behind a capacious orthodoxy was cleverly hinted at by Guarini in his famous poem *Mentre vaga Angioletta*. In its original appearances in print, in 1585 and 1590, the poem's exoteric meaning predominates. It seems to recount how, when the charming Angioletta sings, the very spirit of music becomes embodied in her voice. Manipulating this subtle instrument, the actions of music's spirit are recounted, its fugues and fancies echoed in dizzying text that invites an Orpheus to embody them in his own song. The narrator of the poem, listening to Angioletta sing, finds his heart racing in the experience. At the climax, is it Angioletta herself who turns into a nightingale, taking flight to depart from melancholy? When, however, the poem was republished in the *Rime* of 1598, the first printed collection devoted solely to Guarini's poems, some slight changes allow us to glimpse the poem's esoteric meaning. A comma at the end of line six, not present in the first printings, suggests that the main subject of the twists and turns of melody, now agitated and now at rest, now sparkling and now murmuring low, is not the spirit of music embodied in Angioletta's singing throat, but rather the heart of the listener itself, becoming, he knows not how, the spirit of music. The nightingale takes flight not in order not to be sad (*per non star mesto*), as in the exoteric version, but in order not to stay within (*per non star meco*) the listener. Making a palimpsest of these two versions, we may see the theoretical basis of the guild's practice of psychotherapy take form. The singing voice not only embodies the spirit of music but in turn causes the heart of the listener to embody that spirit. Thus joined, the voice's motions run in parallel with motions in the patient's heart, leading her both to "surcease of sorrow" and to transformation, to be 'let out of herself,' free of her malady.

> When charming Angioletta sings
> Delighting every cultivated heart
> My own heart runs – the sum of things
> Hangs threaded on the sweet sound of her art
> And who know by what means
> But music's spirit seems[,]
> A singing throat which shapes or feigns
> In strangest ways
> Such masterfully speaking strains

> That temper lovely voice with dazzling sound,
> With broken accents turning it around
> With answering twists, a thrust,
> Now slow, now fast.
> With noble sounds, and low, it takes
> To murmuring now, and now changing
> Flights for rests for calm, contented sighs
> Now halting it, now disengaging,
> Pressing, breaking off, and on the brakes,
> It shudders, darting flies,
> Now in a circle takes
> Sometimes, in rambling ways and tremulous
> At others, firm and sonorous.
> Thus she sings, and my own heart re-sings
> (Love's miracle displayed!)
> A nightingale is made
> Which, tarrying not in grief [within], unfolds its wings.

Around this orthodoxy, a plethora of less conventional approaches flourished. One group believed that the transition from the element of water to the element of air experienced by us at birth was of central significance to our spiritual health. Its practitioners would, ludicrously, sometimes begin their performances with their faces submerged in a mazer of water, tinctured with a thimbleful of amniotic fluid preserved from a recent parturition. Raising their faces from the water, they would burst into song with strains resembling the infant's first cry. Others, followers of one Alessandro Franco (possibly kin to Veronica, though his sobriquet *l'ungarese* may indicate altogether different origins), held that the singer could only heal if he or she received healing from the patient in return. The patient not always being a singer, this practice led to the performance of many risible, lop-sided duets. For such profanation of the Muses, Franco and his followers were the subject of wide (though not universal) censure and the poor man died insane. Sometimes, extravagant gestures of the hand accompanied the singing cure, on the grounds that these motions might, like the motions of the voice, enable the listener's heart to move more flexibly. Others, however, such as the members of the famed and much-esteemed *concerto delle donne*, at the court of Ferrara, were strict purists, even to the point of holding the printed music in front of them, emphasizing their hands' immobility.

In fact, the Estense court at Ferrara was home to many who belonged to the *Accademia Orfica*, in addition to Laura Peverara, Livia d'Arco, and Anna Guarini (daughter of the author of *Mentre vaga Angioletta*), the still-handed members of the *concerto delle donne*. The *Orfici* included among their numbers even some from the princely family itself. One such noble healer of souls was Riccardo d'Este, known as *il rosso*. His reputation was great, legendary even among his contemporaries. How sad, then, that all that remains of his *oeuvre* is this solitary aria:

> Non mi dir che sei così cieca
> da non potermi veder….

Giammai ti abbandonerò
Giammai ti deluderò
Giammai errerò né ti lascerò
Giammai lacrimar ti farò
Giammai addio ti dirò
Giammai mentirò né doler ti farò.

M.52 Fuenteovejuna

M.52 Fuenteovejuna Composed: March 21st. Orientation: Original. Font: Arial. TB1: "Who did it?", black. TB2: "Fuenteovejuna did it!", black.

The text of the meme refers to an incident in Spanish history commemorated in the play *Fuenteovejuna* (1619) by Lope de Vega. The incident occurred at the end of the 15th century in a village called Fuenteovejuna. A ruthless and violent military commander who administered the village was murdered by some of the oppressed villagers. When the villagers were tortured to reveal the names of the actual assassins, they would only reply, one and all, "Fuenteovejuna did it." In keeping with its subject matter, this meme is stark and somber. It is, perhaps, the only meme in Evnine's corpus in which there is nothing funny at all. It resembles *My Sister! My daughter!* (M.37) both in its brutality and, relatedly, in use of the slap as an instrument of judicial or quasi-judicial torture, a function the slap has in no other meme. The latter, however, has some little redeeming humor in the clever use of the animated GIF format.

M.58 A Certain Gesture

M.58 A Certain Gesture Composed: March 25th. Posted: March 25th. FIRST PANEL Orientation: Original. Font: Comic Sans. TB1: "HERE IS ONE HAND…", black. TB2: N/a. SECOND PANEL Orientation: Reverse. Font: Comic Sans. TB1: N/a. TB2: … AND HERE IS ANOTHER!", black.

Here is the meme the title of which I have used as a title for this book. Like *My Sister! My daughter!* (M.37) and several later memes, it is designed to appear as an animated GIF, the two panels alternating with each other. The text alludes to the essay "Proof of an External World" by the British philosopher G. E. Moore:

> I can prove now, for instance, that two human hands exist. How? By holding up my two hands, and saying, as I make a certain gesture with the right hand, 'Here is one hand', and adding, as I make a certain gesture with the left, 'and here is another'. And if, by doing this, I have proved ipso facto the existence of external things, you will all see that I can also do it now in numbers of other ways: there is no need to multiply examples. (Moore 1993: 165-6)

Moore, of course, does not say what the "certain gesture" is that accompanies his declarations. One assumes he had in mind a little flourish and not a slap. But sometimes such Moorean certainties can come back at you like a slap:

> There was the famous occasion on which G. E. Moore gave as an example of a certainty, 'I know there is a window in this room' and on which Moore was, in fact, mistaken (Moore was lecturing in a hall at the University of Michigan which had curtains, but no windows behind the curtains). (Putnam 1988: 53)

Moore, a Cambridge professor through the first half of the 20th century, is philosophy's Holy Fool. Or at least, holy to some, fool to others. His work, written with his characteristic dry and pedantic style, apparent in the quotation from "Proof the External World," can often appear startlingly naïve. But not a few highly respected philosophers have professed to find in it unparalleled depths. He was said to be the originator of a sort of open-mouthed gawp in response to unpalatable assertions made by other philosophers, a facial expression that became typical of Cambridge philosophers, passing from Moore to Casimir Lewy to Edward Craig. This gawp is an ancestor, I suppose, of the incredulous stare David Lewis found to be the most common response to his views. (See *The Incredulous Stare* (M.38) and the commentary thereon for an account of Lewis's incredible views.) For an assessment of the anti-skeptical power of Moore's "certain gesture," see the discussion on *I refute him thus* (M.57).

Using the image of Batman slapping Robin in association with Moore's "here is one hand" is not original to Evnine and we know that he saw at least one other effort as early as 2013. I have not, however, found anything earlier which uses the format of an *animated* GIF so in that, at least, the artists showed some originality.

M.60 The Sound of One Hand Slapping (11ignj.jpg)

M.60 The Sound of One Hand Slapping (11ignj.jpg) Composed: March 27th.
Orientation: Reverse. Font: N/a. TB1: N/a. TB2: N/a.

A Certain Gesture (M.58) was posted to Facebook on March 25th, after the completion of the Batman Meme Project, because it is an animated GIF and can only be properly experienced on-line. In the comments to it, two people (apparently independently of each other) commented "the sound of one hand slapping." Whether this suggested the idea of M.60 to the artist, or whether he had already had an idea for a meme along these lines, we cannot determine. It is the only meme in which both speech bubbles are entirely empty and there are no other images or hand-drawn elements.[130]

Despite appearances (or perhaps not!), *The Sound of One Hand Slapping (11ignj.jpg)* is one of the richest and most subtle memes of the entire corpus. The first part of the title, "The Sound of One Hand Slapping," gives access to several layers of meaning. It is clearly adapted from the famous Zen koan devised by Hakuin Ekaku (1686-1768): "You know the sound of two hands

[130] One might think that, at least for a given orientation of the image and with no further additions, only one meme is possible that has no words. In set theory, sets are individuated by their members. Just as there is only one empty set, must there not be just one empty meme (with the qualifications given)? Is not my description of M.60 as the *only* such meme therefore redundant? It is a consequence of Evnine's metaphysics explained in this commentary that artworks in general, including memes, are *not* individuated just by what is in them and that there could, therefore, be many memes – of the same orientation and with no additions – all of which had completely empty speech bubbles. They would be perceptually indiscernible from one another and yet distinct works.

clapping; tell me, what is the sound of one hand?" The koan presents a 'problem,' of course, because it is logically necessary for clapping to involve two hands. Clapping just *is* the beating together of the palms of two hands to produce a sound. Hence, "the sound of one hand clapping" seems like a contradiction in terms. Slapping, on the other hand, requires only one hand (and some body part, usually belonging to another person, against which that hand is struck). There is, therefore, no logical problem with the description "the sound of one hand slapping," and no trouble, in some sense, in conceiving of that sound. Hakuin's koan, however, requires its answerer to *tell* him what the sound of one hand clapping is and one might be flummoxed by the challenge of *telling* someone what the sound of one hand slapping (or of anything at all) is, as well. (See, in this connection, *What Is It Like?* (M.85) and its commentary.) One can, unlike the sound of one hand clapping, produce or imitate or point out the sound of one hand slapping, but does doing any of these amount to telling someone what that sound is? Well, who knows! A lot will depend on what one makes of the notion of "telling what ... is," clearly an interesting and largely indeterminate notion that we cannot stop to illuminate here.

The fact that the meme is simply an image, of course, means that the slapping is depicted visually but there is no accompanying sound. The sound is 'in' the image, in the scene depicted, though not audible. The meme itself, therefore, does not produce, or imitate, or point out the sound of one hand slapping any more than it tells us what that sound is.[131] Indeed, the meme is silent both literally (qua image) and, figuratively, in the absence of any text in the speech bubbles. The empty speech bubbles thus emphasize the way in which the meme does not even accomplish what *is* possible (short of *telling* what the sound of one hand slapping is), namely, producing or imitating that sound. And yet, in its own way, it speaks. It does *represent* the sound of one hand slapping via the conventions for representing sounds in comics. In this respect, it not only speaks, but speaks loudly, for it contains three distinct elements that might be thought to represent in some way the sound of one hand slapping. There is what I call the "whoosh" line that gives the trajectory of Batman's hand on its way towards Robin's cheek, a line that suggests both motion and sound. There is a flesh-toned bloom emanating from Robin's cheek and/or ear, that represents the point of impact between hand and face, suggesting both sound and collision. And finally, there are the upward pointing lines on the red background between the two heads in the image. These suggest the propagation of both sound waves and the energy of the collision, the echoing ring of the slap in the stunned silence that follows it. (Look again at the meme and let yourself 'hear' all this. And note how effective the 'silence' of the empty speech bubbles is in allowing these other visible marks to be 'heard.')

The meme, then, so far suggests the existence of three distinct relations something might have to a given sound. First, something might tell us what the sound is, whatever exactly that involves. The meme does not do this, and perhaps nothing could, but in its title, it directs us to

---

[131] Surely one large part of the impetus for the Batman meme movie *Gone!* must have been the delight in being able to add the sound of the slap to the image in the memes. But see the commentary on *"a glove slapping a human face - forever"* (M.24) for Evnine's realization that the sound he used in the movie, and elsewhere, is the sound of an ungloved hand slapping, while in the image, the hand that is slapping is gloved.

the koan that presupposes that at least some sounds can be 'told.' Secondly, something might share (some of) the acoustic properties of a sound, as an imitation of it would, or a recording, or the sound itself (the special case in which something can represent itself). And finally, something might bear to the sound the relations that the elements of graphic conventions do in a medium that is itself neither conceptual (and hence cannot *tell* us what the sound is) nor sonic (and hence cannot resemble the acoustic properties of the sound). In some ways, this last is the most interesting relation – though we have no ready name for it. And the meme brings out its centrality precisely by omitting any words and, if the reader will forgive the strained metaphor, silently allowing the graphic elements to speak for themselves.

All of this, interesting as it is, is merely one of the dimensions along which this meme is worthy of sustained attention. For we have not yet inquired into the second part of the title that the artist gave the meme: "(11ignj.jpg)." Why has he included in the title what looks like a JPEG file name? Meme generators, including Imgflip, the one used by Evnine, work in the following way. They display the template for a given meme – for example, the picture of Batman slapping Robin, without any additional words – and allow a meme-maker to add text in fields next to the template. They then invite the user to click a button labeled something like "Generate Meme," and in response, produce an image that incorporates the text from the fields into the template. M.60 seems to undercut the distinction between the original template and the outputted meme since they are visually indiscernible. Unlike the template, of course, the meme bears a title, but we might wonder whether all the artist has done is to slap a title on the template and call the result a meme. The second part of the meme's title is, I conjecture, designed to address this suspicion. The meme that is the output of the process performed by the meme generator is a JPEG file to which is assigned a file name that is some apparently random combination of letters and numerals. (In preparing this text, I went through the process and the file produced was given the name "17d2fq.jpg," for example.) The second half of the title of M.60 is a file designation of this kind and its inclusion in the meme's title seems designed to inform us that the artist has not simply taken the original unworked-on image and slapped a title on it; he has deliberately gone through the process of creating a meme but has intentionally done so without the addition of any text or other images. It is his way of telling us that he has worked on the original template (albeit in a minimal way) and that the result is a meme that bears the same relation to the original image as all of the other memes, with added text, bear to the original image. Just as they are distinct from the template that they are 'made out of,' so is M.60.

What makes this interpretation of the second half of the title so plausible is that it exactly follows what the artist himself has written about so-called ready-made works of art, such as Marcel Duchamp's *Fountain*, in his 2016 book, which itself was in the final stages of its production at the hands of the publishers when the Batman memes were being composed. In order, therefore, fully to appreciate M.60, we should pause to understand some of what Evnine wrote about these matters in his more traditional philosophical work.

Evnine develops what he calls a hylomorphic theory of artifacts and organisms. (Its application to organisms is much less convincing than its application to artifacts!) It is founded on what he calls "the matter relation," the relation between an object and its matter. This relation is stipulated to be irreflexive, so a thing is never its own matter, and asymmetric (if A is the matter of B, then B is not the matter of A). Objects can typically change their matter over time (so, strictly, the relation we are interested in is *...is the matter of ... at t*). Such objects have a 'metabolism,' literally in the case of organisms, and figuratively in the case of artifacts. In typical cases, an artifact, such as a bronze statue, is made by work done on some matter (a portion of bronze) by a maker, someone who intentionally manipulates the matter with the intention of making out of it a statue. One can see this as the maker's imposing the concept *statue* onto the bronze. (Imposing a concept on something is not at all to be confused with applying the concept to, or predicating it of, that thing.) Imposing a concept on some matter is a *sui generis* process of creation, correlative with the object that is made out of the matter – itself something that Evnine calls an "ideal" object because it is tied in its very essence to the creative intentions of the maker. It is because of these creative intentions and the role they have played in the maker's manipulation of the bronze (the matter) that we can say, after the manipulation, that we no longer have only the bronze, but now also a further, distinct object, the statue, that has the bronze as its matter.

The reason why, when one wishes to bring into existence an object of a certain kind (say *chair*), one's imposition of the concept onto some appropriate matter is generally part of a process of manipulating, or working on, the matter is that, to put it dramatically, we live in a fallen world where raw materials are not automatically adapted to become the matter of the things we need – tables, chairs, pianos. That matter needs to be beaten into shape. But occasionally, we are lucky enough to find matter already meeting the demands placed by the concept – a tree stump already has the form of a chair, for example. In such a case, the harmony means that no, or minimal, adaptation of the matter will be needed. The maker, then, may bring into existence something, a chair for example, simply by imposing the concept *chair* onto the already suitable matter, the tree stump. The result will be that something new, the chair, comes to exist, in addition to the stuff that is now its matter. In other cases, there may be a harmony that obviates the need for work on the matter, not because the matter happens to conform to the demands of the concept, but because the concept simply imposes very few demands on the matter. Such is the state that the concepts *artwork, painting, statue, sculpture*, etc. came to find themselves in at the outset of the 20th century. Because of the particular history of art, it became possible for someone like Marcel Duchamp to make a sculpture out of a urinal (as its matter) simply by, in effect, declaring it to be so (perhaps by attempting to exhibit it in an art exhibition). Not all concepts allow such universal imposition onto matter – one cannot simply stipulate of a lump of butter that it is now the matter of an airplane. Nor did the concepts *sculpture, artwork*, and the rest always allow such easy imposition onto matter. They are historical concepts and evolved to the point of allowing such imposition only under specific historical circumstances. But evolve in that way they did and so the door was opened to the creation of artworks that became, for obvious reasons, problematic and/or offensive to many.

What Evnine seems to be doing, with M.60, is putting this to the test for himself. The basic image of Batman slapping Robin is like the matter out which these memes are made. (Being virtual or abstract matter, of course, it can be used over and over again, unlike a piece of wood which, once it has become the matter of one chair, cannot become the matter of other things without, in most cases, ceasing to be the matter of that chair.) In most cases, the concept *meme*, or *Batman meme*, or *artwork* is imposed onto the matter through work on it. The work takes the form of the addition of text and other images and drawings to the underlying matter. These are additional elements of virtual or abstract matter and by mixing them appropriately with the image, the artist creates a meme, or artwork. But M.60 is like a Duchampian ready-made. The concept is imposed without any real work of modification or addition. But the presence of the file name in the title alerts us to the fact that the artist is not just presenting here the image as raw material. He wishes us to understand that he has made something *new* out of the image – a meme or an artwork. He has put the image through the electronic process that is initiated by clicking the button "Generate Meme" on the website and the result is the meme generated out of the original image. That meme is distinct from the image itself and has the image as its matter, just as all the more ordinary memes are distinct from the image and just as a chair is distinct from the wood it is made out of and has that wood as its matter.

M.62 Liar

M.62 Liar Composed: March 27th. Orientation: Reverse. Font: Comic Sans. TB1: "What Batman says is true!", white. TB2: "False, Boy Wonder!", black.

The first meme, and one of only four, to use different colored text within the meme. *These Shrooms are Strong* (M.63) uses multi-colored, hand-drawn letters in the first textbox; *Text/Subtext* (M.69) alternates black and white text, as with *Liar*, but across two successive panels (it is an animated GIF), not within a single panel. Only *You demon?* (M.81) has differently colored, printed text within a single panel – and that meme is so different from all others that this alternation is hardly noticeable. *Liar*, therefore, is in some respects unique among the memes and it raises the question why the artist did not use this technique more. Whatever the answer, the differently-colored text in the two speech bubbles works particularly well here because of the content of the meme. The meme presents a version of the self-referential Liar Paradox, one of the Semantic Paradoxes. (See the commentary on *They're Forgetting Slappy* (M.11) for discussion of Grelling's Paradox, another Semantic Paradox, and *Dialetheism* (M.20) and commentary *ad loc.* for the set-theoretic Russell's Paradox.) The standard version of the Liar Paradox uses a sentence such as "This sentence is false," which is *self*-referential. But the same paradoxical consequences of self-reference in the typical Liar sentence are generated equally by two sentences, each of which refers to the other, a phenomenon we might dub "mutual allo-reference." This, of course, produces self-reference indirectly. But the sense of infinite deferral, as each text points back to the other, is amplified in the meme by its having the texts appear in white and black.

Just to make explicit the nature of the paradox, Robin speaks truly if, but only if, Batman speaks truly, since Robin says, precisely, that Batman speaks truly.[132] But Batman will speak truly if, but only if, Robin speaks falsely, since what Batman says is that Robin speaks falsely. Hence, if Robin speaks truly, then Batman speaks truly; and if Batman speaks truly, then Robin speaks falsely. So by transitivity of "if… then…" it follows that if Robin speaks truly, then Robin speaks falsely. Conversely, if Robin speaks falsely, then Batman speaks falsely; and if Batman speaks falsely, then Robin speaks truly. So (again by transitivity) if Robin speaks falsely, then Robin speaks truly. So, finally, Robin speaks truly if and only if he speaks falsely. Parallel reasoning will show the same applies to Batman – he speaks truly if and only if he speaks falsely.

This paradox has been recognized since antiquity but in the 20th century it came to have enormous significance for the development of logic. If a language allows self-reference (or mutual allo-reference) and can say of sentences that they are true or false (or even just true or not true), then paradoxical Liar sentences (or pairs of sentences, as in M.62) will be possible. Surely most, if not all, natural languages meet these conditions. Each by itself seems either harmless or an important resource that we would suffer without. Take self-reference. Perhaps claims made with such sentences as "this sentence is in English" or "this sentence has five words" are not very startling or important, but they seem harmless. And in any case, as mutual allo-reference shows, we don't need self-reference to generate a paradox. Mutual allo-reference is just an inevitable consequence of the ability of one sentence to refer to another, and that is more than just a harmless novelty. We would be unable to teach grammar, engage in proof-reading, and so on, if we couldn't say things like "that sentence is lacking an exclamation mark"!

That any speaker of English (or other natural languages that share these features) can inevitably be confronted by a sentence that they cannot accept as true without having to accept it as false (or not true) may not be much of a worry. But when one wishes to use a specially devised formal language to pursue theoretical activities where freedom from contradiction is a strong desideratum, something has to give. One commonly accepted proposal, deriving from the work of the Polish logician Alfred Tarski (who features in *Snow is white!* (M.70) and *Too Easy, Robin!* (M.75)) is to conceive of such formal languages as involving nested hierarchies of

---

[132] Actually, saying that it is *precisely* what Robin says is a little strong. The sentence he uses to make his assertion is "What Batman says is true!" and, for the paradox to be generated, this must be taken to refer to what Batman says *in his speech bubble*, i.e. what he says next, if we suppose the left-to-right placement of the speech bubbles corresponds to a temporal ordering of earlier-to-later. The intended meaning might have been better expressed by "What Batman is about to say is true!" or something along those lines. As it is, it might, taken on its own, be thought to be either backward looking ("What Batman has just said is true!") or general. If the latter, and we take it in a generic sense, rather than the universal, it will mean "Generally, what Batman says is true!". Neither the backward looking nor the generic reading will yield a paradox. If, however, we take it in the universal sense, then it will mean "Everything Batman says is true!" and the paradox still arises. On the other hand, Batman's "False, Boy Wonder!" is most naturally taken as meaning "What you have just said is false, Boy Wonder!", which is exactly the reading required to generate the paradox.

languages. At the base level, the language will lack the resources of being able to say of sentences at that level that they are true or false. Hence one will simply be unable to formulate a Liar sentence in it. There will literally not be the words to do so in the language. Our desire to attribute truth to sentences at this basic level will be satisfied by the introduction of the next level, which will contain a truth predicate that can only be applied to sentences of the previous level. And so on. Thus, no sentence will be able to say of itself (or of any sentence at the same or higher level in the hierarchy) that it is true or false (or not true) and pairs of mutually allo-referential attributions of truth and falsity will also be impossible. The consequences of this expedient, however, are startling. If we are confined to using a nested hierarchy of languages like this, we can never say anything (however banal) about everything. Totality repeatedly eludes us. Any attempt to grasp it automatically forces us to ascend to a higher level of the hierarchy, thereby undermining our attempt to encompass everything!

M.63 These Shrooms are Strong

M.63 These Shrooms are Strong Composed: March 29th. Posted (privately): April 7th. Orientation: Reverse. Font: Comic Sans. TB1: "Wow! These shrooms are strong!", hand-drawn multi-colored lettering. TB2: "Sober up, Robin. We have crime to fight!", black. Added Image: The Penguin, with thought bubble leading to both Batman and Robin hand-drawn in white around it.

Although several memes have hand-drawn elements, this is the only case of hand-drawn text in the entire corpus. In fact, hand-drawing is the only way the meme generator gives of producing multi-colored text and we may conjecture that the hand-drawing here is mostly done in the service of producing the hallucinatory coloration of Robin's text suitable to its content. (Though of course, the unevenness of the hand-drawn characters is itself also suitable to that content.) This meme is one of only two – the other is *Shhh!* (M.71) – to use thought bubbles. Here, the thought bubble, which is in addition to and not instead of the usual speech bubbles, is the same for both Batman and Robin and contains an image only (The Penguin, as played by Burgess Meredith in the 1960s TV series). For all these reasons, *These Shrooms are Strong* is a strong and technically innovative piece of work.

The multi-colored text works against the logic of the basic template. As I have explained in other, similar cases, the speech bubbles are conventional imagistic devices that signal the writing in them is to be understood as the representation of a spoken utterance. All features of writing that do not contribute to that function are redundant in theory. Yet here the coloring is itself used to convey something in a way distinct from the way associated with speech bubbles. An image in a speech bubble would be even more disconcerting (as we find in *"a glove slapping a human face – forever"* (M.24)). But the conventions associated with a thought bubble are, of course, more lenient. Since thought itself can be linguistic or imagistic, either text or pictures can sensibly be placed in thought bubbles.

M.69 Text/Subtext

M.69 Text/Subtext Composed: April 8th. FIRST PANEL Orientation: Reverse. Font: Comic Sans. TB1: "I assumed you meant...", white. TB2: "Listen to my words!", white. SECOND PANEL Orientation: Reverse. Font: Comic Sans. TB1: "But you said...", black. TB2: "Listen to what I'm not saying!", black.

Another meme in the form of an animated GIF with alternating panels. The potentially infinite repetition of the sequence well captures the instability between the desire to have one's words taken at face value and the desire to be heard deeply. Evnine himself writes about the origin of the meme in a post published on his blog *The Parergon*.

For the Letter Kills, but the Spirit Gives Life

Seven or so years ago, near the beginning of my analysis, I explained to my analyst, after some frustrating experiences, how important it was to me that they always engage with the actual content of what I was saying. I took a huge amount of care in expressing myself – choosing exactly the right words, multiplying distinctions in order to communicate with laser precision – and I didn't want to be 'interpreted' *before* the letter of what I was saying had been fully attended to.

Paul says in 2 *Corinthians* (3:6), distinguishing between Jews and the new Jesus movement, that "the letter kills, but the spirit gives life" and as a Jew, I have always understood that my job is to be for the letter. This has meant two things.

Figure 14 My measurement by a Pauline gauge (image by James LaCroix)

By "the letter," Paul means the old covenant, the Mosaic law and its development by the rabbis of his day, whose views are recorded in the *Mishnah*.[133] This he took to have been annulled by the advent of Jesus with a new covenant. Accordingly, the text of the Old Testament could no longer be read literally, but only "spiritually," by means of allegory, typology, and so on. The Jews were stubborn in continuing, in the face of the new covenant, to read their sacred books by the letter. So, one part of being "for the letter" has been a determination to treat the language I am exposed to from other people literally and precisely – not to try and get the gist or spirit of it, not to look beyond it to see where its originator is coming from.

---

133   [Editor's note:] See the commentary on *The Size of an Olive* (M.12) for some explanation of what the *Mishnah* is.

But there is, alongside this, another way of being "for the letter." R. Akiva, a near contemporary of Paul's, was said to interpret "mounds of rules from every tip of the letters" (TB Menaḥot 29b).[134] The tips were ornamental 'crowns' that adorned the Hebrew script of the time.[135] This type of reading, truly and radically literal (perhaps we should say "letteral"), can stand as synecdoche for a panoply of more or less perverse methods of interpretation associated with the Jews. In the words of John Wilkins, the 17th century inventor of a "real character" (an ideal language which mirrors the structure of reality):

> Amongst the Jewish Rabbies, is not any opinion, whether in nature or policy, whether true or false, but some of them, by a cabalistical interpretation can father it upon a dark place of scripture, or (if need be) upon a text that is clean contrary. There being not any absurdity so gross and incredible, for which these abusers of the text, will not find out an argument.

(The quotation is from his *The Discovery of a World in the Moone* of 1638.)

Figure 15 The title page of John Wilkins's The Discovery of a World in the Moone *(photograph by the editor)*

So, Jews were taken to task, under the guise of the letter, for being both too literal and too fanciful. I have endeavored to honor these twin heritages: a

---

[134] [Editor's note:] "TB" refers to the Babylonian Talmud, the better known of the two Talmuds (the other being referred to as the Jerusalem or Palestinian Talmud). See commentary on *The Size of an Olive* (M.12) for some further explanation.

[135] [Editor's note:] These ornamental crowns are still used in hand-written Torah scrolls.

laborious literalism with respect to what I read and write, hear and say, and an extravagant letterlism, a willingness to associate anything with anything by means of some devious chain, to father monstrous conjunctions of words and meanings through textual abuse. It feels to me as if there must be some relation – quite other than monstrous conjunction – between these two ways of being for the letter, but I cannot easily identify what it is. They are, perhaps, both subsumed by the term "pharisaism." The historical Pharisees, and their successors who compiled the Talmud, stubbornly adhered to the plain meaning of the Bible (in some of their moods) and yet developed complex and sometimes rebarbative methods of interpretation partly to reconcile that text with a much more humane standard of conduct. I would like, therefore, to re-appropriate the term "Pharisee" from the infamy with which the fevered Christian imagination has painted it.

Those seven or so years ago, when I implored my analyst to take me at my word, it was, almost needless to say, only the first way, according to which it contrasts with "spirit," that I had in mind. Two or three years after that, well into the analysis, I was becoming more comfortable and more curious. The tight control over my words – the only real power I could exert to protect myself and ensure the analysis did not unleash anything too scary – came to feel constricting, even suffocating. It was, I suppose, a Damascene moment. I relented, and gave my analyst permission to listen to the spirit of my words and report back on what they heard. (I have no reason to think my analyst's behavior was in any way affected by either my initial injunction or my subsequent permission!) It was around that time that I composed this animated meme [i.e., M.69].

Fast forward in the analysis to last week and a very exhausting and disspiriting session. At the end of the previous session, I had said I thought my presence in our sessions now was very different from how it used to be. My analyst agreed, adding that they, too, were a different analyst now from what they had been. The next day, I said that I would love – if not now, then perhaps towards termination – to hear about the ways in which they thought they had changed as an analyst during the course of my treatment. When my analyst asked what exactly I wanted them to explain, we set off on a frustrating tussle, lasting the whole session, in which I said, over and over again, in every way I could think of, what I wanted and my analyst kept alleging that they didn't understand. Somehow, I don't really understand how, I kind of got through; and my analyst conveyed how their attempt to hear the question behind the question kept them from seeing what I wanted to communicate. At the end I exclaimed "I'd like to go back to that injunction I made right at the start. Please make an effort to engage with the letter of what I am saying before trying to hear what is unsaid." To which they replied, with some, subsequently confessed, hyperbole: "You do realize that is literally the exact opposite of what I'm supposed to be doing?!" (One reason to think that the designation of psychoanalysis as "the Jewish science" may be misleading.) In some sense, of course, what they said is obvious. They are listening for what is unconscious, which is unlikely to be found in the obsessively-controlled language that I wield almost like a weapon. But it startled me nonetheless and I decided to write this post to help work through it.

This post led to a rather amusing exchange. The philosopher Eric Schliesser responded to it with a post of his own. Apparently, when Evnine thanked him for writing about his own post, Schliesser said that he had originally written something notably less sympathetic. Evnine asked to see the earlier draft but Schliesser said it no longer existed. Evnine, therefore, took it upon himself to write Schliesser's more hostile initial response. Here is Schliesser's actual reply.

On Analysis

One recurring fascination is the common root of 'analysis' in analytical philosophy that it shares with the 'analysis' in psychoanalysis. I sometimes wonder why *analyse* and its cognates had such pull over late nineteenth and early twentieth century (Viennese and Cambridge) minds. I was reminded of this by Simon Evnine who regularly calls my attention to his blog, "The Parergon." I hope he does not mind too much being the occasion for these impressions. I treat him here as the everyman of analytic philosophy in which all of us can be substituted into his place, opaque contexts be damned![136]

It is noticeable that Simon treats his precision and "care in expressing" in terms of a "weapon." Even when used in self-defense, weapons are explicitly designed to hurt others.[137] I have noted before (recall) the analytic philosopher's tendency to describe the toolkit of her craft in terms of surgical (and laser-like) instruments, but in those instances the instruments are meant to heal. Of course, Simon's intent is not to hurt others, but self-protection ("the only real power I could exert to protect myself.")[138]

---

[136] [Editor's note:] A reference to the logical problem engendered by linguistic contexts in which one can turn a sentence from true to false, or vice versa, by substituting one proper name for another that refers to the same thing. E.g. "Commissioner Gordon believes that Batman is a crimefighter" is true, but "Commissioner Gordon believes that Bruce Wayne is a crimefighter" is false. "Believes that..." is said to be an opaque context. Of course, the concept doesn't really apply in Schliesser's text, where he is talking about one person standing for others and not about names at all.

[137] [Schliesser's note:] Perhaps the memetic repetition-image of Batman slapping Robin inspired this thought.

[138] [Schliesser's note:] In practice, the toolkit is also deployed to advance careers and schools.

I do not know a better expression of the fragility at the root of much analytic philosophy.[139] Any badly formulated phrase is a misstep of monumental proportions. The robustness of the whole collapses with the weakest link. This fragility is fueled by "frustrating experiences." Once primed by psychoanalysis, it's hard not to discern the dependent child here.

I do not mean to suggest that the analytic philosopher's attitude toward rigor and clarity only expresses fragility. One may as well -- and here I am inspired by Simon's "extravagant letteralism" – read it as pure holiness (recall here on Carnap).[140] After all, a Torah scroll is disqualified if even a single letter is added or a single letter is deleted. Every sign must be correct.

A few days ago a lovely blog post by Liam Kofi Bright inspired me to reflect a bit on what the norms of analytic philosophy would have to be if we "conceived of conceptual engineering as a means to enter into lifeworlds of others." I asserted that the non-dominating way of doing so requires a willingness to be transformed by the experience. What I missed saying explicitly then, and I suspect this omission (recall) is part of my professional deformation, is that one cannot (non-dominatingly) enter into the lifeworld of another without, as Simon shows without saying, being vulnerable.

And here is Evnine's re-imagining of Schliesser's harsher first draft:

On Analysis

One recurring fascination is the common root "analysis" in "analytical philosophy" and "psychoanalysis." I sometimes wonder why *analyse* and its cognates had such pull over late nineteenth- and early twentieth-century (Viennese and Cambridge) minds. (The sympathetic attitude of many members of the Vienna Circle to Freud and psychoanalysis has been somewhat studied And more attention still needs to be given to Roger Money-Kyrle, who studied mathematics in Cambridge in 1919 and then went to Vienna both to be analysed by Freud and do a PhD under Moritz Schlick.[141] I was alerted to Money-Kyrle's importance by David Livingstone Smith, who has drawn on his work on

---

[139] [Editor's note:] The self-exposure and abasement evident in many of Evnine's memes leads one to think he must have been especially pleased by this back-handed compliment.

[140] [Editor's note:] Rudolf Carnap (1891-1970) was one of the Vienna Circle of Logical Positivists. He came to the United States in 1935 and influenced many philosophers here. Both Schliesser and Evnine were taught by students of Carnap. Here, Schliesser is referring to Carnap's high evaluation of clarity for its own sake.

[141] [Editor's note:] Roger Money-Kyrle (1898-1980) was a British psychoanalyst who, as Evnine says, was analyzed by Freud in Vienna from 1919-23 while he also studied philosophy with Moritz Schlick. Schlick (1882-1936) was another member of the Vienna Circle. For the fascinating details surrounding his lurid death, see Edmonds (2020).

propaganda in the light of Jason Stanley's fine work in this area (recall this and this).)

I was reminded of this by Simon Evnine, who sometimes calls my attention to his blog "The Parergon." A recent post of his there, "For the letter kills, but the spirit gives life," makes painfully explicit what psychoanalysis can reveal about one of the worst aspects of analytic philosophy. I have noted before (recall) the analytic philosopher's tendency to describe the toolkit of her craft in terms of surgical (and laser-like) instruments, but in those instances the instruments are meant to heal. Simon gleefully embraces this ("choosing exactly the right words, multiplying distinctions in order to communicate with laser precision") but explicitly and alarmingly casts these tools as instruments of destruction ("the obsessively-controlled language that I wield almost like a weapon").[142]

It is just this literalism that Simon so extols in his post that leads to the unsympathetic readings that analytic philosophers so typically give to all other kinds of philosophy. The tendency to take some sentence or passage by, for example, Marshall McLuhan or Hayden White out of context and subject it to rigorous logical analysis is so distressingly wrong-headed – missing the spirit of the text for its letter.[143] It is as though (I am now inspired by Simon's "letteralism"), if even one single letter in this non-analytic philosophy is found to be out of place, such work will be worthless – like a Torah scroll in which every letter must be perfect. The analytic philosopher likes to see herself as the true protector of intellectual purity.

Simon's embrace of literalism thus seems a sorry spectacle of an all too familiar kind. But what is interesting about his post is the light it inadvertently sheds on this phenomenon. Simon talks of his literalism as arising from "frustrating experiences." One doesn't have to buy into the whole of Freud's theory to see a parallel between the analytic philosopher protecting herself against frustration by obsessive rigour (and it is interesting to remember that "rigidity" comes from "rigour") and the analytic patient who has built a defensive edifice around her neurotic weakness and fragility. Any badly formulated phrase or behaviour becomes a misstep of monumental proportions. The robustness of the whole collapses with the weakest link. Inside of both is a fragile and dependent child.

A few days ago a lovely blog post by Liam Kofi Bright inspired me to reflect a bit on what the norms of analytic philosophy would have to be if we

---

[142] [Schliesser's* note:] Simon, of course, is not actually threatening to harm anyone.

[143] [Editor's note:] There may be an allusion here to *The Medium is the Message* (M.8) and in the commentary there I expatiate on the point made here.

"conceived of conceptual engineering as a means to enter into lifeworlds of others." I asserted that the non-dominating way of doing so requires a willingness to be transformed by the experience. What I missed saying explicitly then, and I suspect this omission (recall) is part of my professional deformation, is that one cannot (non-dominatingly) enter into the lifeworld of another without being vulnerable.

Perhaps philosophers need to think more about the relation between vulnerability and fragility, though. While to be vulnerable is to expose a weakness, the ability to embrace one's vulnerability, if it is the basis for a transformative experience, is also a kind of strength – even a superpower.[144] It is a paradox where weakness itself becomes strength. (Laurie Paul take note![145]) If only Simon, in his post, had been able to relinquish his subservience to the rigid letter and embrace his weakness in the quest for transformation, he might have had something to offer analytic philosophy.

[144] [Editor's note:] Such willingness to accept one's vulnerability might show up as an identification with the figure of Robin in the corpus of Evnine's memes, for example.

[145] [Editor's note:] Laurie Paul's book *Transformative Experience* also shows up in *Transformative Experience* (M.91) and *Transformative Experience (alternate version)* (M.92). I explain some of its contents in my commentary on the first of those memes.

M.72 Vos iz ayer yidisher nomen, Batman?

M.72 Vos iz ayer yidisher nomen, Batman? Composed: April 9th. Orientation: Reverse. Font: Comic Sans. TB1: "Vos iz ayer yidisher nomen, Batman?", black. TB2: "Ruf mikh *Reb* Batman, Boytshik Vunder!", black. TB3: "Un mayn yidisher nomen iz Simcha Bunim.", black, with hand-drawn speech bubble around it leading to Batman.

One of only two memes, the other being the Latin *Filioque* (M.7), entirely in a language other than English. Here the language is Yiddish. Robin says "What is your Jewish name, Batman?". Batman replies "Call me *Mr.* Batman, Boy Wonder!" before answering, in the added speech bubble, "And my Jewish name is Simcha Bunim."

We have some archival material pertaining to the origins of the text in this meme: email correspondence, from April 2016, between the artist and Susanne Shavelson (Associate Director, Mandel Center for Studies in Jewish Education, at Brandeis University), who assisted with the Yiddish. Thanks to this material, the fact that the meme is in translation (and in a language of which the artist did not have first-hand knowledge) renders visible the great attention to detail that must have been operative in general in the composition of the memes.[146]

The artist writes to Shavelson that he started the process of composing the meme with the English text:

Robin: What is your Jewish name, Batman?

---

[146] A similar sense of attention to detail emerges where we have multiple versions of a meme, as in the case of *More Lesbians* (M.43).

Batman: *Reb* Batman to you, Boy Wonder.[147] And my Jewish name is Simcha Bunim.

Using Google Translate, he obtained:

Robin: Vos s eyer idishe nomen, Batman?
Batman: *Reb* Batman tsu ir, Eyngl Vunder! Aun meyn idishe nomen iz Simcha Bunim.

He asks for suggestions for improvements to the translation and Romanization (Yiddish being written in Hebrew characters) and mentions two particular issues. The first is the idiom "X to you," which Google has translated, as one would expect, literally. Perhaps, he wonders, there is some pithier, less literal rendering. The second is the translation of "Boy Wonder." Evnine worries whether Google's "*Eyngl Vunder*" captures the strangeness of Robin's sobriquet.

Shavelson responds by changing the Romanization of the Yiddish to bring it in line with a standard that gives it what she calls a "Lithuanian slant" (see below for more about this). She also renders Batman's first response more idiomatic, and eliminates the "X to you," by introducing a verb ("you may call me") and taking advantage of that to allow Batman to use the informal second person, in contrast to Robin's formal second person in "your name." (Google Translate's "*tsu ir*" [to you] matches Robin's use of the formal mode.) Finally, she suggests "*Vunderkind*" for "Boy Wonder."

The artist replies, appreciating the use of the familiar versus formal "you" and the more idiomatic "you may call me," but wonders whether, perhaps by changes to word order, it would be possible to emphasize the "you" in "you may call me" and whether the "may" might be changed to "must". He is also still concerned over the rendering of "Boy Wonder":

---

[147] Note that Evnine already starts with some Yiddish, the honorific "*Reb*," which I translated above as "Mr." This derives from the Hebrew word "*Rav*" from which we get "Rabbi," but it is used in Yiddish simply to address an adult man, in combination with his given name(s). One may also address a fellow Jew simply as "*Reb Yid*" (Mr. Jew). (Actually, according to the Yiddishist Leonard Prager, "*Reb*" is used only for "respected adult Jewish males" and hence is "far more selective than English *Mr*." (Prager 1985: 77).) Salo Baron (1957: 283) refers to the 15th century R. Simeon ben Zemach Duran (*Magen Avot*, 2:1) who cites a custom according to which Jewish men call each other "Rabbi" whether ordained or not. Duran explains it as having arisen where there were Karaites among the Jews. Karaism, a branch of Judaism that began around 8th century C.E., rejected the rabbinic tradition (and hence the authority of the Talmud) and sought to go back to the Bible directly. Duran's idea is that since Karaites would not use "Rabbi" (or related forms) as an honorific, general use of the term among the so-called Rabbanites (i.e. non-Karaite Jews) was a good way to police the boundaries between the two groups. (In fact, we should be wary of assuming that Karaites would not use forms of "Rabbi." In at least one prominent work of Karaite theology, *Gan Eden* (1354), the author styles himself "Aharon son of Rabbi Eliyahu." I obtained this reference from the bibliography of Gold (2017).) Baron goes on to say that "Rabbanite Jewry has ever since adorned with this title ['Rabbi'] the first names of all its orthodox members" (283). Whether or not Baron had in mind the Yiddish honorific "*Reb*," a pre-15th-century Karaite connection strikes me as fanciful, though not altogether impossible, as an explanation of *that* practice.

And about "Vunderkind," I'm worried that because we use that expression in English for a child prodigy,[148] it will be too unarresting in this context. Are there other options, or is that really the only (or overwhelmingly best and most obvious) way to translate "Boy Wonder"? (Might one invert the word order, as the strange "Boy Wonder" does, to give "Kind Vunder"?)

Shavelson comes back with the introduction of the imperative form of "call" in Batman's first comment, which cleverly addresses both the "may" to "must" issue and the emphasizing of the "you" at one stroke. She also confesses to having "reached the limit (or depth) of my Yiddish ingenuity where Boy Wonder is concerned." It was at this point that Evnine hit on the brilliant, and with hindsight so simple, idea of *"Boytshik Vunder"* for "Boy Wonder," arriving at the final text. (*"Boytshik"* (more commonly spelled in English as "boychik") is a fairly well-known Anglo-Yiddishism that derives from the English word "boy" with a Slavic diminutive ending commonly used in Yiddish. It is so funny here because it captures the original "boy" of "Boy Wonder" but injects a note of tenderness and familiarity absent from the English cognate into the portentous frame of Robin's Homeric epithet.)

Turning to the meme's content, the interaction depicted concerns Batman's *"yidisher nomen"* (Jewish name). What exactly is meant here by this expression? Many Jews recognize a distinction between what they call a *"shem kodesh"* (sacred name) and a *"kinuy"* (nickname, or secular or civic name). The Yiddish for *"shem kodesh"* would be either *"shem koydesh"* (the Yiddishization of the Hebrew expression) or *"ufrufnomen"* (literally "call-up name," since it is the name by which a Jewish man is called up to read from the Torah). The expression *"yidisher nomen"* (which, as we saw, translates the artist's original "Jewish name") is not idiomatic but what *is* idiomatic is the use of "Jewish name" by English-speaking Jews, to mean *"shem kodesh."* That said, however, the distinction between a *shem kodesh* and a *kinuy* as it currently exists in the popular Jewish imagination is somewhat hard to align precisely with Jewish practice, as it has varied across time and in different locations. Thus it is hard to say what, generally speaking, a *shem kodesh* or a *kinuy* is. As far back as Moses, whose name is Egyptian, Jews have had non-Hebrew names.[149] Under waves of Persian, Greek, and Roman ascendancy, and later under the influence of the languages among which the Jews lived in exile, the range of non-Hebrew names used by Jews greatly expanded. Sometimes they would have these non-Hebrew names in addition to Hebrew names but often not. Where a person had more than one name, of which one was Hebrew (or Aramaic), the practice of thinking of the Hebrew (or Aramaic) name(s) as a *shem kodesh* and the other(s) as a *kinuy* gradually arose in some places. The availability of the two expressions in Yiddish, *"shem koydesh"* and *"ufrufnomen,"* seems a great analytical improvement over the single Hebrew expression *"shem kodesh"* or the single English expression "Jewish name." For *"shem koydesh"* appears as a genetic category, classifying based

---

[148] [Editor's note:] The artist makes a mistake here. We use the German cognate *"Wunderkind,"* not the Yiddish version of the word.

[149] Though a Rabbinic text, *Leviticus Rabbah* (32:5), says that one of the reasons the Jews were delivered from bondage in Egypt was that they didn't change their names from Hebrew to Egyptian names.

on the origins of a name (from the primary *loshn koydesh* (holy language), Hebrew; or the secondary one, Aramaic; or from some other source but sanctioned by custom or edict – as with the case of "Alexander," one of the names of the artist's father). "*Ufrufnomen*" ("call-up name"), by contrast, signals a functional category, classifying on the basis of the use that is made of a name.[150] Clearly, these two categories might come apart and someone be called up to read from the Torah by a name which has origins that unfit it for classification as a *shem koydesh*. There is, needless to say, no science to all of this and the distinction I am making is perhaps not one that would be readily accepted. Nonetheless, it appears useful.

The relations between Hebrew/Aramaic and other names borne by a person are various. They may be related by custom, by sameness of meaning, by assonance, or not at all. Presumably Evnine chose "Simcha Bunim" for Batman on account of the assonance between "Batman" and "Bunim." Regarding the name "Simcha Bunim" itself, its two components, "Simcha" and "Bunim," are distinct names which are often, though not invariably, paired with each other (in this order). "Simcha" is a Hebrew name and means "joy." The origins of "Bunim," and the reasons, if any, for its frequent pairing with "Simcha," are less clear. Shmuel Gorr's entry on the name "Bunim" reads:

> Very often combined with the name *Simḥah* (*Simḥah Bunim*). Reason unknown. Some authorities claim that the name derives from the French *bon homme* (a good man). It is this author's contention that the name *Shem Tov* [Good Name] was very popular in pre-expulsion Spain; and this opinion is based on the dozens of Rabbis of pre-expulsion Spain who carried the Hebrew name *Shem Tov*. During the emigration to France, the name was translated to French. During the following centuries of wandering from country to country the two words *Bon Nom* became contracted to one word. Finally, the pronunciation was influenced by local phonetics. (Gorr 1992: 9)

According to either of the etymologies Gorr considers, the name "Bunim" is not of Hebrew origin, but rather French. In the case he favors, we see a fascinating example of the ways in which names used by Jews go in and out of language: a 'Jewish' neologism from a French name from an earlier Hebrew name, Shem Tov (which itself may come from, or have yielded, the name of an important family of Jews, "Kalonymos," which is Greek for "fine or beautiful name").

---

[150] In many Jewish communities, a boy/man is named in ritual contexts (circumcision, being called up to read from the Torah) with the formula "X *ben* (son of) Y" where X is his own *shem kodesh* and Y that of his father. According to this standard, Batman should have answered Robin's question with something like "Simcha Bunim ben Toma." (I speculate here. Bruce Wayne's father was Thomas. The disciple Thomas is called "Toma" in the Syriac version of the New Testament (Syriac being a dialect of Aramaic), from some time before the 5th century C.E. (Incidentally, "Thomas" is a Greek derivative of the Aramaic word for twin ("*t'm*"). One cannot fail to be struck by how apposite the notion of twinning is in this discussion of double naming. And Thomas Wayne was a 'twin' to his son Bruce in that he, too, was, in his day, "a Bat-Man." See *My Sister! My daughter!* (M.37) for reference to another, rather differently inflected confusion between parent and sibling.))

None of these etymologies for "Bunim" provides any reason why it should be regularly paired with "Simcha." There is no connection of meaning and no assonance to relate them. An interesting speculation from the end of the 17th century offers a different etymology which does address that issue. The *Bet Shmu'el* is a work by R. Shmu'el ben Uri Shraga Faivish, a Polish rabbi.[151,152] The work is a commentary on one of the four parts of the *Shulḥan Arukh* of R. Joseph Caro, an extremely important codification of Jewish law made in the 16th century. That part is the *Even Ha'ezer*, which deals with issues of marriage and divorce. Because it was important for *gittin*, decrees of divorce, to have the names of the parties recorded correctly, the *Bet Shmu'el* contains an appendix with information about common Jewish names and their various forms. Here is what he writes about "Bunim":

> The name "Bunim" – It comes from the name "Benjamin"[153] which comes from the name "Ben Oni" [son of my sorrow][154] which is why they call him [i.e. one named "Bunim"] "Simcha." (Appendix on Names, Names for Men, Bet)

The *Bet Shmu'el*'s idea is that the sorrowful connotations suggested by the name "Bunim" are, when put in combination with the name "Simcha," counteracted by the latter's meaning of "joy." (This doesn't, of course, explain why the joyful connotations of "Simcha" should be muted by its combination with "Bunim." Perhaps there are some who, for whatever reason, particularly want the name "Bunim" and therefore seek the amelioration given by the addition of "Simcha.")

Some remarks from a little earlier in the *Bet Shmu'el*'s discussion, however, are of even greater interest. In a formal document, the author says, we should not write the name "Bunim" for those who are generally called "Bunim." This will appear perplexing:

> On the face of it, it's difficult to understand why we don't write the *kinuy* "Bunim" given that it corresponds to a different *shem kodesh*, "Simcha," and I've already written about how, when the *shem kodesh* and the *kinuy* are different, one must [also] write the *kinuy*. [But in *Naḥalat Shiv'ah*, R. Shmuel ben David Moshe] explains that those [who bear the name "Bunim"] who are [also] called "Simcha" are in the minority. Most Bunims have as their *shem kodesh*

---

[151] I was alerted to this reference by Davidson (n.d.). Many thanks to Rabbi Davidson for helping me track down the original source and informing me of the further passage from the *Bet Shmu'el* that I discuss below.

[152] Shraga Faivish was a name much loved by Evnine's father, a humorous-sounding 'old-fashioned' Jewish name. Given this, it is hard to imagine that the artist didn't consider using it as Batman's Jewish name. It would have illustrated some of the issues around the contrast between a *shem kodesh* and a *kinuy* much as Simcha Bunim does. "Shraga Faivish" is treated as a unit, as part of the *Bet Shmu'el*'s Jewish name. "Shraga" is the Aramaic for illumination. "Faivish," however, is derived from the *Greek* name "Phoebus," the name of the sun god.

[153] [Editor's note:] The *Bet Shmu'el* doesn't say how, exactly, but presumably by familiar contraction.

[154] [Editor's note:] "And it came to pass, as her [Rachel's] soul was in departing, (for she died) that she called his name Benoni: but his father called him Benjamin" (*Genesis* 35,18, KJV).

"Benjamin." So there is no need to write "Bunim" as we go with the more common case.

(The reasoning is that those whose *shem kodesh* is "Benjamin" but who are called "Bunim," i.e., the majority of Bunims, don't fall under the previously cited precept that where *kinuy* and *shem kodesh* are different, we must write the *kinuy* too. This is because, as we saw, the *Bet Shmu'el* takes "Bunim" to derive from "Benjamin" and hence, evidently, not to be a different name.)

This passage is interesting from multiple points of view. First, we learn from it that "Bunim," at least in the author's environment, was not frequently conjoined with "Simcha." Yet the association was already established enough that he anticipates an objection based on it. Secondly, in the compound "Simcha Bunim," the author treats "Simcha" as a *shem kodesh* and "Bunim" as a *kinuy*. Yet nowadays the combination itself is likely to function as a *shem kodesh* and people be called up to read from the Torah by the two names together (as happens with many Hebrew-Yiddish combination names such as "Menaḥem Mendel"). (In the meme, Batman gives the combined form as the answer to the question about his "Jewish name.") Thirdly, there is an issue about what counts as a name's derivation. We saw above that some authorities take the name "Bunim" to come either from "*bon nom*" or "*bon homme*." Let us suppose this is correct. Yet the *Bet Shmu'el* takes it to derive from a quite different source. Even if the *Bet Shmu'el*'s view were false, even if he knew it were false, if people were calling those named "Benjamin" "Bunim," this would indeed justify, for example, not including both "Benjamin" and "Bunim" in a divorce document on the grounds that they are, in *some* sense, the same name. There is thus a logical distinction between a name's deriving from another (a historical fact independent of usage and belief), and a person's deriving that name from another. But there must surely come a time when, after enough people have derived the name A from B, a name, either A itself or one homophonic with and indistinguishable from A, does itself derive from B. Fourthly, the *Bet Shmu'el* believes that "Bunim" is derived from "Benjamin." Yet he still refers to the first as a *kinuy* and the latter as a *shem kodesh*. This indicates that he does not take the distinction as one between a 'holy' name in Hebrew and a 'secular' name from the surrounding language. It seems rather to be a distinction between a formal and an informal name. The translation of "*kinuy*" as "nickname" seems exactly right here. There is no indication that those called "Benjamin," whose nickname (*kinuy*) is "Bunim," have in addition a German or Polish name. The distinction between *shem kodesh* and *kinuy*, for the *Bet Shmu'el*, is not necessarily diasporic, as it is, I believe, in the imagination of most contemporary Western Jews (and as it was, evidently, in the imagination of the artist in composing this meme).

I return, now, to the comment made by Susanne Shavelson in the archival material referred to at the outset that, in changing the Romanization of the meme's text in line with a widely-accepted standard, she was giving it a "Lithuanian slant." I have discussed, in the Introduction and elsewhere, how these memes provide the backdrop for an extended, practical meditation on the relation of speech to writing. Each meme is a picture, an image, that includes, as a pictorial element, a representation of a written text. This, in turn, by its location in a speech bubble, functions as a representation of an imaginary act of speaking. There is thus ample room, richly mined by the artist, for play around the relations of speech, writing, and image.

This meme is a dramatic instance of that, though its play will be almost entirely concealed without some knowledge of the issues surrounding the orthography and Romanization of Yiddish.

Figure 16 Map of central Europe (public domain)

The origins of Yiddish are disputed. In a previous generation, the prominent Yiddish linguist Max Weinreich cautioned us against seeing Yiddish as "the German language plus some additives... Yiddish... is a fusion language" (1967: 2209) with input from Western and Southern Laaz[155] (medieval Judeo-French and Judeo-Italian spoken by the ancestors of those who moved into Ashkenaz – Germany and Northern France), Slavic (after the eastward shift of the Jews began in the 13th century), and, most prominently, the medieval low German of its initial geographical environment and the Hebrew/Aramaic used by Jews continuously in religious contexts. Recent opinion, for example that of Alexander Beider (2015), identifies Yiddish (or rather its main dialects) with one or another dialect of German, plus some additives, just the view Weinrich urged us to reject. Whatever its origins, it eventually came to encompass two variants (each with many subvariants): Western Yiddish, spoken in Ashkenaz (Germany and Northern France) and Eastern Yiddish, spoken in what is now Central and Eastern Europe. By the 19th century, Western Yiddish was dying out as a result of increasing assimilation and Eastern Yiddish was becoming the main form of living Yiddish. This, in turn, comes in three main dialect variants: Northeastern (Lithuanian), Central (Polish), and Southeastern (Ukrainian), the latter two forming a southern counterpoint to the northern Lithuanian dialect. Starting in the second half of the 18th century, Jewish proponents of the Enlightenment began to stigmatize Yiddish as merely a debased form of German that kept its native speakers from accessing European high culture. The image of Yiddish as a comic, backward, folksy language began to take shape, in contrast to dominant European languages, on the one hand, and Hebrew, on the other – an image that even many subsequent supporters of Yiddish have been

---

[155] "Laaz" is a rich and complex word but in one of its uses, it signifies Jewish languages built on Romance foundations.

happy to accept.[156,157,158] From its beginnings, Yiddish was written as well as spoken and, like Jewish languages in general, written in Hebrew characters. For most of its history, this was

[156] It is a very vexed question whether the artist is himself guilty of relying on this comic image of Yiddish here in M.72. David L. Gold gives the text of a Yiddish story about indigenous Americans (see the following footnote for more about this) and identifies a phenomenon in which 'declining' languages like Yiddish become "ludic languages, that is, languages used largely for jocular purposes, often only for low comedy and vulgar humor" (Gold 1983: 113). (He presents no evidence for this phenomenon with respect to languages other than Yiddish and it would be most interesting to know if his claim is borne out in such cases. One would need to distinguish between different venues for the humor, too – in-group ones and out-group ones. That surely makes some difference to whether the phenomenon is offensive or not.) One *is* tempted to say that there is something funny about seeing Batman and Robin, of all people, speaking in Yiddish. To which Gold might object that if we can have, as we do, a Yiddish Homer, Shakespeare, Milton, Spinoza, Dickens, Marx, Whitman, Dickinson, Gilbert and Sullivan, Freud, and Einstein (to name just a few), without humor (or more humor than found in the originals), then why not a Batman meme in which there is no extra humor deriving from the fact that the meme is in Yiddish? On the other hand, the humor here might be at the expense of Batman and Robin who, as wealthy establishment Wasps, are heirs to a tradition that has been haunted for centuries by the figure of the Yiddish-speaking European Jew. The meme might, then, be analogous to parodying a misogynist man by representing him as (or by) a woman, not because there is something inherently "ludic" about women but because it plays on the insecurities of the man so portrayed. To complicate matters further, in the case of this meme, the text is humorous for the fact that it presents Batman and Robin not just as *speaking Yiddish*, but as *being Jewish* (see also *You don't look Jewish* (M.18) for a similar gesture). This humor is, notionally, quite independent of the language of the meme. That said, of course, it is obviously reinforced by having the meme in a Jewish language, in this case Yiddish. (Indeed, it would be reinforced less by having the meme, say, in contemporary Israeli Hebrew since that is now the language of a nation-state that has deformed the inheritance of Judaism by forcing it into a highly uncongenial form.) Gold is definitely right to focus our attention on how the choice of language, as such, may play a role in attempting (possibly offensively) to elicit a laugh. But the interplay between the content of the meme and the language that content is delivered in is far from simple in this instance. (This is not the only place where the artist may risk being offensive.)

[157] In the previous footnote, I mentioned a paper by David L. Gold, the title of which is "A Story about Pocahontas, Geronimo, and Sitting Bull in Yiddish" (1983). The story is an instance of the "ludic" use of Yiddish that Gold is bothered by. It involves a father "dzheronevits" (Geronimo), a mother "pokeyente" (Pocahontas), their daughter "mine-horevits" (Minnehaha), along with "siting-bulvan" (Sitting Bull), and "meshugn-ferd" (Crazy Horse). Two indigenous tribes are mentioned: "shvarts-fusike" (Blackfeet) and "shmohoker" (Mohawks). Gold calls these names "Yiddishizations" or "partial Yiddishizations." (Of course, what they are (partial) Yiddishizations of are probably not the original names in indigenous languages but the Anglicizations (or possibly, depending on the story's origins, the Russifications, or Polifications, or Germanifications) of those originals. The Yiddishizations work both by translation ("meshugn-ferd" for "Crazy Horse") and assonance ("dzheronevits" for "Geronimo"), two relations, as we have seen, that often relate a *kinuy* to a *shem kodesh*.) Gold says the story is *about* Pocahontas, Geronimo, and Sitting Bull. But Pocahontas and Geronimo were not married, lived in different centuries, thousands of miles from each other, and did not have Minnehaha (a fictional character) as a daughter! Does the story really say *of them* that they were and did? Other than being indigenous Americans, there is no resemblance at all between the characters in the story and the people Gold says the story is about. Robin Jeshion (2002) has emphasized the way in which proper names, as such, can enable thought and talk *about* their bearers (*de re* thought and talk, to use the philosophical jargon), regardless of which features those bearers are represented as having or not having. (See the commentary on *Who knows two?* (M.29) for an account of Jeshion's views on this matter.) Jeshion draws on Saul Kripke's seminal work (1980) according to which names are generally bestowed on things in acts of naming and then

passed along through historical chains that allow later people to refer to the original bearers of the name despite possibly having no direct access to them. Gold's claim that the Yiddish story in question is about Pocahontas, etc., is a good case study. For while, we may suppose, there were historical links between the Yiddish names in the story and the original names of the people referred to by Gold in his title, the story itself does not use those bestowed names but rather names that *might* be considered to be *different*, though resembling, names. Gold's claim about the story's subject matter shows that a view like Jeshion's really must work hand in hand with an account of the identity of names. When are two variants considered forms of the same name (and hence both giving access to *de re* thought about the same bearer) and when of different names? And conversely, reflection on the philosophy of proper names shows that a claim like that in Gold's title must really be offered only with great caution. It is not at all uncontroversial to say that the story in question is *about* Pocahontas, Geronimo, and Sitting Bull.

[158] In the previous footnote, I brought to bear Kripke's views on proper names on a claim made by David Gold in the title of his 1983 paper. As it happens, the artist himself, in a blog post, brought to bear David Gold's complaints about the use of Yiddish as a ludic language, discussed two footnotes above, on Kripke's 1980 book *Naming and Necessity*. I quote:

> What kind of relation is like identity but holds between a thing and itself (rather than between necessarily co-referring names, for example) *by stipulation*? Why, shmidentity, of course! The term "shmidentity" (actually "schmidentity," but see infra on the spelling) was introduced by Saul Kripke in *Naming and Necessity* and, following his example, the "sh-" or "shm-" prefix is now often used in philosophy for properties or relations that resemble other properties or relations but have some feature that may be controversial in the case of the prototypes built in by stipulation.
>
> The linguist David L. Gold, in a paper in the *Jewish Language Review* (volume 3, 1983), entitled "A Story about Pocahontas, Geronimo, and Sitting Bull in Yiddish," refers to the fact that languages in decline (such as Yiddish) often become "ludic languages, that is, languages used largely for jocular purposes, often only for low comedy and vulgar humor" (113). Having made this claim he cites, without quoting, a responsum by him to a reader's query in an earlier issue of the journal which I here excerpt:
>
>> Since Yiddish word-initial /š/ + consonant sounds "funny" to a sizable number of English ears, any Yiddish word containing it is automatically recategorized [as humorous] when entering English (e.g. *shmir*). Perhaps the fact that initial /šm/ is a pejorizer in Yiddish and EAE [Eastern Ashkenazic English]... has contributed to this feeling among English-speakers. (1982: 302)
>
> The use of the term "shmidentity," therefore (and similar neologisms in the philosophy literature) is culturally insensitive, appealing to the 'funny'-sounding phonemes of a language that translated Freud, Einstein, Shakespeare, and Emily Dickinson, among countless others, for a quick laugh now that that language has fallen on hard times and is forced to wear the fool's motley. I recommend this usage be avoided in philosophy henceforth.
>
> As for the spelling, "schmidentity" (the form used by Kripke himself) reflects the efforts of those who have sought to cast Yiddish as low German and transcribe it into Latin characters on the model of German spelling. It is, therefore, another blow to the dignity of Yiddish. Standard Yiddish Orthography romanizes /š/ as "sh." If one must, therefore, continue to use this offensive neologism, I recommend that at least the spelling "shmidentity" be given.

done according to orthographic principles that, like those governing English, were not consistent and uniform. But, more or less in step with the surrounding European communities, the encroachments of modernity (nationalism, increasing print publication, participation in international scholarship, the press, organized educational projects, etc.) led to a desire for systematicity. And like other languages subject to regional variation, the question of Yiddish orthography and its interaction with variations in pronunciation has been problematic.[159] These problems have been amplified by the stateless position of the Jews in the Yiddish homelands, the political vicissitudes to which they were subject by a variety of states, and the ideologies through which they met those vicissitudes (religious Orthodoxy, Yiddish nationalism, Zionism, International Socialism).

There are two directions in which one can be pulled in introducing or regularizing an orthographic system for a language spoken in different ways (e.g. with different accents, class inflections, and so on). One goal is a uniform system of written representations (words or sentences). With an alphabetic writing system, that means a uniform system of spelling, where the common graphic representations may be pronounced differently by different speakers (e.g. Londoners and Glaswegians). At the limit, one could have a writing system pronounced in entirely disanalogous ways by different speakers. That, I believe, is the situation with Chinese writing and it is certainly the case with non-linguistic written codes such as mathematics. A mathematical formula will be read out loud in English and Hebrew in ways that have only coincidental phonetic similarities. Going in the opposite direction, one might think about employing a stock of written symbols that have fixed pronunciations. Those in London and Glasgow would pronounce letters in exactly the same way. Consequently, they would write down (i.e. spell) London or Glaswegian spoken words differently, even when the words spoken were, by semantic and syntactic standards, the same. This is how something like the International Phonetic Alphabet works. Such a system would be entirely inappropriate for autonomous writing – writing that is not a record of or direction for speech. Think of a novelist writing with the phonetic alphabet. A narrator, even one not appearing in the work, would have to be given an 'identity' since the words "It was a dark and stormy night..." would have to be written to sound in a determinate way: as spoken by a Londoner or a Glaswegian, of this or that class. (But think how much more appropriate the phonetic approach would be for writing the words *spoken* by characters – in the speech bubbles of our meme, for example! See the artist's use of the International Phonetic Alphabet in *Cicero**!* (M.56)). In fact, familiar alphabetic writing systems mostly fall in between the two extremes. They accord a certain autonomy to the written. An author does not have to write a novel in a way that forces it to be English or Scottish. But they are not entirely non-phonetic and speech variations can be, and sometimes are, indicated by variations in spelling (as when authors seek to reproduce the sound of the words spoken in dialect by characters). Words from other languages can be written in the

---

[159] See Gold (1977) for a comprehensive overview of efforts at systemization in orthography. And see Romaine (2011) for a wonderful, if heartbreaking, treatment of systemization in the context of language revitalization.

Roman (or Hebrew) alphabet, relying on, if not a precise phonetic value for each letter, at least a range of permissible values that will enable one to approximate, more or less, the sounds of unfamiliar words, as spoken by their native speakers, through their written representations.

Coming specifically to the case of Yiddish, we must keep in mind that the situation was one of standardizing on-going orthographic practices over a range of different pronunciations. Although it was hoped to make a standard orthography that was dialect-neutral, in practice some people's practices and pronunciations would be better suited to a given standard than others. The Lithuanian dialect had changed less, with respect to vowels, than the southern dialects and so was considered 'purer.' As a result, Lithuanian Yiddish enjoyed a "near-perfect one-to-one correspondence of letter and sound" (Katz 1998: 190). A standard orthography (and pronunciation) based on Lithuanian Yiddish, i.e., a linguistically more conservative standard with respect to phoneme-grapheme correspondence, was taken up and promoted by YIVO, the *yidisher visnshaftlekher institut* (Jewish/Yiddish Scientific Institute; now known as the *YIVO Institute for Jewish Research*) founded in 1925 to promote Yiddish culture. This is now known as Standard Yiddish Orthography (though in fact it is not standard).

All of these issues are recapitulated (though as Gold (1977: 330) points out, with much less passion) when we turn to Romanization. Here we introduce another set of letters, with their more or less constrained phonetic values, into service of writing that will be pronounced in ways like, or unlike, one or another dialect of Yiddish. Actually, Romanization is a tricky concept altogether. Since the letters of the Roman alphabet, *per se*, do not have fixed, but only constrained, phonetic values (think of the ways the same letter can be pronounced differently in English, French, Italian, Polish, and so on), we again face two choices – between uniform Romanizations of Yiddish that will be pronounced differently by English and Italian speakers, or developing Romanization systems not for an alphabet alone but for an alphabet and a language (or an alphabet, language, region, social class...) – thus, schemes for Romanizing into English, into Italian, etc.[160] All these issues were discussed in the period after the great debates about orthography, and there are several different systems in use for Romanization.[161] One of these was proposed by YIVO which, again, is thought to have a Lithuanian slant to it. This is the scheme used by Shavelson in her initial revision of the text produced by Google Translate. Hence, finally, we are in a position to understand what is meant by saying that she was giving the text a "Lithuanian slant."

The question of the Lithuanian slant, however, is not fully captured by these purely linguistic matters. Jewish Lithuania (*Lita* – which comprises also Belarus, Latvia, and parts of Russia and Poland) was, for several hundred years, home to one of the most intellectually

---

[160] Gold (1977: 357, fn. 73) briefly alludes to discussions of this issue: "Some discussants spoke of 'transcription in English' (i.e. a national Romanization for English-speaking countries or perhaps only for the United States), but A. A. Roback wanted the Romanization to be international if possible." It is unclear to me how any such scheme could be international, unless it relied on people's antecedent knowledge of how the language was supposed to sound.

[161] See Weinberg (1995), written from the very practical point of view of a library cataloguer!

vigorous religious and secular traditions in the history of the Jews – "a place of Torah, the likes of which were unknown in the history of the Jewish Diaspora with the exception of ancient Mesopotamia" (Samuel Mirsky, quoted in Schochet (1998: 207)). In the 18th century, it was home to the Vilna Gaon, Eliyahu ben Shlomo Zalman (1720-97), one of the most important figures in Jewish religious history.[162] The Vilna Gaon was the most significant of the opponents (*mitnagdim*) of the burgeoning Hasidic movement, the center of gravity of which was further south, in Poland and Ukraine. His intellectual rigor and the importance he placed on study stood in opposition to the high premium Hasidism placed on emotional and ecstatic prayer-based religious experiences. Followers in his footsteps established through *Lita* a number of the most important yeshivas (religious academies) since the academies of Sura and Pumbedita in Mesopotamia in the second half of the first millennium, pre-eminent amongst them, the yeshiva of Volozhin (see Stampfer 2012). In the 19th century, Vilna was home to an important part of the Jewish Enlightenment movement and secular scholarly studies were strong there. (The Vilna Gaon himself was well-versed in languages and mathematics and stressed the need for study in these subjects.) When YIVO was formed, in the 1920s, its headquarters were to be in Berlin. But it became apparent very quickly that Vilna was a much better choice and that is where the institute was located until it moved to New York in 1940.[163] Associated with these impressive achievements, a certain character type came to occupy a place in the Jewish imagination: the Litvak (Jew from *Lita*). The Litvak is characterized by

> rationality and intellectuality, love and breadth of learning, intellectual discipline and independence, reticence and emotional restraint, modesty and privacy, ethical sensitivity and moral discipline. (Schochet 1998: 207)[164]

Thus, when we talk about the Lithuanian slant to Standard Yiddish Orthography (and pronunciation and Romanization), we must understand it against the background of a culture in which the Litvak element was both admired and resented. The Litvaks included only a minority of Yiddish speakers but saw themselves as an intellectual elite with a distinguished history. To others, however, they may have appeared haughty and cold, eschewing emotionality in favor of the life of the mind, whether in religious or secular guise. Cultural and religious divisions between, say, Hasidism and its opponents get mapped onto linguistic differences between the southern dialects of Yiddish and the northern, Lithuanian dialect. (Needless to say, these mappings are not precise or exceptionless.)

The artist is heir to the Litvak tradition. We know that he grew up hearing about the contrast between Litvaks and Galitzianers (a term for Jews from the more southern province of Galicia,

---

[162] For the link between the prestige of the Gaon and the prestige of Lithuanian Yiddish, see Katz (1998).

[163] Kuznitz (2014: *passim*, and 112ff.) for the vacillations between Berlin and Vilna.

[164] Stressing the Litvak's need to be convinced by empirical evidence, Schochet, later in his article, compares him to "a man from Missouri" (214)! This seems to me altogether a discordant note relative to the description given in text.

in Poland/Ukraine), learning about the notorious Litvak "ey"[165], without really understanding what any of it meant. He is related, on his father's side, to several Litvak rabbis at least one of whom attended the yeshiva of Volozhin. (I provide a bibliography of the religious writings of these paternal relatives at the end of this commentary.) Finally, all who know him will agree how well the stereotype of the Litvak personality quoted above captures him.

We may conclude by returning to the original meme to say something about how it plays with the relations between image, speech, and writing. The meme is a picture that represents a situation in which two people are speaking with each other. They are speaking Yiddish. What do they sound like? We cannot say, of course. Are they speaking with their wholesome American accents? Should we imagine the voices of Adam West and Burt Ward in the 1960s TV show stumbling over these unfamiliar words in another language? Do they pronounce the "r"s in the usual, rounded American way (in Yiddish, the so-called *kanadisher reysh*, or Canadian "r")?[166] Or do Batman and Robin suddenly sound like two native Yiddish speakers? And if they do, what kind of Yiddish? Are they using Lithuanian pronunciation? Standard Yiddish Pronunciation (close to Lithuanian)? Or should we imagine their speech as better represented by the following version of the text, informally rendered so as to suggest a Polish Yiddish:

> Robin: Vus iz ayer yidisher numen, Batman?
> Batman: Rif mikh *Reb* Batman, Boytshik Vinder! In maan yidisher numen iz Simkhe Binem.[167]

In any case, the text in the speech bubbles that represents Batman's and Robin's Yiddish speech does so with Roman letters. There is thus a missing, purely hypothetical visual element, intermediate between the meme as we have it and the spoken situation it depicts, which represents their speech in Hebrew characters. What would this look like? It might use the Standard Yiddish Orthography, with its Lithuanian slant, or one of the other varieties advocated, such as the 'Orthodox' system of Solomon Birnbaum (1891-1989), more closely associated with Central or Southeastern Yiddish. How should the choice of orthography here relate to the phonic qualities of the depicted speech? Further, an issue of particular interest would arise in this hypothetical visual element, namely, the rendering of the name "Simcha Bunim" (specifically, the rendering of its first component). One of the main issues facing orthographers of Yiddish was how to deal with words of Hebrew (or Aramaic) origin. These words were represented by Hebrew letters long before those letters were put to work representing words of Germanic and other origins. The use of those letters, therefore, was not always consistent with the conventions that developed specifically for the parts of the language derived from non-Hebrew sources, such as German. Orthographers therefore faced a choice.

---

[165] To rhyme with "day," the main respect in which the vowels of Lithuanian Yiddish were not pure, so that a Litvak would pronounce the word "*torah*" as "*teyrah*" and the Galitzianer as "*toyrah*."

[166] For reasons that I think are not entirely understood, Yiddish schools in Canada did not correct the North American "r" in their students in the way that Yiddish schools in the United States did. Thanks to David Roskies, himself a native Yiddish speaker from Canada, for confirming this fascinating fact.

[167] Many thanks to Leyzer Burko for the rendition.

They could leave alone the traditional spellings of words of Hebrew origin, so that they looked like the Hebrew words they were (or came from), but at the cost of an orthographic system that worked one way for words of one origin and a different way for words of another. Or they could use a single set of orthographic conventions and bring into line the spelling of the words of Hebrew origin with the spelling of words of German origin. The cost, in this case, is that 'one and the same' word will be spelled differently in Yiddish and Hebrew. The so-called Soviet Yiddish orthographic system, employed with some state support in the Soviet Union, opted for the latter – consistency at the expense of tradition; Standard Yiddish Orthography and Birnbaum's 'Orthodox' approach went with the former – tradition at the expense of consistency. In the meme, the name "Simcha" well illustrates the issue. In Standard Yiddish Orthography it would be written שׂמחה (which is how the Hebrew word for "joy" is spelled in Hebrew) while in the Soviet system it would be סימכע. Even without a knowledge of the Hebrew alphabet, one can see that there is only one letter in common, the letter that represents the sound /m/.

Finally, we come to the meme as we have it, in which the text is in Roman characters. All the issues about what Batman and Robin are supposed to sound like still exist, but now arise at one further remove. We are dealing with a visual representation of a visual, but merely implicit or hypothetical object, which itself represents the spoken scene depicted. Despite the visual differences between the actual meme and the hypothetical missing link, they depict the same scene. The means of depiction, as they relate to the speech involved, are different. And in a sense, we can go straight from the actual meme to the depicted speech (just as we could if the speech in an English-language meme were represented, say, by the International Phonetic Alphabet, rather than by ordinarily-spelled English); and yet the representation of speech by one or another writing system is itself loaded with meaning. (We have seen the significance of the 'Lithuanian slant.')

If the text in the actual meme is a Romanization, of which implicit written text is it a representation? Does the YIVO-inspired system of Romanization that Shavelson used imply (or require?) that the missing visual element itself uses Standard Yiddish Orthography? That it includes "שׂמחה" rather than "סימכע," for example? With respect to the name, in any case, the artist has deliberately denied us any clue, for he has in fact opted to Romanize Batman's 'Jewish name' as if he were Romanizing Hebrew, not Yiddish.[168] The Romanization from Yiddish of Batman's combined name would be "simkhe-bunim," with a hyphen, no capitals, and "khe" rather than "cha." "Simcha" is, rather, a traditional and familiar rendering in English of a *Hebrew* name. In the choice between "Simcha Bunim" and "simkhe-bunim," therefore, the artist faced the same kind of choice faced by Yiddish orthographers that I described in the previous paragraph, the choice between tradition and consistency. And he opted for tradition at the cost of consistency.

[168] Though not, be it said, according to the same system of transliteration that I have generally employed in this book. According to the system I use here, the name should be rendered in Roman letters as Simḥah. I have preserved Evnine's choice of Romanization for that name throughout this commentary, however.

Appendix: Bibliography of Religious Works by the Artist's Paternal Ancestors

Note on onomastics: The artist's name is "Evnine." The name exists in several forms among his extended family. Relatives in Israel bore (and bear) the name Yevnin (יבנין), some by secondary reversion from "Evnine" (including the artist's father and brother) and some directly from the name in its old-world form. Why this variation? Family legend had it that the name, in its Anglicized form, lost its original initial "y" sound because if the name were written in Cyrillic, the first letter would be "Е" (pronounced "ye"; as opposed to Э, which is pronounced "e") and this must have been mistaken, by impatient immigration officials, for the English "E." In fact, this story is almost certainly mistaken. First, members of the family came on three independent occasions from Russian-speaking to English-speaking locations and in all cases ended up with an Anglicized version of the name beginning with "E" not "Y." Although not impossible, it is unlikely that the origins story of the name given above played out on three independent occasions. The artist's great-great-great-uncle Bezalel came to the US in 1880 and became "Ewnin." His great-uncle Oscar came to the US in the 1920s and became "Evnin." And his grandfather went to the UK in the 1920s and became "Evnine." But even more tellingly, on the title pages of several of the works below, the name is spelled in Cyrillic characters and appears there as "ЭВНИН," *not* as "ЕВНИН." Thus, in the Cyrillic spelling itself there is no initial "y" sound. On the other, the name of the artist's ancestor was spelled "Jewnin" in the *Jewish Encyclopedia* (1904), which gives the German orthography for "Yevnin" and the name appears in some publications with the Yiddish spelling יעוונין, also pronounced "Yevnin."

The truth of the matter, according to Beider (2008: 347 and 450), is that both forms of the name, "ЭВНИН" (Evnin) and "ЕВНИН" (Yevnin), were to be found in Eastern Europe. The latter was prevalent in a number of areas (Belostok, Grodno, Novgrudo, Bobrujsk, and Kiev) while the former was found only in one of these areas (Belostok) and should be regarded as a corruption of the more prevalent spelling, its authenticity attested to by its etymology (see the next paragraph) as well as its greater prevalence. (In fact, Evnine's ancestors were connected with Grodno and so the corrupted spelling was found there as well as in nearby Belostok.) It appears that there was a certain freedom in which form of the name was used, perhaps varying by individual, context, and alphabet.

The name "Yevnin" itself, "in Eastern Slavic languages, means 'of Yevna' (i.e. son of Yevna), where Yevna was a common male given name in Lithuania and Belorussia, the Slavonized form of Yevne, one of the Lithuanian Yiddish phonetic variants of biblical Jonah" (Beider, personal communication; the material is presented in his 2001: 454-5). Thus the artist's middle name Jonah, taken immediately from his grandfather, who must have gotten it from *his* grandfather Abraham Jonah, is deeply connected with his name and ancestry in *Lita*.

A) Abraham Jonah (Avraham Yonah, son of Isaiah), 1813-1848 (Grodno).[169]

---

[169] According to his tombstone, he died on December 6th. This is the day of the year on which his namesake, the artist of the memes, was born.

A1) Glosses on Maimonides's *Sefer HaMitzvot*, published in *Maḥshevet Moshe* (Vilna, 1866), an edition of part of Maimonides's *Sefer HaMitzvot*, with commentaries and glosses by various authors. The book is named for the principal commentary, *Maḥshevet Moshe*, by Moshe ben Gershon Mendil. The glosses by Abraham Jonah, published posthumously, are introduced by his son Samuel.

A2) *Nimuqe Maharay* (Maharay is an acronym that stands for Morenu HaRav [our teacher the rabbi] Rabbi Avraham Yonah) on Maimonides's *Mishneh Torah* (Warsaw, 1882).[170]

B) Samuel (Shmu'el, son of Abraham Jonah), 1830-? (Grodno).[171]

B1) *Divre Ḥefetz* (Odessa, 1872). Comments on selected parts of the Pentateuch. Samuel says they are taken from, or inspired by, Elkhanan Spektor, Yosef Dov HaLevi Soloveitchik, and Zvi Leib Berlin (the *Netziv*), all renowned Torah scholars. The last was head of yeshiva at Volozhin for much of the second half of the 19th century, probably while Samuel was a student there.

B2) *Imre Shmu'el*. Commentary on a posthumous publication of sayings by the Vilna Gaon, *Se'arat Eliyahu* (Warsaw, 1877, Vinograd 1360; Vilna, 1889, Vinograd 1361; Vilna 1894, Vinograd 1362). Published as part of a collection of three works by the Vilna Gaon, *Sifre Hagra* (Jerusalem, 1983).

B3) *Naḥalat Olamim* (Warsaw, 1882). A collection of epitaphs from the Jewish cemetery in Warsaw.

---

[170] Jay M. Harris mentions, as one of the prominent innovations in religious study associated with Lithuania in the 19th century, "the 'rediscovery' of Maimonides' comprehensive law code, the *Mishneh Torah*... [which] most closely corresponds to the intellectual ideals of this elite, precisely because of its encyclopedic character... In the commitment to the study of Maimonides we find yet again a reflection of the Gaon's commitment to study the totality of the rabbinic tradition" (1998: 94).

[171] The birth dates, and even the birth order, of Abraham Jonah's two eldest sons, Samuel and Nathan Neta, are perplexing. Eisenstadt (1900) gives the dates and order as follows: Nathan Neta 1838 and Samuel 1839. *The Jewish Encyclopedia* (1904), however, records that Samuel was born in 1830 and Nathan Neta in 1835. Samuel, in his notes in A1, refers to his younger brother "Neta" so the *Jewish Encyclopedia* is surely to be preferred.

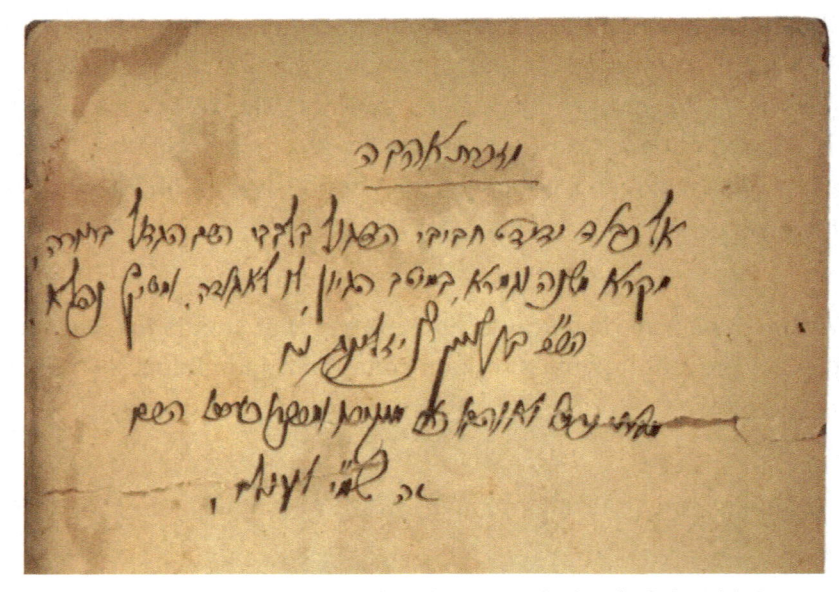

Figure 17 An inscription in a copy of Naḥalat Olamim *in the hand of Shmu'el Yevnin, to Rabbi Benjamin Schlesinger. Inscription transcribed and translated by Gedalyahu Wittow. Image courtesy of Kestenbaum & Company Auction House*

מזכרת אהבה
אל כבוד ידידי חביבי הדגול בלבבו הרב הגדול בתורה,
מקרא, משנה וגמרא, במיטב הגיון, לו לאגדה, ובשטף נפלא
הר"ר בנימין שליזנגר נ"י
מאיתי מחבבו ואוהבו כאח מוקירו ומכבדו כערכו הרם
זה שמ"י לעולם

A memento of love

To my honorable dear friend, a great-hearted Rabbi and giant of Torah

Bible, Mishnah, and Gemara, of legendary and excellent clarity and wonderful eloquence

Rabbi Benjamin Schlesinger, may his light shine,

From me, one who loves him like a brother, who cherishes him and honors him in keeping with his lofty worth

"This [Shmu'el Yevnin] is 'my name' forever."[172]

---

[172] See the footnote to the last line of the following inscription.

B4) *Imre Shmu'el*. [Same title, but different work from B2.] Commentary on a book recounting the deeds of the Vilna Gaon by his son, *Ma'aseh Rav* (Vilna 1887 Vinograd 816; Vilna 1888 (reprint of 1887) Vinograd 817). Published as part of a collection of three works by the Vilna Gaon, *Sifre Hagra* (Jerusalem, 1983).

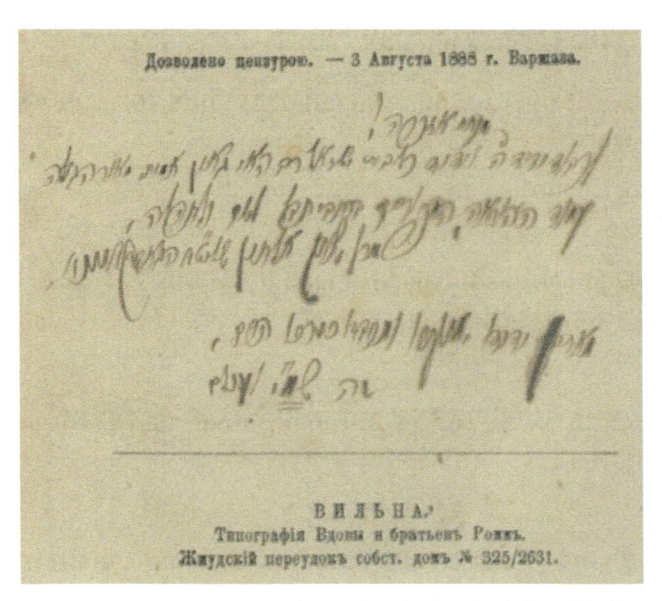

Figure 18 An inscription on a copy of Ma'aseh Rav *in the hand of Shmu'el Yevnin, to R. Yitzkhak Elkhanan Spektor (1817-1896), one of the titans of 19th century Lithuanian Jewry. Inscription transcribed and translated by Israel Sandman. Image courtesy of Kedem Auction House*

מנחת אזכרה!

לכבוד ידיד ה' וידיד כל בית ישראל רב האי גאון אמיתי מאור הגולה

עמוד ההוראה המפורסם ברחבי תבל לשם ולתהלה

מרן יצחק אלחנן שליט"א הגאבד"ק וענו',

מאת בן ידידו, מוקירו ומכבדו כערכו הרם,

זה שמ"י לעולם

A memento[173]

For the honor of the one who is precious to God and precious to all the House of Israel, this true rabbi and Gaon, light of the Diaspora

Pillar of legal decisions, whose reputation and praise are renowned throughout the breadth of the earth

Our master Isaac Elhanan, may he live for long, good days, amen, Gaon and head of the holy court of law, yet humble

From the son of his dear friend, who cherishes him and honors him in keeping with his lofty worth

"This [Shmu'el Yevnin] is 'my name' forever."[174]

B5) *Shem MiShmu'el*. Listed by Eisenstadt (1900: 22) as a manuscript. No further bibliographic record found.[175]

C) Nathan Neta (Natan Net'a, son of Abraham Jonah and great-great-grandfather of the artist), 1835 (Grodno)-1914.

C1) *Nit'ey Or*, 2 vols. (Vilna, 1900). Essays on Talmudic matters. As is often the case in rabbinic works, the title plays on the author's name. "*Net'a*" means "seedling" and the title of the book is "Seedlings of Light." After his own name, there remain four letters in the book's title, a yod from the end of *nit'ey* and the

---

[173] [Translator's note:] This dedication contains a rhyme scheme, explicated below, indicated by its layout. Lines one and two both end with the sound "_la." My reading of the end of line three, the middle line, is speculative, but it is buttressed by positing an internal rhyme: words two and three of the first half of this line end with "_aq" and "_an," respectively; so I sought and seemingly found these same endings on words two and three of the second half of this line. Lines four and five both end with the "_am" sound. Also, much of line four contains layers of internal rhyme: "_do"; "(_ro)_do"; ("_rko").

[174] [Translator's note:] This line, in which the author alludes to his name, is a quote from *Exodus* 3:15 and it contains multiple puns: [1] the Hebrew word for "my name," *shemi* / שמי, is written here accompanied by double underlining and acrostic marks, calling attention to the fact that it is an acrostic of the author's name; and [2] the word "forever" renders the Hebrew *le'olam* / לעולם, on which Rashi comments that the spelling in the Torah implies the reading *le'alem* / לעלם, meaning "to hide" – which is what the author does, only alluding to his name but not making it explicit.

[175] In the *Mishnah (Shabbat* 12.3), it is asserted that one is liable for having violated the prohibition against writing on the Sabbath not just if one writes a whole word, but if one writes even two letters, since two letters might make a little word within a bigger word. For example, if one were writing the name "Shmu'el" – the rabbis use this very example, along with "Shimon," coincidentally part of the *shem kodesh* of the artist – but only got as far as the first two letters, one would still have written an entire word, "*shem*" (name). Perhaps Shmu'el Yevnin's work *Shem MiShmu'el* (*The* Shem *(Name) from Shmu'el*) was a commentary on this part of the *Mishnah*, to which he was no doubt attracted owing to his evident delight in wordplay around his name. See the inscriptions discussed in the text.

aleph, vav, and resh that make up the word *or*. The aleph, he tells us, is the first letter of his father's name (Abraham) and the resh, the first letter of his mother's name, Rebecca Rayna, joined by the vav that can mean "and" – thus the word for light signifies "Abraham-and-Rebecca-Rayna" (he writes this all as one word). The yod stands for his father's second name, Jonah, and is the middle of his mother's second name, Rayna.

C2) *Ner Tamid* (Warsaw, 1914; reprinted Jerusalem 1962). A collection of 20 sermons on Talmudic matters, to which are appended the answers to various questions raised in connection with *Nit'ey Or* (C1).

C3) *Binyan Yerushalayim*. A commentary on the Passover *Haggadah*, published posthumously in an edition of *Haggadah Shel Pesaḥ* (Warsaw 1914) by his son Bezalel. (See the commentary to *Thirteen Holes* (M.30) for some discussion of its contents.)

C4) *Agudat Ezov*. Sermons (*drushim*). This work is listed by Eisenstadt (1900: 22) as a manuscript. No further bibliographic trace found.

D) Bezalel (son of Abraham Jonah), 1840 (Grodno)-1909 (Detroit).

D1) *LeMazkeret* (New York, 1892).

D2) *Hashkem VeDaber* (Part I, Chicago, 1895; Part II Milwaukee, 1903). (In Yiddish, but with an English title-page stating "A complication of experiences, at the earliest of the daily speakable matters of facts, reffering [sic] to the Judaism in America," a polemical work against Reform Judaism and Anarchist Jewish movements).

D3) *The Faithful Portrayal, composed of various revelations upon the climax of an anti-semitic topic, on American soil* (New York, 1907). (In English, concerning the disruptions of the funeral of Rabbi Jacob Joseph allowed by the New York police).

M.74 Politeness is so important

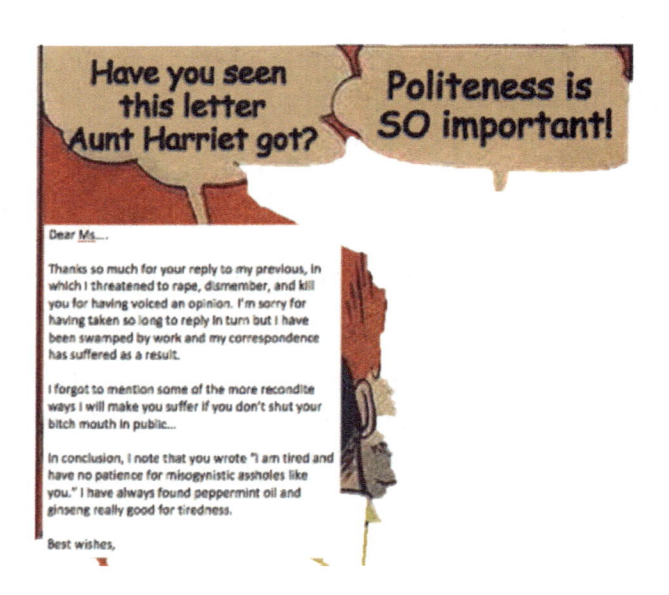

M.74 Politeness is so important Composed: April 10th. Orientation: Reverse. Font: Comic Sans. TB1: "Have you seen this letter Aunt Harriet got?", black. TB2: "Politeness is SO important!", black. Added Image: A letter, obscuring Robin's head and left hand, with the text "Dear Ms..../Thanks so much for your reply to my previous, in which I threatened to rape, dismember, and kill you for having voiced an opinion. I'm sorry for having taken so long to reply in turn but I have been swamped by work and my correspondence has suffered as a result./I forgot to mention some of the more recondite ways I will make you suffer if you don't shut your bitch mouth in public.../In conclusion, I note that you wrote "I am tired and have no patience for misogynistic assholes like you." I have always found peppermint oil and ginseng really good for tiredness./Best wishes,"

This meme involves more text, by far, than any other. As always when there is longer text, but here especially, the limitations imposed by the speech bubbles and by the demands of visibility are acutely felt. In this case, the artist has chosen a radical and (as we shall see) rather interesting approach used nowhere else in the corpus. In one of the alternate versions of *He thought that he thought...* (M.27), a meme which has a fairly lengthy response from Batman, Evnine wrote the text for each of the speech bubbles in a Word document, took screen captures of them, and then inserted the images into the bubbles. (See the commentary on M.27 for further discussion.) In *Politeness is so important*, he seems to have employed the same technique but this time, instead of trying to cram the text into Robin's speech bubble (which would, of course, have clearly rendered it illegible), to represent a scene in which Robin *reports* the contents of the letter received by Aunt Harriet, he has chosen to represent the letter outside any speech bubble.

This decision leaves the total image somewhat hard to decode. What is the scene depicted in it? Not, we have just noted, one in which Robin reports the contents of letter. The text does not appear inside a speech bubble and so does not function to represent an act of speaking. But also not one in which Robin is depicted, say, as *giving* the letter to Batman to read for himself. For the letter is wildly out of proportion. (If it were in proportion, its text would be illegible.) And although the letter covers Robin's otherwise-visible left hand, it is not really put into relation with it. Robin is not depicted as holding the letter, as he is depicted as holding things in *The Language of Flowers* (M.51), *Not What You're Thinking* (M.93), and *The Origins of Neo-Platonist Metaphysics* (M. 96). The letter's placement near the bottom-left corner of the frame seems rather designed simply to leave us an unobstructed view of Batman's face. Somewhat analogous to *Some Idiot* (M.22), the meme deploys a *sui generis* mode of depiction that offers to the viewer the contents of the letter, and represents Robin as transmitting those contents to Batman, while remaining indeterminate about how exactly the transmission occurs. The meme as a whole is no longer to be read as a simple image but as a kind of rebus, with distinct elements between which the viewer has to construct a relation.

This conclusion is borne out by the appearance of the letter itself which is a curious hybrid of a textual and pictorial representation. Its text is disposed in traditional epistolary fashion, with a greeting and a parting salutation of "best wishes." Even without Robin's words, we would immediately identify the object as a letter by its visible appearance. And yet, it is not an *image* of a letter, exactly, since it contains editorial ellipses. The name of the addressee is missing, an absence made especially prominent by the fact that the three dots used to indicate missing text, coming right after the period after "Ms," have rendered the formal title into something that Microsoft Word identifies, by the wavy red line underneath, as a mistake.[176] (Perhaps, for all we know, the artist deliberately failed to put "Ms. Cooper," Aunt Harriet's name, to obtain this effect in order to "heighten the contradictions" implicit in the letter's mode of representation. After all, he does have Robin tell us who the addressee is so why should the name not have appeared here in the letter?) There is a further ellipsis in the second paragraph where, thankfully, we are spared the horror of the letter-writer's violent fantasies. Finally, there is no name at the bottom, though the appearance of "best wishes" clearly suggests one ought to be present. We thus have, in this item, something that is between an image and an editorially-curated quotation. Perhaps an epistolary picture of a quotation, or a pictorial quotation of an epistle. In any case, the unclear status of the letter's representation works synergistically with the *sui generis* mode of representation in the meme as a whole.

Regarding the meme's content, it is one of only two to refer to Robin's aunt, Harriet Cooper. (The other is *#JeSuisRobin* (M.59).) It is essential, of course, to the meme's allusion to the shocking amounts of sexual harassment to which women who express opinions in public are subject that it should find a woman in the world of the Batman story to serve as the letter's addressee. Aunt Harriet is a rare such presence. As for the details of the letter, it seems as if it combines three real incidents in which harassment was mixed with curious politeness (or

---

[176] See the similar phenomenon in the comparable variant of *He thought that he thought...* (M.27).

apparent solicitude), all of which coincidentally came to the attention of the artist around the time he composed this meme. 1) Evnine attended a lecture by Professor Mary Anne Franks at a conference organized by the University of Miami in April 2016 in which the speaker related a story about having replied to a harasser and then receiving a follow-up in which the harasser apologized for the delay in his reply. This is the origin of the letter's first paragraph. 2) Professor Tamsin Shaw related on Facebook a case of having received a harassing letter that was, mystifyingly, signed "Best wishes." This accounts for the letter's final greeting (and perhaps by extension for its polite address, "Dear Ms."). 3) The artist's friend Dane Harris, an English teacher resident in Taiwan, showed him extensive harassing communication from a woman who, responding to Harris's complaints of physical ill-being, suggested he treat himself with hot milk. This has been transformed into the recommendation of ginseng and peppermint oil as a remedy for tiredness in the letter's third paragraph.

This strange combination of harassment and concern is not really addressed by Batman's tone-deaf reply. Batman, in this meme, certainly does not 'sweeten' his own abuse of Robin with any form of 'politeness.' His tone is harsh and glib as he extolls the importance of politeness. In the other meme that alludes to Aunt Harriet, Robin more or less denounces Batman himself as an abuser for his repeated slapping. It is interesting that the artist only seems able to address the abusive pattern of violence he has set in motion through his repeated use of this image in connection with practically the only allusions in the whole corpus to a woman.

This meme will be explained in the accompanying book

Il n'y a pas de hors-texte!

M.77 find this out; but

> Three minutes' thought would suffice to...
>
> Thought is irksome and three minutes is a long time!!!

M.77 find this out; but Composed: April 20th. Orientation: Reverse. Font: Comic Sans. TB1: "Three minutes' thought would suffice to...", black. TB2: "Thought is irksome and three minutes is a long time!!!", black.

This meme uses a well-known quotation from the poet and classicist A.E. Housman: "Three minutes' thought would suffice to find this out; but thought is irksome and three minutes is a long time" (Housman 1905: xi). Although a number of the memes use quotations, only this and two others - *The Medium is the Message* (M.8) and *Seek Simplicity* (M.10) - take a sentence that originally belongs to a single voice and break it up between the two voices of Batman and Robin. In M.8, the effect is to make it seem as if the actual end of the quotation is replacing what Robin would have said if allowed to finish. Here, as in M.10, the effect is quite different because the quotation is itself a conjunction the conjuncts of which are already counterposed to each other and this contraposition is only heightened by the division of the whole into the two adversarial 'slots' provided by the image. (Here in *find this out; but* the two parts are joined by "but"; in *Seek Simplicity* they are joined by "and," but "and" used with the sense of "but.") Thus, although Batman is clearly interrupting Robin, he is not hijacking the conversation to reframe Robin's sentiment. Rather, the rhetorical effect of the entire original quotation is preserved intact.

What is not preserved intact, however, is the text of the original quotation. The artist has extracted part of the original from Batman's and Robin's encounter. Even with this text missing, their dialogue is entirely comprehensible but in fact, the extracted text is not completely absent and shows up as (or in?) the meme's title. The context from which it has been removed, in the meantime, has been slightly altered. Robin's part of the original has had three dots added at its end. Nor, surely, are these the three dots of ellipsis, signaling that some text has gone missing. Their function is to indicate, rather, that Robin's speech has been interrupted. (This function they discharge largely by graphic means. They are like perforations along which the text is torn in two.) Batman's segment of the original has its first letter capitalized. (It also has three exclamation marks not in Housman but that is not relevant to the title-text's immediate surroundings.) Thus, having been extracted, the title-text can fit back properly into its original context at neither end. It is like a jigsaw piece the tabs and blanks of the neighboring pieces of which have been damaged. It has, to all intents and purposes, become an orphan, ripped from a home it can no longer return to.[177]

[177] *find this out; but* is certainly an odd-looking title. Its fragmentary nature, the initial lower-case letter, the incongruous (without context) semi-colon all contribute to this strangeness. But the strangeness helps to highlight an interesting set of issues concerning titles of artworks generally. Jerrold Levinson (1985), restricting himself to authorially-chosen titles, argues that titles of works are proper names of the works they entitle. If so, they are, as Levinson admits, an unusual and distinctive type of proper name, for two reasons. For first, on the plausible assumption that a title is a part of the work it entitles, such a title would be the name of something of which it itself was a part. Usually, of course, a name and that which it names are ontologically distinct. And secondly, titles of artworks have interpretive significance for understanding what they are names of in a way in which ordinary proper names do not. (This requires, and receives from Levinson, some qualification but I shan't dwell on that here.) But if the titles of artworks are proper names of those artworks, a whole range of further issues come into view as well. In the commentary on *Perimeter* (M.79), I shall discuss some recent philosophical issues surrounding names. To anticipate briefly, on the one hand, there are those who take the relation between a name and its bearer to be mediated by some descriptive content associated with the name. On one extreme version of this, a name abbreviates a definite description (e.g. "Walter Scott" abbreviates "the author of *Waverley*") and the name refers to its bearer because the bearer is that which satisfies the description. On the other hand, there is the view that names are bestowed on their bearers directly and refer to them owing to these historical facts, without that link's being mediated by any descriptive content attaching to the name. Against the background of this dichotomy, consider titles of artworks. They are clearly bestowed on their bearers (by the artist - and it is for this reason only that they bear on the interpretation of the works they entitle). Yet they often have content (without which they would have little to offer to the effort of interpreting the works they entitle). That content may be a description or it may be something else. And where it is a description, it may or may not describe the entitled work. Yet even if it does, it does not refer to the work owing the work's satisfying that description.

Consider the following cases. 1) *Robert Elsmere*. This is the title of a novel by Mary Augusta Ward. It is derived from, and homomorphic with, "Robert Elsmere," which is the name of the main character in Ward's novel. (I leave out of consideration here the issues raised by so-called empty names or fictional names. That is a different topic.) But the two are distinct proper names, for one names a character and the other the novel. 2) *The Mayor of Casterbridge*. This is the title of a novel by Hardy. It is homomorphic with the description "The Mayor of Casterbridge," which applies to a character within the novel. (Again, I set aside the issue of empty or fictional descriptions.) As title of the work, *The Mayor of Casterbridge* does not describe, or purport to describe, anything. It certainly does not refer to the work in virtue of the work's satisfying the description since the work itself is not the mayor of Casterbridge. Yet the title's status as a description is still important. It is significant in understanding the work that its name is a description which is satisfied (fictionally) by one of the novel's characters. 3) *The Love Song of J. Alfred Prufrock*. This is the title of a poem by Eliot. It has the form of a definite description and the description is, presumably, meant to be, and is, satisfied by the work that is so entitled. That poem itself is J. Alfred Prufrock's love song. (This supposes that the descriptive phrase "The Love Song of J. Alfred Prufrock" *is*

Turning to the content of Housman's sentence, let us ask the obvious question: what is it, exactly, that three minutes' thought would find out were thought not so irksome and three minutes not such a long time? The text is from the preface to his edition of the satires of Juvenal. Housman is discussing the principles of textual criticism and taking to task many of his contemporaries and predecessors. One fault many of these are alleged to have is a mechanical reliance on rules in editing. The 18th century, he says, had as its rule to go with the reading (if there is one) found in a simple majority of manuscripts. The rule of the second half of the 19th century, by contrast, is always to go with the reading of the best manuscript unless what it has is utterly impossible (by which he seems to mean principally ungrammatical or unmetrical). (He describes this as the "fashion of leaning on one manuscript like Hope on her anchor and trusting to heaven that no harm will come of it" (1905: v).) This rule might find expression in an editor's preface in such words as "I have made it my rule to follow *a* wherever possible, and only where its readings are patently erroneous have I had recourse to *b* or *c* or *d*" (xi) (though Housman writes acerbically that no eminent scholar would state the rule thus baldly, only his "unreflecting imitators"). Housman then poses a dilemma. Either *b*, *c*, and *d* are derived from *a*, in which case they should never be preferred to it, or they are not, in which case the rule assumes what is clearly false, that all errors in *a* will be "impossible readings." It is this dilemma

the title; one might feel inclined to say that the phrase occurs *in* the title, implying that the title and the phrase are not identical. A full accounting of this issue exceeds the scope of this note.) Strangely, if the descriptive phrase is supposed to be satisfied by the work the phrase entitles, it seems that the work could not fail to satisfy it. What if an artist entitled a poem *The Last Poem I'll Ever Write* and then, subsequently, wrote another poem? Presumably, in that case, we would allow that the title still named the same poem, but the poem would not satisfy the description that is the title. So some descriptions can be 'falsified' and some (like "The Love Song of J. Alfred Prufrock") cannot. Presumably, this has to do with the way the description relates to the entitled work. In the case of Prufrock, the description works through the fictional world of the poem; in the case of "The Last Poem I'll Ever Write" it describes via the poem's place in the actual world. 4) *The Lark Ascending*. This is the title of a composition by Vaughan Williams. The description does not describe anything, exactly. Not the piece itself, nor something in the piece. But the piece does evoke something that might be described by the title. Why, one might wonder, is the piece not called *A Lark Ascending*? Why the definite description? There are, of course, works whose titles are indefinite descriptions, including 5) *A Shropshire Lad*, by A.E. Housman! (Could that have been entitled *The Shropshire Lad* equally well, as in the Vaughan Williams case? Surely not.) There are, however, titles with contents that are not descriptions at all (though they may contain descriptions). For example, 6) *I met Heine on the Rue Fürstenburg*, a composition by Morton Feldman. Assuming that the "I" of the title is taken as referring to the composer (but why should we assume that?), the sentence that is the title of this work is actually true (according to Feldman). It is not at all clear what the meaning of the sentence has to do with the work it entitles. Qua title, it is a (simple) noun phrase that refers to the work (if titles are names, as Levinson argues) and clearly would have to refer quite independently of its content since although the content is an important part of the title, it cannot function to relate the title to the work (as can the description "The Love Song of J. Alfred Prufrock"). Are there two homophonous linguistic expressions, one a sentence and one a (simple) noun phrase? Or does a single expression function simultaneously in two different ways? Finally, we may add 7) *find this out; but*. Unlike titles that are proper names of characters or places, or indefinite or definite descriptions, or sentences, this title is not a natural linguistic unit. It has content, though its content is neither a sentence nor a description. But it, as anything, can still be pressed into service as a title (and name) of the work it entitles, namely the meme M.77.

which three minutes' thought would find out. Instead of the mechanical application of rules, Housman thinks critics should exercise their faculty of discernment and judgment. Each textual uncertainty will be attended by any number of circumstances a critic may take into account. One cannot detect errors only on the grounds of impossibility but must pay attention, above all, to the sense of what is expressed. A manuscript reading may be judged in error because it describes something implausible or inconsistent with other parts of the text too. (Which is not to say, of course, that these should be turned into new rules and an author never allowed, on principle, to be implausible or inconsistent.)

Housman returns to these themes in his well-known piece "The Application of Thought to Textual Criticism" (1921) sixteen years later, though there are some subtle differences between the preface to Juvenal and the later lecture. In the earlier piece, though he does talk of inferior critics' having become "entangled in a task for which nature has neglected to equip them," he dwells much more on their moral failings and lack of appropriate training. The deplorable state of criticism in his day he ascribes to the combined effects of sloth and vanity. Sloth prevents the critic from "learning his trade" or being willing to "toil" over difficult passages; vanity prevents him from admitting his inability and refraining from editing. The section of the Juvenal preface from which the meme's quotation is taken is said by Housman to be

> meant for one only of the three classes into whose hands this book will come. It is not for those who are [true] critics: they know it already and will find it nothing but a string of truisms. It is not for those who never will be critics [i.e. most of those who take themselves already to be critics]: they cannot grasp it and will find it nothing but a string of paradoxes. It is for beginners; for those who are not critics yet, but are neither too dull to learn nor too self-satisfied to wish to learn. (xi)

In the later lecture, much more emphasis is laid on inborn talent. Adapting the Roman proverb about poets, he says "*criticus nascitur, non fit*" - a critic is born, not made. Criticism "cannot be taught at all" (1921: 69). The role of education (habit) is not to supply a deficiency of birth but to limit the damage it can do in one determined to practice criticism.

Another difference between the two works is a little harder to make precise. Though both works are equally opposed to the dominance of rules in criticism, there seem to be different conceptions of rules at work in each. In the earlier piece, we are given two examples of offensive rules, as we have seen. "If a majority of manuscripts agree on a certain reading, go with that" and "if the best manuscript has a certain reading, go with that unless it is impossible." The first is a bad rule because not all manuscripts are equal in their value, the second because scribes can make mistakes that are not ungrammatical or unmetrical. In both cases, one must attend to the particulars of any situation to determine the best reading. The nature and role of these particular considerations is not susceptible to codification. Anything, potentially, might be relevant and only judgment can determine how. In the later essay, though some of the language is the same, the context is slightly different. There, Housman argues that textual criticism is both science and art: "the science of discovering error in texts and the art of removing it." But it is not an exact science. Hence, unlike mathematics, it is not subject to hard-and-fast rules. Such rules "will lead you wrong; because their simplicity will render them inapplicable to problems which are not simple, but complicated by the play of personality" (68). There seem to be three separate, though possibly connected, issues at play here. First there is the matter of simplicity versus complexity. But in the Juvenal preface, he does not argue against the proposed rules because they are too simple. And, indeed, one could imagine similar rules to them, inadequate just as they are, and yet vastly more complex. Secondly, there is the nature of the subject matter of a rule. Mathematics has hard and fast rules because its subject matter is lines and numbers. Criticism's subject matter, though, involves the play of personality. But the reason that the play of personality may make hard and fast rules impossible may have nothing to do with complexity - it is simply the wrong kind of domain to sustain such rules.[178] Thirdly, there is the issue of uncodifiability, of rule versus (to use the language of the philosopher John McDowell) the ability to perceive what is salient in a given situation. This contrast exists whatever the nature of the rules in question is, though emphasizing the importance of the perception of salience may be compatible with allowing the use of rules of thumb or heuristic principles. (For example, there may be no applicable rule that helps someone determine the size of a given object – but a rule of thumb, such as trying to imagine the object against an object of known size, may be helpful nonetheless. Rules of thumb, of course, are *better* if they are simple, not worse.)

Housman attempts to drive his point home, in the later discussion, with a simile no less perplexing than it is charming. The critic, he says, "is not at all like Newton investigating the motions of the planets: he is much more like a dog hunting for fleas. If a dog hunted for fleas on mathematical principles, basing his researches on statistics of area and population, he would never catch a flea except by accident" (69). Is the dog, in the simile, hunting for any old fleas? Then he *should* go where the fleas are likely to be, "basing his research on statistics of area and population." Or is the dog aware of some particular flea he wishes to catch? Then of course, he should just try and catch that flea. But then he needs no science at all – though the skill of catching will be helpful. Given this simile, and given the rather inconsistent position on rules, then, it seems obscure why Housman thinks of criticism as like a science in any sense.

I dwell on these matters at such length because I am struck, especially in his, I think, superior treatment in the Juvenal preface, by the similarity between Housman's conception of criticism and the way ethical theories are nowadays framed. There is an opposition, among ethical theories, between those which are rule-based and those which are not. Of the former, Kantianism and Utilitarianism are the most prominent. Kant tells us not to perform any action whose maxim (i.e. the description under which it is performed intentionally) cannot be made

---

[178] Here Housman may be echoing the distinction drawn by Wilhelm Dilthey between *Naturwissenschaften* (natural sciences) and *Geisteswissenschaften* (human sciences). Dilthey argued that the *Geisteswissenschaften* relied on a hermeneutic methodology quite different from the methodology of the natural sciences. I don't know if Housman knew Wilhelm Dilthey's work but he certainly knew the work of his younger brother Karl, who was a prominent classicist and he was, in general, a great admirer of German scholarship.

a universal rule. Utilitarianism, more simply, gives us a single rule directly: among the alternative actions you can undertake at any moment, always perform that which produces the greatest amount of some designated value (pleasure, utility, goodness, etc., according to the different varieties of Utilitarianism). Over against these stands virtue ethics. Here the emphasis is on the person who is acting. A virtuous person will, in any given set of circumstances, see what the right thing to do is. But since the circumstances are infinitely variable, no possible rule can codify this knowledge of the virtuous person. In Aristotle's version of the theory, a person becomes virtuous by some mixture of first and second natures. First nature is what one is born with; second nature is what one acquires through training and education. Clearly Housman, though wavering between the relative importance of first and second natures, is like the Aristotelian virtue ethicist. Like that of the virtuous person, the skill of the critic is uncodifiable; she will, in particular circumstances, exert her judgment to arrive at a conclusion about the correct reading. She is not infallible, any more than the virtuous person is infallible. But both rely on a skill that cannot be reduced to the application of rules to a situation. And in both cases, this is because situations are too rich, too replete with indefinite detail any part of which might be relevant to a given decision, ethical or textual.

M.78 Not a Strict Freudian

M.78 Not a Strict Freudian Composed: April 21st. Orientation: Reverse. Font: Comic Sans. TB1: "My analyst said she missed me over the break!", black. TB2: "So, she's not a strict Freudian?", black.

Like *Jamaica?* (M.31), this meme speaks to the issue of breaks in analysis. Anyone with experience here will know how much analysts are inclined to interpret on the basis of the patient's feelings about an upcoming break in the treatment. (And there is always an upcoming break somewhere on the horizon!) The artist may be gently turning the tables on analysts here by representing Robin's analyst as the one suffering from longing over the separation of a break.

But regardless of the artist's intentions, how are we to read what is going on *inside* the meme? I must confess, here, to an embarrassing editorial mistake. For a long time, pondering the meaning of this meme, I misread Batman's text as "So, she's not a strict Freudian!". In other words, I mistook the question mark for an exclamation mark. I saw the scene as one in which Batman was emphatically expressing a (derisive) opinion of the reported action of Robin's analyst or, possibly, a (derisive) response to an earlier claim by Robin that his analyst was a Freudian. As a question, however, Batman's text is much harder to interpret, and with it, the scene as a whole. Although, in the other memes, it is not common for Batman's text to be in the form of a question, there are a few such cases. Some of these questions are clearly rhetorical, which gives them the force of an exclamation. (See, for example, *Haven't You Heard?* (M.53).) In others (*Who knows two?* (M.29) and *Thirteen Holes* (M.30), for example) the question is genuine but the use of the original orientation of the image, with Batman on the left, means that Robin supplies the answer in his speech bubble. In the current case, however, the question is clearly not rhetorical and there is nothing to indicate what sort of answer the question is eliciting, what its point is. Its interpretation is not helped by the fact that that the question's verb is not in the interrogative mood, requiring us, therefore, to imagine its being said with the rise in tone one has to use (in English) to make it clear that an indicative sentence is being used to ask a question. The required tone of voice, needless to say, is at odds with the assertiveness of the accompanying slap. Thus, the rhetorical and dramatic structure of the encounter depicted is very hard to make sense of. One is almost tempted to suppose that the artist committed a parapraxis and meant to write an exclamation mark! But who can say?[179]

What of the term "Freudian"? It is a highly equivocal term and its use to signal some kind of identity can function in very different ways. In my initial misreading of the meme (which, if the hypothesis of a parapraxis on the artist's part is correct, may still be on the right lines), it seems to function as a term of esteem, as if Robin's analyst is falling short of some ideal suggested by the epithet "strict Freudian." But taking the meme's text as it stands, it is possible to read the term "Freudian" with either a positive or a negative valence, in the one case making Batman's question a tentative expression of scorn, in the other, of relief. In fact, "Freudian" does often function almost as a term of abuse. David Anderegg (2005) has an amusing and insightful discussion of how a therapist can respond to the hostile question "You're not a Freudian, are you?". He suggests three identities the therapist can take on in response: martyr, deserter, seducer. The martyr accepts the description, knowing it will be off-putting (perhaps repelling a potential client) but valuing truthfulness even to their own detriment. The deserter fears the consequences of being seen as a Freudian and (insincerely) disavows the description. (Anderegg invokes Peter's betrayal of Jesus here.) The seducer avoids a direct answer and simply practices their Freudianism, bringing the questioner (say, a patient) along with them until the questioner herself is too compromised to make the hostile question anything other than part of a farce. Although Robin's analyst is not present in the meme, we can imagine versions of these responses in possible follow-ups to Batman's question. And since we are now imagining the epithet as hostile, Robin's responses would inevitably merge with possible responses to the slap. So, as martyr: "And what if she were? What's wrong with that? I'm ready for another if that's how you want to play it!". As deserter: "Oh my God, no! And please stop!". As seducer: "You and I are both orphans. Maybe each of us is finding a missing parent in the

---

[179] If it were a parapraxis, how might we analyze it? Badly, of course, in the absence of a lot more information about the context in which it was committed. (A parapraxis is, of necessity, an action – a miswriting, a misspeaking, a misreading; hence a written text, as we have here, can only be a parapraxis in a derivate sense, as the product of a parapraxic action. That's why the context of its commission is essential to understanding it.) But to hazard a few generalities, we might note that the change effects the substitution of uncertainty for emphatic certainty. So perhaps some anxious but repressed uncertainty was seeking an outlet and seized on the fact that punctuation has no semantic content, and hence that the substitution can be made without reaching any form of semantic awareness, to make itself felt. Uncertainty about what? Here we resort to pure conjecture in suggesting uncertainty about the artist's Batman meme project, or about his analysis, or perhaps (and now I come to it, this seems the most plausible) about whether his own analyst was a strict Freudian (in whatever sense we give that term).

other. Are you slapping me because you are scared my analyst's love for me means I wouldn't miss you if you went away?".

We still, though, have not adequately addressed what is meant by "Freudian," whether it is used in a hostile way or not. The biggest fault-line in its meaning is between a wider and a narrower sense. Sometimes it is used as a synecdoche for *psychoanalytic* or something even wider, the world of psychoanalytic psychotherapy (those, for example, at whom McWilliams (2004) is aimed). But there are many within that large group who would abjure the term in a narrower sense, in which it principally refers to practitioners of the kind of ego-psychology that was once dominant in mainstream psychoanalysis but has, in the last thirty to forty years, receded to become just one current among many in a much more diverse psychoanalytic environment. (Mitchell and Black (2016) provide a good overview of the emergence of this diverse landscape, organized largely around the move from so-called one-person models of the analytic encounter – the analysis is a space into which the patient's psyche unfolds, with the analyst there to monitor the space and help the patient understand – to so-called two-person, or relational, models – the analysis is essentially about a relationship between analyst and patient.)

Ambiguity between the wider and narrower sense is relevant to the meme since one of the differences between Freudians, narrowly construed, and many more contemporary styles of psychoanalysis (Freudianism in the wider sense) concerns the way in which (and the degree to which) the analyst practices abstinence and neutrality in the analysis. Batman's use of "strict" suggests that he is reacting to the self-disclosure that Robin reports his analyst as engaging in and that he concludes, from that self-disclosure, that the analyst must not be a Freudian in the narrow sense.[180,181] Whether Freudians in the wider sense would be likely to tell their patients that they missed them is another matter. A harrowing paper by an analyst in the relational tradition (so "not a strict Freudian") in fact concerns precisely the question of the analyst's speech around this issue. Michelle Shubin (2018) recounts the case of a patient whose analysis was forced, by external circumstances, to end before patient and therapist were ready. As the last session approached, Shubin felt herself become emotionally distant, unable to meet the patient's increasing need for some sign that the analyst matched her emotions about the enforced separation. But,

---

[180] We must, however, bear in mind that Robin might be an unreliable informant about what his analyst told him, magnifying a more restrained comment, such as "I looked forward to resuming our work after the break," through the lens of intense wish-fulfillment. That in itself would surely merit a slap!

[181] "The classical practitioner of the craft knew she should remain scrupulously nongratifying (so the patient's drives would not find satisfaction and thereby elude the frustration that motivates thought), blankly anonymous (so the patient's transferences would emerge uncontaminated by the person of the analyst), and dispassionately evenhanded (so as not to exert any personal influence of the patient's autonomous working through of their own internal conflicts).... It was this strict emphasis on asceticism and restraint that was reflected in the once popular term 'strict' Freudian" (Mitchell 1997: 177).

the more [the patient] wanted me to express my affection and grief, the more I withdrew. My silence felt penetrating and profound to us both. "Fucking shit," she yelled. "Why is it such a big deal to say you'll miss me? I always tell you everything I'm feeling. Now you decide to withhold? Isn't this supposed to be a collaboration?" (176)

If the analyst withholds and avoids, at least in general, saying "I missed you," how, if at all, is the analysis a "collaboration"? There is no doubt that it is an utterly unique and *sui generis* kind of collaboration and understanding it means tackling this notion of withholding, or abstinence, on the analyst's part. This is a much-discussed topic and I want merely to emphasize one aspect of it here. The patient and analyst are two people who meet regularly in a single space, interacting mostly through their speech with each other. In that context, the patient's energy is centrifugal. She talks to the analyst not only about the analytic situation but also about her life outside. She is, frequently, curious about the analyst too, her unexpressed feelings and thoughts, her other patients, and her life outside the consulting room. In some sense, it is the analyst's job to resist this force with a centripetal force of her own, focusing everything, as far as is possible, back on to the patient. Another metaphor, alongside that of the opposing forces, for what transpires is that the analyst is the guardian of a projection of the three-dimensional into the two-dimensional. The three dimensions are the patient, the analyst, and all the 'thirds' that they are connected to outside the consulting room. The two dimensions are those of the analytic dyad formed by the patient and analyst, which is to say, the patient as she presents and represents herself and the analyst as she interacts with the patient and appears in the patient's fantasy.

The projection of the three-dimensional into the two-dimensional is a glamour. In its unprojected three-dimensional state, reality is unmanageable by the patient and analyst, unmanageable because it vastly exceeds them and their sphere of action. By means of the projection, it is unstably rendered in a form susceptible to their (and especially the patient's) agency.[182] But the glamour *is* unstable. It is sustained only by a constant effort of suppression and transmutation and it falls to the analyst to perform this labor. This is her 'abstinence': the active and intense effort to suppress and transmute in order to keep the glamour flickering. The glamour is dangerous, too. It contains more than it has space for, not quantitatively (like an overstuffed suitcase) but ontologically – like an impossible object – three dimensions projected into two. As such an impossible object, too much contact with it can make you mad. The patient both longs for the intrusion of the real, to break the spell, and desperately wishes to cling to the enchantment. Consequently, the analyst's abstinence, her guardianship of the projection, is both resented and welcomed. Inevitably, sometimes things 'get through' without transmutation. Reality and its demands will impinge on the ephemeral, fantasy-laden projection that exists inside the analysis. The analysis itself extends beyond the analytic

---

[182] I feel compelled to say that with the words "a form susceptible to their... agency," where it may appear that some literality is breaking through the metaphor of the glamour, I take myself to be at my most metaphorical.

situation. So not only is the work of the analysis directed at the glamour, the two-dimensional projection that is susceptible, at least in small measure, to the patient's agency. It must also be the business of the analysis to manage its own parerga, the realities that flutter like bats at its fragile windows; to confront the impossibility of the analytic dyad in its purity; to incorporate what cannot be incorporated, to assimilate the unassimilable.

I have spoken metaphorically and in a highly-charged register to capture what the experience is like. But in concrete detail and described impersonally, the issues may appear much more prosaic. Let us look at some examples. A patient dreams she is in a room with another person and her associations to this person connect them with the analyst. But in the dream, she also has a shadowy sense of another figure in the room. In fact, the patient is a control case for the analyst's candidacy and is aware that there is a supervisor to whom her analyst talks about her. She has a shadowy sense of this other person in the room with them. Wendy Greenspun's paper "Three Dimensional Treatment" (2011) recounts how one analysis was affected, over the years, by the analyst's having had four different supervisors for it, one of them twice, for two non-consecutive periods. Here, one might say, the analysis is not just taking place, but taking place dramatically and with important vicissitudes, in times and places where the patient is not present. Yet while the supervisor is, in fact, a part of the analysis, they will not be there in the consulting room with patient and analyst; nor will what the supervisor says be discussed with the patient. The analyst *abstains* from speaking of that, making herself a kind of transformer through which all of that 'external' part of the analysis gets rendered in the two-dimensions of the interaction between analyst and patient. Three-dimensional treatment in a two-dimensional space. No wonder a patient may feel an analyst as sadistic! The analyst twists and squeezes the analysis as a whole, something which in reality includes the supervisor, ontologically deforming it in the attempt to fit it all into the consulting room where there is only the analyst and patient. And not only do supervisors play a part in an analysis. They also show up in the patient's transference. Philip Luber (1991) distinguishes between cases where a transferential reaction to the analyst is, for various reasons, split up, so that part is experienced towards the analyst and part towards the supervisor (or even training institute) and cases of what he calls "genuinely triadic transference" phenomena. Yet, of course, the object of part of this triadic transference, though intimately connected to the analysis, is allowed in only as mediated by the analyst.

The phenomenon of supervision and the way it impinges on the analysis and in turn may reflect the analysis, is much studied today.[183] For another, quite different, example of what I call

---

[183] I note here in passing that the idea of requiring supervision for analysts in training was pioneered, and eventually made hegemonic within training institutes, by the artist's relative, Max Eitingon. (Eitingon was the artist's second cousin, three times removed but this makes the connection seem more distant than it was. The Eitingons were a family that managed its own parerga in a lively way. Max's cousin and brother-in-law Motty – Motty married Max's sister Fanny – likely had a role in bringing about the meeting of the artist's father and mother. See the commentary on *Thirteen Holes* (M.30) for a little more about the Eitingons.) Eitingon, indeed, was himself the first analytic supervisor, in a formal sense, as director of the Berlin Polyclinic he founded in 1920, along with Karl Abraham and Ernst Simmel.

the projection of the three-dimensional into the two-dimensional, consider a case discussed by Agnès Fabrikant (1997). Fabrikant describes an analysis she conducted with a middle-aged woman, Luce, whose partner, Mireille, was being treated by another analyst, Dr. X, in the same town. When Fabrikant began seeing Luce, Mireille, who was sickly and unable to work, was already in treatment and their common, but diminished, finances were just about able to absorb the cost. Fabrikant agreed to see Luce for a very reduced fee since treatment would otherwise have been impossible. At a certain point, Fabrikant recounts how she began to feel put upon by this arrangement.

> Luce would talk about the reduced fee with guilt but she was vague about her finances because her anxiety kept her from getting a clear view. She indicated that it was a difficult subject for her to discuss with Mireille, and in any case, Mireille's situation with Dr. X could not be altered. Dr. X had made clear that he would not accept a reduced fee. The only way out of the quandary, Luce said, would be either for her or Mireille to come less frequently. Luce's guilt, and my knowledge of Mireille's need, complicated my own desire to raise the fee which was, in truth, extremely low and had remained so for a number of years. I felt increasingly as if I were colluding with Luce in protecting her from a confrontation with Mireille over the material limitations they faced, a confrontation that might be very painful for one or both of them in its outcome. I was resentful of Dr. X and wished that Luce had started seeing me first, so that I would be the fixed point the others would have to arrange themselves around. And I became angry with Luce because it seemed to me as if she had forced me to subsidize Mireille's treatment. Obviously I needed to get ahold of myself and understand what was going on and what I should do.
>
> Yet thinking this through proved very hard. On the one hand, everything had to happen between Luce and I. The analytic third[184] was composed of us and us only. But at the same time, it seemed that there was a very complex interaction going on between three interlocking systems. Each system comprised a dyad: me + Luce, Luce + Mireille, and Mireille + Dr. X. (Of course I knew Dr. X professionally, which didn't make things any easier.) In a certain sense, it would have been ideal for the four of us to meet and hammer out the just distribution (to Dr. X and me) of the total Luce and Mireille could afford to pay for therapy. I would gain something; Dr. X. would lose something. But we could not do this. Instead, a series of interlocking vectors of force were at play, so that each couple was affected unpredictably by what transpired in the other two couples. The behavior of no couple, around this problem, could be thought of in isolation.
>
> Analysts talk of the frame of an analysis, referring to such things as fee, time, and location. Art critics have 'the parergon,' meaning the frame of a painting. I

---

[184] [Editor's note:] Fabrikant is here referring to a paper published not long before her own by Thomas Ogden (1994). See *infra* for discussion.

use the expression *analytic parergon* to mean something broader than the usual analytic frame. In the situation I described the third created by the analyst and analysand does not exhaust the scene of the analysis. When it came to the very practical issue of the fee, the third formed by Luce and myself was experienced by us as a fragment of a larger system. We would need to bring in a fourth and fifth. To discuss the issue *à deux* was to unnaturally force a larger system into a smaller space. Just as a viewer's experience of a painting is necessarily affected by the painting's frame, so an analysis is necessarily affected by the way the dyad is framed by containing systems. (138)

Fabrikant comes very close to the language I used above but she is stymied in the attempt to conceptualize the situation she writes about because of the seduction, or interference, of Ogden's framework. For Ogden, the "third" is an entity somehow emergent from the analyst and analysand, something almost with a mind of its own.[185] It is part of the work of analysis, according to Ogden, for both patient and analyst to disentangle themselves from this symbiotic entity. But the relevant 'third' Fabrikant is struggling with is not the third that encompasses the two, the analyst and patient, but the third that exceeds them. Talk of the fourth and fifth is quite misleading and unhelpful since it makes the problem seem to concern simply the enlargement of something that begins in the consulting room. Rather, the 'third' in question is something that is both at odds with the emergent dyad (how confusing that what is called by some "the dyad" should be called by Ogden "the third"!) and yet, as parergon, inseparable from it.

---

[185] Sometimes, one gets a sense, a 'mind' conveniently invoked as the subject of the analyst's own failings, a way for the analyst to off-load her own missteps onto an entity that involves the patient too, a device to convert "I fucked up" to "we fucked up." Is this, too, demanded by the analyst's abstinence? (This is not a rhetorical question.)

M.80 The Slap Itself

M.80 The Slap Itself Composed: April 24th. Orientation: Reverse. Font: Arial. TB1: "I am being slapped by Batman.", black. TB2: "I am slapping Robin.", black.

I HAVE CAST MY COMMENTARY ON M.80 IN THE FORM OF ANOTHER KIND OF MEME KNOWN AS "INCREASINGLY VERBOSE." IN INSTANCES OF THE INCREASINGLY VERBOSE MEME, A GIVEN IMAGE IS PAIRED WITH SOME TEXT, USUALLY SIDE BY SIDE, THOUGH IN THIS CASE THE TEXT IS INTEGRATED INTO THE IMAGE. THE IMAGE AND TEXT PAIR ARE THEN ITERATED TWO OR THREE TIMES, WITH THE IMAGE BECOMING INCREASINGLY ABSTRACT AND THE TEXT BECOMING INCREASINGLY VERBOSE. OBVIOUSLY THE NAME "INCREASINGLY VERBOSE" FOR THIS MEME DERIVES FROM WHAT HAPPENS TO THE TEXT ALONE. OTHER NAMES FOR IT FOCUS ON THE IMAGE, SUCH AS "MEME DECAY" OR "DECONSTRUCTED MEMES." FOR ME, THE CHARM OF THIS MEME LIES IN THE WAY THE INCREASING VERBOSITY, WHICH INEVITABLY INVOLVES AMPLIFICATION, IS NONETHELESS OFFERED TO THE VIEWER AS "SAYING THE SAME THING." (THIS PRESUPPOSES THAT THE ORIGINAL TEXT IS A REPRESENTATION OF A SPEECH ACT, ELSE WHAT SENSE COULD BE MADE OF MERELY IMPLICIT CONTENT?) IN THIS CASE, I USE THE ARTIST'S ORIGINAL MEME AS THE FIRST PANEL OF AN INCREASINGLY VERBOSE MEME. THE SUBSEQUENT TWO ITERATIONS, IN WHICH THE "SAME THING" THAT IS SAID IN THE MEME IS SAID WITH INCREASING VERBOSITY, CONSTITUTE MY COMMENTARY ON IT. THIS FORM OF COMMENTARY SEEMS PARTICULARLY APPROPRIATE FOR THIS MEME SINCE THE MEME ITSELF PLAYS WITH THE MINIMAL DIFFERENCE BETWEEN TEXT AND NO-TEXT. SINCE BATMAN AND ROBIN SAY SIMPLY THAT THEY ARE PERFORMING AN ACTION WHICH IS ENTIRELY MANIFEST, IT IS ALMOST AS IF THEY ARE SAYING NOTHING AT ALL. AS THE COMMENTARY DEVELOPS, THOUGH, ENTIRELY NEW CONTENT, DERIVING FROM FREUD AND FROM THE PHILOSOPHER OF LANGUAGE JOHN PERRY, TURNS THE ALMOST-SILENCE INTO A POSITIVE EXPLOSION OF MEANING!

See M.55, on increasing degrees of abstraction in musical analysis (Heinrich Schenker).

The first panel of the commentary reproduces the original meme. That meme, therefore is both itself and part of a commentary on itself.

In the second panel, the indexical expressions of the first panel are replaced by proper names and hence the first-person of the verbs is replaced by the third-person. (This shows something interesting. The person of the verb, first or third, seems to be sensitive to the means by which the subject is referred to and not just by the relation the subject has to the speaker. One might have thought the first-person would be used whenever the subject is the speaker, but in fact, it only occurs with the pronoun "I." Other expressions that also refer to the speaker, such as the speaker's name, do not take the first person. And so, *mutatis mutandis*, for the third-person.) Yet the pronouns have not disappeared, and resurface in the Robin's statement "I like this" and Batman's "I don't want this."

In the third panel, the pronouns and names are brought together in an allusion to John Perry's classic paper "The Essential Indexical." Perry argues that when we use indexicals, we express propositions that can be expressed without them, but in distinctive manners keyed to the indexicals we use. Thus, if Batman were to say "I am slapping Robin," the proposition he expresses could also be expressed by an utterance, by anyone, of the sentence "Batman is slapping Robin." Batman's manner of expressing this proposition, however, is first-personal and is tied to the use of the pronoun "I." Robin can also express something using this manner, were he to utter the sentence "I am slapping Robin," but what he would express in that manner would be a different proposition, namely, the proposition anyone could express by uttering the sentence "Robin is slapping Robin" (which of course is false).

Indexical expressions are expressions that vary their reference in a systematic way in response to context. Here the commentary on the commentary is referring to the "I" in both Robin's and Batman's speech bubbles. "I" varies its referent systematically, referring, on any given occasion, to its utterer on that occasion. Other indexical expressions include "now" and "here." They are keyed to the time and place of utterance, rather than the utterer.

In containing only redundant text, M.80 is in some way equivalent to M.60, a meme without text at all.

Cf. Nancy McWilliams: "The recurrence in the therapeutic relationship of the main emotional currents in the client's history is a wondrous phenomenon. What makes it especially fascinating is that both parties to therapy start out earnestly resolving that what happened to the client earlier will not happen this time around. The patient is looking to undo the prior damage and thus tries to choose a therapist who offers a contrasting experience to the one internalized in childhood; the therapist longs not to fail the patient as the early caregivers did. And yet with stunning inevitability, both parties find themselves caught up in repetition" (259).

See M.41 on pronouns and indexicals. See M.59 on sentences such as "I am Robin." Here discussed by Perry in M.59, as discussed by Strawson.

See M.6 and commentary ad loc. See also M.91 and M.92 on intrapsychic conflict versus collaboration.

There is psychoanalytic theme running through the commentary which brings out the interplay of masochistic and sadistic currents contained in the image and the artist's use of it. Robin's "I like this" and "Do I want this?" suggest an ambivalent masochistic pleasure in being slapped. Ditto for Batman's "I don't want this" and "I need this." (And my use of "want," "need," and "like" also suggests variability in the modality of desire.)

In the second panel, Robin describes his own situation in terms of the title of Freud's classic paper on on beating fantasies. Batman stresses the inevitability with which the pair fall into this violent pose, as analyst and patient will, inevitably, re-enact the patient's trauma. Yet the trauma they are forced into repeating remains a mystery as yet. The image of the meme is given without context, a mysterious and mysteriously repeated primal scene.

Batman's final assertion that he is Robin brings out to what degree the artist's use of the image in his memes is designed to express intrapsychic conflict. The beater and the beaten are the same person and this person both wants and does not want the slapping.

The fluid identities of Batman and Robin in this context are connected to the issue of pronouns and the manners of saying things discussed by Perry in "The Essential Indexical." Does either know who he really is in this scenario? Are they interchangeable? Is what differs only the manner of their occupancy of common roles?

M.91 Transformative Experience

M.91 Transformative Experience Composed: May 12th. Orientation: Reverse. Font: Comic Sans. TB1: "These memes have really been a transformative experience for us!", black. TB2: "Right? And we had no idea at the beginning!", black.

This and *Transformative Experience (alternate version)* (M.92) function as a pair, both composed on the same day and employing exactly the same text, with the same visual appearance, in Robin's speech bubble. They give a more co-operative and less angst-ridden picture of Batman's and Robin's relationship than most of the other memes. Robin's use of "us" in the text common to both M.91 and M.92 is its only occurrence in all of the memes. In M.91, the "us" is echoed by Batman's "we," which appears only rarely. M.92 shows Batman candidly admitting to a lack of certainty and clarity that is at odds with his usual persona. It is as if, in these two memes, Batman and Robin are figuring something out together. What might they be figuring out? That will surely depend on how we understand the reference of "these memes." The expression might be referring to some non-specified memes that exist as part of the world represented in the memes, as if Robin were to say "these costumes" or "these villains." But this would leave us with no way of understanding the memes. Much more attractive is the hypothesis that the memes are 'meta' memes and that "these memes" refers to some or all of Evnine's Batman memes themselves. Perhaps it is supposed to refer only to M.91 and M.92 but I think much greater sense can be made of them if we assume (as surely all readers will have already assumed) that the expression refers to Evnine's Batman memes in general. On this interpretation, one has the overwhelming sense that the artist is speaking directly to his viewers. The two figures, Batman and Robin, rather than dramatizing the artist's intra-psychic conflicts, as they so often do, are channeling a single voice, and so what they are figuring out is what the project of creating these Batman memes meant to the artist, what the nature was of his experience in engaging in the whole creative enterprise of which these two memes are a small (but highly significant) part.

According to Robin, at least part of the character of that experience was that it was transformative for the artist. This reference to transformative experience is almost certainly an allusion to the work of the philosopher Laurie Paul, whose book *Transformative Experience* was still making waves, after its 2014 publication, around the time the memes were composed in May 2016. In order to understand these memes, then, and with them, to gain some insight into what the artist is trying to tell us here about what his work meant to him, we should look at the main ideas of that book. Paul's book is about whether, and if so how, we can make a certain species of important decisions – decisions about transformative experiences – rationally. By making decisions rationally, she means within the framework of decision theory. To illustrate this framework, suppose an agent faces a choice between two actions, A and B. A may be "go on a picnic" and B may be "stay at home." She assesses the possible outcomes if she does A. Perhaps those outcomes depend entirely on the weather. If the weather stays fine, she will have a good time; if it rains, the outing will be miserable. Let us suppose she can represent these outcomes numerically, say in terms of units of happiness or satisfaction, m units for a good time, n units for a miserable time. She then multiplies these numbers by the probability of the states they depend on. If it's 90% likely to stay sunny and 10% likely to rain, then multiply m by 0.9 and n by 0.1. Now add the results. This gives you what is called the expected utility of doing A – a single number that reflects, in the way just described, the values, to you, of the possible outcomes of the act and the probabilities of those outcomes. Do the same for B to obtain its expected utility. The rational agent, on this model of decision making, acts so as to maximize her expected utility, i.e., she chooses whichever of A or B has the higher expected utility. I have given a very simple example but of course, in real life cases, it will generally be very hard, for many decisions, to reach an exact view (let alone to represent it numerically) about how good or bad an outcome is for you. And there will be plenty of imponderables in assessing likelihoods of various states of the world that outcomes will depend on. But setting those general and looming worries aside, there is a particular kind of case that Paul thinks poses a special problem for this model.

Alongside the goal of acting rationally, Paul supposes there is, especially in the contemporary and developed world, a goal of acting authentically. In broad terms, this means acting to achieve self-realization. But what, more specifically, does it entail? Among the considerations we weigh in making choices, some are what Paul characterizes as objective, or third-personal considerations and some are subjective, or first-personal. Very roughly, the objective considerations are ones that, even if you apply them to yourself, could be applied to anyone. Subjective considerations are ones where you think about how the outcome will be for you in particular, from the inside, as it were.[186] Under optimal circumstances, as we attempt to choose rationally (i.e., attempt to maximize expected utility), we take into consideration subjective considerations and in this way also act authentically. Self-realization means, in this context, acting on the basis of considerations about how we think our choices will be for us, from the inside. But there are certain classes of decisions, concerning what Paul calls transformative experiences, where, for reasons to be explained, we cannot appeal to subjective considerations in the ordinary way and hence where rationality and authenticity appear to be at odds. This brings us to the key question for understanding M.91 and M.92 – what are transformative experiences?

There are two key features of transformative experiences. First, they are epistemically transformative. That is, what it is like to have them is something that can only be known by having them. A person who has never eaten a food with a distinctive taste cannot know what that experience will be like, from the inside, except by having it. Secondly, they are personally transformative. They will change how you value and think about your experiences (and other aspects of your life). So even if you knew what the experience would be like, you couldn't now know whether (and how strongly) you will value that experience once you have it. A good example of a transformative experience, one that Paul discusses extensively, is having a (first) child. It will lead to experiences (of feeling a certain kind of love for your child) that you just can't know what it's like to have, from the inside, unless you actually have them. And it may affect your preferences not just by introducing new ones that rank the new experience against other things, but also by rearranging existing preferences that don't involve the new kind of experience. For example, it may lead you to prioritize your relationship with your own parents over your career, the opposite of your pre-child preferences.

If this is right, then for decisions about transformative experiences, for example, decisions about whether to have a child or not, we cannot satisfy the demands of authenticity in the framework required for rationality. We cannot satisfy the need to make the decision an aspect of our self-realization by plugging into the decision matrix values for what the experience will be like – we don't know what it will be like, and even if we did, we don't know how we'll value that what-it-is-like after we have the experience. (Think of how often people who do not want children are told that if they have them, their preferences will change and they will be glad they had them.) So, if we want our decisions in these cases to be authentic, by taking into account subjective factors, it cannot be by plugging into the framework of rational decision making some values about the outcomes of our choices; and if we want out decisions to be rational, in

---

[186] In his book *Epistemic Dimensions of Personhood* (2008), Evnine has a chapter titled with the name Paul Ricoeur gave to one of his books, "Oneself as Another." The chapter carries as epigraph this passage from Bernard Malamud's book *The Fixer* (1966), describing Spinoza's philosophy: "It's as though a man flies over his own head on the wings or reason, or some such thing. You join the universe and forget your worries" (85). The topic of the chapter is the conflicts between seeing oneself 'from the inside' and 'as another' (or as 'just anyone').

the sense of maximizing expected utility, we will have to work only with the objective outcomes of our choices.

However, according to Paul, all is not lost. There is a way to be both authentic and rational in decisions about transformative experiences, and that is to 'reframe' or 'reconfigure' the decision. Rather than making the decision in terms of the subjective aspects of what it would be like to have the experience in question, we can make a decision about whether we want to discover the kind of person that having the experience will make us. Paul calls the acquisition of knowledge about how we will change in certain circumstances *revelation*. Satisfying preferences regarding revelation, to know or not to know how the experience will remake us, is genuinely authentic, in the appropriate sense. And it is also something we can know about from the inside, even without (yet) having the experiences, and hence that we can plug into a rational decision matrix.

Having offered this description of Paul's views, perhaps I might be allowed to make two comments on them before returning to my primary duty – the interpretation of M.91. First, the idea of reframing or reconfiguring the choice situation seems problematic. It is often assumed, with great plausibility, that in making rational choices, one should do so on the basis of *all* available relevant considerations. These considerations may include both subjective and objective ones and in each category there may be various distinct considerations. None of this prevents the initial problem that Paul diagnoses from arising since, as she points out, unless the objective reasons 'swamp' the subjective ones that are imponderable owing to the transformative nature of the experience that the decision is about, their imponderability will still make it impossible to attempt to maximize expected utility. But when she tells us that we should reframe the decision by focusing on whether we want to find out what sort of a person we will become, we must remember that these considerations are *already* supposed to be part of the decision process, owing to the requirement to base our decisions on the totality of relevant considerations. In other words, even before the reframing, we should have been taking into account how much we value learning about the kind of person we might become as a result of a transformative experience. Thus, reframing the decision seems to be merely letting go of the attempt to incorporate in our decision process an 'inside' appreciation of what it will be like for us to undergo the experience and basing our decision on the remaining factors, the objective ones and the subjective ones about the value to us of revelation, that were already supposed to be taken into account. Perhaps the point that Paul wants to emphasize here is that among the remaining considerations, there are still some which are able to speak to the demand for authenticity; by excluding the considerations about what the experience would be like for us, we have not thereby reduced ourselves to a purely objective take on our own lives but can still, authentically, give voice to something concerning self-realization, indeed something about how it will be for us personally, only now, it is not the imponderable what-it-would-be-like-for-us-to-have-the-experience, but the more ponderable what-it-would-be-like-for-us-to-learn-about-the-kind-of-person-we-will-become.

My second point concerns the description of the rational, authentic decision *not* to have the experience in question. Paul says that saying "no" to a transformative experience is a decision to "reject this kind of revelation" (120). If the decision not to have a transformative experience is characterized in this way, then given the way our culture privileges continuous change, dynamism, and growth, decisions to forgo various kinds of transformative experience will inevitably be cast by Paul's reframing as failures: loss of nerve, absence of courage, retreat, playing it safe, stagnation, stasis, and so on. How can a decision to "reject" revelation about what you will become, about how you will change, appear in any other light? The reframing, therefore, seems to me prejudicial to those who say "no"!

Returning now to an examination of M.91, Robin (as I conjectured, channeling the artist's voice directly) seems to suggest that the memes have been a transformative experience. The artist seems to be saying that the process of creating the memes has made available to him certain kinds of experience he simply could not have imagined and, more than that, has changed him in some relatively profound ways. I will discuss, in my comments on M.92, what those experiences and changes might be, as best as I can from the outside. Here I will only note that Batman's answer in M.91 brings out a feature of transformative experience that is not one highlighted in Paul's treatment of it (though there is no reason to think she would disagree with anything I say here). Paul's book is focused on a decision problem – how do we (rationally and authentically) make decisions about whether to have transformative experiences. What Batman brings out is that in many cases, experiences turn out to be transformative without our having known, in advance, that they would be. Hence, the question is moot of whether to decide to have them. There are at least two reasons for this. First, when we make decisions, we are considering types of experience. We wonder whether to have a child or to taste a new food. Having a child is a type of experience. And decisions, of course, have to focus on types since they concern the as-yet unrealized future. There is no particular experience of my having a child when I am deciding about whether to have one. But what will or will not be transformative is some particular experience. And that means that an experience might be transformative owing to features that are only incidental to its falling under the type in terms of which I deliberate about it. For example, I might deliberate about going to the store, and then go to the store, and part of my experience in going to the store might involve meeting someone who changes my life. Actually going to the store, on that occasion, turned out to be transformative but not for the facts about it that made it a going to the store, which was what I deliberated about. So, in this case, the artist may have deliberated about making a lot of Batman memes, and the experience of making them may have been transformative, but not for anything about it that is implied by the type of experience *making Batman memes*.

But beyond this, there is, I think, a deeper reason why the artist might not have had any idea, prior to making a lot of Batman memes, that this was going to be a transformative experience. How, exactly, does the continuous stream of a life gel into discrete experiences of which we can even ask whether they are transformative or not? The artist must have begun by making a few memes without much thought for a project. Certainly the memes were unified by the sameness of the image, and perhaps by some other factors. But was there yet something of which Robin could have said "these memes have been a transformative experience for us"? I would say not. It was probably only well into the making of the memes that the artist must have become aware that there was a single, discrete experience, the making of "these memes." As Kierkegaard says, "life can only be understood backwards; but it must be lived forwards." (See in this regard my commentary on *…a meme in which I'm being…* (M.1) and on the artist's own paratextual remark on *A Character in a Novel* (M.3).) There could have been no prior deliberation on the artist's part about whether to accept or reject the revelation consequent on this transformative experience. Not just because of the reasons given in my previous paragraph, that the transformational features of it may have had no essential connection to the kind *making Batman memes* under which it would have been deliberated about; but more importantly, because it was only once things were well underway that there crystallized, partially retrospectively, a single experience.

So, when Robin says "these memes have really been a transformative experience for us," and Batman answers "we had no idea at the beginning," I hear the artist trying to convey to us how much he was taken by surprise; how – as when one journeys by train and, coming from the countryside, begins to see a house here and a mysterious storage facility there, and then, somehow, without understanding when, one realizes one is now already in a city – the modest and inconsequential activity of making a few Batman memes gave way to "these memes"; how he must have been able to look back and realize that he had been having a transformative experience without having known, for most of its duration, that he had been having any kind of experience at all.

M.92 Transformative Experience (alternate version)

M.92 Transformative Experience (alternate version) Composed: May 12th. Orientation: Reverse. Font: Comic Sans. TB1: "These memes have really been a transformative experience for us!", black. TB2: "Yes and no!!", black.

M.92 belongs with M.91, the two of them making a pair in which Robin has the same text but Batman gives different responses. See the commentary on M.91 for some general comments on the two memes and for an extensive explanation of the concept of transformative experience that informs Robin's text. In this commentary, I shall assume familiarity with all that, and with my hypothesis that in these two memes the artist is speaking about his own experience in making his Batman memes, and get straight to a discussion of what he might be trying to say through Batman's "yes and no!!".

"Yes and no." How are we to understand such a claim? On its face, it is self-contradictory – the memes both were and were not transformative. Though the artist raises the prospect of true contradictions in *Dialetheism* (M.20), common sense rebels. Contradictions cannot be true and Batman is surely saying something that at least *might* be true. But more importantly, supposing Batman were uttering such a contradiction, it would be an interpretive dead-end. It would not assign the reader any clearly identifiable interpretive task. Much more plausible is the supposition that Batman's apparent contradiction is in fact no contradiction at all, but contains implicit appeal to respects in which the memes were transformative and (different) respects in which they were not. The interpreter, in that case, would be directed to uncover what those respects were. In what ways were the memes transformative and in what ways were they not? But if that is the interpreter's task, another implicit restriction must be understood to be at play. It will be of interest if we can find *any* respects in which the memes were transformative, for transformation, in the relevant sense, is a rare and significant phenomenon. But precisely on that account, failure to be transformative is commonplace and, for the most part, uninteresting. Thus it will not do, as an interpretation, simply to find *some* respects in which the memes were not transformative. For Batman's utterance to have a point, the respects in which the memes were not transformative must be suitably related to those in which they were. This, then, is the framework for understanding the meme: it calls on us to understand a way in which the memes were genuinely transformative for the artist and an intimately connected way in which they were somehow stymied in their transformative potential. It points, in other words, to an ambivalence at the heart of the entire project. But how to give substance to this skeleton of understanding? Our evidence is exiguous and we can only hope to say something by supplementing it with a large dose of fantasy.

Evnine began his university studies in music and only switched to philosophy after his first degree. Prior to the creation of these memes, Evnine's public philosophical work always took the form of traditional monographs and journal articles. (See the entries to the bibliography of this volume for a sampling of these offerings.) However, we also notice a strange lack of constancy in subject matter. The books and papers range over many topics, some topics appearing in one work, never to be seen again. The form or the shell of the work is normal, but there is a restlessness on the inside. So, we have an early misstep, followed by an apparent consistency in area that may conceal some continued dissatisfaction. In early 2016, he began to produce, and publish on Facebook, the Batman memes collected here, many of which allude to philosophical issues (as, indeed, do M.91 and M.92 themselves, which in some way 'comment' on the topic of transformative experience). The memes exhibit the same restlessness as the more traditional work – touching on a vast variety of topics, and not just philosophical – but now, the ephemeral and outsider nature of the outer form reflects the restless lack of center of the inner movement. The memes, therefore, seem to represent a transformation in which something hidden, or repressed, begins to surface and reshape what contains and conceals it. (If the artist could only have found a way to write *around* the memes, and not just *in* them, he could have transformed his way of doing philosophy even more.)

But Robin's text says that the memes have been a transformative experience for "us," the figures – Batman and Robin – whom we have assumed to be speaking for the artist himself. There seems, therefore, to be a more personal element connected to the process of philosophical transformation enacted by the memes. Personal transformation, at least in very broad outline, is easy to locate in the artist's life, since a few years before his memetic activity began, he started psychoanalysis, an obvious source of potential transformation. But how are we to connect personal and philosophical transformation? What, in psychoanalysis, could connect to the shift in style of philosophical output from traditional papers and books to the fragmentary, playful, and hyper-expressive medium of the memes? I suggest that the presence of the child, Robin, in the image, and the concept of childishness that his depiction suggests, provide a powerful key for understanding the co-incidence of personal and philosophical transformation and, as we shall see, for understanding also the ambivalence suggested by Batman's "and no!!".

We may begin by quoting some remarks by the artist from a presentation he made of some of his memetic work to philosophy departments in 2017:

> In 1969, the expression "the personal *is* political" was coined by feminist thinkers to challenge the idea that there is a disjuncture between the personal and the broader structures of power in which individuals are inscribed. If we interpret "political" broadly, so as to include all forms of public, institutional discourse, a special case of the expression would be "the personal *is* philosophical." This special case would cover efforts to overcome the gap between the personal and the conventions and norms of philosophy as a discipline. Those norms enjoin authors to keep their own personalities out of their work, enjoin readers to focus only on the 'ideas' in the text, ideas that are supposed to be able to circulate without any vital connection to the lives and circumstances of their authors. This privileging of objectivity and impersonality, with its effacement of the people who produce philosophy and the ways their individuality affects their philosophy, has left the discipline shrunken and shriveled, deprived of the nourishing life-blood of the real people who make it. What is desperately needed for the reinvigoration of philosophy is the rude and forceful interpellation of our stunted disciplinary norms by the subject, in all her strange specificity and individuality. Auto-theory is one form this interpellation can take: the calling out of a moribund modality of philosophy by the subject, slowly and seductively revealing her own face. But because each subject is singular, unique, and real, the face of her desire, even as it reveals itself, will always retain an element of inscrutability to the other. "Fetish" is the name we give to what is inexplicable, or surd, in desire.
>
> My project is a work of auto-theory, conducted under the sign of this image [here the image of Batman slapping Robin was displayed, along with a slapping sound effect] in which the joyful, liberating, fetish-clad warrior, in his idiosyncratic singularity, forces the intrusion of the personal onto the stunted, childish discipline of academic philosophy, trying, with a slap, to bring the blood to its face, trying to rouse it from its valorization, at once perverse and torpid, of the production of philosophy without a visible human face.

These powerful words seem to connect the philosophical transformation with a sense of personal liberation of the kind that we might well associate with psychoanalysis: a liberation from the imprisonment we suffer by our childish forms of adaptation, the sense of torpidity such imprisonment produces in the form of neurosis and, perhaps more fundamentally, character formation. At the same time, the use of the image is playful and original, placing itself well outside the boundaries of the usual disciplinary parameters. It interpellates traditional philosophy in the name of personal liberation. The Batman Meme Project, and its parerga, are the work of someone coming into his own, fusing his revisionary aspirations for philosophy with a sense of his own emotional liberation, and tapping into a childish and playful vigor.

In fact, going further out on a limb, we can hypothesize a more intimate link between the two kinds of transformation. Analytic philosophy, as its practitioners will know well, appeals largely because of its care with language. It is the philosophy of verbal distinctions, definitions, precision, and small but crucial differences between various formulations of ideas. For many, this functions like water to a parched desert traveler, struggling through the endless dunes of ordinary interactions where such care is not only useless but often counterproductive. Yet the careful, even over-careful, control of language has its own perils and can naturally become the tool of repression. One variety of psychotherapy is Primal Scream Therapy; but even without elevating the need for a primal scream to starring role of psychotherapy, it is easy to see the point of the idea. The very notion of free association in psychoanalysis (for more on which, see *Free Association* (M.14) and the commentary thereon) suggests the importance of throwing off the shackles of care and precision in self-expression, as if the voice of the unconscious must be always, to some extent, inarticulate, fragmentary, and confused.

To summarize so far, then, a symbolic association of Robin, receiving a slap, with a style of philosophy that was once a valued home to the artist, after his early misstep in the direction of music, but came to be felt as constricting, in the way our childish modes of adaptation (including, for those destined for analytic philosophy, an iron mastery over the means of self-expression) are initially valuable defenses but become hindrances as our circumstances change and might be shed during the course of analysis. And so also, perhaps as part of that very process, with the unlocking of other childish forces, the former objects of repression now unleashing themselves gleefully in a new kind of philosophical play. All of this might be read into the "yes" of Batman's "Yes and no!!". And yet, there is also that "no," that qualification of the transformative experience associated with "these memes." What is that qualification? At the very least, what seems to have unlocked, or provided a focus for, these positive forms of transformation is an image that shows an adult slapping down a child's attempt to speak. Perhaps the artist felt free to take the steps he has taken only because the very form of those steps signals a disapproval of the childish voice struggling to make itself heard. The transformation has had to carry within itself its own dismissal. Allowing identification with both Robin and Batman, the image used in this body of work says at one and the same time "look at me!" and "shut up!". If identification with Batman, in the image, signifies joyful liberation from, or rebellion against, faceless and immature norms internalized by the artist, identification with Robin surely signifies a sense of self-censoring, of putting oneself down, of revulsion, even, at the child within, the child who, in the very Batman Meme Project (and its parerga!) wants to come out and play. The image thus serves several psychic functions at the same time; its use is, as psychoanalysts would say, overdetermined. And in fact, in the same remarks from which we quoted above about the liberatory potential of the image, we also find these words by the artist, giving a quite different take on that image:[187]

> The childish desire to show one's face is met, as it were, with a slap by the reality principle that knows that to be seen, a face must mask itself in some way to make it enticing to the viewer. The upwelling or over-flowing needs of the id must be tamped down by the ego and super-ego... This is what I see in [the] image. An enthusiastic, youthful Robin, as yet unsuccessful in making himself visible to us, is schooled by the older Batman. "No-one is interested in you, Robin," the image itself seems to say. "Wear a mask!"

[187] These remarks, and those quoted above, come from two of four 'incompatible' introductions to the presentation, all of which were delivered by Evnine on each occasion he made the presentation.

M.96 The Origins of Neo-Platonist Metaphysics

M.96 The Origins of Neo-Platonist Metaphysics Composed: May 18th. Orientation: Reverse. Font: Comic Sans. TB1: "WHAT'S THE MATTER, BATMAN?", black. TB2: "NOTHING IS THE MATTER!", black. TB3: "THE ORIGINS OF NEO-PLATONIST METAPHYSICS", white. Added Image: A mirror in Robin's left hand, reflecting Batman and his speech bubble, with the words "THE MATTER IS NOTHING!!", in black.

From a technical point of view, this may be the most dazzling meme in the entire corpus. Evnine has taken Batman's head and speech bubble from a specially made meme with the image in its original orientation, inserted it into a mirror frame, and rotated both frame and image at an angle which, while not actually possible, suggests the reflection while still allowing us to read it. A couple of other details will be mentioned in due course.

To understand the content of the meme, we must go back to Evnine's early 'book,' *The Incoherence of the Incoherence* (see *Incoherence* (M.95) and *The Sound of Your Blood...* (M.42) for a description of and another excerpt from it, respectively). It includes the following, self-contained passage:

The Origins of Neo-Platonist Metaphysics

Plotinus sat with a girl standing just in front of him. He said (or at least Porphyry said he said, for Porphyry, being something of a voyeur was at that time concealed in the room), he said, "So, if we strip off the accidents or qualities - or 'forms' as Aristotle named them - such as colour (and by way of demonstration, off came her scarf and jewellery), texture (her skirts and petticoats), height (her shoes), extension (her farthingale), figure or outline (her corset), moistness (her underwear), dryness (he cleared his throat), we are left with the matter. The matter in hand, as it were." He flushed. But then his face clouded with the memory of an unsolved philosophical problem.

"What's the matter?" said the girl.

He found the solution and his face cleared. "Oh, it's nothing, my dear. Nothing at all," he said, and continued his exposition.

++++++++++++++++++++++++++++++

From which incident Porphyry was led to conclude that Plotinus held matter to be something with hardly any real existence, yet still a theoretical construct, as opposed to Gregory, who dispensed with this mystical pectin altogether and made his jam all from predicates, claiming, implicitly, that they needed nothing of which to be predicated.

In another sense this is exactly what Plotinus said, supposing that qualities were predicated of matter and that matter was nothing, or rather "a shadow, and on this shadow is traced a sketch – the world of appearance." (*Enniads* VI)

Neo-Platonism (so named only since the 19th century) is a phase in the history of ancient, Plato-inspired philosophy that is taken to have emerged in the 3rd century C.E. with Plotinus (204/5 – 270). Plotinus's writings were collected after his death and published as the *Enniads* by his pupil and biographer, Porphyry. In Evnine's vignette we see Plotinus engaged in a studied mix of Eros and philosophy. The intertwining of the two is itself, of course, a well-known theme of Platonic philosophy, as witnessed by Diotima's speech to Socrates in Plato's *Symposium*. Diotima there recounts to Socrates the true method of philosophy, ascending through erotic love to a higher form of love exemplified in the pure contemplation of the Forms, the immaterial source of what is only approximated in the world of mere appearance, the home of sexual desire. Porphyry is depicted as eavesdropping but mishearing or misunderstanding what he hears.[188] He thereby accidentally 'discovers' one of neo-Platonism's fundamental assumptions – the unreality, or lesser reality, of matter.

---

[188] A case of learning through inappropriate voyeurism is present in another cultural tradition roughly contemporaneous with Porphyry – the Talmud! In TB *Berakhot* 62a we learn: "**Rav Kahana entered and lay beneath Rav's bed. He heard** Rav **chatting and laughing** with his wife, **and seeing to his needs,** i.e., having relations with her. Rav Kahana **said to** Rav: **The mouth of Abba,** [i.e., Rav] **is like** one who **has never eaten a cooked dish,** i.e., his behavior was lustful. Rav **said to him: Kahana, you are here? Leave, as** this **is an undesirable mode of behavior.** Rav Kahana **said to him: It is Torah, and I must learn**" (text in bold represents the words of the Talmud, the rest is supplied by the translator Adin Steinsaltz; I have made a few trivial, silent changes). Interestingly, this anecdote is inserted into a lengthy discussion concerning how, when, and where one may defecate. Returning to Plotinus, his translator Stephen MacKenna writes: "He builds the soul a fairy palace; enchanted, you follow him through the lovely labyrinthine structure; you mount, breathless, by successive stairways of the spirit, each more pure, more tenuous, more aspiring than the last – but sooner or later there comes a time when you ask

The issue under discussion is one that has haunted Western philosophy almost since its inception: what is the relation between the qualities of an object and the object as such. It is an attractive starting point to think that underlying (*hypokeimenon* was Aristotle's term) the qualities is a substance that the qualities are qualities of. This is sometimes called 'matter' (*hyle* in Aristotle). This simple idea, however, gives rise to myriad philosophical perplexities. Must the underlying thing, as it is in itself, be free of all qualities? And if it is, how can we grasp it or conceptualize it? Substance as unknowable (Aristotle's prime matter, Locke's "something, I know not what," or Kant's *noumenon*) is a recurrent theme in Western philosophy. In the face of these puzzling views, another approach has arisen, both in ancient and modern guise, that does away with the underlying substance for the qualities altogether and treats an object simply as the 'bundle' of its qualities. A dance around these ideas is depicted in Evnine's early piece. Plotinus is said to have not quite given up on the idea of underlying matter, in contrast to Gregory of Nyssa, the fourth-century Cappadocian father of the church, who is associated with a pure bundle theory. I describe the exchange as a dance because Plotinus's view is something of a moving target here. The underlying substance is both something and nothing, and the nothing is not quite nothing, but a shadow. (Evnine's use of "theoretical construct" to capture Plotinus's view is jarring and off the mark; "mystical pectin" might be much better though its metaphorical register makes it hard to say.)

At the time he wrote The Origins of Neo-Platonist Metaphysics, around 1981-4, Evnine was attending lectures at the University of London on post-Aristotelian philosophy given by the distinguished scholar Professor Sir Richard Sorabji. It was Professor Sorabji's practice to distribute in class mimeographed handouts replete with quotations from ancient, and occasionally more modern, sources. Although my researches have been unsuccessful in locating a mimeographed handout with quotations from Plotinus and Gregory of Nyssa that might provide the source material for Evnine's piece, Sorabji's book *Matter, Space, and Motion: Theories in Antiquity and Their Sequel* was published in 1988 and the handouts were, I think, often-handwritten drafts of parts of that book. One can read there the following obscure passage from Plotinus, the glosses in square brackets being my own attempts to elucidate it:

> There should be no objection, if we make perceptible substance [the ordinary world of tables and chairs] out of non-substances [i.e. qualities]. For not even the whole [of perceptible substance] is true substance; it imitates it [the fundamental Platonist insight to capture the relation between the mundane and what is truly real], for true substance has being independently of the others which accompany it [its qualities? the mundane world which imitates it?] and the others which are generated out of it, because it truly is. But here [i.e., with perceptible substance] what underlies [i.e., matter] does not generate [the qualities], and it is not adequate to be a being, because the others do not come from it, but it is a shadow, and a shadow upon a shadow, a picture and an

yourself where the W.C. is" (an unpublished letter quoted by E.R. Dodds in the preface to MacKenna (1936: 69-70)).

appearance. (*Enneads* 6.3.8, translated by Armstrong, quoted in Sorabji 1988, 51-2)

Immediately following the Plotinus passage in his 1988 book, Sorabji introduces Gregory of Nyssa and provides three quotations which, again, must have been part of Evnine's unrecovered mimeographed source. Gregory's reason for adopting the bundle theory is that it solves, he alleges, the problem of how an immaterial God could create a material world. Here is an excerpt from one of the three passages. Again, the square brackets are my added glosses.

> You can hear people saying things like this: if God is matterless, where does matter come from? How can quantity [a quality of material things] come from non-quantity [God is himself without any quantity], the visible from the invisible… [The answer to these questions is that God] established for the creation of things all the things through which matter is constituted [the notion of constitution doing the work here of contrasting with the non-bundle theory's idea that matter is something independent that has these qualities, rather than being made up of them]: light, heavy, dense, rare, soft, resistant, fluid, dry, cold, hot, colour, shape, outline, extension. All of these are in themselves thoughts and bare concepts [hence immaterial and consistent with creation by an immaterial God]; none is matter on its own. But when they combine, they turn into matter [i.e., their combination is just what matter is]. (*in Hexaemeron* col. 69-BC, quoted in Sorabji 1988: 52; I assume the translation is by Sorabji)

The few words from Plotinus that Evnine quotes – "a shadow, and on this shadow is traced a sketch – the world of appearance" – are evidently those translated in the passage from Sorabji's book as "a shadow, and a shadow upon a shadow, a picture and an appearance." Does this undermine the claim that Evnine's source was a handout distributed by Sorabji? No. The discrepancy is easy to explain. Evnine's wording comes from the translation of Plotinus made by Stephen MacKenna, between 1905 and 1930. Sorabji footnotes the Plotinus paragraph in his book to thank A.H. Armstrong for letting him see his translation, which was not published until 1988, the same year as Sorabji's book. So, when Sorabji was preparing the mimeographs in the early 1980s, the (unfound) source for Evnine's work must have employed the MacKenna translation. By the time Sorabji published the work, he had switched to using Armstrong's.

Evnine's sketch is quite cleverly done but reading it now, one cannot help but feel how 'off' it is. The double wordplay around "matter" (connecting its philosophical use with the two English idioms "the matter in hand" and "what's the matter?") is clearly the lynchpin of the scene.[189] But the very young man, writing in the dark ages of the early 1980s, is completely

---

[189] There is, I hasten to add, no reason at all to think that Plotinus's actual pedagogy in any way resembled his approach in Evnine's lurid depiction, although we know he had women among his pupils. In fact, one anecdote concerning his teaching speaks very highly of Plotinus, portraying him, indeed, as something of a third-century Wittgenstein: "He was always as ready to entertain objections as he was powerful in meeting them. At one time I myself kept interrogating him during three days as to how the soul is associated with the body, and he continued explaining; a man called Thaumasius entered in the midst of our discussions; the visitor was more interested in the general drift of the system than in particular

oblivious to the sordor of the conjured encounter. Academia, as I write this in 2022, is still convulsing with the attempt to rid itself of sexual harassment and the sexualization of the teacher-student relationship and in that context, one can hardly approve of Evnine's attempt at humor. I mentioned above Diotima's speech from the *Symposium* and the idea that pedagogy is somehow essentially erotic. The idea persists to this day. Here is Jane Gallop, in her *Feminist Accused of Sexual Harassment*:

> At its most intense – and, I would argue, its most productive – the pedagogical relation between teacher and student is, in fact, a "consensual amorous relation." And if schools decide to prohibit not only sex but "amorous relations" between teacher and student, the "consensual amorous relation" that will be banned from our campuses might just be teaching itself. (Gallop 1997: 57)

In fact, Gallop seeks to make of the entanglement of sex and pedagogy a distinctively feminist strategy: "It is because of the sort of feminist I am that I do not respect the line between the intellectual and the sexual" (12). It seems to follow from this (am I being too literal?) that if large parts of the population are not to be excluded from intellectual nurturing by a given teacher, that teacher must be pansexual, that their students must be attractive to them, and so on. Are unprepossessing students of the wrong gender simply to be denied an education by a particular teacher? What of the asexual or aromantic, either as students or teachers? Are they unable to experience pedagogy at its most productive? Adrienne Rich wrote a famous essay called "Compulsory Heterosexuality." Gallop seems to be guilty of something more generic, compulsory sexuality.

Evnine's scene is both better and worse than the kind of thing Gallop envisages. Better, because it strips off the smugness (out comes "I do not respect the line between the intellectual and the sexual"), the cooptation of liberatory ideology ("it is because of the sort of feminist I am"), the erasure of asexuality ("might just be teaching itself") and leaves us with the bare matter at hand: "amorous relations" between teacher and student. Worse, because it evinces a perverse degree of objectification and absence of desire (notwithstanding the allusion to Plotinus's flushing and the evidence of the girl's (sic) arousal). It has its virtues but is, perhaps, saved from being utterly cringeworthy only by its status as near-juvenilia.

We may return, finally, to the meme. The meme attempts to express the central joke of the written piece – the transition from the colloquial "nothing is the matter" to the neo-Platonist idea of matter as nothing – in its highly compressed and visual medium. This could have been done so as to maintain the device of misunderstanding what is heard. For example, using the original orientation of the image, Batman could have said "Nothing's the matter!!!!" and Robin answered "What did you say? Matter is nothing?" Instead, Evnine has chosen to do something far superior – to translate the mistake into a visual one. The trick is done through the insertion

---

points, and said he wished to hear Plotinus expounding some theory as he would in a set treatise, but that he could not endure Porphyry's questions and answers: Plotinus asked, 'But if we cannot first solve the difficulties Porphyry raises what could go into the treatise?'." (Porphyry, *Life of Plotinus*, 13, trans. by MacKenna)

into the image of a mirror, presenting an imperfect reflection of Batman's words. One reason this is so clever is that neo-Platonism uses the metaphor of reflections, along with paintings and shadows, to represent the relation between the material world and the ideal, immaterial world that is the home of true being. (We see this in the final part of the Plotinus quotation above.) In the meme, however, the usual hierarchy is deconstructed since it is only through the reflection of Batman's words that the truth about the material world is seen. This subversion is emphasized by a detail almost too subtle to be noticed. If one enlarges the end of the text reflected in Robin's mirror, one sees this:

Figure 19 Detail showing two exclamation marks in the reflection

Barely visible are *two* exclamation marks where the original has only one. The mirror has thus, in a sense, increased rather than decreased reality, the reality of Batman's imperatival force.

In fact, turning the joke into a visual one, because of its occurrence in the essentially visual medium of the meme, is only half of the story. As I have noted in various places, the use of speech bubbles in the meme's template functions to represent what are spoken words via an image of their written representation. The reflection of the filled speech bubbles is therefore an image of an image (a shadow of a shadow) of the spoken reality. Offering a visual reflection of the speech bubble and its writing is metaphysically incongruous. First, it is not (even very approximately) a true visual reflection. It is what we might think of as a semantic reflection, inverting the order of the words rather than the shape of the letters. But secondly, it treats something that is merely an artifact of the medium of representation (using a picture of words where the depicted scene includes only spoken words) as if it were part of the depicted scene itself. This is highlighted by Evnine in his decision to include in the mirror reflection not just the words in Batman's speech bubble but also the speech bubble itself. And continuing in the same vein, he also includes the force lines arising from the impact of Batman's hand on Robin's cheek. Would it have been funnier to omit all of this and to include within the mirror only the reflected words, with no red background, no Batman-head, no speech bubble, no force lines – the words appearing against the crosshatching used to indicate that a virtual image has a transparent background? I don't know.

Figure 20 The meme with only the words reflected in the mirror. Executed, for the editor, by Jennifer Watson

M.97 He Forgot the Meme

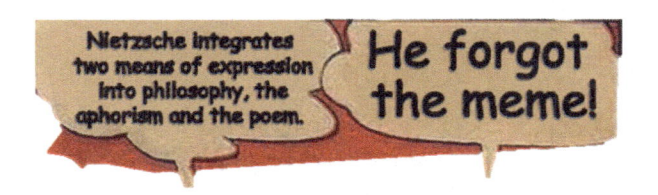

M.97 He Forgot the Meme Composed: May 20th. Orientation: Reverse. Font: Comic Sans. TB1: "Nietzsche integrates two means of expression into philosophy, the aphorism and the poem.", black. TB2: "He forgot the meme!", black.

Robin's text is adapted from Gilles Deleuze's book on Nietzsche:

> Nietzsche brings into philosophy two modes of expression, the aphorism and the poem. These very forms imply a new conception of philosophy, a new image of the thinker and the thought. (1965: 17)

How this text, with Batman's addition, could serve as an epitome of what Evnine is attempting in his memes! A new image of the thinker and the thought! But what, exactly, is this new image, this new conception of philosophy? I quote here extensively from a piece written by Evnine on philosophy through memes. Philosophy *through* memes is not the same as incorporating memes, as a new mode of expression, into philosophy, so this piece by Evnine should be thought of as only the first step in understanding the reference to Deleuze's Nietzsche in M.97.

> The native medium of philosophy is language, generally in the form either of discursive text or Socratic discussion. Since, as we have seen, memes often include language, one obvious way in which philosophy can be done *through* memes is that it can be done *in* memes. Recognizably philosophical text, either extant or original, can appear in a meme. If we stop here, though, we will achieve only an etiolated sense of philosophy through memes for a couple of reasons. First, given existing formats for memes, the amount of text that can

appear is very small. One can, no doubt, make allusions to already famous philosophical text in this way but that is hardly doing philosophy.

Figure 21 Socratic dialog, adapted from Plato's Euthyphro, *in the format of the American Chopper Argument meme, by Evnine.. One has to know the text already to appreciate it and the meme format just adds a bit of humor*

The only inventive and original philosophical text that could appear would have itself to be in the form of an aphorism or koan. Andrew Hui (2019) remarks that "aphorisms seem appropriate yet ill-matched to [the] cultural climate of the short attention span" exemplified by "tweets, memes, [and] GIFs" (177) and the same might be said for the koan. Appropriate, because short and quick to consume; ill-matched, because, as Hui puts it, they are "hermeneutically dense" and so in need of lengthy pondering. In any case, there is little evidence that meme-makers have aspired to hermeneutic density in the *language* inside memes (as opposed to in memes as wholes) – though that does exist as a possibility.

A second reason discursive philosophy *in* memes would be not all that interesting is that it would leave the role of the image (or other elements) and the meme format itself unintegrated into the philosophy being done. A successful meme ought to rely on all its elements. It is a controversial view that pictures can have propositional content (Grzankowski 2015), but if they can, then discursive philosophy within a meme might rely on both text and image. In that way, a meme could present a complex thesis, or even an argument, in an integrated way (see Birdsell and Groarke (2007) for exploration of visual arguments).[190]

Insisting on propositionality as a requirement for doing philosophy, however, leaves the scope of philosophy through memes fairly limited. If we seek something more exciting, we will have to have a wider conception of what counts as philosophy and an interpretation of "through" according to which it doesn't mean just "in." (Many philosophers, myself included, may require a Leap of Faith here. See Livingston (2006).) One possibility is to look at the ways that images can color the way in which we take in some philosophical text.

---

[190] I owe the thought that memes might present visual arguments to Wen Xianda, who also pointed me to the relevant literature.

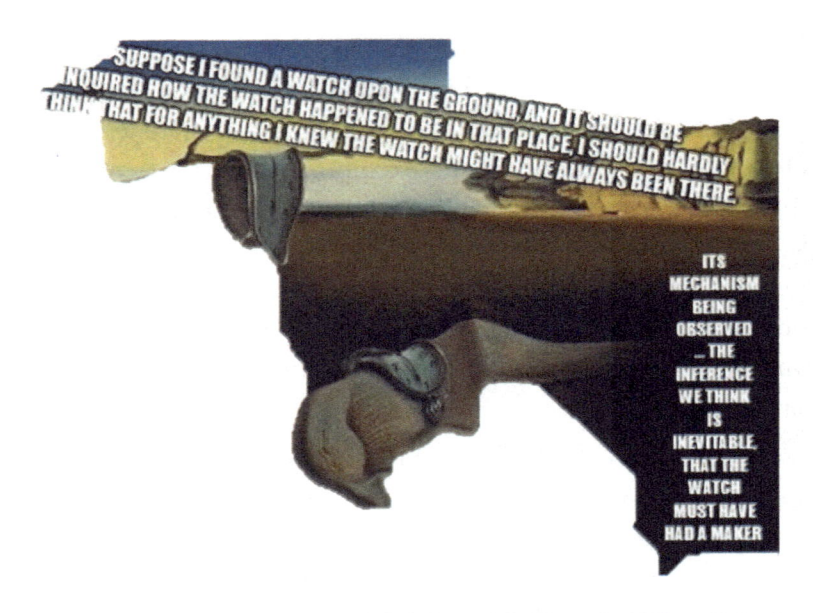

Figure 22 A one-off meme, by Evnine, in which (slightly modified) text by William Paley is cast in a different light by the image (Dali's The Persistence of Memory*). Note how the text itself is positioned to imitate the very far from 'perfect' watches*

One may not be able to give propositional expression to the overall effect of putting Paley's argument from design, which invokes the watch as an instance of reliable precision, over Dali's surreal, drooping watches, but it does encourage us to be skeptical about the argument. Another possibility is to think of memes in which text appears as labels of elements in an image as maps, for the non-propositional understanding of which several proposals have been made (e.g. Camp 2018).

The most developed proposals I am aware of for thinking about how philosophy may be done nonpropositionally, however, arise in connection with the arts. Martha Nussbaum (1992) describes how literature can also be moral philosophy (the philosophy done by literature is not to be identified with the propositions that constitute a literary text); Thomas Wartenberg (2007) argues that philosophy can be screened (in film); Cynthia Freeland (2010) discusses portraiture in terms of what it can offer with respect to character and the relation of mind and body; and there are other examples. A general framework for thinking about the issue (though not one which the authors just mentioned would necessarily accept), rather than in connection with a specific art form, is provided by Alva Noë (2015). Noë develops a view on which the arts involve philosophical *practice* by aiming at explicit representations of first-order activities we engage in spontaneously and unreflectively. By doing this, they show us to ourselves and enable us to 're-organize' those first-order activities (so that life may imitate, and be enriched by, art). Choreographed dance, for example, provides representations of our spontaneous dancing and movement;

it is an embodied philosophy of human motion. If we were to ask what choreographed dance says about human motion, of course, it would be clear that we were asking an inappropriate question. And the philosophy at issue comes to us *through* choreography not by way of the appearance *in* choreography of traditional philosophy but in some other way. Here, then, there is the potential for a more interesting way of thinking about philosophy through memes.

Applying Noë's framework to memes faces a couple of problems. The goal is to find some ordinary activities that reach deeply into what it is to be human (as movement and spontaneous dance do) and that give rise to memes as a meta-level representation of them. One problem is that memes, as such, are not tied to any particular medium. They can involve images alone, images with words, video with words, words alone, and human behaviors. Indeed, potentially anything can be part of a meme. Whatever these media can do in the way of philosophy might be done by memes that utilize them. But we want a way in which memes, as such, reflect on deep-seated facets of human existence and not just through the elements out of which singular memes are made. A second problem is that memes are highly ephemeral and many of them, let us say it, entirely inconsequential. It may simply stretch credibility to maintain that putting the text "I can has cheezburger?" over a picture of a cat could amount to a philosophical representation of anything important to us.

The answer to both problems is to pitch the discussion at a certain level of abstraction. There are some fairly general features of memes that obtain whatever the media of particular memes may be and it is to these features that we should look for representations of, and reflections on, first-order activities. This, in turn, will direct our attention principally to the activity of making memes, rather than to what is accomplished philosophically by singular memes. Hence, we need not worry that the philosophical interest of memes will be undermined by the silliness of many of them. I suggest there are two features of human existence that stand to meme-making in something of the same relation as movement does to choreography. These features are *bricolage* and ownership.

Bricolage

Bricolage is tinkering or jury-rigging and the *bricoleur*, someone who engages in it. She is likely to have a little hoard of cast-off bits and pieces and, when things need fixing or improving, sees what she has that can do the job – perhaps in some roundabout or unorthodox way. The concept was first made theoretical use of by Claude Lévi-Strauss (1966) who sees it as a practical analogue of the mental operations involved in mythmaking, to be contrasted with engineering as mythmaking is with science. Unlike the engineer, the *bricoleur* "works with what is at hand... a treasury" of "pre-constrained elements" the possibilities of which "always remain limited by the particular history of each piece and by those of its features which are already determined by the use for which it was originally intended or the modifications it has undergone for other purposes" (17-19). Although not everyone is a *bricoleur* in the narrow sense, *bricolage* is a fundamental aspect of human existence. It has to do, not with finding meaning where there is none, but with recycling meaning, imposing a new meaning on something that already has one. In this sense, it is a task imposed on all of us who live in history since we are always already in a world full of meanings that are given to us and that provide us with the materials out of which we must fashion our own meanings.

This is something that is central to meme-making.[191] The meme-maker works with a treasury (albeit a vast one, owing to the internet) of pre-constrained elements: pictures of celebrities, stills from films, references to song lyrics, cultural stereotypes, current affairs, and, of course, other memes. She does not have a relatively fixed goal, and a body of resources finalized towards achieving that goal – as is perhaps nearer the case with more traditional forms of artistic creativity – but rather responds to the moment, suddenly wanting to express herself on something and casting around for templates, images, words that will do the job. And she doesn't use these cultural artifacts simply for their material properties but for the meanings they carry with them.

Following Noë's lead, then, we can say that the production and circulation of memes provides a representation of our historicity, a spectacle in which we can see traced out the ways of re-use, of how meaning made arises from meaning found. But the connection between memes and *bricolage* goes deeper. Roland Barthes, writing very much in the same vein as Lévi-Strauss, says: "Mythical speech is made of a material which has already been worked on so as to make it suitable for communication: it is because all the materials of myth (whether pictorial or written) presuppose a signifying consciousness, that one can reason about them while discounting their substance" (1972: 108; by "substance" I understand something like "material properties"). Memes, "speech... made of a material which has already been worked on," themselves constitute something like a mythology.[192] This is borne out not just by the formal feature that Barthes describes but by their content. The vast majority of

---

[191] A point recognized in existing work on memes. Milner (2016) counts "re-appropriation" as one of the five fundamental "logics of memes" (11-42).

[192] A resemblance between memes and mythology's cousin, folklore, has been noted by Shifman (2014: 15) and Phillips and Milner (2017: 21-57).

image-based memes use representations of people and anthropomorphized animals (themselves a staple of myth). These can be grouped under a taxonomy of mythological types: hero, villain, everyman, sage, trickster, and so on. Drake, in this common meme template, for example, plays the role of sage, offering knowledge of what to value:

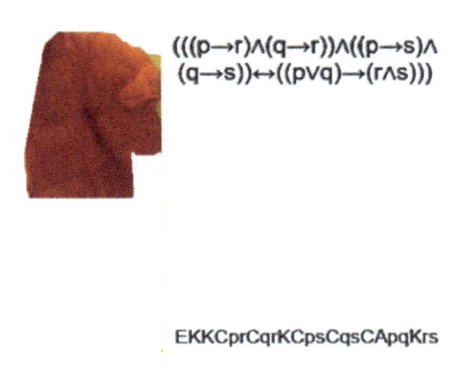

$(((p\rightarrow r)\wedge(q\rightarrow r))\wedge((p\rightarrow s)\wedge(q\rightarrow s))\leftrightarrow((p\vee q)\rightarrow(r\wedge s)))$

EKKCprCqrKCpsCqsCApqKrs

Figure 23 A Drake meme, by Evnine, in which in which Drake recoils from the use of the usual logical notation but embraces the more obscure Polish notation

The same function is absolved, in a structurally similar way, by the Marie Kondo meme ("this one sparks joy… this one does not spark joy…") and, with a different structure, by many "advice animal" memes.

Wojak is an everyman:

Figure 24 Wojak, or Feels Guy

as are the variants on it (NPC, Doomer, Doomer Girl, etc.). (This everyman quality is inherited by the internet abbreviation "TFW" ("that feel when") that derives from Wojak memes.) Feminist Ryan Gosling memes portray Gosling as a hero, both for his good looks and his commitment to sexy feminism. Other memes invoke mythical situations. The American Chopper Argument meme above invokes a battle of the gods. And the meme template instanced here depicts the frustration of mortals in the face of the inscrutable:

Figure 25 A Woman Yelling at a Cat meme (by Evnine) that brings out the human experience of frustration in the face of the inscrutable. The woman's words come from the film 2001: A Space Odyssey, *when the astronaut Dave pleads with Hal the computer to let him back into the ship. The cat replies with Hal's words, but with the name changed from "Dave" to "Karen," which connects human bafflement with the outrage of the entitled White woman associated with that name. The picture of the yelling woman (Taylor Armstrong) is from an episode of* Real Housewives of Beverley Hills. *Armstrong was shouting because of remarks someone made concerning abuse she was subject to from her husband, who killed himself a year or two later. Armstrong has since posted the meme in an approving way*

Care needs to be taken, however, in assigning the figures in memes to mythological types. One of the most important criteria in the assessment of memes by the cognoscenti is irony (see Her and Zharova 2017). Irony, though, is often, by design, hard to detect. This means there is often a certain difficulty in knowing how to take the figures in memes (given an associated text). For example, in the Drake meme above, is Drake really offering a sage-like recommendation of Polish over Principia-style notation for logic? Or to put it another way, would the joke of the meme have been any less effective, indeed any different at all, had I reversed the texts? Drake, therefore, in memes made with this template, may well embody a kind of impostor and not a genuine sage. This situation is ubiquitous in memes. In such memes, figures, despite some superficial appearance of belonging to another mythological type, actually exemplify the trickster. Hynes (1993) tells us that:

> At the heart of... manifest trickster traits is (1) the fundamentally ambiguous and anomalous personality of the trickster. Flowing from this are such other features as (2) deceiver/trickplayer, (3) shape-shifter, (4) situation-invertor, (5) messenger/imitator of the gods, and (6) sacred/lewd bricoleur. (34)

The trickster is, without a doubt, the tutelary spirit of memes and their makers.

Ownership

Ownership is a fundamental feature of human life. It extends well beyond our material possessions to encompass our words, ideas, and actions. A number of prominent forms of collective work break down into a series of interventions, either synchronic or diachronic, each of which is owned by some individual or individuals. (Think of Western philosophy.) This conception of joint activity, however, comes under pressure from two complementary sources. First, there are many collective projects that do not, actually, function this way. I have used the term "creative curation" (2016: 153) to describe the ways in which people create and maintain in existence such things as languages, nations, and cities. Although people, of course, are engaged in owned actions that contribute to such entities, the function of these actions does not require their ownership by, or attribution to, individual agents. Secondly, and explicitly, fifty or so years ago, theory began to announce the 'death of the author' (Foucault... and others).

Foucault suggests that

> as our society changes ... the author function will disappear, and in such a manner that fiction and its polysemous texts will once again function according to another mode.... All discourses... would then develop in the anonymity of a murmur. (1984: 119)

Despite such pronouncements, however, the way we experience (both as producers and consumers) such discourses as art, literature, and philosophy has not really relinquished the role of the author, the owner of the work, the view, the argument.

Memes, though, constitute one area of creative activity where the death of the author really has taken hold. They truly are produced and circulated in the "anonymity of a murmur." Taken together, they serve a double function of revealing to us at a relatively explicit level something of the nature of collective curation and simultaneously, breaking new ground in the development of a mode of discourse which, I think, we are still very reluctant to embrace.

I say they reveal such things in a relatively explicit way. Patrick Davison (2012) draws a contrast between what he calls the restricted and the unrestricted web. The former is home to well-regulated platforms like Facebook and Twitter that provide security at the cost of creativity. The unrestricted web includes platforms (such as imageboards like 4chan) that forego security in the name of the freedom of the imagination. Many meme templates originate in the unrestricted web and are subsequently "normified" as they move to the restricted web where most of us encounter them. Davison writes:

> The memes of the unrestricted web... not only often disregard attribution and metadata; they are also frequently incorporated into systems and among practices that actively prevent and dismantle attribution. (132)

One can see this idea at work in a manifesto written by Seong-Young Her (2016), one of the founders of *The Philosopher's Meme*:

> The task is not the destruction of the meme, but rather the destruction of the ownership of the meme which manifests as the invisible hand of conservative prescriptivism -- comments, screeching from Imgur and Reddit; "you're using that meme wrong!" The elimination of the very notion of personal property in this area is what once made ironic memes so great: the meme was true only to itself.

Even if a Golden Age has now been lost, it remains true that most memes circulate, even on the restricted web, without attribution.[193]

Memes reveal something about ownership to us in another way. Davison conjectures that one of the reasons why the unrestricted web eschews attribution is that this bypasses the whole question of copyright. Memes, because they are works of *bricolage*, draw freely from many sources that are not, strictly speaking, free. In fact, there have been some notable examples of copyright holders asserting their rights over people who have used their material. In 2010, Constantin Films, who hold the rights to the film about Hitler, *Downfall* (*Der Untergang*), demanded that Youtube remove the many parody videos in which users add their own subtitles to the German script of a particular scene. (See Schwabach (2012) for a discussion of this and similar cases from the legal point of view.) Getty, who own the rights to a photograph of a penguin that appears in the Socially Awkward Penguin meme, have

---

[193] One-off memes are of interest here. Since they do not use a template, they participate less in the sharing economy of memes and therefore can be more easily considered as authored works, subject to the full range of hermeneutic tools suitable for such works. One might almost call such things "anti-memes."

successfully levied payment from people who have posted such memes on a website.

Figure 26 Not the original template image for Socially Awkward Penguin, which I would not dare print, but a substitute created to get around Getty's enforcement of their rights to the original

It is clear that current copyright law in the US does not work in the interests of freedom and creativity and this is particularly the case with memes, one of the points of which, as we have seen, is their appropriation of existing cultural material. Memes thus provide an avenue, similar to that provided by appropriation art, through which, as Elizabeth Cantalamessa (2020) argues, artists and others can help to conceptually engineer concepts like *work of art*, *originality*, *copy*, and *authorship*. (See also Hick 2017.) As the invocation of the idea of conceptual engineering indicates, this work is itself a kind of practical philosophy that can be done through memes.

M.101 Even You?

M.101 Even You? Composed: June 11th, 2017. Posted: June 11th, 2017. Orientation: Reverse. Font: Arial. TB1: "Batman, will even you die some day?", black. TB2: "Only when I'm very old, Robin. And you'll be all grown up by then!!", black.

Adam West, who portrayed Batman in the 1960s TV series, died on June 9th, 2017, two days before this meme was composed and posted on Facebook. There can be no doubt that it was intended as a tribute to him. The meme has great pathos, owing, I think, to the discrepancy between Robin's age and the much younger manner in which he expresses himself. (In this incongruity, it resembles *Mr. Peabody* (M.25).) Robin sounds like a child of six or seven, beginning to confront the reality and the universality of death. Batman plays the role of the loving parent, attempting, but inevitably failing, to make this unacceptable fact acceptable. The slap, so at odds with the love and care Batman exhibits towards Robin in his words (love and care he exhibits nowhere else in Evnine's memes), actualizes the way in which no amount of tenderness can mitigate the slap in the face that is death, and loss in general. (See also *Wrong!* (M.21) and the commentary thereon.)

Appendix: Memes Omitted from Volume I

M.3 A Character in a Novel Composed: February 20th. Posted: February 20th. Orientation: Reverse. Font: Impact, with font shadow. TB1: "THERE CAN BE NO DOUBT THAT... IT WAS BECAUSE IT REPRESENTED THAT SAME GAIT THAT AN ANCIENT MARBLE RELIEF ACQUIRED SUCH GREAT IMPORTANCE FOR NORBERT HANOLD...", white, with black borders. TB2: "FOOL! HE'S A CHARACTER IN A NOVEL!", white, with black borders.

M.7 Filioque Composed: February 21st. Posted: February 21st. Orientation: Reverse. Font: Impact, with font shadow. TB1: "Et in spiritum sanctum qui ex patre procedit.", white, with black borders. TB2: "FILIOQUE!", white, with black borders.

M.16 Yeah, Yeah Composed: February 23rd. Posted: February 27th. Orientation: Reverse. Font: Arial. TB1: "...but in no language does a double positive express a negative.", black. TB2: "Yeah, yeah!", black.

M.20 Dialetheism Composed: February 29th. Posted: March 2nd. Orientation: Reverse. Font: Arial. TB1: "But if there is a set of all non-self-members, then it both is and isn't a member of itself.", black. TB2: "AND????", black. TB3: "Dialetheism", white, with black borders.

M.21 Wrong! Composed: February 24th. Posted: March 2nd. Orientation: Reverse. Font: Impact, with font shadow. TB1: "Better to have loved and lost than never...", white, with black borders. TB2: "Wrong! Wrong! Wrong!", white, with black borders.

M.23 Whereof one cannot speak... Composed: March 2nd. Published: March 3rd. Orientation: Reverse. Font: Comic Sans. TB1: "Whereof one cannot speak, thereof one must be silent.", white. TB2: N/a.

M.26 God loves the number 5 Composed: March 2nd. Posted: March 6th. Orientation: Reverse. Font: Comic Sans. TB1: "God loves the number 5.", black. TB2: "He loves all numbers equally!", black.

M.27 He thought that he thought... Composed: March 3rd. Posted: March 7th. Orientation: Reverse. Font: Arial. TB1: "What, reduced to their simplest reciprocal form, were Bloom's thoughts about Stephen's thoughts about Bloom and about Stephen's thoughts about Bloom's thoughts about Stephen?", black. TB2: "He thought that he thought that he was a jew whereas he knew that he knew that he knew that he was not.", black.

M.33 I thought your boat... Composed: March 2nd. Posted: March 10th. Orientation: Reverse. Font: Comic Sans. TB1: "I thought your boat was longer than it is.", black. TB2: "Wrong! It's exactly as long as it is!", black.

M.34 Distinguo, Batters Composed: March 9th. Posted: March 11th. Orientation: Original. Font: Comic Sans. TB1: "You've become a pompous fool, Robin! A bumptious oaf!", black. TB2: "Distinguo, Batters, distinguo!", black.

M.35 ... more like a visible one Composed: March 3rd. Posted: March 12th. Orientation: Reverse. Font: Comic Sans. TB1: "Capitalism! As if an invisible hand...", black. TB2: "... more like a visible one!", black.

M.38 The Incredulous Stare Composed: March 11th. Posted: March 14th. Orientation: Reverse. Font: Arial. TB1: "There are many possible worlds, concrete, spatio-temporally inaccessible from each other; actuality is indexical...", black. TB2: "?!?!?!?", black. TB3: "Incredulous stare," white.

M.39 It's Greek! Composed: February 22nd. Posted: March 14th. Orientation: Reverse. Font: Arial. TB1: "Linear B is Etruscan.", black. TB2: "It's Greek!", black.

M.40 Maudlin Trash Composed: March 16th. Posted: March 16th. Orientation: Reverse. Font: Arial. TB1: "I just love "Cinema Paradiso.", black. TB2: "Maudlin trash. I prefer Նռան գույնը by Սերգեյ Փարաջանով", black.

M.41 Galbungus says it does Composed: March 15th. Posted: March 16th. Orientation: Reverse. Font: Comic Sans. TB1: "Terrentius says 'ego' has no vocative.", black. TB2: "But Galbungus says it does!", black.

M.44 Vish! Composed: March 10th. Posted: March 18th. Orientation: Reverse. Font: Comic Sans. TB1: "Precious: highly esteemed or cherished. Cherish: to hold dear. Dear: highly valued or precious.", black. TB2: "Vish!!", black.

M.47 Are you even listening? Composed: March 5th. Orientation: Reverse. Font: Comic Sans. TB1: "A table is just a classical mereological fusion of momentary table-like entities at successive times.", white. TB2: "Are you even listening to yourself?", white.

M.51 The Language of Flowers Composed: March 21st. Orientation: Reverse. Font: Arial. TB1: "I just wanted to say how much…", black. TB2: "The only sentence in the language of flowers is "I fucked up"!", black. Added Image: A daffodil, in Robin's left hand.

M.53 Haven't You Heard? Composed: March 22nd. Orientation: Reverse. Font: Comic Sans. TB1: "I dress like this for myself!", black. TB2: "Haven't you heard of false consciousness?", black.

M.54 There was a ship… Composed: March 22nd. Orientation: Reverse. Font: Comic Sans. TB1: "There was a ship…", black. TB2: "Now wherefore stopp'st thou me?", black.

M.55 My favorite notes Composed: March 23rd. Orientation: Reverse. Font: Comic Sans. TB1: "… so basically, all classical pieces come down to:", black. TB2: "You left out all my favorite notes!!", black. TB3: "{whistles}", white, placed underneath the image of musical notation. Added Image: Musical notation, in which the line in the treble clef descends, in joined minims, from E to D to C (the octave above middle C) and the line in the bass clef, in similar rhythm, rises from C below middle C, to G, and back down to C. Above the notes in the treble clef is the notation "3 2 1", underneath those in the bass clef, "I, V, I".

M.56 Cicero!** Composed: March 24th. Orientation: Reverse. Font: Arial. TB1: "According to Cicero*…", black. TB2: "Cicero**!", black. TB3: "*This is a written representation of the spoken name [ˈsɪsəɹəʊ].", white. TB4: "**This is a written representation of the spoken name [ˈkɪkəɹəʊ].", white.

M.57 I refute him thus Composed: March 25th. Orientation: Reverse. Font: Comic Sans. TB1: "Berkeley says the material world isn't real.", black. TB2: "I refute him thus!", black.

M.59 #JeSuisRobin Composed: March 26th. Orientation: Reverse. Font: Comic Sans. TB1: "Stop the slapping @Batman! #NotAllSuperheroes Help me Aunt @Harriet @SacredRiver #JeSuisRobin", black. TB2: "Sorry, Robin, I don't twitter!", black.

M.61 And this is not a slap Composed: March 27th. Orientation: Reverse. Font: Comic Sans. TB1: "Ceci n'est pas un mème Batman.", black. TB2: "And this is not a slap!", black.

M.64 An Error in the Reckoning Composed: March 30th. Orientation: Reverse. Font: Comic Sans. TB1: "At the death of Adrian the Fifth, Pedro Juliani, who should be named John the Twentieth, was through an error in the reckoning elevated to the papal chair as John the Twenty-first.", black. TB2: "That was careless!", black.

M.65 I am Spartacus! Composed: April 4th. Orientation: Reverse. Font: Arial. TB1: "I am Spartacus!", black. TB2: "I am Spartacus!", black.

M.66 Slap Negation Composed: April 8th. Orientation: Reverse. Font: Comic Sans. TB1: All negation must be represented in a sentence.", black. TB2: "All negation must be represented in a sentence.", black. TB3: "Slap negation", white, with black borders.

M.67 I am no-one Composed: April 8th. Orientation: Reverse. Font: Comic Sans. TB1: "I am no-one.", black. TB2: "Yes you are. But that won't help you escape a slap!", black.

M.68 The Age of Grief Composed: April 8th. Orientation: Reverse. Font: Comic Sans. TB1: "It feels like there is a vast ocean of sadness just behind my head, waiting to engulf me!", white. TB2: "You have reached the Age of Grief!", white.

M.70 Snow is white! Composed: April 8th. Posted: April 8th. FIRST PANEL Orientation: Original. Font: Arial. TB1: ""Snow is white!" is true!", black. TB2: N/a. SECOND PANEL Orientation: Reverse. Font: Arial. TB1: N/a. TB2: "Snow is white!", black.

M.71 Shhh! Composed: April 9th. Orientation: Original. Font: Comic Sans. TB1: "Shhh, Robin! Not a word.", black. TB2: "The longer he goes without hearing another human voice, the happier he is.", black. Added Image: Robin's speech bubble redrawn as a thought bubble.

M.73 Strong Female Lead Composed: April 10th. Orientation: Original. Font: Comic Sans. TB1: "It doesn't question the underlying structures of patriarchy!", black. TB2: "But it has a strong female lead!", black.

M.75 Too Easy, Robin! Composed: April 11th. Orientation: Reverse. Font: Comic Sans. TB1: "My turn. '"David Soul is dreamy" is true if and only if David Soul is dreamy.'", black. TB2: "Too easy, Robin! Tarski and Hutch!", black. TB3: "Combatting The Riddler has left the Dynamic Duo grappling with PTSD.", white.

M.79 Perimeter Composed: April 23rd. Posted: April 23rd. Orientation: Reverse. Font: Comic Sans. TB1: "Perimeter College? Does that mean it runs around…", black. TB2: "The Holy Roman Empire was neither holy, Roman, nor an empire!", black.

M.81 You demon? Composed: April 25th. Posted: April 25th. Orientation: Reverse. Font: Comic Sans. TB1: "You demon?", brown. TB2: "Eudaimon!!", blue. Various colored scribbles over the whole image.

M.82 Not a Performative Composed: April 29th. Orientation: Reverse. Font: Comic Sans. TB1: ""I slap you!" is not a performative.", black. TB2: "So much the worse for you, then!", black.

M.83 "Sorry!" (Not Sorry!) Composed: April 29th. Orientation: Reverse. Font: Comic Sans. TB1: "What seems to be the hardest word, Batman?", black. TB2: ""Sorry"! (Not sorry!)", black.

M.84 Fail Better! Composed: April 30th. Orientation: Reverse. Font: Comic Sans. TB1: "Batman, I failed!", black. TB2: "Fail again! Fail better!", black.

M.85 What Is It Like? Composed: April 30th. Orientation: Reverse. Font: Comic Sans. TB1: "Batman, what is it like to be…", white. TB2: "a) Like this!", white. TB3: "a) Batman?", white. TB4: "b) a bat?", white. TB5: "c) a bat, man?", white. TB6: "d) a Batman?", white. TB7: "b) Abstract from the 'what it is like' of experiences in each of a bat's sensory modalities to what it is like to experience in that modality, and then aggregate these!", white. TB8: "c) Don't call me "man"!", white. TB9: "d) The question is ill-formed! "Batman" is not a general term!!", white.

M.86 The Sleep of Reason Composed: May 3rd. Orientation: Reverse. Font: Comic Sans. TB1: "Poetry heals the wounds inflicted by reason.", black. TB2: "But the sleep of reason produces monsters!!!", black.

M.87 A Pair of Fine Eyes Composed: May 4th. Orientation: Reverse. Font: Comic Sans. TB1: "How I wish I lived in a Jane Austen novel.", black. TB2: "You do have a pair of fine eyes!", black.

M.88 Bibliophagia Composed: May 8th. Orientation: Reverse. Font: Comic Sans. TB1: "I think I may be bibliophagic!", black. TB2: "Well that would explain why you write like shit!", black.

M.89 The Cheat of Words Composed: May 10th. Orientation: Reverse. Font: Comic Sans. TB1: "It is easy to perceive what imperfection there is in language, and how the very nature of words…", black. TB2: "The English language is incomparably rich and can convey every thought accurately and elegantly.", black.

M.90 Widdershins Composed: May 10th. FIRST PANEL (top left) Orientation: Reverse. Font: Comic Sans. TB1: "Is this widdershins, Batman?", black. TB2: "No, you idiot. The other way!!", black. SECOND PANEL (top right) *Idem*, with image rotated 90' clockwise. THIRD PANEL (bottom right) *Idem*, with image rotated another 90' clockwise. FOURTH PANEL (bottom left) *Idem*, with image rotated another 90' clockwise. In each case, the text remains at the top.

M.93 Not What You're Thinking Composed: May 12th. Orientation: Reverse. Font: Comic Sans. TB1: "Yeah, lesbians rule!", black. TB2: "No, Robin! A lesbian rule!!", black. Added Image: A lesbian rule in Robin's left hand.

M.94 A Girl Has No Name Composed: May 14th. Orientation: Reverse. Font: Arial. TB1: "What was she called, Batman?", black. TB2: "A girl has no name!!!!", black.

M.95 Incoherence Composed: May 17th. Orientation: Reverse. Font: Arial. TB1: "The incoherence of philosophy!", black. TB2: "No! The incoherence of the incoherence!", black.

M.98 Synthesis Composed: May 21st. Orientation: Reverse. Font: Arial. TB1: "The situation is deadlocked. The dialectic tension has come to a point where something has to happen.", black. TB2: "Like a slap in the face?!", black. TB3: "The Logic of Hegel's Dialectic: Synthesis", white.

M.99 Jerusalem Composed: May 23rd. Orientation: Reverse. Font: Comic Sans. TB1: "Batman? And was Jerusalem….", orange, with brown borders. TB2: "Yes! Among these dark Satanic Mills!", orange, with brown borders.

M.100 Change Composed: May 28th. Orientation: Original. Font: Arial. TB1: "When it is not necessary to change…", white. TB2: "… it is necessary not to change!", white.

M.102 Groovy Composed: August 16th, 2017. Orientation: Reverse. TB1: "When the students find out who you really are, they'll hate you forever", black. TB2: "I planned it all this way", black. TB3: "Groovy!", multicolored, with hand-drawn speech bubble around it leading to Robin. All text is represented in braille.

M.103 Squiggle Composed: March 18th, 2018. Orientation: Reverse. TB1: N/a. TB2: N/a. Added images: a tangled black line in Robin's speech bubble and a straight black line in Batman's

M.104 Dinner's Ready Composed: December 26th, 2022. Orientation: Reverse. Font for first three text boxes: Comic Sans. TB1: "If it weren't for the problem of how to get the kids to come in to dinner, I'd be inclined to just junk [proper names].", black. TB2: "If it weren't for the problem of how to interpellate the subject, I'd be inclined to just junk [proper names].", black. TB3: "Batman! Boy Blunder! Dinner's ready!", black, with hand-drawn speech bubble around it leading to the Joker. Font for last three text boxes: Impact with font shadow. TB4: "BROKE", white with black outline. TB5: "WOKE", white with black outline. TB6: "BESPOKE", white with black outline. Added image: The Joker.

BIBLIOGRAPHY

Adelman, Eliahu (2015) "Ehad Mi Yod'ea – Its Sources, Variations, and Parodies," Hebrew University of Jerusalem Website http://www.jewish-music.huji.ac.il/content/ehad-mi-yod'ea-its-sources-variations-and-parodies (accessed 26th October, 2022).

Ahmed, Sara (2004) *The Cultural Politics of Emotion* (Edinburgh: Edinburgh University Press).

Ahmed, Sara (2017) *Living a Feminist Life* (Durham: Duke University Press).

Aldrich, Henry (1691) *Artis Logicae Compendium* (Oxford: Sheldonian Theatre).

Anderegg, David (2005) "'You're Not a Freudian, Are You?' Secret Identities in the Lives of Working Clinicians," *American Journal of Psychoanalysis* 65, 333-9.

Anon (n.d.) *The Mystery of Green Grow the Rushes Oh!*, E.F.D.S.S. leaflet no. 10 (London: English Folk Dance and Song Society).

Austin, J.L. (1975) *How to Do Things with Words,* second edition (Cambridge: Harvard University Press).

Balint, Michael (1959) *Thrills and Regressions* (London: Maresfield Library).

Balint, Michael (1968) *The Basic Fault: Therapeutic Aspects of Regression* (London: Tavistock).

Baron, Salo Wittmayer (1957) *A Social and Religious History of the Jews*, vol. 5 (New York: Columbia University Press).

Barthes, Roland (1972) *Mythologies*, Annette Lavers (trans.) (New York: Farrar, Strauss, & Giroux).

Beider, Alexander (2001) *A Dictionary of Ashkenazic Given Names: Their Origins, Structure, Pronunciation, and Migrations* (Teaneck, NJ: Avotaynu).

Beider, Alexander (2008) *A Dictionary of Jewish Surnames from the Russian Empire*, revised edition (Teaneck, NJ: Avotaynu).

Beider, Alexander (2015) *Origins of Yiddish Dialects* (Oxford: Oxford University Press).

Birdsell, David and Leo Groarke (2007) "Outlines of a Theory of Visual Argument," *Argumentation and Advocacy* 43, 103-13.

Bollas, Christopher (2009) *The Evocative Object World* (London: Routledge).

Bourke, Anthony and John Rendall (1971) *A Lion Called Christian* (New York: Broadway Books).

Brentano, Robert (1988) *Two Churches: England and Italy in the Thirteenth Century* (Berkeley: University of California Press).

Breuer, Josef and Sigmund Freud (1893-5) *Studies on Hysteria* in *The Standard Edition of the Complete Psychological Works of Sigmund Freud*, v.2.

Cage, John (1961) *Silence: Lectures and Writings* (Middletown, CT: Wesleyan University Press).

Cage, John (2016) *The Selected Letters of John Cage*, Laura Kuhn (ed.) (Middletown, CT: Wesleyan University Press).

Camp, Elisabeth (2018) "Why Maps Are Not Propositional," in Alex Grzankowski and Michelle Montague (eds.), *Non-Propositional Intentionality* (Oxford: Oxford University Press), 19-45.

Cantalamessa, Elizabeth (2020) "Appropriation Art, Fair Use, and Metalinguistic Negotiation," *British Journal of Aesthetics* 60, 115-29.

Cronin, Brian (2009) "Batman Slaps Robin – The Origin of the Panel" https://www.cbr.com/batman-slaps-robin-the-origin-of-the-panel/ (accessed 20th October, 2022).

Daly, Lloyd W. (1967) *Contributions to a History of Alphabetization in Antiquity and the Middle Ages* (Brussels: Latomus).

Davidson, Baruch (n.d.) "Why is Simcha Bunim a Common Combination?" https://www.chabad.org/library/article_cdo/aid/1018509/jewish/Why-Is-Simcha-Bunim-a-Common-Combination.htm (accessed 28th October, 2022).

Davison, Patrick (2012) "The Language of Internet Memes," in Michael Mandiberg (ed.), *The Social Media Reader* (New York: NYU Press), 120-34.

De Morgan, Augustus (1847) *Formal Logic or the Calculus of Inference Necessary and Probable* (London: Taylor and Walton).

Delafield, Catherine (2020) *Women's Letters as Life Writing 1840-1885* (New York: Routledge).

Deleuze, Gilles (1965) *Nietzsche* (Paris: Presse Universitaire de France).

Derrida, Jacques (2016) *Of Grammatology*, Gayatri Spivak (trans.) (Baltimore: Johns Hopkins University Press).

Deutscher, Max (2014) "'Il n'y a pas de hors-texte' – Once More," *Symposium* 18, 98-124.

Edmonds, David (2020) *The Murder of Professor Schlick: The Rise and Fall of the Vienna Circle* (Princeton: Princeton University Press).

Eifermann, Rivka (1997) "The Exceptional Position of 'A Child is Being Beaten' in the Learning and Teaching of Freud," in Ethel Person (ed.), *On Freud's 'A Child is Being Beaten* (London: Karnac Books), 157-78.

Eisenstadt, Benzion (1900) *Dor Rabanav ve-Sofrav* (Vilna).

Evans, Gareth (1982) *Varieties of Reference* (Oxford: Clarendon Press).

Evans, Gareth (1985) *Collected Papers* (Oxford: Clarendon Press).

Evnine, Simon (1989) "Freud's Ambiguous Concepts," *Journal of Speculative Philosophy* 3, 86-99.

Evnine, Simon (1991) *Donald Davidson* (Stanford: Stanford University Press).

Evnine, Simon (2008) *Epistemic Dimensions of Personhood* (Oxford: Oxford University Press).

Evnine, Simon (2015) "'But Is It Science Fiction?': Science Fiction and a Theory of Genre," *Midwest Studies in Philosophy* 39, 1-28.

Evnine, Simon (2016) *Making Objects and Events: A Hylomorphic Theory of Artifacts, Actions, and Organisms* (Oxford: Oxford University Press).

F.C.H. (1868) "Old Latin Religious Song," *Notes and Queries*, 4th series, 2, 557.

Fabrikant, Agnès (1997) "The Analytic Parergon," in Barend Smilovic (ed.), *Filthy Lucre: Psychoanalysis and Money* (London: Octagon Press), 132-56.

Fish, Stanley (1980) *Is There a Text in this Class* (Cambridge: Harvard University Press).

Forster, E.M. (1927) *Aspects of the Novel* (New York: Harcourt).

Foucault, Michel (1978) *History of Sexuality, vol 1: An Introduction* (New York: Random House).

Foucault, Michel (1984) "What is an Author?" in Paul Rabinow (ed.), *The Foucault Reader* (New York: Pantheon Press), 101-20.

Foucault, Michel and Richard Sennett (1981) "Sexuality and Solitude," *London Review of Books* 3.9 http://www.lrb.co.uk/v03/n09/michel-foucault/sexuality-and-solitude_(accessed 25th October, 2022).

Fournier, Lauren (2021) *Autotheory as Feminist Practice in Art, Writing, and Criticism* (Cambridge: MIT Press).

Freeland, Cynthia (2010) *Portraits and Persons* (Oxford: Oxford University Press).

Freud, Sigmund (1913) "On Beginning the Treatment," in *The Standard Edition of the Complete Psychological Works of Sigmund Freud*, v.12, 121-44.

Freud, Sigmund (1915) "The Unconscious," in *The Standard Edition of the Complete Psychological Works of Sigmund Freud*, v.14, 159-218.

Freud, Sigmund (1919) "'A Child is Being Beaten': A Contribution to the Study of the Origin of Sexual Perversions," in *The Standard Edition of the Complete Psychological Works of Sigmund Freud*, v.17, 175-204.

Freud, Sigmund (1925) "Negation," in *The Standard Edition of the Complete Psychological Works of Sigmund Freud*, v.19, 235-42.

Gallop, Jane (1997) *Feminist Accused of Sexual Harassment* (Durham: Duke University Press).

Gedo, John (1981) *Advances in Clinical Psychoanalysis* (New York: International Universities Press).

Genette, Gérard (1997) *Paratexts: Thresholds of Interpretation* (Cambridge: Cambridge University Press).

Gold, David L. (1977) "Successes and Failures in the Standardization and Implementation of Yiddish Spelling and Romanization," in Joshua Fishman (ed.), *Advances in the Creation and Revision of Writing Systems* (The Hague: Mouton), 307-69.

Gold, David L. (1982) Response 857/1, *Jewish Language Review* 2, 302.

Gold, David L. (1983) "A Story about Pocahontas, Geronimo, and Sitting Bull in Yiddish," *Jewish Language Review* 3, 113-5.

Gold, David L. (2017) "A Student of Jewish Languages Reads Michał Németh's Unknown Lutsk Karaim Letters in Hebrew Script (19th–20th Centuries). A Critical Edition," *Almanach Karaimski* 6, 17-118.

Gorr, Shmuel (1992) *Jewish Personal Names: Their Origin, Derivation and Diminutive Forms* (Teaneck: NJ, Avotaynu).

Graeber, David (2012) "On Batman and the Problem of Constituent Power," reprinted and enlarged in David Graeber, *The Utopia of Rules: On Technology, Stupidity, and the Secret Joys of Bureaucracy* (New York: Melville Press, 2015), 207-26..

Greeenspun, Wendy (2011) "Three Dimensional Treatment," *Contemporary Psychoanalysis* 47, 386-405.

Grice, H.P. (1991) *Studies in the Way of Words* (Cambridge: Harvard University Press).

Grossman, David (2017) *A Horse Walks into a Bar*, Jessica Cohen (trans.) (New York: Knopf).

Grzankowski, Alex (2015) "Pictures Have Propositional Content," *Review of Philosophy and Psychology* 6, 151-63.

Harris, Jay M. (1998) "Rabbinic Literature in Lithuania after the Death of the Gaon," in Izraelis Lempertas (ed.), *The Gaon of Vilnius and the Annals of Jewish Culture* (Vilna: Vilnius University Publishing House), 88-95.

Harris, Jay M. (2010) "Talmud Study," *YIVO Encyclopedia of Jews in Eastern Europe.* https://yivoencyclopedia.org/article.aspx/Talmud Study (accessed 17th December, 2022).

Her, Seong-Young (2016) "The Post-Pepe Manifesto," *The Philosopher's Meme* https://thephilosophersmeme.com/2016/01/29/the-post-pepe-manifesto/ (accessed 30th October, 2022).

Her, Seong-Young and Masha Zharova (2017) "Post-Irony Against Meta-Irony," *The Philosopher's Meme* https://thephilosophersmeme.com/2017/03/10/post-irony-against-meta-irony/ (accessed 30th October, 2022).

Hick, Darren Hudson (2017) *Artistic License: The Philosophical Problems of Copyright and Appropriation* (Chicago: Chicago University Press).

Hoffer, Axel and Virginia Youngren (2004) "Is Free Association Still at the Core of Psychoanalysis?" *International Journal of Psychoanalysis* 85, 1489-92.

Hoffman, Irwin (2006) "The Myths of Free Association and the Potentials of the Analytic Relationship," *International Journal of Psychoanalysis* 87, 43-61.

Hornsby, Jennifer (1995) "Disempowered Speech," *Philosophical Topics* 23, 127-47.

Housman, A.E. (1905) *D. Iunii Iuuenalis saturae* (London).

Housman, A.E. (1921) "The Application of Thought to Textual Criticism," *Proceedings of the Classical Association* 18, 67-84.

Housman, Clemence (1905) *The Life of Sir Aglovale de Galis* (London: Methuen).

Hui, Andrew (2019) *A Theory of the Aphorism: From Confucius to Twitter* (Princeton: Princeton University Press).

Hynes, William (1993) "Mapping the Characteristics of Mythic Tricksters: A Heuristic Guide," in William Hynes and William Doty (eds.), *Mythical Trickster Figures: Contours, Contexts, and Criticisms* (Tuscaloosa: University of Alabama Press), 33-45.

Idel, Moshe (1991) "Rabbinism versus Kabbalism: On G. Scholem's Phenomenology of Judaism," *Modern Judaism* 11, 281-196.

Jeshion, Robin (2002) "Acquaintanceless *De Re* Belief," in Joseph Keim Campbell, Michael O'Rourke & David Shier (eds.), *Meaning and Truth: Investigations in Philosophical Semantics* (Seven Bridges Press), 53-74.

Jewnin, Nathan Neta (1914) *Binyan Yerushalayim* (Warsaw).

Johnson, Samuel (1973) *Early Biographical Writings of Samuel Johnson* (Westmead: Gregg International Publishers).

Johnson, W.E. (1921-4) *Logic* (Cambridge: Cambridge University Press).

Joseph, H.W.B. (1906) *Introduction to Logic* (Oxford: Clarendon Press).

Katz, Dovid (1998) "The Religious Prestige of the Gaon and the Secular Prestige of Lithuanian Yiddish," in Izraelis Lempertas (ed.), *The Gaon of Vilnius and the Annals of Jewish Culture* (Vilna: Vilnius University Publishing House), 187-99.

Keynes, J.N. (1884) *Studies and Exercises in Formal Logic* (London: Macmillan).

Klein, Melanie (1955) "The Psychoanalytic Play Technique: Its History and Significance," in Melanie Klein, Paula Heimann, and Roger Money-Kyrle (eds.), *New Directions in Psychoanalysis* (London: Tavistock), 1-22.

Kneale, William and Martha Kneale (1962) *The Development of Logic* (Oxford: Clarendon Press),

Korsmeyer, Carolyn (2019) *Things: In Touch with the Past* (Oxford: Oxford University Press).

Kretzmann, Norman (1966) *William of Sherwood's* Introduction to Logic (Minneapolis: University of Minnesota Press).

Kripke, Saul (1980) *Naming and Necessity* (Cambridge: Harvard University Press).

Kris, Anton (1996) *Free Association: Method and Process*, revised edition (Hillsdale: The Analytic Press).

Kuznitz, Cecile Esther (2014) *YIVO and the Making of Modern Jewish Culture: Scholarship for the Yiddish Nation* (Cambridge: Cambridge University Press).

Laber-Warren, Emily (2012) "Unconscious Reactions Separate Liberals and Conservatives," originally published under the title "Calling a Truce in the Political Wars," https://www.scientificamerican.com/Article/calling-truce-political-wars/ (accessed 20th February, 2022).

Ladd-Franklin, Christine (1883) "On the Algebra of Logic," in C. S. Peirce (ed.), *Studies in logic by members of the Johns Hopkins University* (Boston: Little, Brown and Co), 17-71.

Le Besco, Soazig (2016) "Animal Crackers: Patients and Analysts Decode the Bestiary," *Abreactions: A Journal of Psychoanalysis* 14, 72-113.

Lemma, Alessandra (2014) "Off the Couch, into the Toilet: Exploring the Psychic Uses of the Analyst's Toilet," *Journal of the American Psychoanalytic Association* 62, 35-56.

Leslie, Sarah-Jane (2007) "Generics and the Structure of the Mind," *Philosophical Perspectives* 21, 375–403.

Leslie, Sarah-Jane and Adam Lerner (2022) "Generic Generalizations," *The Stanford Encyclopedia of Philosophy* https://plato.stanford.edu/archives/fall2022/entries/generics (accessed 20th October, 2022).

Levinson, Jerrold (1985) "Titles," *Journal of Aesthetics and Art Criticism* 44, 29-39.

Lévi-Strauss, Claude (1966) *The Savage Mind* (Chicago: Chicago University Press).

Lichtenberg, Joseph and Floyd Galler (1987) "The Fundamental Rule: A Study of Current Usage," *Journal of the American Psychoanalytic Association* 35, 47-76.

Livingston, Paisley (2006) "Theses on Cinema as Philosophy," *Journal of Aesthetics and Art Criticism* 64, 11-18.

Luber, M. Philip (1991) "A Patient's Transference to the Analyst's Supervisor: Effect of the Setting on the Analytic Process," *Journal of the American Psychoanalytic Association* 39, 705-25.

Machado, Carmen Maria (2019) *In the Dream House: A Memoir* (Minneapolis: Graywolf Press).

MacKenna, Stephen (1936) *Journals and Letters* (London: Constable).

Mahony, Patrick (1987) *Psychoanalysis and Discourse* (London: Tavistock).

Mahony, Patrick (1997) "'A Child is Being Beaten': A Clinical, Historical, and Textual Study," in Ethel Person (ed.), *On Freud's 'A Child is Being Beaten* (London: Karnac Books), 47-66.

Malamud, Bernard (1966) *The Fixer* (New York: Farrar, Strauss and Giroux).

Mansel, Henry (1849) *Artis Logicae Rudimenta, from the Text of Aldrich, with Notes and Marginal References* (Oxford: William Graham).

Mayhew, A.L. (1907) "Peccavi: 'I Have Sindh'," *Notes and Queries*, 10th series, 8, 345-6.

McGinn, Colin (2013a) "Respectability Regained," (July 14th 2013) now only available https://www.goodreads.com/author/show/12834.Colin_McGinn/blog?page=5 (accessed 28th October, 2022).

McGinn, Colin (2013b) "Out on a Limb," *Harper's Magazine*, November https://harpers.org/archive/2013/11/out-on-a-limb/ (accessed 28th October, 2022).

McLuhan, Marshall (1964) *Understanding Media: The Extensions of Man* (New York: McGraw Hill).

McWilliams, Nancy (2004) *Psychoanalytic Psychotherapy: A Practitioner's Guide* (New York: The Guilford Press).

Milner, Ryan (2016) *The World Made Meme* (Cambridge: MIT Press)

Mitchell, Stephen (1997) *Influence and Autonomy in Psychoanalysis* (London: Routledge).

Mitchell, Stephen and Margaret Black (2016) *Freud and Beyond: A History of Modern Psychoanalytic Thought*, updated edition (New York: Basic Books).

Montague, Stephen (1985) "John Cage at Seventy: An Interview," *American Music* 3, 205-16.

Monteiro, George (2010) "The Bat and the Raven," *Edgar Allan Poe Review* 11, 105-20.

Moore, G.E. (1993) *G.E. Moore: Selected Writings*, Thomas Baldwin (ed.) (London: Routledge).

Nelson, Maggie (2016) *The Argonauts* (Minneapolis: Graywolf Press).

Newell, William Wells (1891) "The Carol of the Twelve Numbers," *The Journal of American Folklore* 4, 215-20.

Noë, Alva (2015) *Strange Tools: Art and Human Nature* (New York: Hill and Wang).

Nussbaum, Martha (1992) *Love's Knowledge: Essays on Philosophy and Literature*, revised edition (New York: Oxford University Press).

Nye, Andrea (1990) *Words of Power: A Feminist Reading of the History of Logic* (London: Routledge).

Ogden, Thomas (1994) "The Analytic Third: Working with Intersubjective Clinical Facts," *International Journal of Psychoanalysis* 75, 3-19.

Ogden, Thomas (1996) "Reconsidering Three Aspects of Psychoanalytic Technique," *International Journal of Psychoanalysis* 77, 883-99.

Paleotti, Gabriele (2012) *Discourse on Sacred and Profane Images*, William McCuaig (trans.) (Los Angeles: Getty Research Institute).

Paul, Laurie A. (2014) *Transformative Experience* (Oxford: Oxford University Press).

Peacocke, Antonia (2023) "How to Think Many Thoughts at Once: Content Plurality in Mental Action," in Michael Brent and Lisa Miracchi Titus (eds.) *Mental Action and the Conscious Mind* (London: Routledge), 31-60.

Perry, John (1979) "The Problem of the Essential Indexical," *Noûs* 13, 3-21.

Phillips, Whitney and Ryan Milner (2017) *The Ambivalent Internet: Mischief, Oddity, and Antagonism Online* (Cambridge: Polity Press).

Prager, Leonard (1985) "Two Yiddish Tales about Sir Moses Montefiore (Text and Commentary)," *Jewish Language Review* 5, 64-84.

Putnam, Hilary (1988) *The Many Faces of Realism* (LaSalle: Open Court).

Romaine, Suzanne (2011) "Revitalized Languages as Invented Languages," in Michael Adams (ed.), *From Evlish to Klingon: Exploring Invented Languages* (Oxford: Oxford University Press), 185-226.

Rouse, Richard and Mary Rouse (1982) "*Statim Invenire*: Schools, Preachers, and New Attitudes to the Page," in Robert Benson and Giles Constable (eds.), *Renaissance and Renewal in the Twelfth Century* (Cambridge: Harvard University Press), 201-25.

Rushdie, Salman (2011) *Shame* (New York: Random House).

Russell, Bertrand (1903) *Principles of Mathematics* (Cambridge: Cambridge University Press).

Sartre, Jean-Paul (1956) *Being and Nothingness*, Hazel Barnes (trans.) (London: Methuen).

Schenk, Gabriel (2017) "'Arthur the King' and 'Arthur the Man' in Clemence Housman's *The Life of Sir Aglovale De Galis*," *The Housman Society Journal* 43, 52-71.

Schochet, Elijah (1998) "The Nature of Lithuanian Jewry: The Legacy of the Gaon of Vilna," in Izraelis Lempertas (ed.) *The Gaon of Vilnius and the Annals of Jewish Culture* (Vilna: Vilnius University Publishing House), 206-22.

Schwabach, Aaron (2012) "Reclaiming Copyright from the Outside In: What the Downfall Hitler Meme Means for Transformative Works, Fair Use, and Parody," *Buffalo Intellectual Property Law Journal* 8, 1-25.

Scott, W. Clifford (1958) "Noise, Speech, and Technique," *International Journal of Psychoanalysis* 39, 108-11.

Sedgwick, Eve Kosofsky (2000) *A Dialogue on Love* (Boston: Beacon Press).

Searle, John (1995) *The Construction of Social Reality* (New York: The Free Press).

Shaen, Margaret Josephine (1908) *Memorial of Two Sisters, Susanna and Catherine Winkworth* (Longmans, Green).

Sharp, Cecil J. (1916) *One Hundred English Folksongs* (Boston: Oliver Ditson Company).

Shifman, Limor (2014) *Memes in Digital Culture* (Cambridge: MIT Press)

Shubin, Michelle (2018) "What's So Great About Authenticity Anyway? The Therapeutic Function of an Analyst's Lie," *Psychoanalytic Dialogues* 28, 175-82.

Sidoli, Mara (1996) "Farting as a Defense Against Unspeakable Dread," *Journal of Analytical Psychology* 41, 165-78.

Simons, Peter (2000) *Parts: A Study in Ontology* (Oxford: Oxford University Press).

Sorabji, Richard (1988) *Matter, Space, and Motion: Theories in Antiquity and Their Sequel* (Ithaca: Cornell University Press).

Spacal, Savo (1990) "Free Association as a Method of Self-Observation in Relation to Other Methodological Principles of Psychoanalysis," *Psychoanalytic Quarterly* 59, 420-36.

Spade, Paul Vincent (2007) *Thoughts, Words and Things: An Introduction to Late Mediaeval Logic and Semantic Theory*, Version 1.2. https://hdl.handle.net/2022/18939 (accessed 25th October, 2022)

Spillius, Elizabeth et al. (2011) *New Dictionary of Kleinian Thought* (London: Routledge).

Sprague de Camp, L. and Fletcher Pratt (1975) *The Compleat Enchanter: The Magical Misadventures of Harold Shea* (New York: Ballantine Books).

Stampfer, Shaul (2012) *Lithuanian Yeshivas of the Nineteenth Century: Creating a Tradition of Learning* (Oxford: The Littman Library of Jewish Civilization).

Steinsaltz, Adin (1976) *The Essential Talmud* (New York: Basic Books).

Stewart, Bob (1977) *Pagan Imagery in English Folksong* (Atlantic Highlands, NJ: Humanities Press).

Stott, Rebecca (2012) *Darwin's Ghosts: The Secret History of Evolution* (New York: Spiegel and Grau).

Tabory, Joseph (2008) *JPS Commentary on the Haggadah: Historical Introduction, Translation, and Commentary* (Philadelphia: The Jewish Publication Society).

Thomason, Krista (2014) "Shame, Violence, and Morality," *Philosophy and Phenomenological Research* 91, 1-24.

Thompson, M. Guy (2004) *The Ethic of Honesty: The Fundamental Rule of Psychoanalysis* (Amsterdam: Rodopi).

Tokarczuk, Olga (2022) *The Books of Jacob*, Jennifer Croft (trans.) (New York: Riverhead Books).

Tompkins, Jane (1987) "Me and My Shadow," *New Literary History* 19, 169-78.

Uckelman, Sara L. (2017) "Syllogism Mnemonics," https://medievallogic.wordpress.com/2017/11/16/syllogism-mnemonics/ (accessed 25th October 2022).

Uckelman, Sara L. (2021) "What Problem Did Ladd-Franklin (Think She) Solve(d)?" *Notre Dame Journal of Formal Logic* 62, 527-552.

Ulrich, Johann Caspar (1768) *Sammlung Jüdischer Geschichten in der Schweiss* (Basel).

Vinograd, Yeshayahu (2003) *Otsar sifre ha-Gera : bibliyografyah meforeṭet u-muʻeret shel sifre ha-gaʾon he-ḥasid Rabi Eliyahu ben Rabi Shelomoh Zalman mi-Vilna, zatsal* (Jerusalem: Kerem Eliyahu).

Waltz, Robert B. (ed.) (2018) "Green Grow the Rushes-O (The Twelve Apostles, Come and I Will Sing You) entry in The Traditional Ballad Index: An Annotated Source to Folk Song from the English-Speaking World," version 4.4, https://www.fresnostate.edu/folklore/ballads/ShH97.html (accessed 27 October 2022).

Wartenberg, Thomas (2007) *Thinking on Screen: Film as Philosophy* (London: Routledge).

Weinberg, Bella Hass (1995) "Ambiguities in the Romanization of Yiddish," *Judaica Librarianship* 9, 58-74.

Weinreich, Max (1967) "The Reality of Jewishness versus the Ghetto Myth: The Sociolinguistic Roots of Yiddish," in *To Honor Roman Jakobson: Essays on the Occasion of his Seventieth Birthday*, vol. 3 (The Hague: Mouton), 2199-221.

Weldon, Glen (2016) *The Caped Crusade: Batman and the Rise of Nerd Culture* (New York: Simon and Schuster).

Whitehead, A.N. (1920) *The Concept of Nature* (Cambridge: Cambridge University Press).

Whitehead, A.N. and Bertrand Russell (1910-3) *Principia Mathematica* (Cambridge: Cambridge University Press).

Wilmers, Mary-Kay (2009) *The Eitingons: A Twentieth-Century Story* (London: Faber and Faber).

Winkworth, Susanna (1883) *Letters and memorials of Catherine Winkworth* (E. Austin).

Wistreich, Richard (2017) "'Inclosed in this tabernacle of flesh': Body, Soul, and the Singing Voice," *Journal of the Northern Renaissance* 8, 1-31.

Woolf, Virginia (1933) *Flush: A Biography* (London: Hogarth Press).

Zimmer, Ben (2008) "Jottings on the 'Jamaica' Joke," *Language Log* http://languagelog.ldc.upenn.edu /nll/?p=591 (accessed 28th October, 2022).

Zwartjes, Arianna (2019) "Autotheory as Rebellion: On Research, Embodiment, and Imagination in Creative Nonfiction," *Michigan Quarterly Review* https://sites.lsa.umich.edu/mqr/2019/07/autotheory-as-rebellion-on-research-embodiment-and- imagination-in-creative-nonfiction/ (accessed 28th October, 2022).

INDEX OF MEMES

M.1	xix, 2, 113, 228
M.1-M.2	14
M.1-M.4	2, 136
M.1-M.8	14
M.2	3-5, 6
M.3	2, 3, 13, 228, 253
M.3-M.100	14
M.4	7, 11, 13
M.5	11
M.5-M.8	136
M.6	13, 22, 70
M.7	100, 184, 253
M.8	14, 22, 30, 182, 208
M.9	27, 30
M.9-M.104	14
M.10	30, 71, 208
M.11	35, 171
M.12	38, 103, 177, 178
M.13	23, 36, 42, 112
M.14	49, 64, 133, 232
M.15	xix, 19, 65
M.16	253
M.17	46, 74, 81
M.18	76, 191
M.19	xix, 78, 122
M.20	36, 71, 80, 110, 129, 171, 229, 253
M.21	252, 253
M.22	38, 46, 75, 80, 205
M.23	82, 253
M.24	82, 167, 175
M.25	46, 85, 115, 252
M.26	253
M.27	204, 253
M.28	65, 87
M.29	xix, 88, 97, 191, 214
M.30	xix, 88, 97, 112, 203, 214, 218
M.31	110, 214
M.32	xix, 78, 111, 115
M.33	23, 254
M.34	125, 254
M.35	254
M.36	115
M.37	121, 163, 164, 187
M.38	129, 165, 254
M.39	254
M.40	254
M.41	254
M.42	xix, 123, 234
M.43	127, 184
M.43a	128-130
M.43b	128-130
M.44	254
M.45	1, 19, 50, 131
M.45a	131-134
M.46	14, 136
M.47	3, 14, 31, 255
M.49	110, 157
M.50	xix, 159
M.51	80, 127, 205, 255
M.52	163
M.53	214, 255
M.54	255
M.55	12, 74, 255
M.56	48, 193, 255
M.57	165, 255
M.58	83, 164, 166
M.59	46, 205, 255
M.60	24, 166
M.61	255
M.62	36, 171
M.63	171, 174
M.64	256
M.65	65, 256
M.66	256
M.67	46, 256
M.67-M.71 (the Depressive Cluster)	15
M.68	256
M.69	xix, xxii, 39, 171, 176, 179
M.70	15, 53, 172, 256
M.71	47, 125, 174, 256
M.72	xix, 47, 65, 76, 101, 113, 184, 191
M.73	256
M.74	xix, 204
M.75	65, 129, 172, 256
M.76	24
M.76-M.77	15
M.77	xx, 14, 39, 45, 107, 129, 208, 210
M.78	62, 132, 214
M.79	23, 209, 257
M.80	xx, 24, 221
M.81	171, 257
M.82	24, 36, 92, 257
M.83	111, 257
M.84	15, 257

M.85	167, 257
M.86	257
M.86-M.87	15
M.87	257
M.88	133, 257
M.89	15, 94, 257
M.90	258
M.91	xx, 4, 183, 223, 229, 230
M.92	xxii, 183, 223, 225, 227, 229
M.93	80, 130, 205, 258
M.94	65, 258
M.95	123, 234, 258
M.96	xx, 80, 120, 129, 234
M.97	xx, 241
M.97-M.100	15
M.98	258
M.99	258
M.100	258
M.101	252
M.101-M.104	14
M.102	36, 258
M.103	31, 258
M.104	94, 110, 157, 259

Index of Names

Abaye 40
Abraham, Karl 218
Abulafia, Abraham 56
Adelman, Eliahu 98
Aglovale de Galis 45-47
Ahmed, Sara xvii
Akiva, Rabbi 178
Aldrich, Henry 69-70, 73
Allen, Woody 110
Amphlett, Chrissy 86
Anderegg, David 215
Angioletta 159-160
Archilei, Vittoria 159
Aristotle 65-68, 71, 213, 234, 236
Armstrong, A.H. 237
Armstrong, Taylor 248
Augustine, Saint 45
Austin, J.L. 31, 54, 125
Balint, Michael 60
Baring-Gould, Sabine 102-103
Baron, Salo 185
Barthes, Roland 246
Beardsley, Monroe 99-100
Beasley, Edward 44
Beider, Alexander 190, 198
Berlin, Zvi Leib 199
Billimoria, N.M. 44
Birdsell, David 243
Birnbaum, Solomon 196, 197
Black, Margaret 50, 216
Bollas, Christopher 56
Boulez, Pierre 87
Bourke, Anthony 51
Brentano, Robert 53
Breuer, Joseph 54, 56
Bright, Liam Kofi 25, 26, 181, 182
Brontë, Charlotte 44
Bunsen, Chevalier 44-45
Burko, Leyzer 196
Caccini, Giulio 159-160
Cage, John 123-126
Camp, Elisabeth 244
Cantalamessa, Elizabeth 251
Carlyle, Thomas 44
Carnap, Rudolf 181
Caro, Joseph 188

Catwoman 28, 95
Cherfas, Teresa 43
Collie, Susan 43
Cooper, Harriet 15, 204-206
Craig, Edward 165
Cristina of Lorraine 160
Cronin, Brian xxii
Cunningham, Merce 126
d'Arco, Livia 161
d'Este, Riccardo 161
Dali, Salvador 244
Daly, Lloyd William 68
Davidson, Baruch 188
Davidson, Donald 53
Davison, Patrick 250
De Morgan, Augustus 68
de' Bardi, Giovanni 159-160
de' Cavalieri, Emilioi 159
de' Medici, Ferdinando 160
Delafield, Catherine 43-44
Deleuze, Gilles 241
Dickens, Charles 44, 191
Dickinson, Emily 191, 192
Dilthey, Karl 212
Dilthey, Wilhelm 212
Diotima 235, 238
Dissertator, Anonymous 14-21, 70
Drake 247-248
Duchamp, Marcel 168, 169
Dunaway, Faye 122
Duran, Simeon ben Zemach 185
Edmonds, David 181
Eifermann, Rivka 16
Einstein, Albert 191, 192
Eisenstadt, Benzion 199, 202, 203
Eitingon, Fanny 218
Eitingon, Leonid 109
Eitingon, Max 109, 218
Eitingon, Motty 109, 218
Eitingon, Zissia 109
Eliot, T.S. 209
Ellenborough, Lord 42
Emmy von N 56
Evans, Gareth 57, 92, 94
Evnin, Oscar 198
Evnine, Abraham Jonah (Brunya) 108, 198

Evnine, Ariel	36
Evnine, David	*See* Yevnin, David
Evnine, George	76, 187, 188, 198
Evnine, Jeremy	18-21
F.C.H.	103
Fabrikant, Agnès	62, 219, 220
Feldman, Morton	210
Fish, Stanley	100
Forster, E.M.	57
Foster, Jodie	86
Foucault, Michel	85-86, 249
Franco, Alessandro	161
Franco, Veronica	161
Franks, Mary Anne	206
Freeland, Cynthia	244
Freud, Anna	16
Freud, Sigmund	16, 17, 53-58, 62, 109, 181, 182, 191, 192
Galilei, Vincenzo	159
Galler, Floyd	57, 59, 60
Gallop, Jane	238
Gaskell, Elizabeth	44
Gaskell, William	43
Gedo, John	59
Gilbert, W.S.	12, 191
Gold, David L.	185, 191-194
Gordon, James	15, 180
Gorr, Shmuel	187
Gosling, Ryan	248
Graeber, David	15
Grayson, Dick	15, 48, 112, 113
Greenspun, Wendy	218
Gregory of Nyssa	235-237
Grice, Paul	100, 125
Groarke, Leo	243
Grossman, David	xvii
Grzankowski, Alex	243
Guarini, Anna	161
Guarini, Giovanni Battista	159-161
Gurney, T.A.	42
Hakuin, Ekaku	167
Hamilton, Edmond	xxi, xxii
Hardy, Thomas	209
Harris, Dane	206
Harris, Jay	77, 199
Her, Seong-Young	248, 250
Hick, Darren Hudson	251
Hoffer, Axel	57, 63
Hoffman, Irwin	58, 63
Homer	191
Hornsby, Jennifer	62-63
Housman, A.E.	45, 208-213
Housman, Clemence	45, 47
Hui, Andrew	243
Hynes, William	249
Idel, Moshe	102
Jeshion, Robin	90-95, 191-192
Jewnin	*See* Yevnin
Johnson, Samuel	xvii
Johnson, W.E.	72
Joker, The	28, 157, 158
Joseph, H.W.B.	73
Judson, Whitcomb	92, 94
Julius	*See* Judson, Whitcomb
Kahana, Rav	235
Kant, Immanuel	80, 212, 236
Katz, Dovid	194, 195
Keynes, John Neville	73
Khokhlov, Nikolai	109
Kierkegaard, Søren	228
Kingsley, Charles	44
Klein, Melanie	32-34, 58-60
Kleis, John Christopher	45
Kneale, Martha	69
Kneale, William	69
Kobes, Bernard	13-14
Kondo, Marie	247
Korsmeyer, Carolyn	83-84
Kretzmann, Norman	67
Kripke, Saul	191-192
Kris, Anton	50
Kube, Wilhelm	109
Kuznitz, Cecile Esther	195
Laber-Warren, Emily	25
Ladd-Franklin, Christine	70
Laing, R.D.	xxii
Lambrick, H.T.	44
Lawrence, Gavin	36
Le Besco, Soazig	50-52
Ledger, Heath	28
Leiter, Brian	27-29
Lemma, Alessandra	132-134
Lennon, John	126
Lerner, Adam	8
Leslie, Sarah-Jane	8-9
Leverrier, Urbain	91
Levinson, Jerrold	209-210
Lévi-Strauss, Claude	245-246
Lewis, Dan	83
Lewis, David	165
Lewy, Casimir	165
Lichtenberg, Joseph	57, 59, 60

Livingston, Paisley	243
Locke, John	236
Lope de Vega, Felix	163
Luber, Philip	218
Luther, Martin	44
Machado, Carmen Maria	xvii
MacKenna, Stephen	236, 237, 238
Mackintosh, Catherine	43-44
Mahony, Patrick	17, 56
Maimonides	199
Malamud, Bernard	225
Malcolm, Norman	125
Malory, Thomas	45
Mansel, Henry	73
Marx, Karl	191
Matey, Jennifer	78
Maxwell, Lindsey	126
Mayhew, A.L.	43
Mazzini, Giuseppe	44
McDaniel, Kris	27
McDowell, John	212
McGinn, Colin	116-119
McLuhan, Marshall	22-24, 26, 182
McWilliams, Nancy	216, 222
Me'ir, Rabbi	38-40
Mendil, Moshe ben Gershon	199
Mercader, Ramón	109
Meredith, Burgess	174
Milner, Ryan	246
Milton, John	191
Mirsky, Samuel	195
Mitchell, Stephen	50, 216
Money-Kyrle, Roger	181
Montague, Stephen	126
Monteiro, George	114
Monteverdi, Claudio	159
Moore, G.E.	125, 165
Morrison, Grant	112-113
Napier, Alan	48
Napier, Sir Charles	42-44, 48
Newell, William Wells	98-99, 100
Nicholson, Jack	28, 122
Niebuhr, Barthold Georg	44
Nietzsche, Friedrich	241
Noë, Alva	xvii, 244-246
Nussbaum, Martha	244
Nye, Andrea	78
O'Hara, Clancy	15
O'Sullivan, Gilbert	12
Ogden, Thomas	63, 64, 219-220
Ono, Yoko	126
Orwell, George	82, 83, 84
Paleotti, Gabriele	xviii
Paley, William	244
Parsifal	45
Paul, Laurie	183, 224-227
Paul, St.	177-178
Peacocke, Antonia	58
Peano, Giuseppe	71
Penguin, The	28, 174
Pennyworth, Alfred	15, 46, 48, 112
Peri, Jacopo	159
Perles, Joseph	98
Perry, John	222
Pessoa, Fernando	114
Peters, Ellis	45
Peverara, Laura	161
Phillips, Whitney	246
Philoponus, John	66
Plato	235, 242
Plotinus	234-239
Poe, Edgar Allen	111-114
Pompele, Giovanna	89
Porphyry	234-235, 238
Prager, Leonard	185
Pratt, Fletcher	70-73
Putnam, Hilary	165
Pym, Arthur Gordon, of Nantucket	114
Rashi	viii, 105, 106, 202
Rav	235
Rendall, John	51
Reynolds, Reginald	45
Rich, Adrienne	238
Ricoeur, Paul	225
Riddler, The	28
Roback, A.A.	194
Romaine, Suzanne	193
Romero, Cesar	157
Rosen, Michael	82, 83, 84, 97, 109, 110
Roskies, David	196
Rouse, Mary	68
Rouse, Richard	68
Rushdie, Salman	xvii
Russell, Bertrand	23, 36, 71, 72
Russell, John Morris	125
Sandman, Israel	104, 201
Satie, Erik	125
Savile, Anthony	80
Schenk, Gabriel	45
Schlesinger, Benjamin	200
Schlick, Moritz	181
Schliesser, Eric	180-182

Schochet, Elijah	195
Scholem, Gershom	102
Schönberg, Arnold	74
Schwabach, Aaron	250
Scott, Clifford	59
Searle, John	95
Sedgwick, Eve Kosofsky	xvii
Sennett, Richard	86
Shaen, Agnes	43
Shaen, Margaret	43-44
Shakespeare, William	191, 192
Sharp, Cecil	100, 108
Shavelson, Susanne	184, 185, 186, 189, 194, 197
Shaw, Tamsin	206
Shifman, Limor	246
Shmu'el ben David Moshe	188
Shmu'el ben Uri Shraga Faivish	188
Shubin, Michelle	216
Sidoli, Mara	61
Simmel, Ernst	218
Simons, Peter	30, 31
Smith, David Livingstone	181
Socrates	235
Soloveitchik, Yosef Dov HaLevi	199
Sorabji, Richard	236, 237
Spacal, Savo	54, 58, 63
Spade, Paul Vincent	65, 68
Spektor, Elkhanan	199, 201
Spillius, Elizabeth	32
Spinoza, Benedict	191
Sprague de Camp, L.	69, 70-73
Stanley, Jason	182
Steinsaltz, Adin	77, 235
Stewart, R.J.	99, 100-104, 106-107
Stott, Rebecca	xviii
Sullivan, Arthur	12, 191
Swan, Curt	xxi, xxii
Tabory, Joseph	88, 98, 105
Tarski, Alfred	172
Templier, Pierre-Daniel	125
Thackeray, William Makepeace	44
Thomason, Krista	46-47
Thompson, M. Guy	57
Thompson, Raymond E.	45
Tokarczuk, Olga	xviii
Tolley, Clinton	70
Tompkins, Jane	xvii
Trotsky, Leon	97, 108-109
Uckelman, Sara	67, 70
Ulrich, Johann Caspar	98
Vaughan Williams, Ralph	210
Vilna Gaon	*See* Zalman, Eliyahu ben Shlomo
Volta, Ornella	125
Waltz, Robert B.	98, 99, 100
Ward, Burt	196
Ward, Mary Augusta	209
Warner, William Lee	43
Warren, Mark	7
Wartenberg, Thomas	244
Watney, David	112
Watson, Jennifer	240
Watson, Tim	83
Wayne, Bruce	15, 46, 48, 95, 112-113, 180, 187
Wayne, Thomas	187
Weinberg, Bella Hass	194
Weinreich, Max	190
Weldon, Glen	112, 113
Wertham, Fredric	112
West, Adam	196, 252
White, Hayden	182
Whitehead, A.N.	30-31, 71, 72
Whitman, Walt	191
Wilkins, John	94, 178
William of Sherwood	67, 69
Wilmers, Mary-Kay	109
Wimsatt, William	99-100
Winkworth, Alice	43
Winkworth, Catherine	43-45
Winkworth, Jessie	43
Winkworth, Susanna	43-45
Wistreich, Richard	xix
Wittgenstein, Ludwig	125, 237
Wittow, Gedalyahu	200
Woolf, Virginia	xvii
Woollcott, Walter	43
Xianda, Wen	243
Yate, A.C.	43-44
Yehuda HaNasi	39
Yehuda, Rabbi	38-40
Yevnin, Abraham Jonah	198-199, 202-203
Yevnin, Bezalel	198, 203
Yevnin, Bezalel (son of Nathan Neta)	108, 203
Yevnin, David	19, 198
Yevnin, Nathan Neta	88, 101, 104-108, 199, 202
Yevnin, Rebecca Rayna née Ginzburg	203
Yevnin, Samuel	199-202
Yoḥanan, Rabbi	39-40
Youngren, Virginia	57, 63
Zalman, Eliyahu ben Shlomo	195, 199, 201
Zetland, Lord	43-44
Zharova, Masha	248
Zimmer, Ben	110

INDEX OF SUBJECTS

Alphabetic order 68
Analytic philosophy 22-6, 164-5, 180-3, 231-3
Authorship 249-51
Bathroom access 16-21, 131-4, 235-6
Batman Meme Project .... xxi-xxii, 3-5, 13-4, 19, 157, 227-8, 230-3
Bricolage 245-9
Childishness .... xvii, 18-21, 85-6, 230-3, 252
Clarity 25-6, 31-3, 177-83
Cumulative songs 88-90, 97-109
Death 252
Essential indexicality 222
Evnine family history 88, 101-9, 195-6, 198-203, 218
Generics 8-10
Hand job .... *See* Sex, masturbation
Harassment 119-20. 204-6, 234-5, 238
Hylomorphism 168-70
Intentional Fallacy 99-100
Interpretation 99-107, 112-3, 177-80, 229-30
Judaism 76-7, 88-9, 184-97
    Karaism 185
    Rabbinic 38-41, 77, 101-7, 177-9, 222, 235-6
    Relation to Christianity 3-4, 177
Language 36-7, 40-1, 115-20, 190-7
    Indirect speech 115-20, 180
    Use vs. mention 111
Masculinity 78-9
Matter 169-70, 236-7
Memes, Evnine's
    Occasional 7, 13
    Periodization 14
    Technique 2, 6, 11, 27, 30, 38, 40-1, 80, 82, 110, 121, 128-9, 136, 157, 171, 174, 204-6, 234, 238-40
Memes, in general 241-51
    Identity conditions of 166
Music 11-12, 74-5, 87, 123-6, 159-62
Naming 65, 90-6, 184-97
Neo-Platonism 234-40
Origins stories 4-5, 14, 113-4
Paradoxes
    Grelling's 36-7
    Liar 36, 171-3
    Russell's 36
Parergon .... xviii, 219-20
Parthood 3-4
Psychoanalysis 16-21, 110, 131-4, 177-80, 214-20, 222, 230-1
    Free association 32, 49-64
    Freudian 54-8, 215-7
    Kleinian 32-4, 59-63
    Projective identification 32
    Relational 63-4
Root vegetables 126
Sex 83-4, 234-6
    Incest 121-2, 187
    Masturbation 52, 85-6, 115-20
    Sodomy 112
Shame .... xvii, 45-8, 74, 78-9, 80-1, 112
Slap .... xvii-xviii, xxiii, 15-21, 166-8, 232
    Absurd xxiii
    Antiphonal .... xxiii, 22, 30, 88-9, 111, 208
    Corrective .... xxiii, 111
    Demonstrative .... xxiii, 2, 24, 115, 136
    Gloved 83-4
    Interruptive .... xxiii, 111, 208
    Punitive .... xxiii, 89
    Shame 46, 112
    Torture 122, 163
Speech act theory 54-63, 91-6
Syllogism 65-70
Textual criticism 39-40, 208-13
Thought 174-5
    De re 91-6
    Expression of 54-8
    Transparency thesis 57
Titles 13-14, 209-10
Transformative experience 183, 223-33
Victoriana 42-6
Violence .... xvii, 14-21, 47, 78-9, 112, 122
Virtue ethics 212-3
Writing speech . xxii-xxiii, xvii, 7-8, 11-12, 22-3, 35-6, 40-1, 47-8, 71, 101, 166-8, 174-5, 190-7, 205-6, 239-40
Yiddish 88, 108, 184-97